For my brother.

Just imagine what he's
had to put up with all
these years.

Jane's World 1

BY PAIGE BRADDOCK

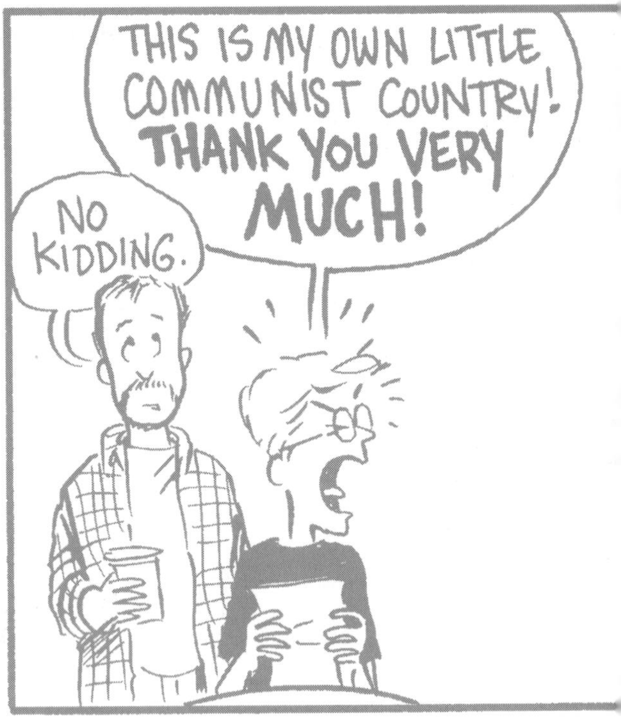

THIS IS MY OWN LITTLE COMMUNIST COUNTRY! THANK YOU VERY MUCH!
NO KIDDING.

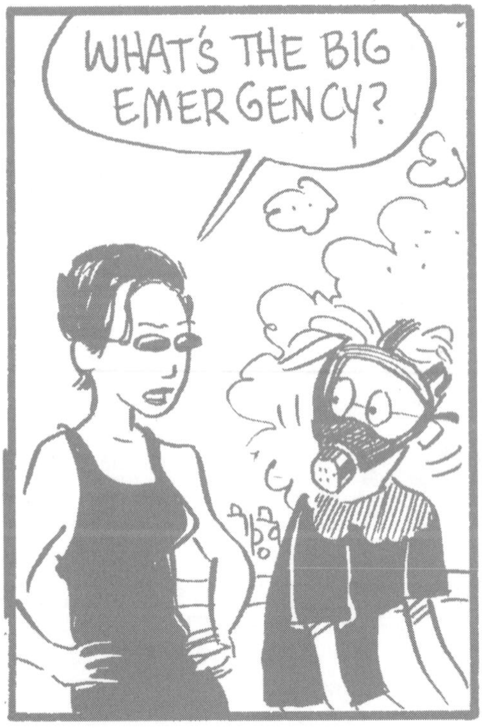

WHAT'S THE BIG EMERGENCY?

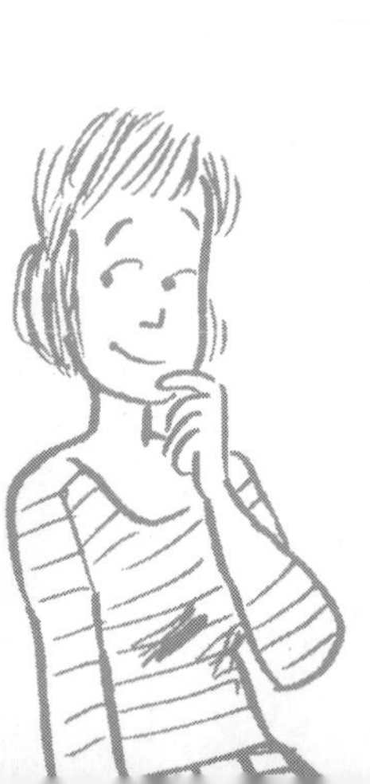

Chapter 1

The clown princess

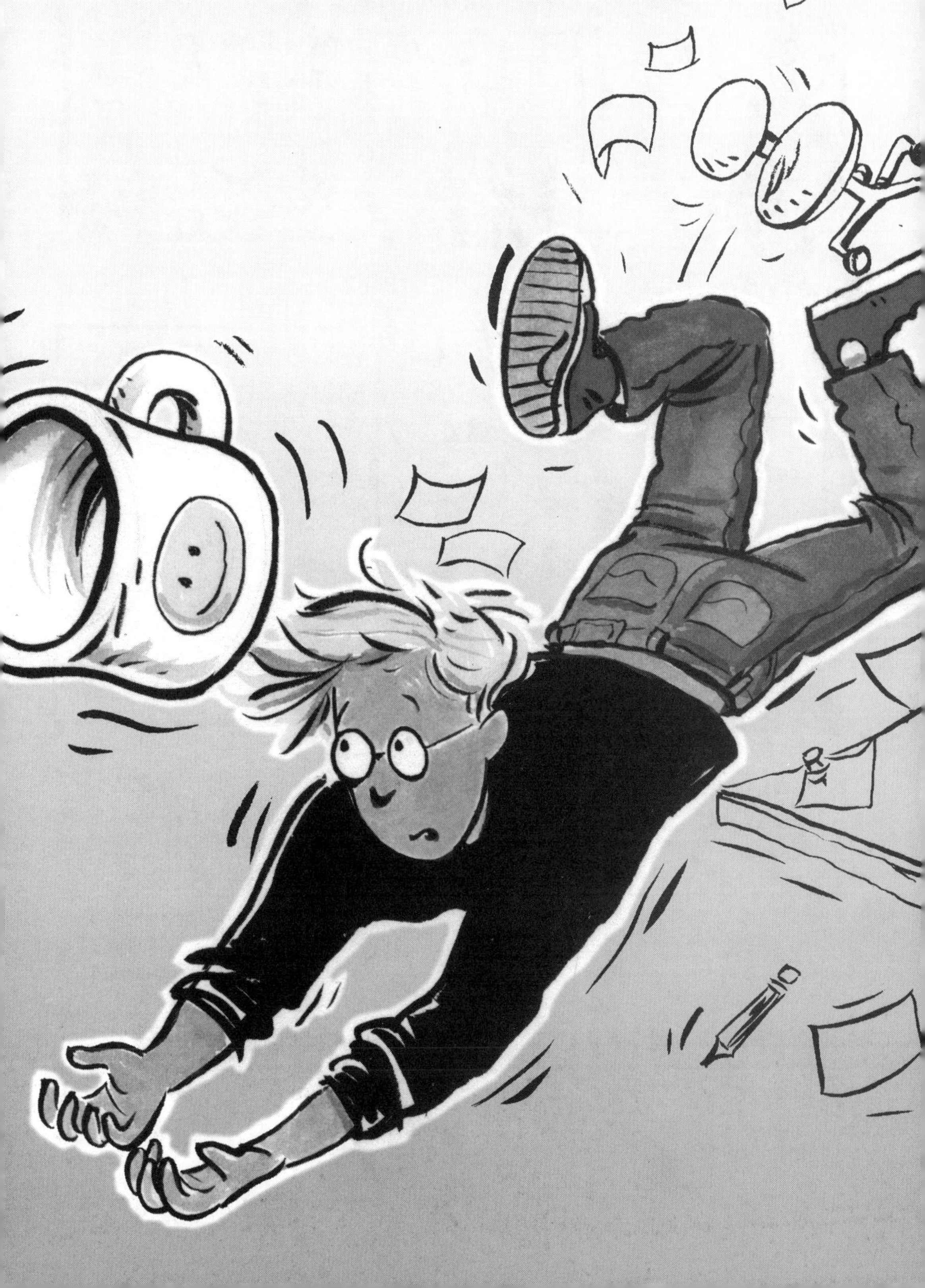

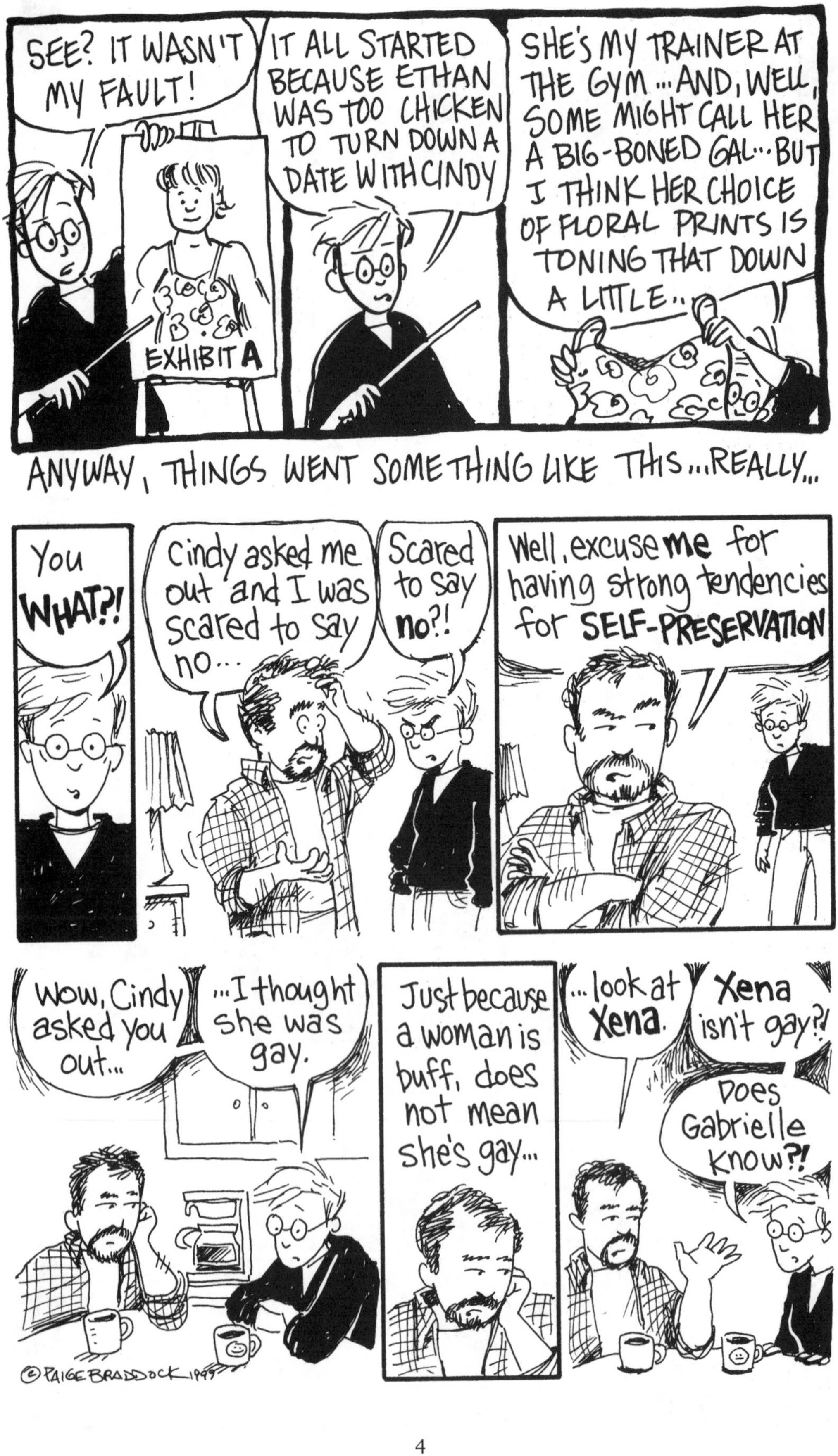
SEE? IT WASN'T MY FAULT!
EXHIBIT A
IT ALL STARTED BECAUSE ETHAN WAS TOO CHICKEN TO TURN DOWN A DATE WITH CINDY
SHE'S MY TRAINER AT THE GYM ... AND, WELL, SOME MIGHT CALL HER A BIG-BONED GAL... BUT I THINK HER CHOICE OF FLORAL PRINTS IS TONING THAT DOWN A LITTLE..
ANYWAY, THINGS WENT SOMETHING LIKE THIS... REALLY...
You WHAT?!
Cindy asked me out and I was scared to say no...
Scared to say no?!
Well, excuse me for having strong tendencies for SELF-PRESERVATION
Wow, Cindy asked you out...
...I thought she was gay.
Just because a woman is buff, does not mean she's gay...
...look at Xena.
Xena isn't gay?!
Does Gabrielle know?!
© PAIGE BRADDOCK 1999

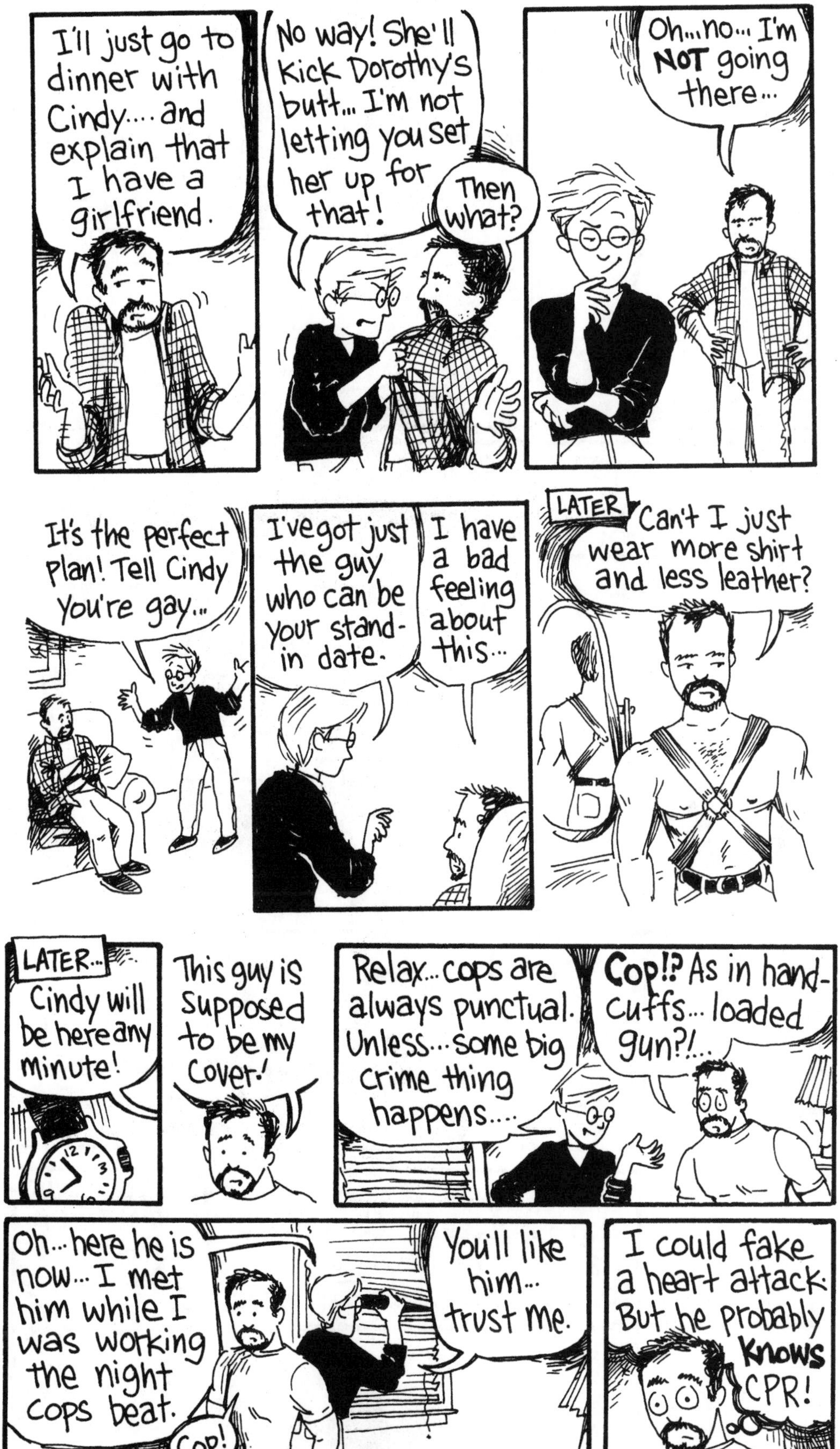
I'll just go to dinner with Cindy.... and explain that I have a girlfriend.
No way! She'll kick Dorothy's butt... I'm not letting you set her up for that!
Then what?
Oh... no... I'm NOT going there...
It's the perfect plan! Tell Cindy you're gay...
I've got just the guy who can be your stand-in date.
I have a bad feeling about this...
LATER
Can't I just wear more shirt and less leather?
LATER...
Cindy will be here any minute!
This guy is supposed to be my cover!
Relax... cops are always punctual. Unless... some big crime thing happens....
Cop!? As in hand-cuffs... loaded gun?!...
Oh... here he is now... I met him while I was working the night cops beat.
Cop!
You'll like him... trust me.
©PAIGE BRADDOCK 1999
I could fake a heart attack. But he probably knows CPR!

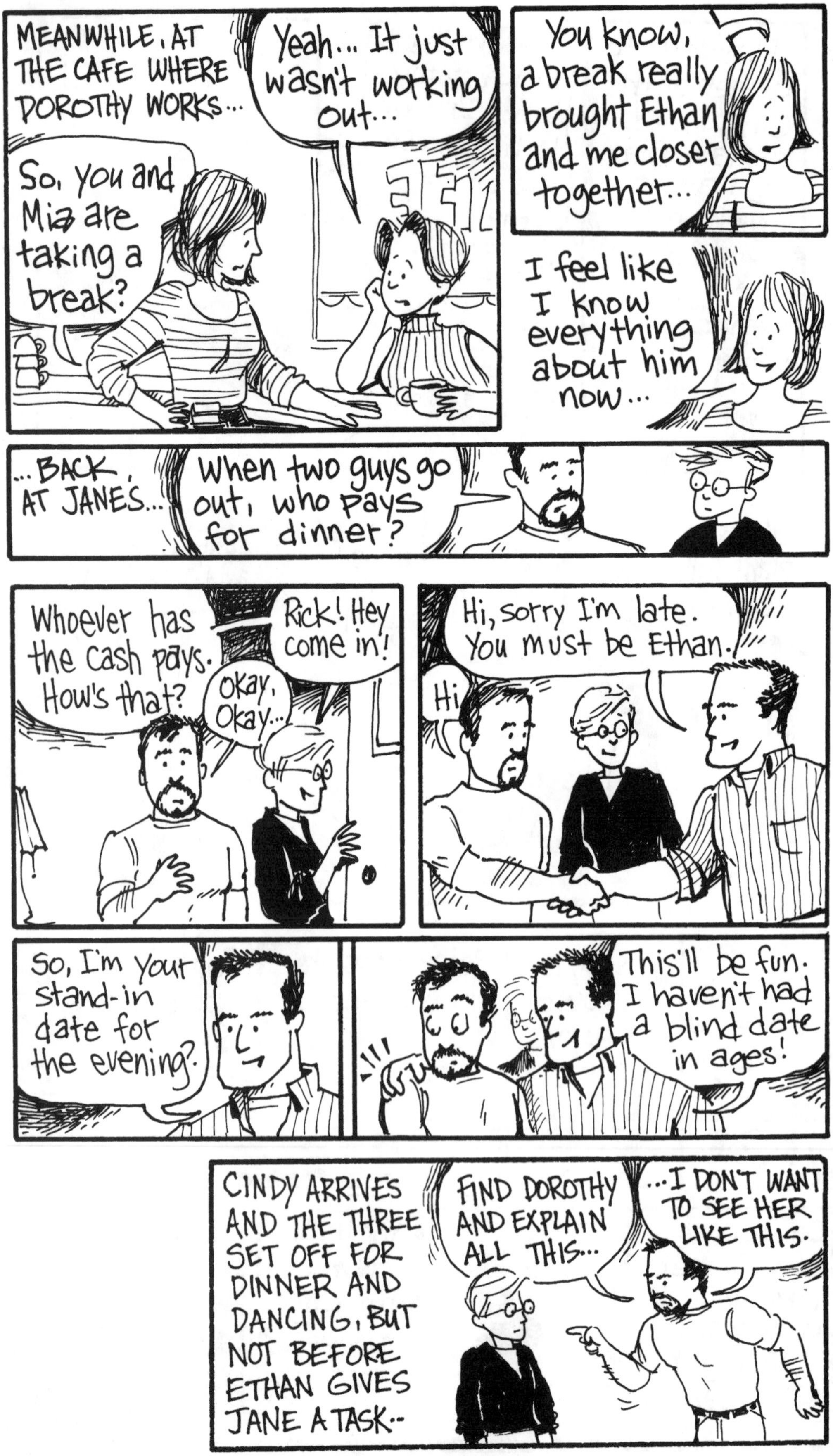
MEANWHILE, AT THE CAFE WHERE DOROTHY WORKS...
Yeah... It just wasn't working out...
So, you and Mia are taking a break?
You know, a break really brought Ethan and me closer together...
I feel like I know everything about him now...
...BACK AT JANE'S...
When two guys go out, who pays for dinner?
Whoever has the cash pays. How's that?
Rick! Hey come in!
Okay, Okay...
Hi, sorry I'm late. You must be Ethan.
Hi
So, I'm your stand-in date for the evening?
This'll be fun. I haven't had a blind date in ages!
CINDY ARRIVES AND THE THREE SET OFF FOR DINNER AND DANCING, BUT NOT BEFORE ETHAN GIVES JANE A TASK--
FIND DOROTHY AND EXPLAIN ALL THIS...
...I DON'T WANT TO SEE HER LIKE THIS.

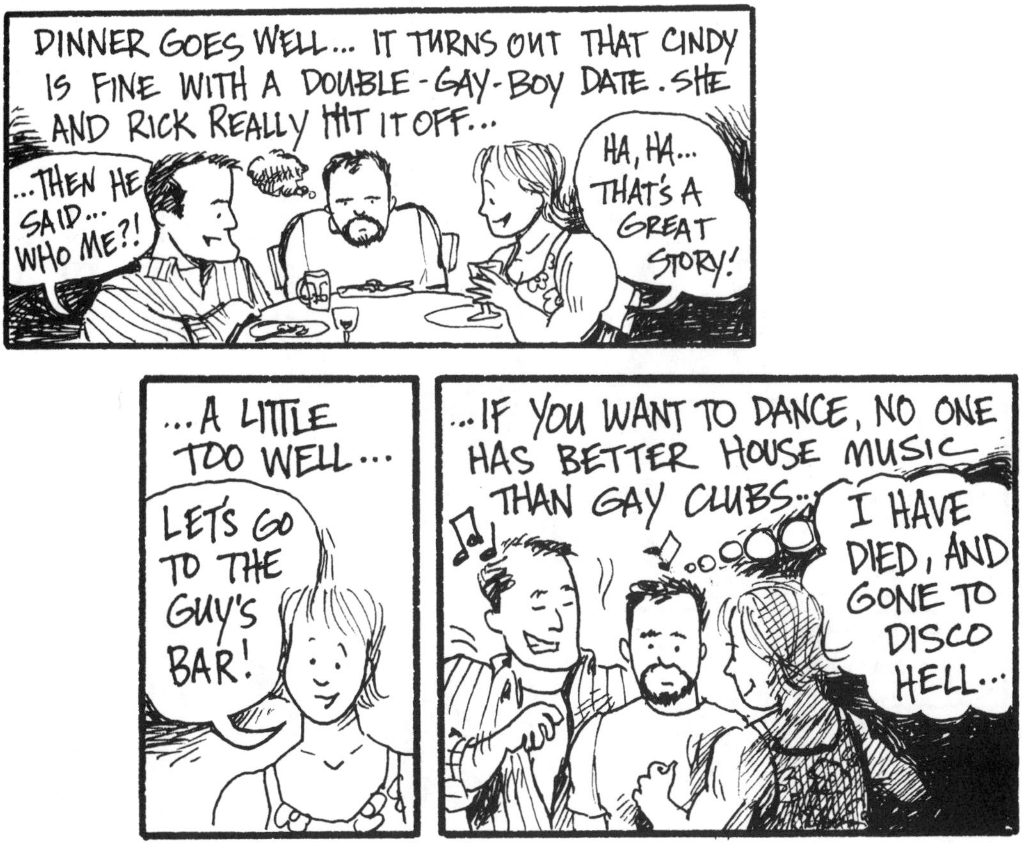
DINNER GOES WELL... IT TURNS OUT THAT CINDY IS FINE WITH A DOUBLE-GAY-BOY DATE. SHE AND RICK REALLY HIT IT OFF...
...THEN HE SAID... WHO ME?!
HA, HA... THAT'S A GREAT STORY!
...A LITTLE TOO WELL...
LET'S GO TO THE GUY'S BAR!
...IF YOU WANT TO DANCE, NO ONE HAS BETTER HOUSE MUSIC THAN GAY CLUBS...
I HAVE DIED, AND GONE TO DISCO HELL...

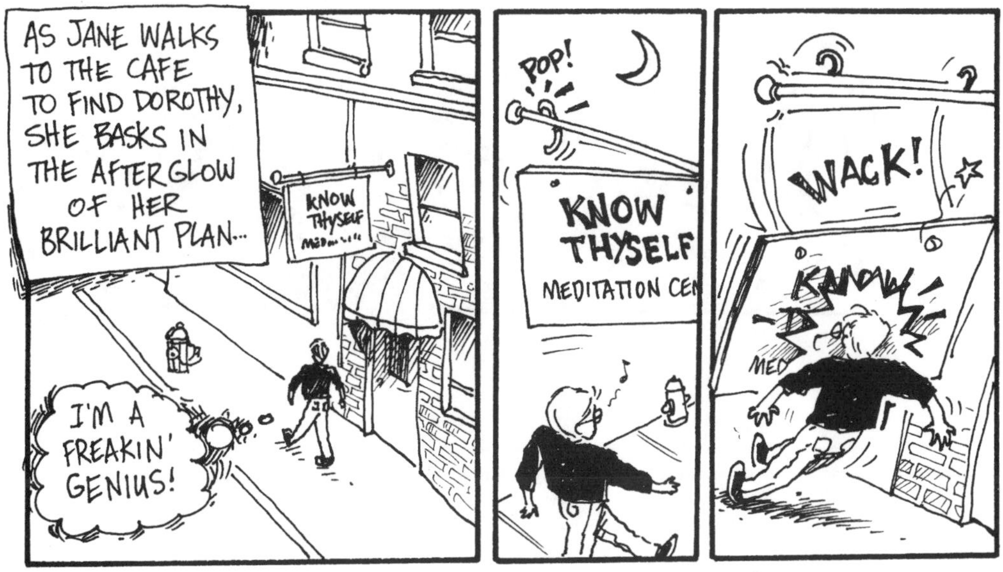
AS JANE WALKS TO THE CAFE TO FIND DOROTHY, SHE BASKS IN THE AFTERGLOW OF HER BRILLIANT PLAN...
KNOW THYSELF
I'M A FREAKIN' GENIUS!
POP!
KNOW THYSELF
MEDITATION CEN
WACK!
KAPOW!
MED

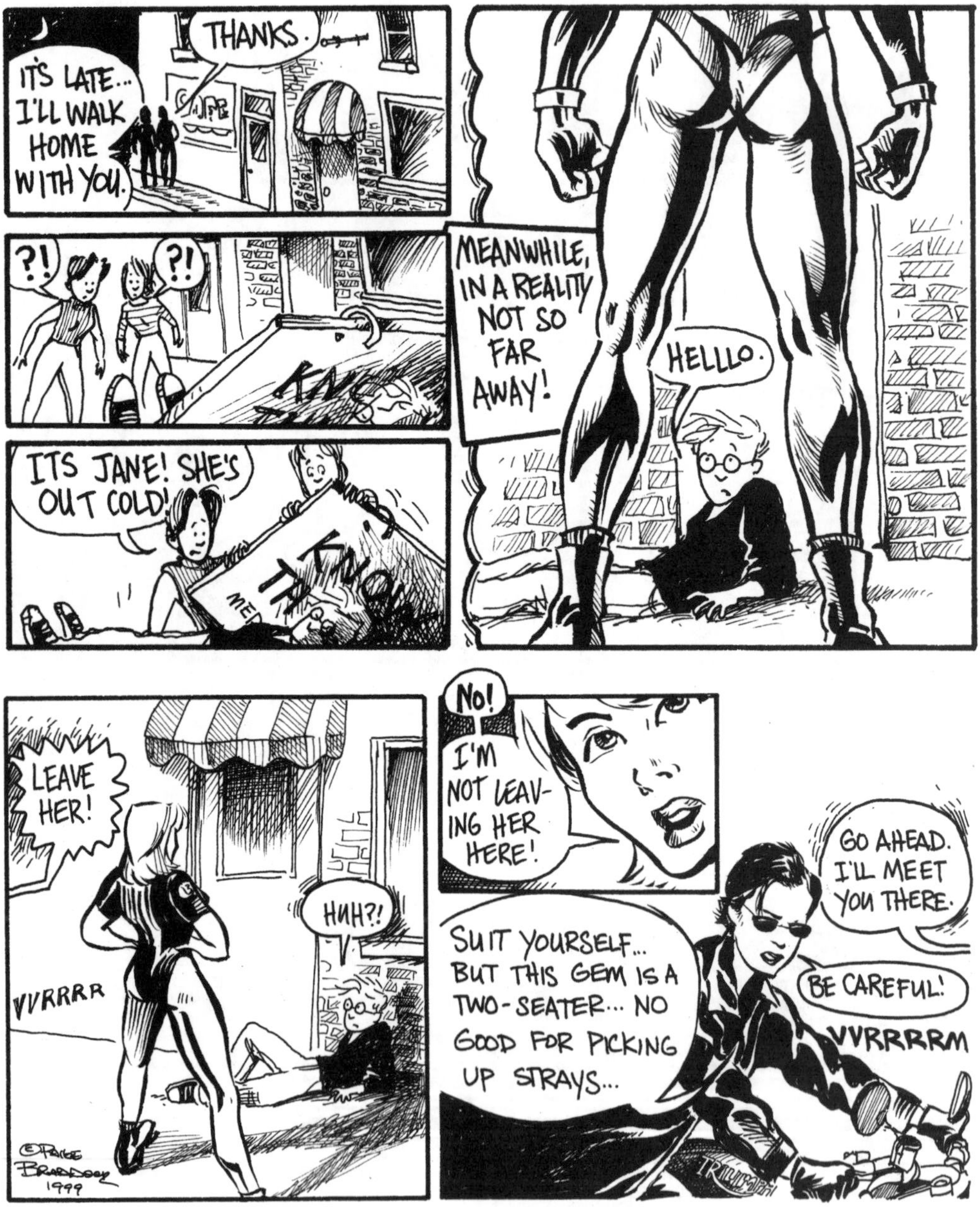
IT'S LATE... I'LL WALK HOME WITH YOU.
THANKS.
?!
?!
ITS JANE! SHE'S OUT COLD!
MEANWHILE, IN A REALITY NOT SO FAR AWAY!
HELLLO.
LEAVE HER!
VVRRRR
HUH?!
©PAIGE BRADDOCK 1999
No!
I'M NOT LEAVING HER HERE!
SUIT YOURSELF... BUT THIS GEM IS A TWO-SEATER... NO GOOD FOR PICKING UP STRAYS...
GO AHEAD. I'LL MEET YOU THERE.
BE CAREFUL!
VVRRRRM

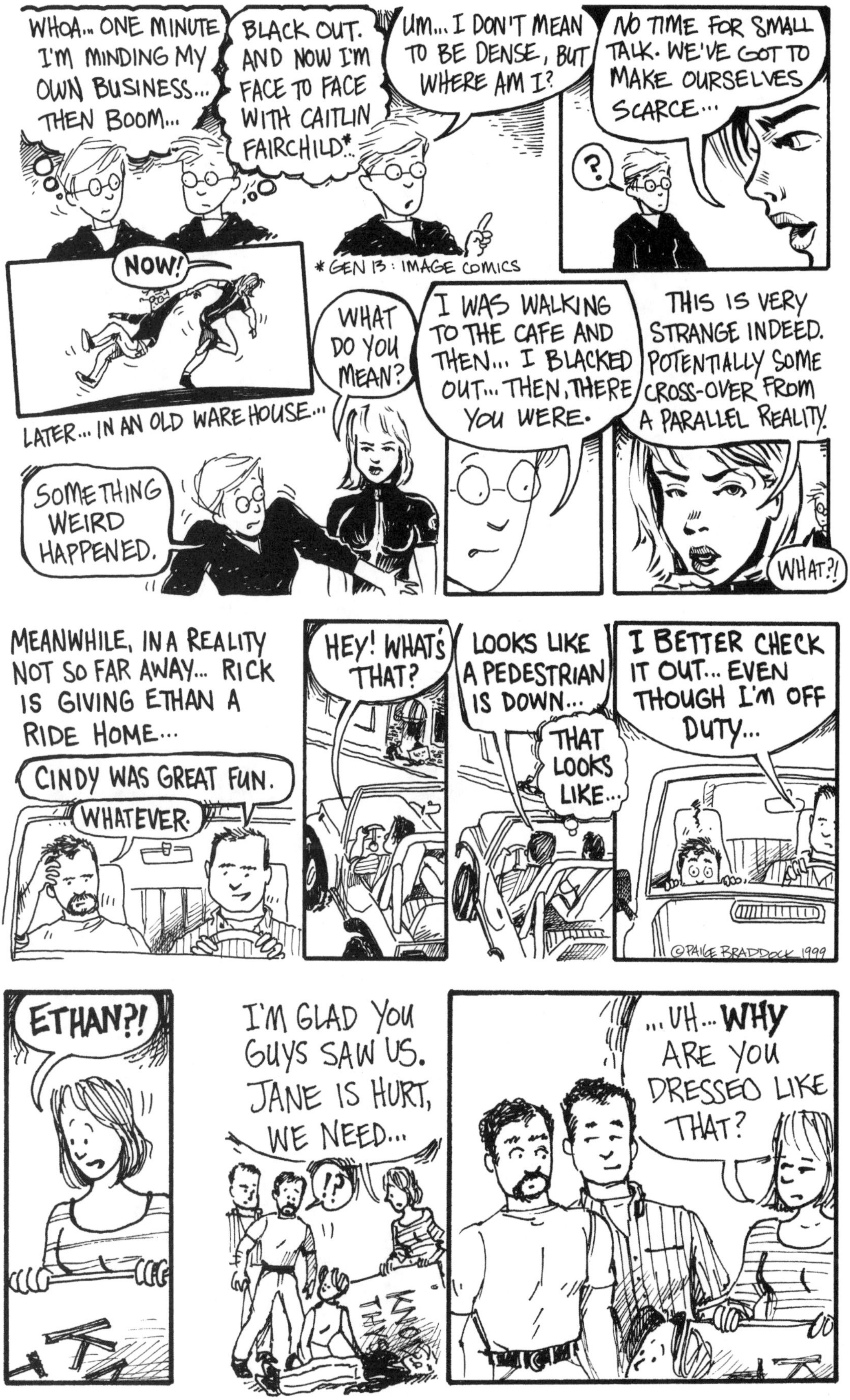

WHOA... ONE MINUTE I'M MINDING MY OWN BUSINESS... THEN BOOM...
BLACK OUT. AND NOW I'M FACE TO FACE WITH CAITLIN FAIRCHILD*...
UM... I DON'T MEAN TO BE DENSE, BUT WHERE AM I?
NO TIME FOR SMALL TALK. WE'VE GOT TO MAKE OURSELVES SCARCE...
?
* GEN 13 : IMAGE COMICS
NOW!
LATER... IN AN OLD WARE HOUSE...
SOMETHING WEIRD HAPPENED.
WHAT DO YOU MEAN?
I WAS WALKING TO THE CAFE AND THEN... I BLACKED OUT... THEN, THERE YOU WERE.
THIS IS VERY STRANGE INDEED. POTENTIALLY SOME CROSS-OVER FROM A PARALLEL REALITY.
WHAT?!
MEANWHILE, IN A REALITY NOT SO FAR AWAY... RICK IS GIVING ETHAN A RIDE HOME...
CINDY WAS GREAT FUN.
WHATEVER.
HEY! WHAT'S THAT?
LOOKS LIKE A PEDESTRIAN IS DOWN...
THAT LOOKS LIKE...
I BETTER CHECK IT OUT... EVEN THOUGH I'M OFF DUTY...
©PAIGE BRADDOCK 1999
ETHAN?!
I'M GLAD YOU GUYS SAW US. JANE IS HURT, WE NEED...
!?
...UH... WHY ARE YOU DRESSED LIKE THAT?

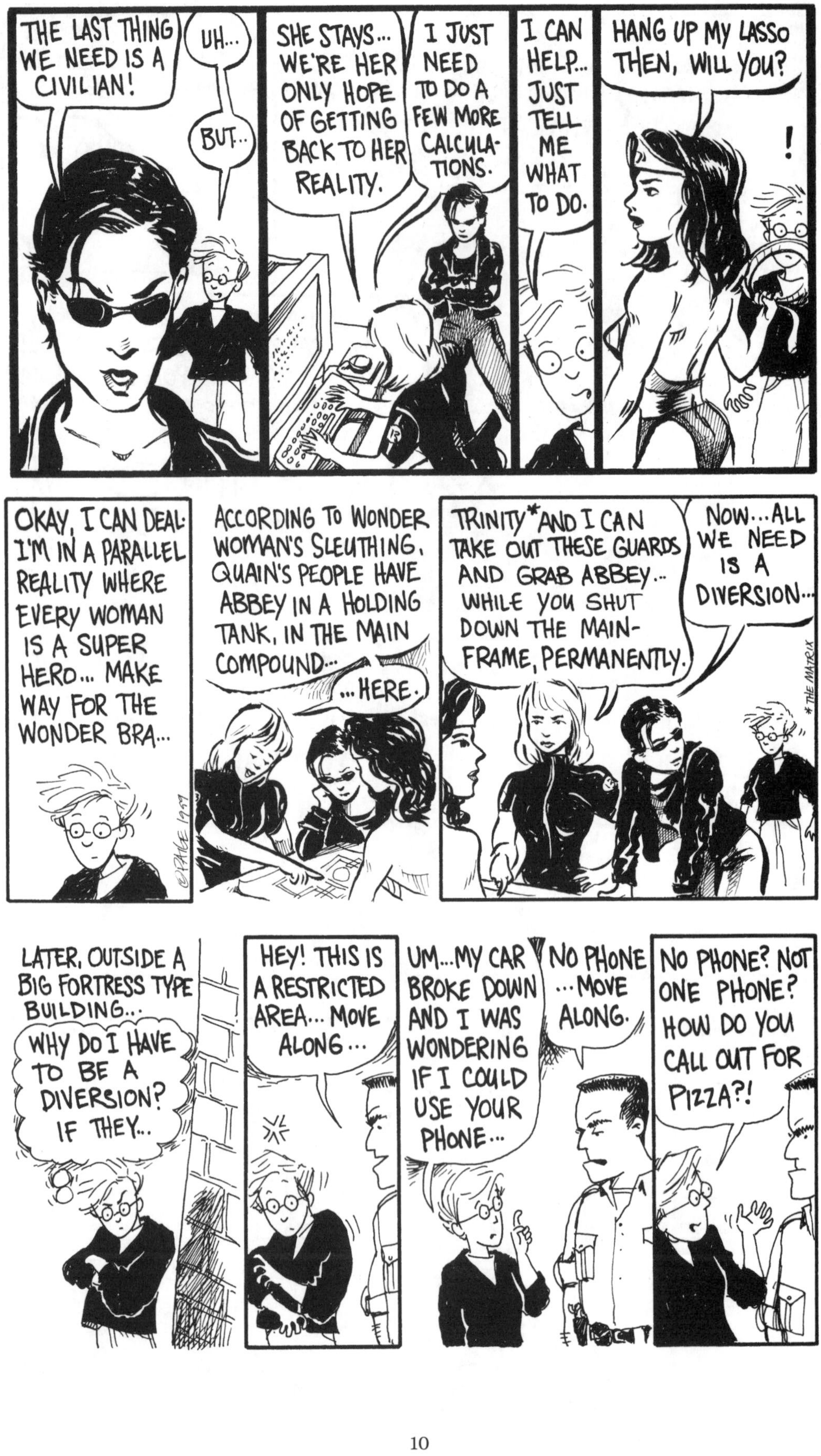
THE LAST THING WE NEED IS A CIVILIAN!
UH...
BUT...
SHE STAYS... WE'RE HER ONLY HOPE OF GETTING BACK TO HER REALITY.
I JUST NEED TO DO A FEW MORE CALCULATIONS.
I CAN HELP... JUST TELL ME WHAT TO DO.
HANG UP MY LASSO THEN, WILL YOU?
!
OKAY, I CAN DEAL: I'M IN A PARALLEL REALITY WHERE EVERY WOMAN IS A SUPER HERO... MAKE WAY FOR THE WONDER BRA...
©PAIGE 1999
ACCORDING TO WONDER WOMAN'S SLEUTHING, QUAIN'S PEOPLE HAVE ABBEY IN A HOLDING TANK, IN THE MAIN COMPOUND...
...HERE.
TRINITY* AND I CAN TAKE OUT THESE GUARDS AND GRAB ABBEY... WHILE YOU SHUT DOWN THE MAINFRAME, PERMANENTLY.
NOW... ALL WE NEED IS A DIVERSION...
* THE MATRIX
LATER, OUTSIDE A BIG FORTRESS TYPE BUILDING...
WHY DO I HAVE TO BE A DIVERSION? IF THEY...
HEY! THIS IS A RESTRICTED AREA... MOVE ALONG...
UM... MY CAR BROKE DOWN AND I WAS WONDERING IF I COULD USE YOUR PHONE...
NO PHONE ... MOVE ALONG.
NO PHONE? NOT ONE PHONE? HOW DO YOU CALL OUT FOR PIZZA?!

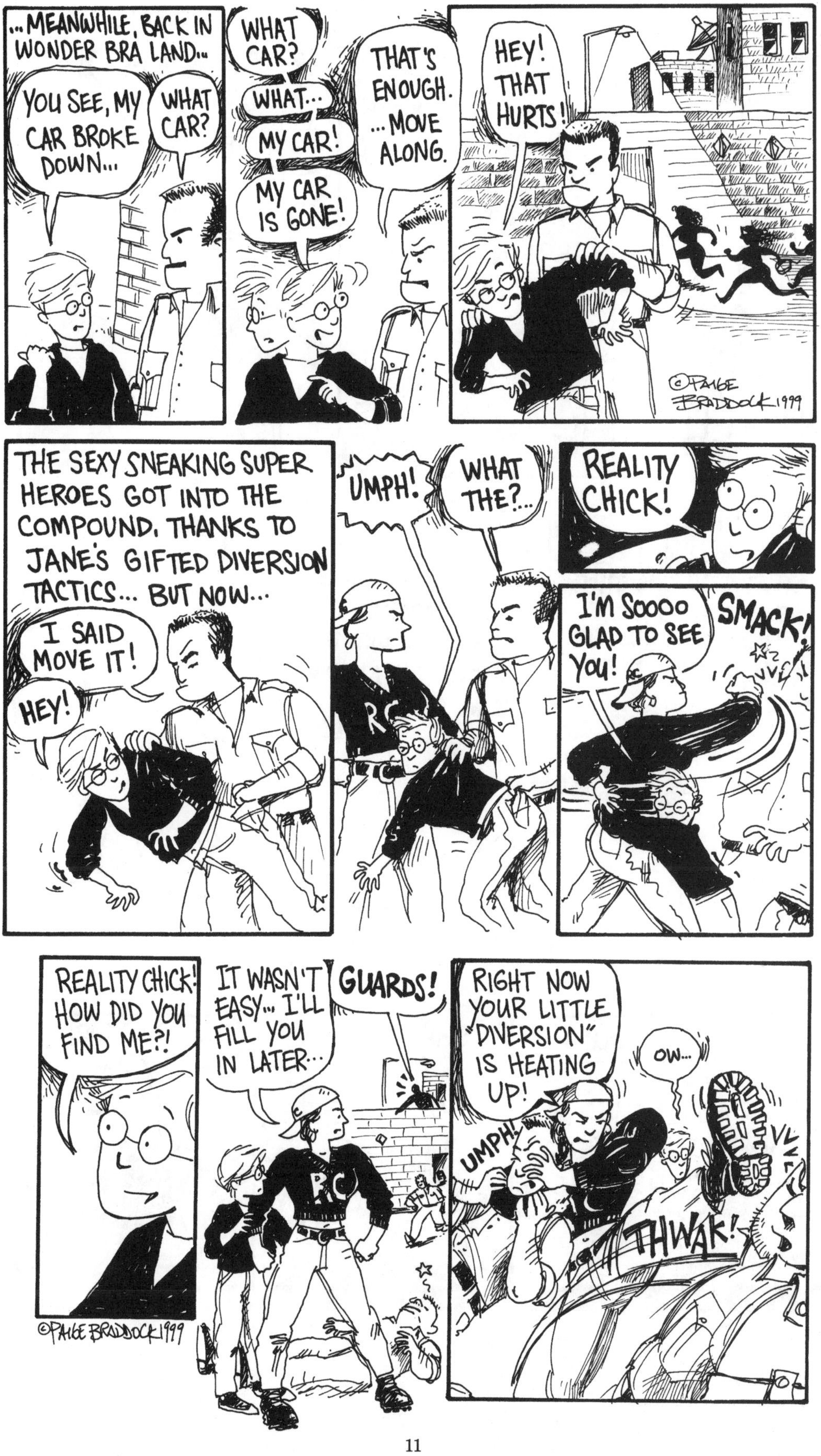
...MEANWHILE, BACK IN WONDER BRA LAND...
YOU SEE, MY CAR BROKE DOWN...
WHAT CAR?
WHAT CAR?
WHAT...
MY CAR!
MY CAR IS GONE!
THAT'S ENOUGH. ...MOVE ALONG.
HEY! THAT HURTS!
©PAIGE BRADDOCK 1999
THE SEXY SNEAKING SUPER HEROES GOT INTO THE COMPOUND, THANKS TO JANE'S GIFTED DIVERSION TACTICS... BUT NOW...
I SAID MOVE IT!
HEY!
UMPH!
WHAT THE?...
REALITY CHICK!
I'M SOOOO GLAD TO SEE YOU!
SMACK!
REALITY CHICK! HOW DID YOU FIND ME?!
©PAIGE BRADDOCK 1999
IT WASN'T EASY... I'LL FILL YOU IN LATER...
GUARDS!
RIGHT NOW YOUR LITTLE "DIVERSION" IS HEATING UP!
OW...
UMPH!
THWAK!

Reality Chick encourages Jane to leave, for her own safety...

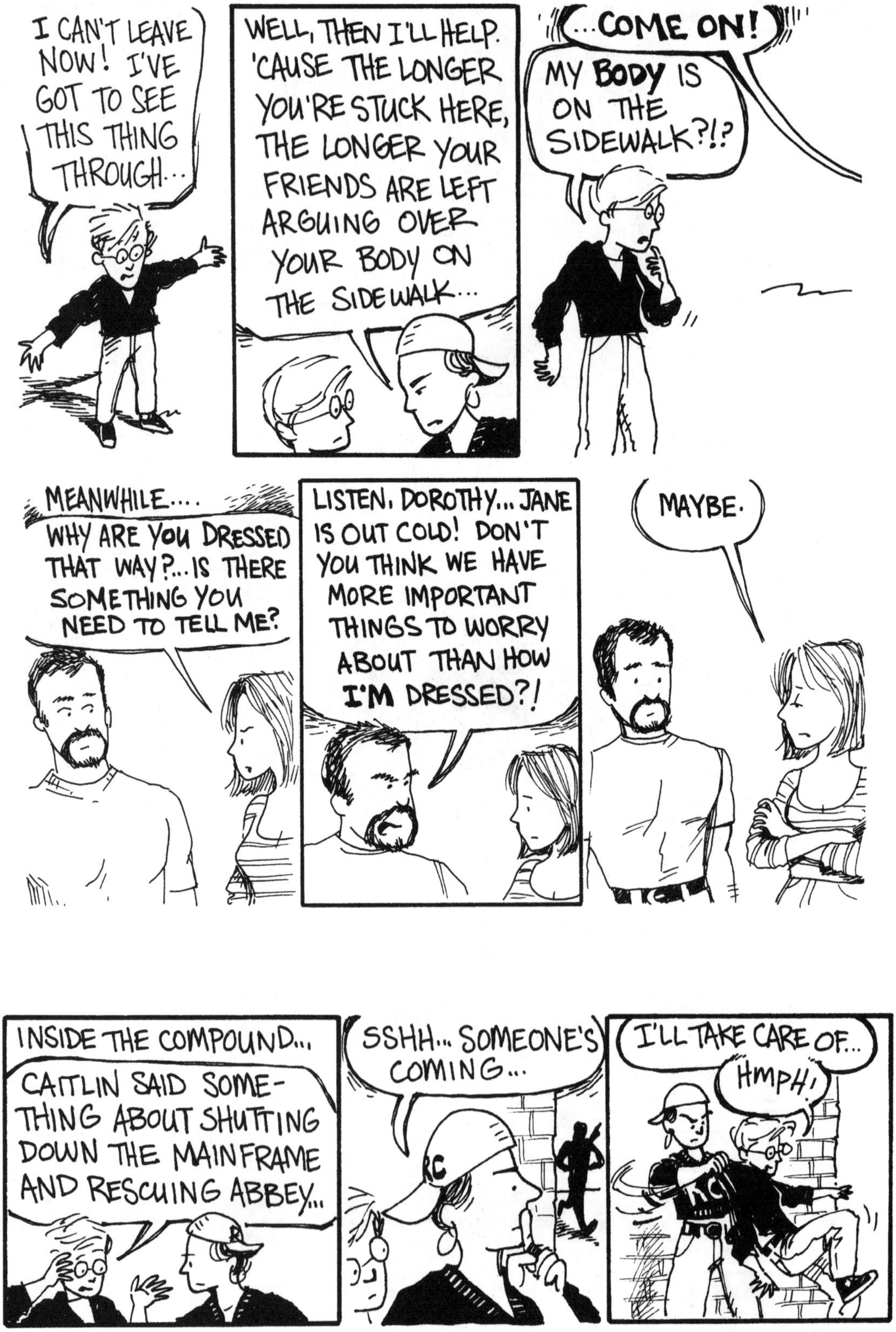

I CAN'T LEAVE NOW! I'VE GOT TO SEE THIS THING THROUGH...
WELL, THEN I'LL HELP. 'CAUSE THE LONGER YOU'RE STUCK HERE, THE LONGER YOUR FRIENDS ARE LEFT ARGUING OVER YOUR BODY ON THE SIDEWALK...
...COME ON!
MY BODY IS ON THE SIDEWALK?!?
MEANWHILE....
WHY ARE YOU DRESSED THAT WAY?...IS THERE SOMETHING YOU NEED TO TELL ME?
LISTEN, DOROTHY... JANE IS OUT COLD! DON'T YOU THINK WE HAVE MORE IMPORTANT THINGS TO WORRY ABOUT THAN HOW I'M DRESSED?!
MAYBE.
INSIDE THE COMPOUND...
CAITLIN SAID SOMETHING ABOUT SHUTTING DOWN THE MAINFRAME AND RESCUING ABBEY...
SSHH... SOMEONE'S COMING...
I'LL TAKE CARE OF...
HMPH!

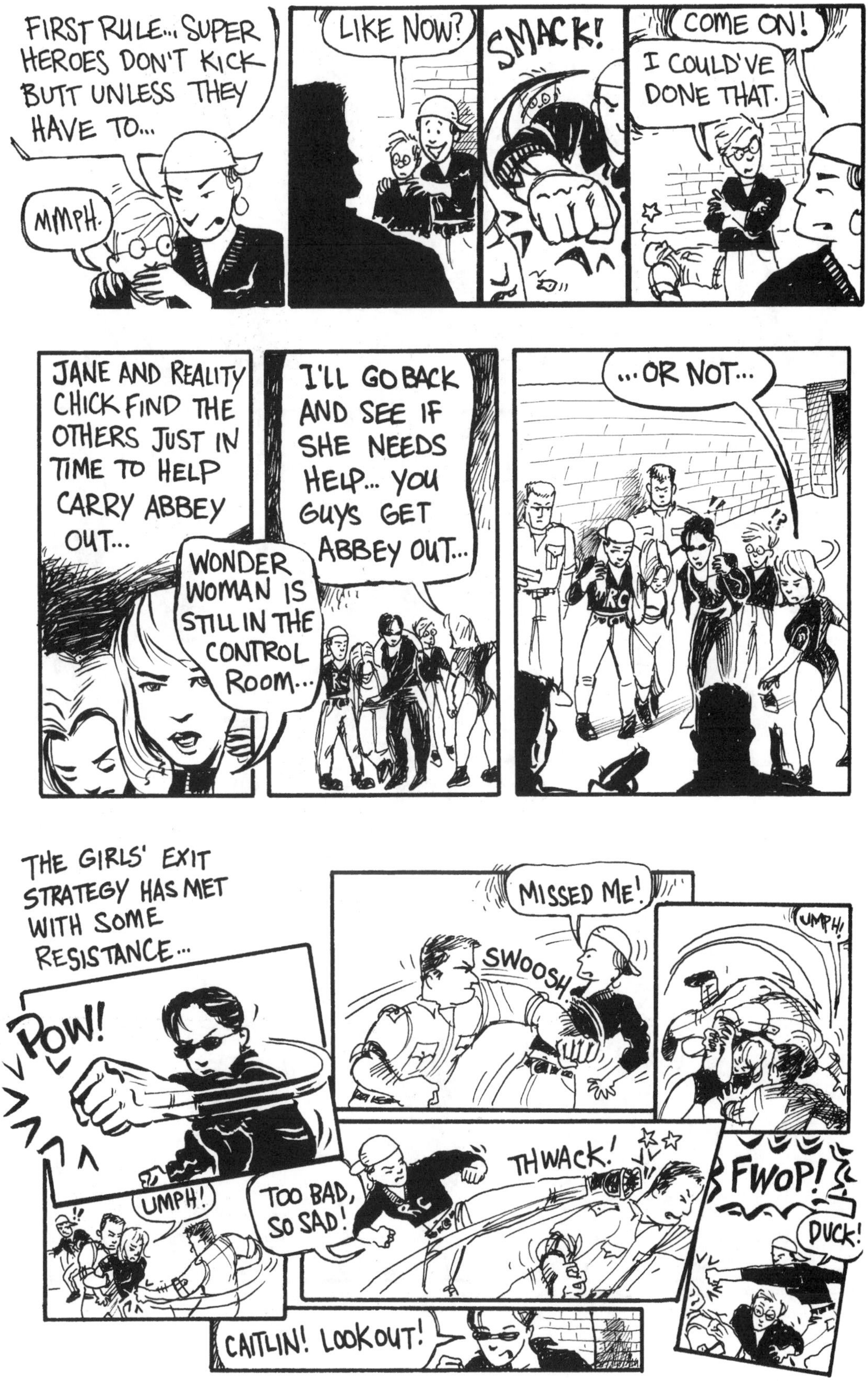
FIRST RULE... SUPER HEROES DON'T KICK BUTT UNLESS THEY HAVE TO...
MMPH.
LIKE NOW?
SMACK!
COME ON!
I COULD'VE DONE THAT.
JANE AND REALITY CHICK FIND THE OTHERS JUST IN TIME TO HELP CARRY ABBEY OUT...
WONDER WOMAN IS STILL IN THE CONTROL ROOM...
I'LL GO BACK AND SEE IF SHE NEEDS HELP... YOU GUYS GET ABBEY OUT...
...OR NOT...
THE GIRLS' EXIT STRATEGY HAS MET WITH SOME RESISTANCE...
POW!
MISSED ME!
SWOOSH
UMPH!
UMPH!
TOO BAD, SO SAD!
THWACK!
FWOP!
DUCK!
CAITLIN! LOOKOUT!

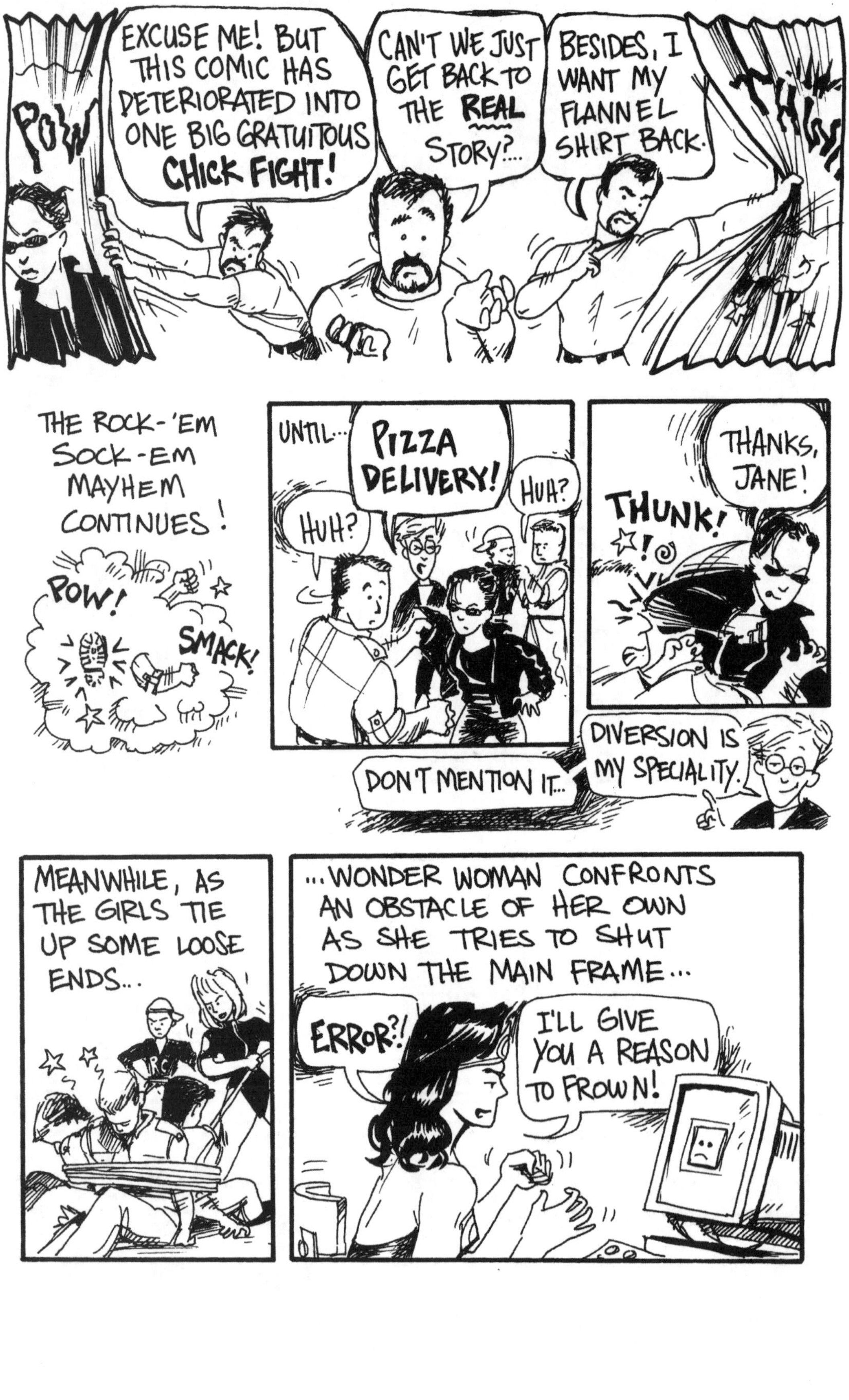

POW
EXCUSE ME! BUT THIS COMIC HAS DETERIORATED INTO ONE BIG GRATUITOUS CHICK FIGHT!
CAN'T WE JUST GET BACK TO THE REAL STORY?...
BESIDES, I WANT MY FLANNEL SHIRT BACK.
THE ROCK-'EM SOCK-EM MAYHEM CONTINUES!
POW!
SMACK!
UNTIL...
PIZZA DELIVERY!
HUH?
HUH?
THANKS, JANE!
THUNK!
DON'T MENTION IT...
DIVERSION IS MY SPECIALITY.
MEANWHILE, AS THE GIRLS TIE UP SOME LOOSE ENDS...
...WONDER WOMAN CONFRONTS AN OBSTACLE OF HER OWN AS SHE TRIES TO SHUT DOWN THE MAIN FRAME...
ERROR?!
I'LL GIVE YOU A REASON TO FROWN!

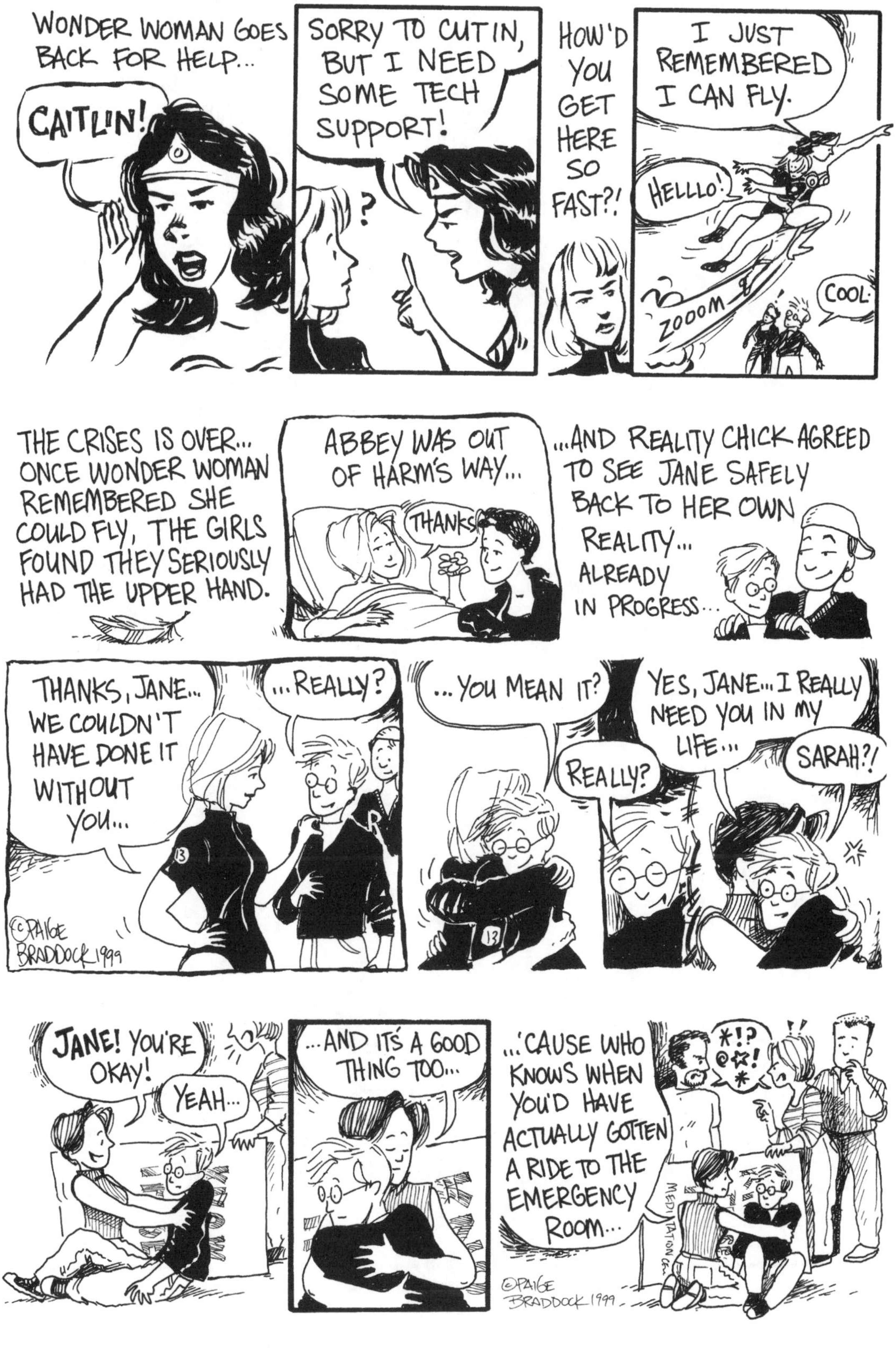

WONDER WOMAN GOES BACK FOR HELP...
CAITLIN!
SORRY TO CUT IN, BUT I NEED SOME TECH SUPPORT!
?
HOW'D YOU GET HERE SO FAST?!
I JUST REMEMBERED I CAN FLY.
HELLLO!
ZOOOM
COOL!
THE CRISES IS OVER... ONCE WONDER WOMAN REMEMBERED SHE COULD FLY, THE GIRLS FOUND THEY SERIOUSLY HAD THE UPPER HAND.
ABBEY WAS OUT OF HARM'S WAY...
THANKS
...AND REALITY CHICK AGREED TO SEE JANE SAFELY BACK TO HER OWN REALITY... ALREADY IN PROGRESS...
THANKS, JANE... WE COULDN'T HAVE DONE IT WITHOUT YOU...
...REALLY?
©PAIGE BRADDOCK 1999
...YOU MEAN IT?
REALLY?
YES, JANE... I REALLY NEED YOU IN MY LIFE...
SARAH?!
JANE! YOU'RE OKAY!
YEAH...
...AND IT'S A GOOD THING TOO...
...'CAUSE WHO KNOWS WHEN YOU'D HAVE ACTUALLY GOTTEN A RIDE TO THE EMERGENCY ROOM...
MEDITATION Co.
©PAIGE BRADDOCK 1999

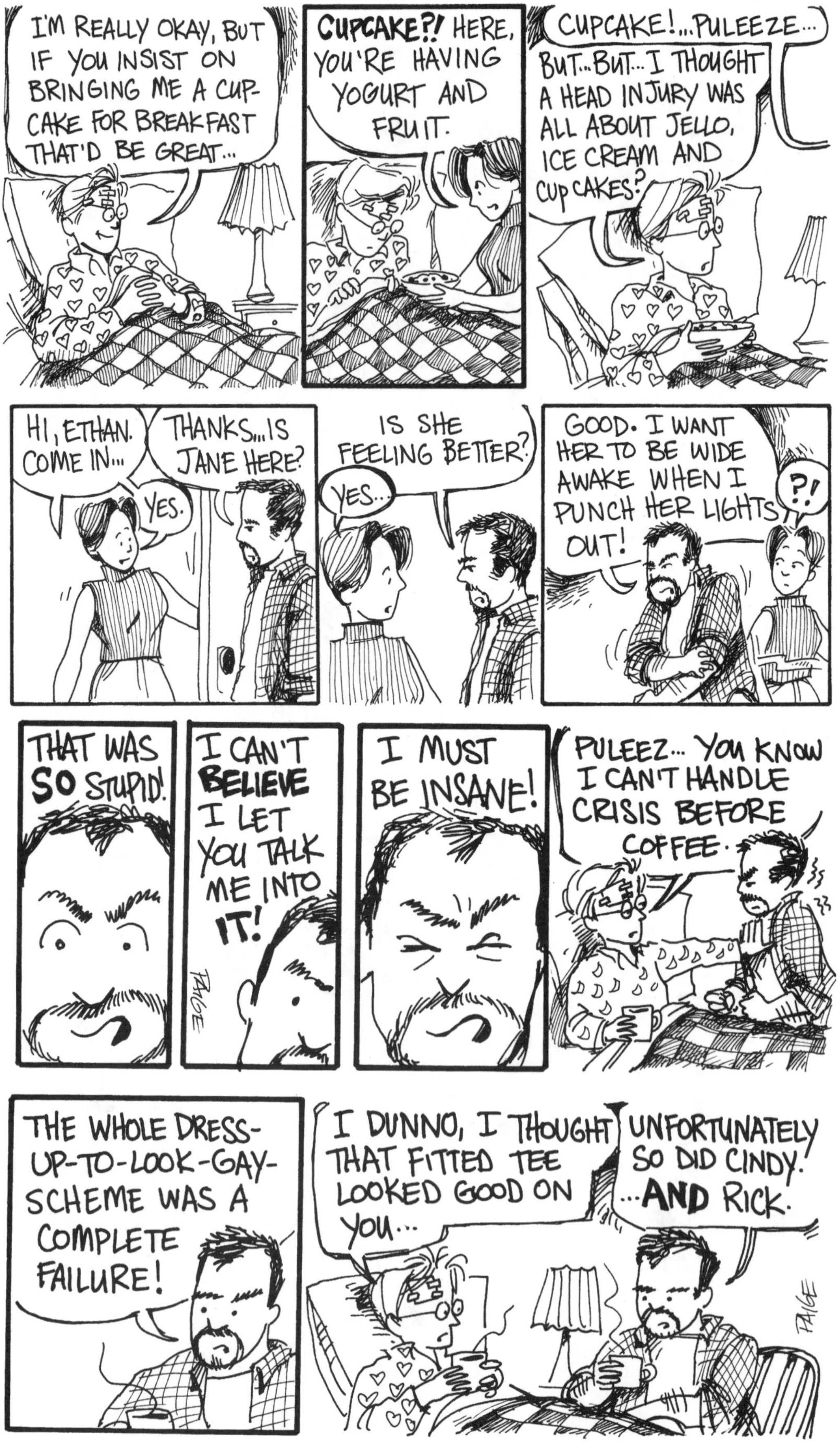
I'M REALLY OKAY, BUT IF YOU INSIST ON BRINGING ME A CUPCAKE FOR BREAKFAST THAT'D BE GREAT...
CUPCAKE?! HERE, YOU'RE HAVING YOGURT AND FRUIT.
CUPCAKE!...PULEEZE...
BUT...BUT...I THOUGHT A HEAD INJURY WAS ALL ABOUT JELLO, ICE CREAM AND CUP CAKES?
HI, ETHAN. COME IN...
THANKS...IS JANE HERE?
YES.
IS SHE FEELING BETTER?
YES...
GOOD. I WANT HER TO BE WIDE AWAKE WHEN I PUNCH HER LIGHTS OUT!
?!
THAT WAS SO STUPID!
I CAN'T BELIEVE I LET YOU TALK ME INTO IT!
PAIGE
I MUST BE INSANE!
PULEEZ... YOU KNOW I CAN'T HANDLE CRISIS BEFORE COFFEE.
THE WHOLE DRESS-UP-TO-LOOK-GAY-SCHEME WAS A COMPLETE FAILURE!
I DUNNO, I THOUGHT THAT FITTED TEE LOOKED GOOD ON YOU...
UNFORTUNATELY SO DID CINDY. ...AND RICK.
PAIGE

MY BOSS COULD CARE LESS... SEE, I'M A COG IN THIS CORPORATE MEDIA MACHINE, ONCE FONDLY REFERRED TO BY MY GRANDPA AS A "DAILY **NEWS**-PAPER"!... YEAH... MAYBE IN HIS DAY... NOW, IT'S "SEXY" NEWS THAT SELLS... SCANDAL IS WHAT EVERYONE WANTS. UNFORTUNATELY FOR ME, I'M NOT ON THE "SEXY" BEAT...

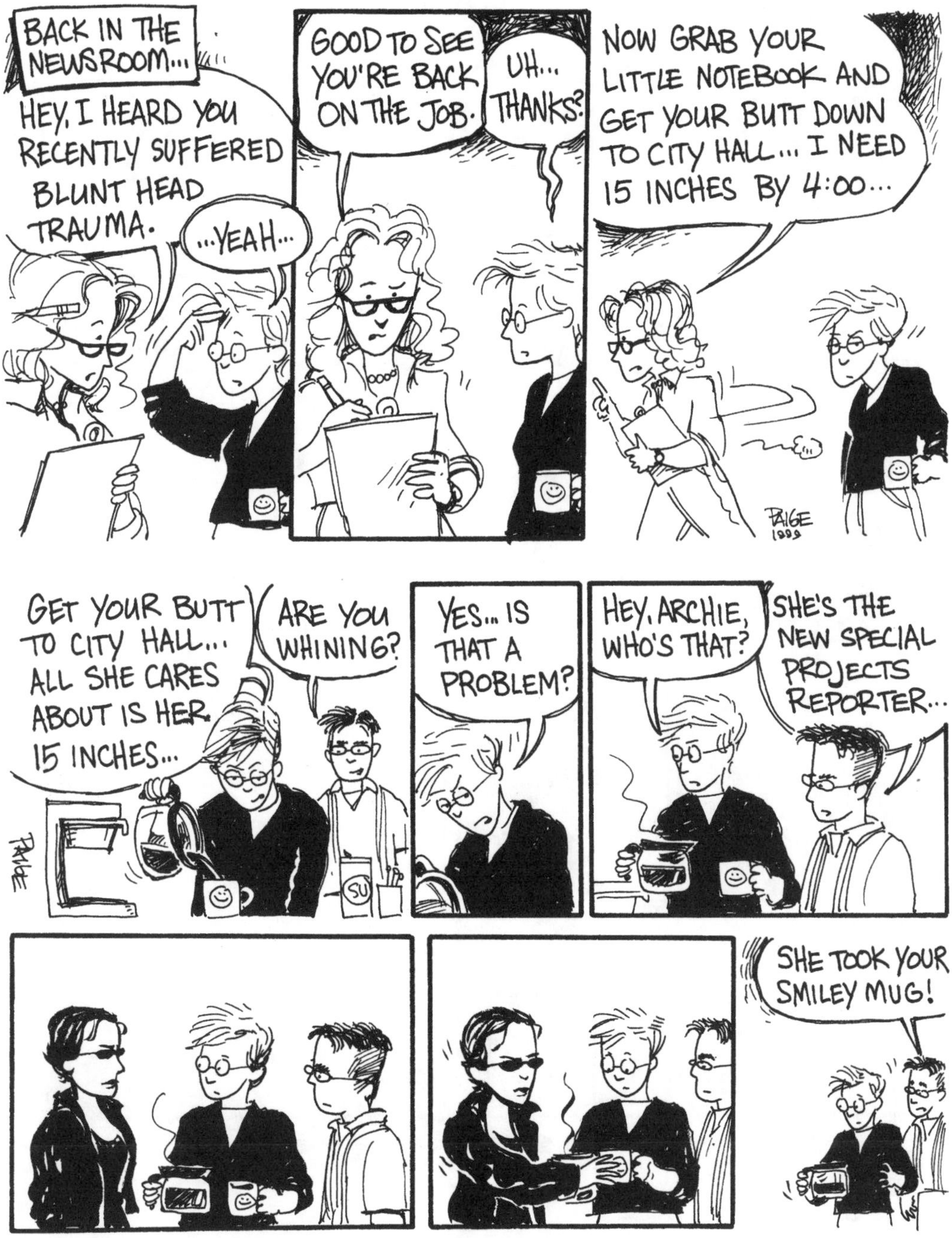
BACK IN THE NEWSROOM...
HEY, I HEARD YOU RECENTLY SUFFERED BLUNT HEAD TRAUMA.
...YEAH...
GOOD TO SEE YOU'RE BACK ON THE JOB.
UH... THANKS?
NOW GRAB YOUR LITTLE NOTEBOOK AND GET YOUR BUTT DOWN TO CITY HALL... I NEED 15 INCHES BY 4:00...
GET YOUR BUTT TO CITY HALL... ALL SHE CARES ABOUT IS HER 15 INCHES...
ARE YOU WHINING?
YES... IS THAT A PROBLEM?
HEY, ARCHIE, WHO'S THAT?
SHE'S THE NEW SPECIAL PROJECTS REPORTER...
SHE TOOK YOUR SMILEY MUG!

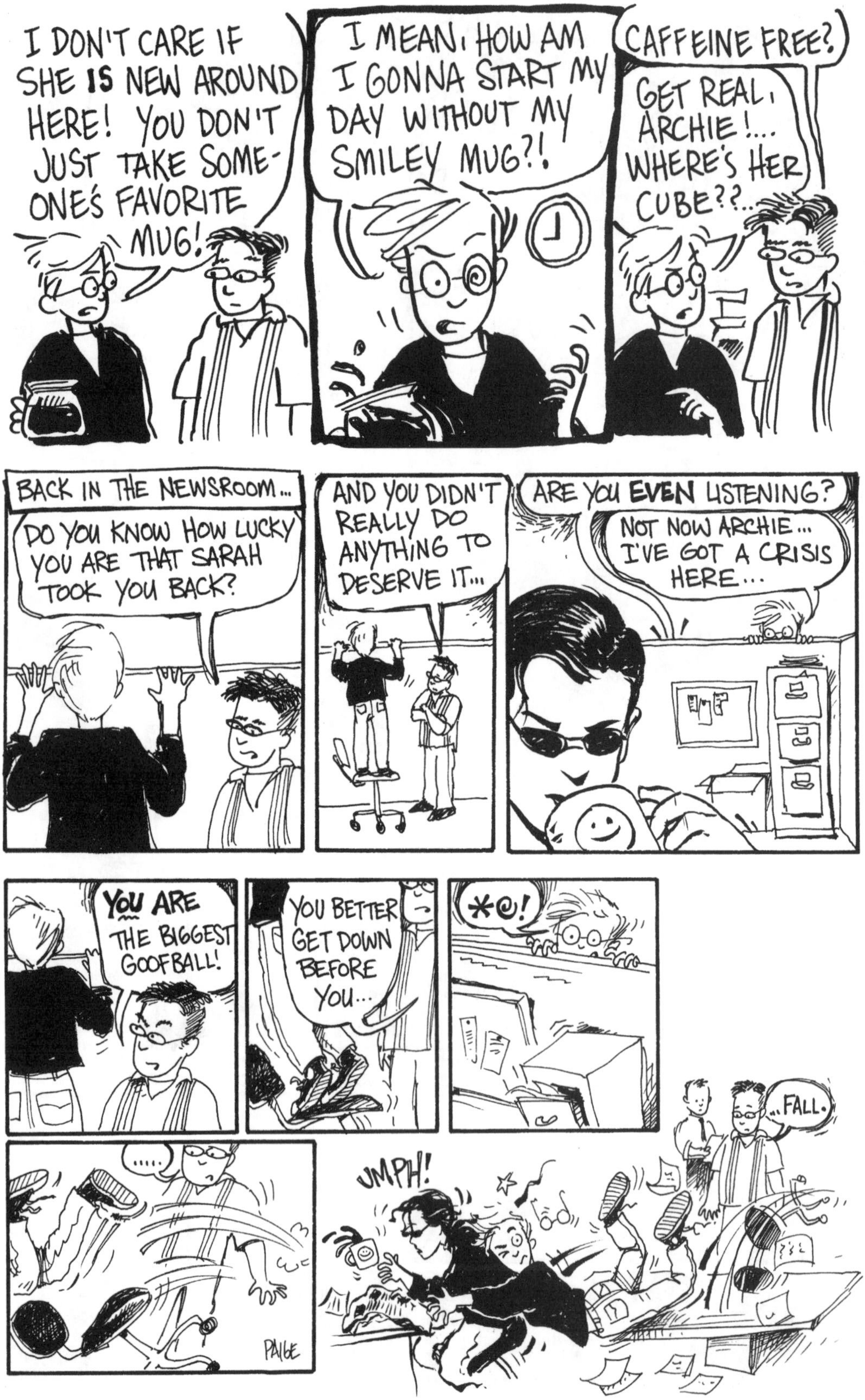
I DON'T CARE IF SHE IS NEW AROUND HERE! YOU DON'T JUST TAKE SOME-ONE'S FAVORITE MUG!
I MEAN, HOW AM I GONNA START MY DAY WITHOUT MY SMILEY MUG?!
CAFFEINE FREE?
GET REAL, ARCHIE!... WHERE'S HER CUBE??...
BACK IN THE NEWSROOM...
DO YOU KNOW HOW LUCKY YOU ARE THAT SARAH TOOK YOU BACK?
AND YOU DIDN'T REALLY DO ANYTHING TO DESERVE IT...
ARE YOU EVEN LISTENING?
NOT NOW ARCHIE... I'VE GOT A CRISIS HERE...
YOU ARE THE BIGGEST GOOFBALL!
YOU BETTER GET DOWN BEFORE YOU...
*@!
...FALL.
.....
UMPH!
PAIGE

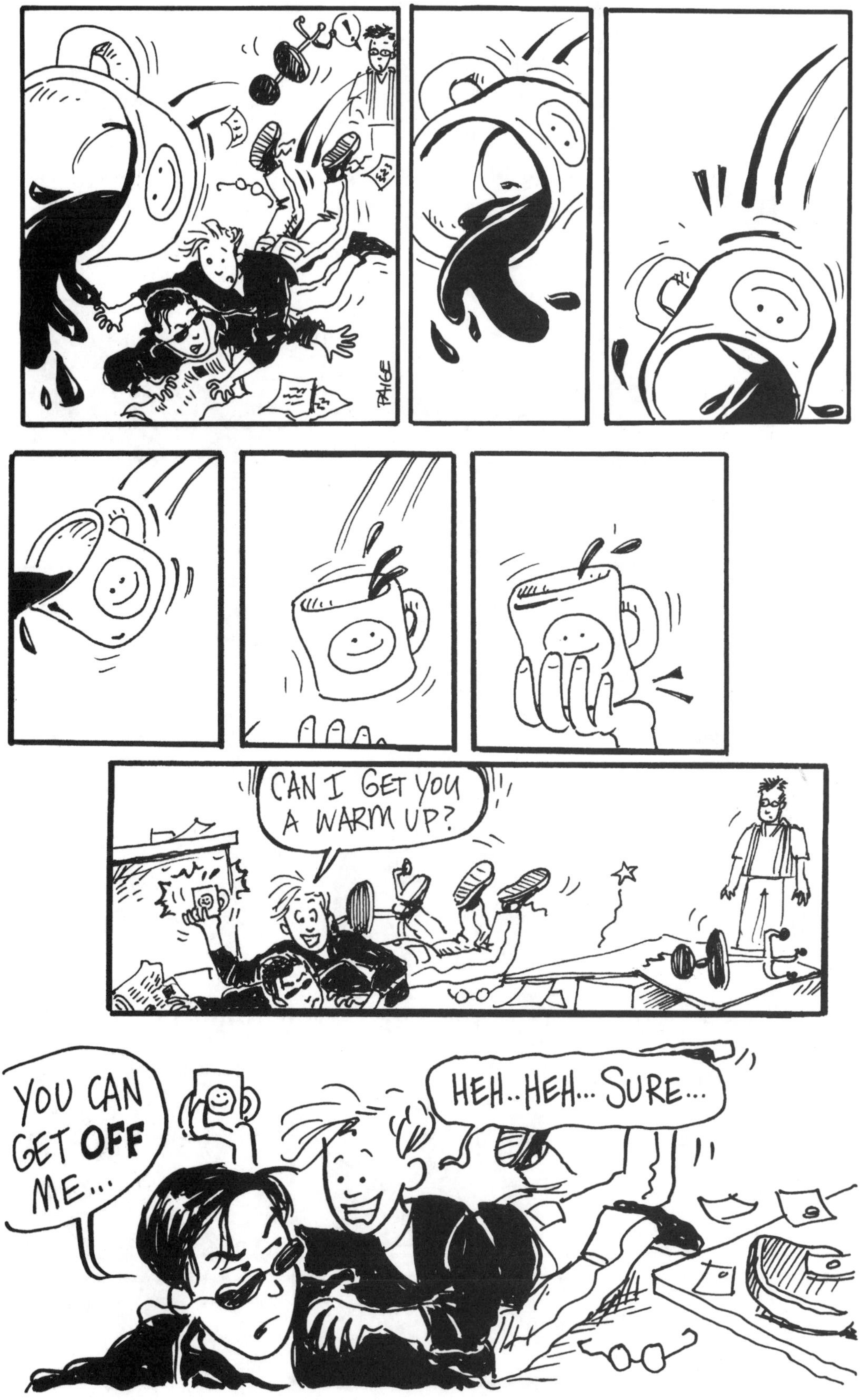
!
PAIGE
CAN I GET YOU A WARM UP?
YOU CAN GET **OFF** ME...
HEH..HEH... SURE...

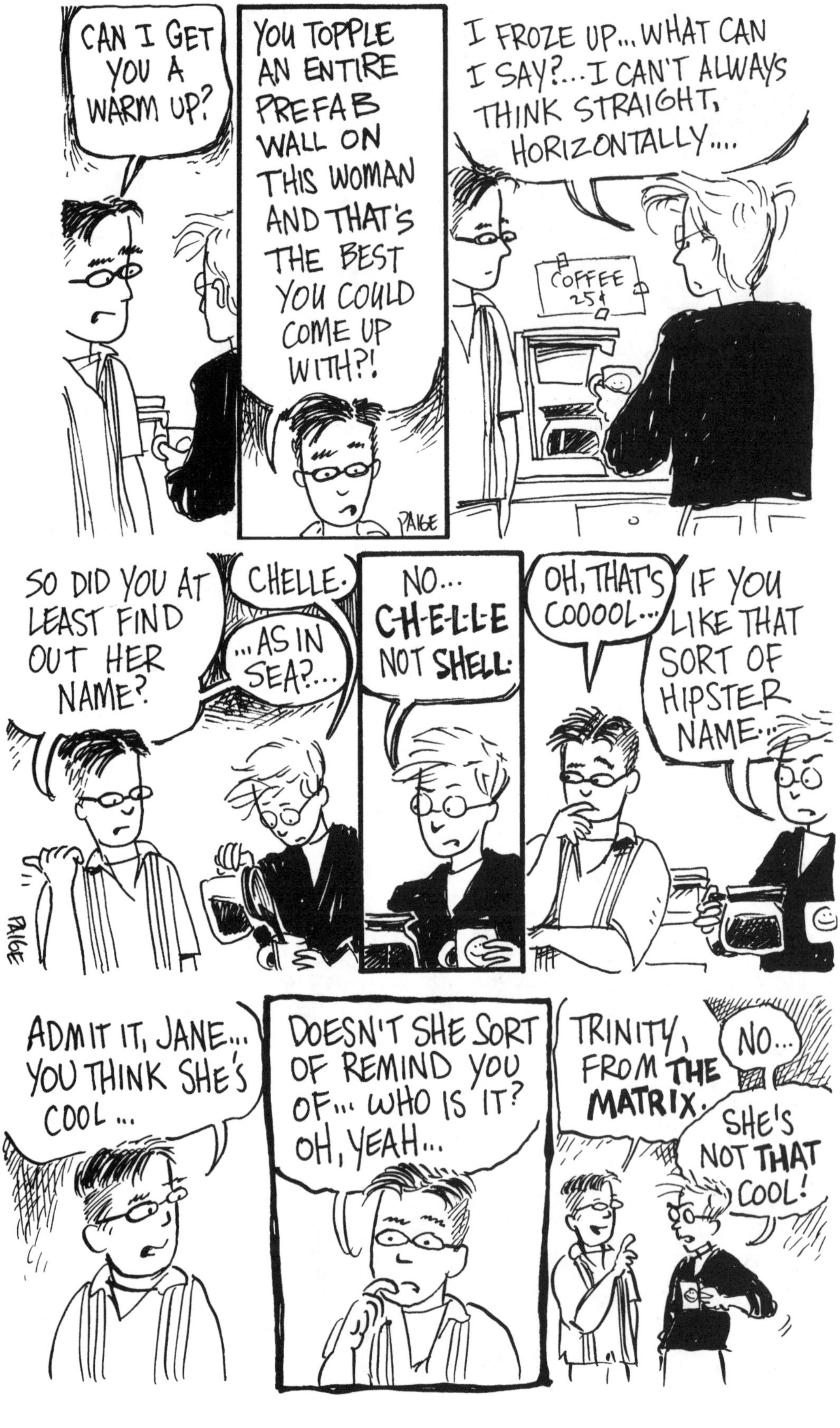
CAN I GET YOU A WARM UP?
YOU TOPPLE AN ENTIRE PREFAB WALL ON THIS WOMAN AND THAT'S THE BEST YOU COULD COME UP WITH?!
PAIGE
I FROZE UP... WHAT CAN I SAY?... I CAN'T ALWAYS THINK STRAIGHT, HORIZONTALLY....
COFFEE 25¢
SO DID YOU AT LEAST FIND OUT HER NAME?
CHELLE.
...AS IN SEA?...
NO... C-H-E-L-L-E NOT SHELL.
OH, THAT'S COOOOL...
IF YOU LIKE THAT SORT OF HIPSTER NAME...
PAIGE
ADMIT IT, JANE... YOU THINK SHE'S COOL...
DOESN'T SHE SORT OF REMIND YOU OF... WHO IS IT? OH, YEAH...
TRINITY, FROM THE MATRIX.
NO...
SHE'S NOT THAT COOL!

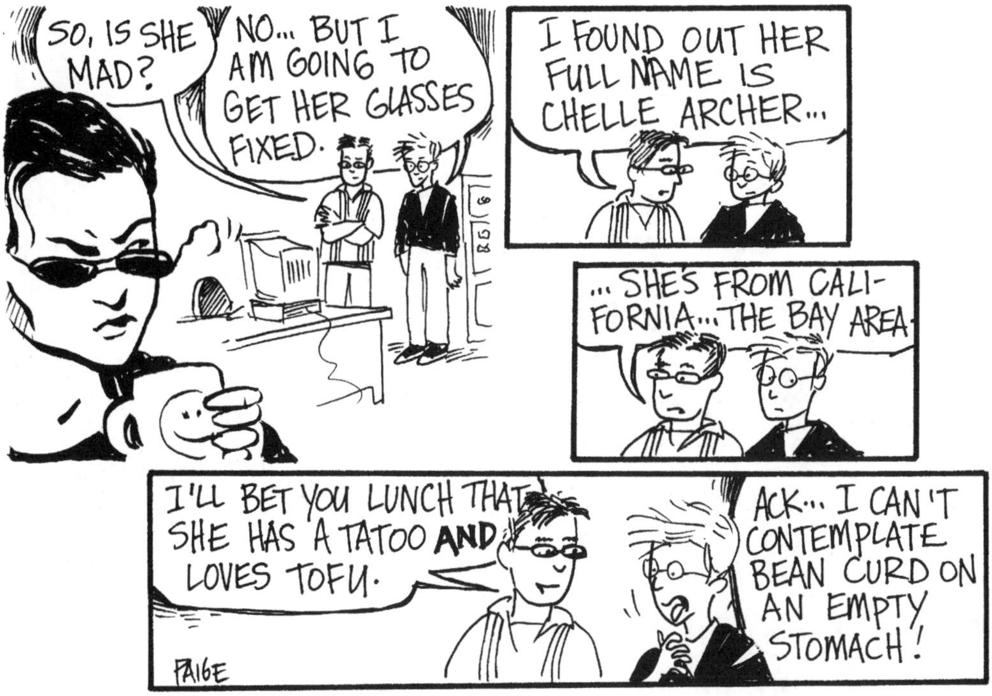
SO, IS SHE MAD?
NO... BUT I AM GOING TO GET HER GLASSES FIXED.
I FOUND OUT HER FULL NAME IS CHELLE ARCHER...
...SHE'S FROM CALIFORNIA... THE BAY AREA.
I'LL BET YOU LUNCH THAT SHE HAS A TATOO **AND** LOVES TOFU.
ACK... I CAN'T CONTEMPLATE BEAN CURD ON AN EMPTY STOMACH!
PAIGE

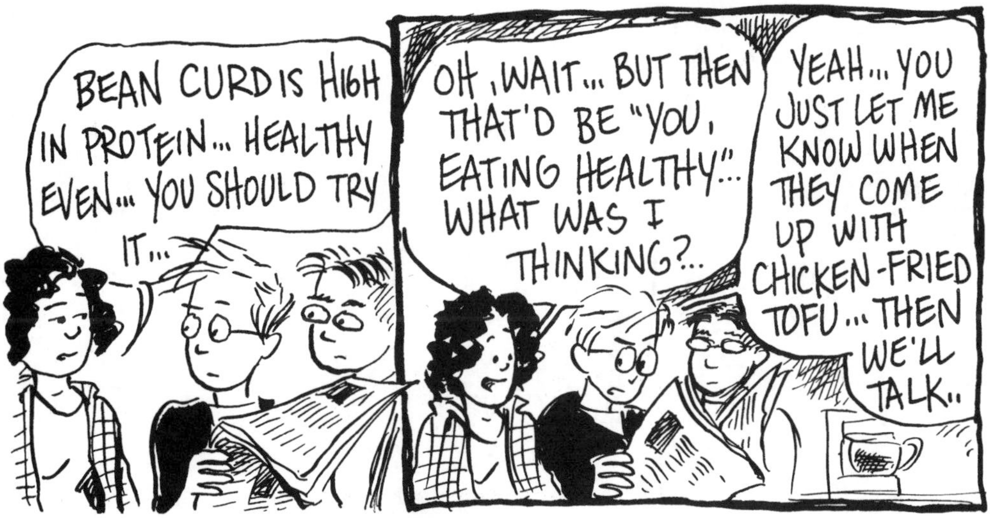
BEAN CURD IS HIGH IN PROTEIN... HEALTHY EVEN... YOU SHOULD TRY IT...
OH, WAIT... BUT THEN THAT'D BE "YOU, EATING HEALTHY"... WHAT WAS I THINKING?...
YEAH... YOU JUST LET ME KNOW WHEN THEY COME UP WITH CHICKEN-FRIED TOFU... THEN WE'LL TALK..

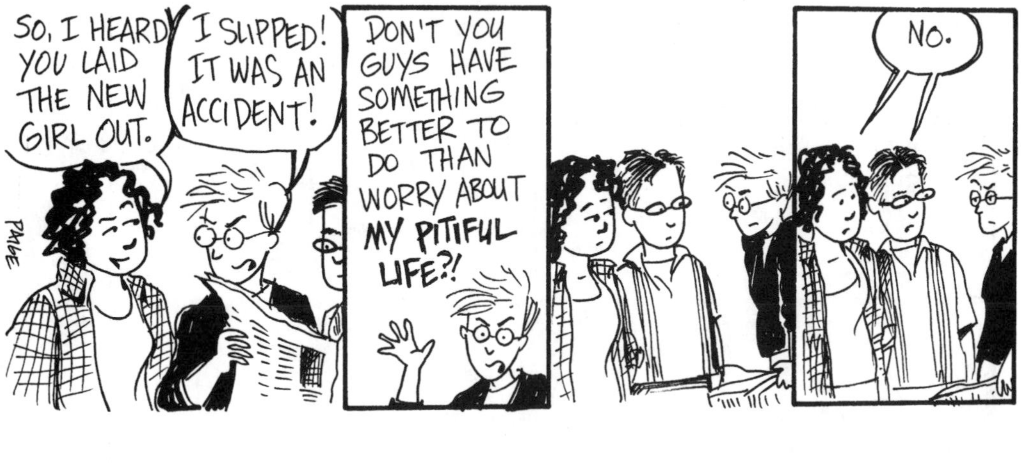
SO, I HEARD YOU LAID THE NEW GIRL OUT.
I SLIPPED! IT WAS AN ACCIDENT!
PAIGE
DON'T YOU GUYS HAVE SOMETHING BETTER TO DO THAN WORRY ABOUT **MY PITIFUL LIFE?!**
NO.

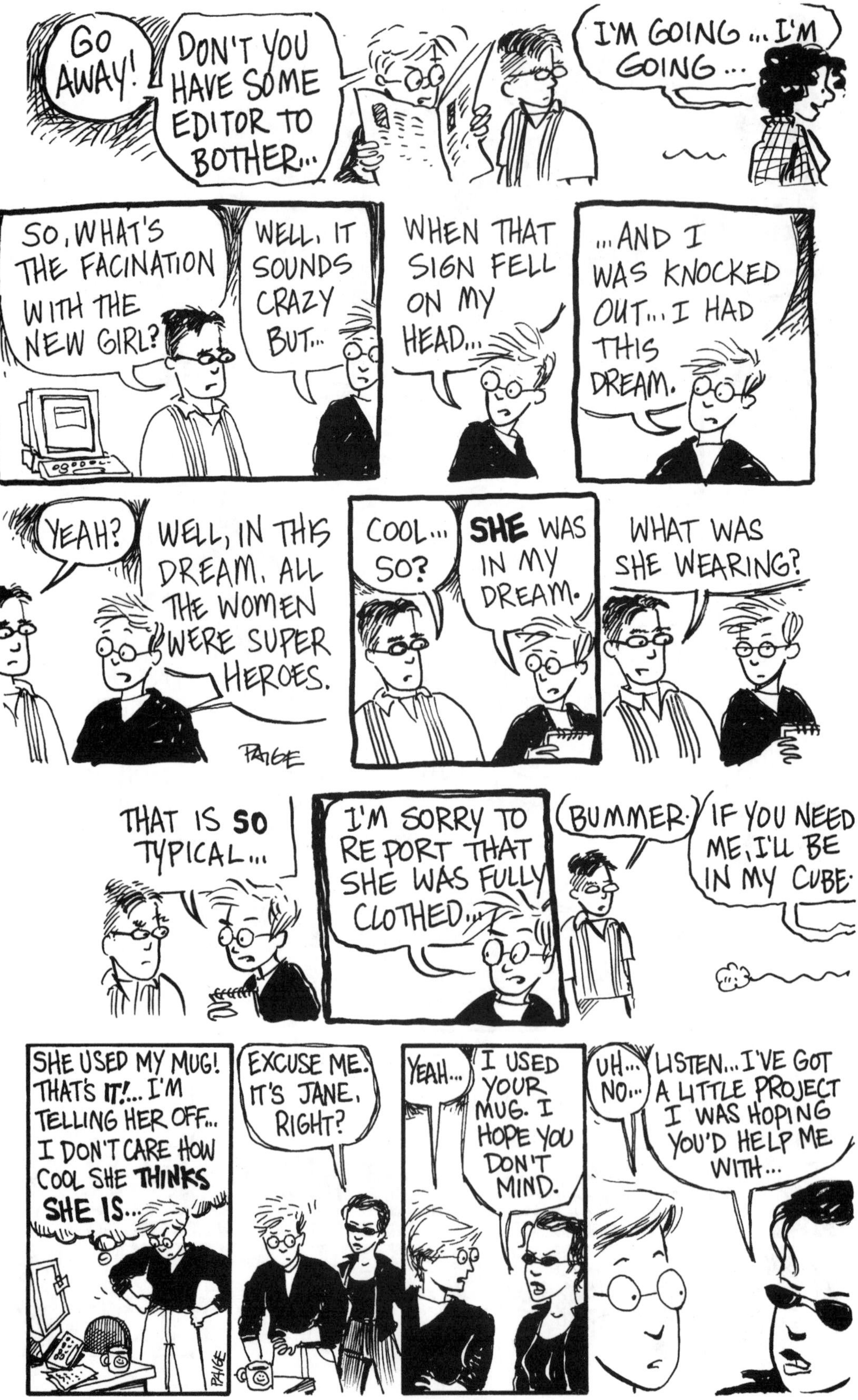
GO AWAY!
DON'T YOU HAVE SOME EDITOR TO BOTHER...
I'M GOING... I'M GOING...
SO, WHAT'S THE FACINATION WITH THE NEW GIRL?
WELL, IT SOUNDS CRAZY BUT...
WHEN THAT SIGN FELL ON MY HEAD...
...AND I WAS KNOCKED OUT... I HAD THIS DREAM.
YEAH?
WELL, IN THIS DREAM, ALL THE WOMEN WERE SUPER HEROES.
PAIGE
COOL... SO?
SHE WAS IN MY DREAM.
WHAT WAS SHE WEARING?
THAT IS SO TYPICAL...
I'M SORRY TO REPORT THAT SHE WAS FULLY CLOTHED...
BUMMER.
IF YOU NEED ME, I'LL BE IN MY CUBE.
SHE USED MY MUG! THAT'S IT!... I'M TELLING HER OFF... I DON'T CARE HOW COOL SHE THINKS SHE IS...
PAIGE
EXCUSE ME. IT'S JANE, RIGHT?
YEAH...
I USED YOUR MUG. I HOPE YOU DON'T MIND.
UH... NO...
LISTEN... I'VE GOT A LITTLE PROJECT I WAS HOPING YOU'D HELP ME WITH...

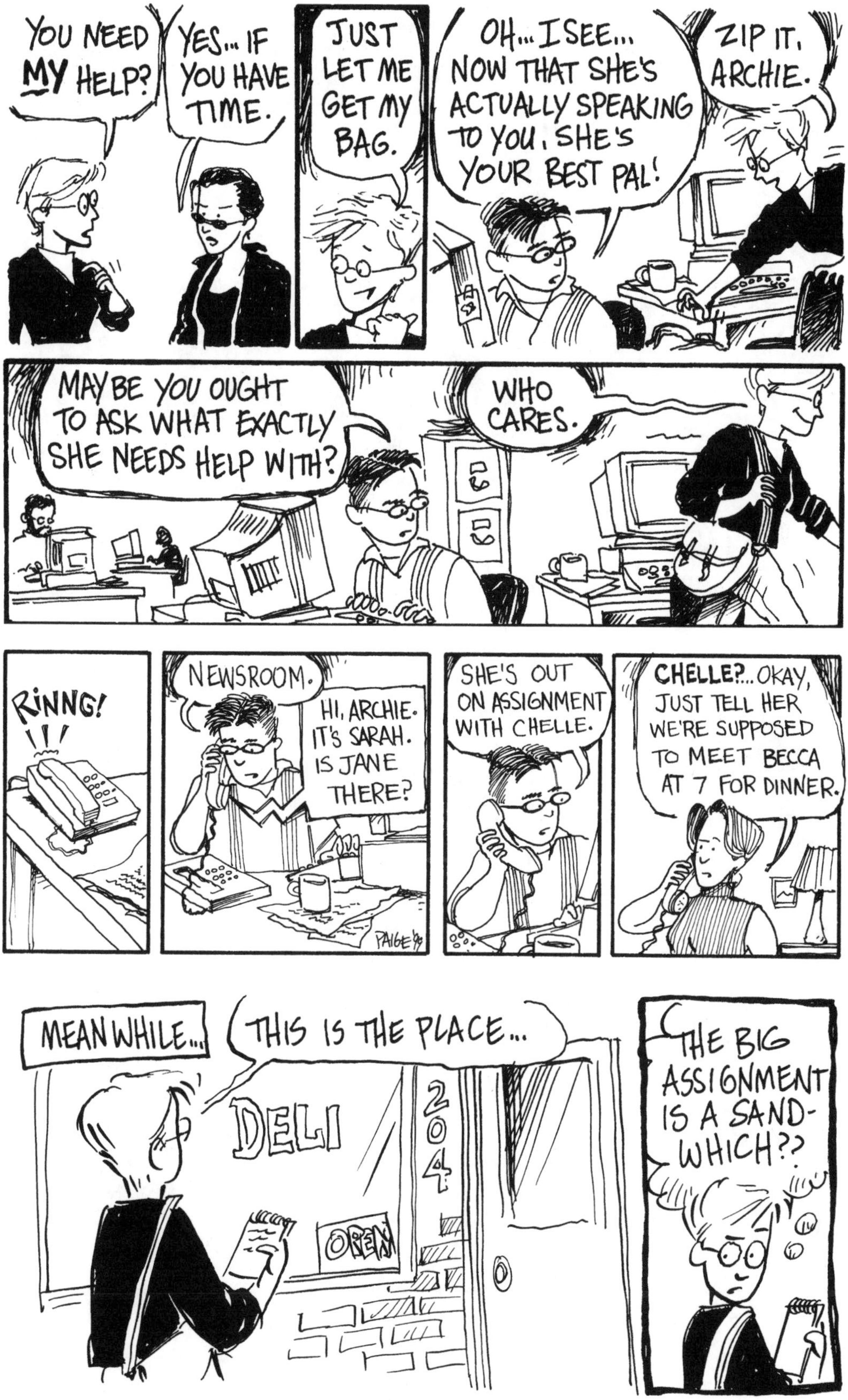
YOU NEED MY HELP?
YES... IF YOU HAVE TIME.
JUST LET ME GET MY BAG.
OH... I SEE... NOW THAT SHE'S ACTUALLY SPEAKING TO YOU, SHE'S YOUR BEST PAL!
ZIP IT, ARCHIE.
MAYBE YOU OUGHT TO ASK WHAT EXACTLY SHE NEEDS HELP WITH?
WHO CARES.
RINNG!
NEWSROOM.
HI, ARCHIE. IT'S SARAH. IS JANE THERE?
PAIGE '99
SHE'S OUT ON ASSIGNMENT WITH CHELLE.
CHELLE?... OKAY, JUST TELL HER WE'RE SUPPOSED TO MEET BECCA AT 7 FOR DINNER.
MEANWHILE...
THIS IS THE PLACE...
DELI
204
OPEN
THE BIG ASSIGNMENT IS A SAND-WHICH??

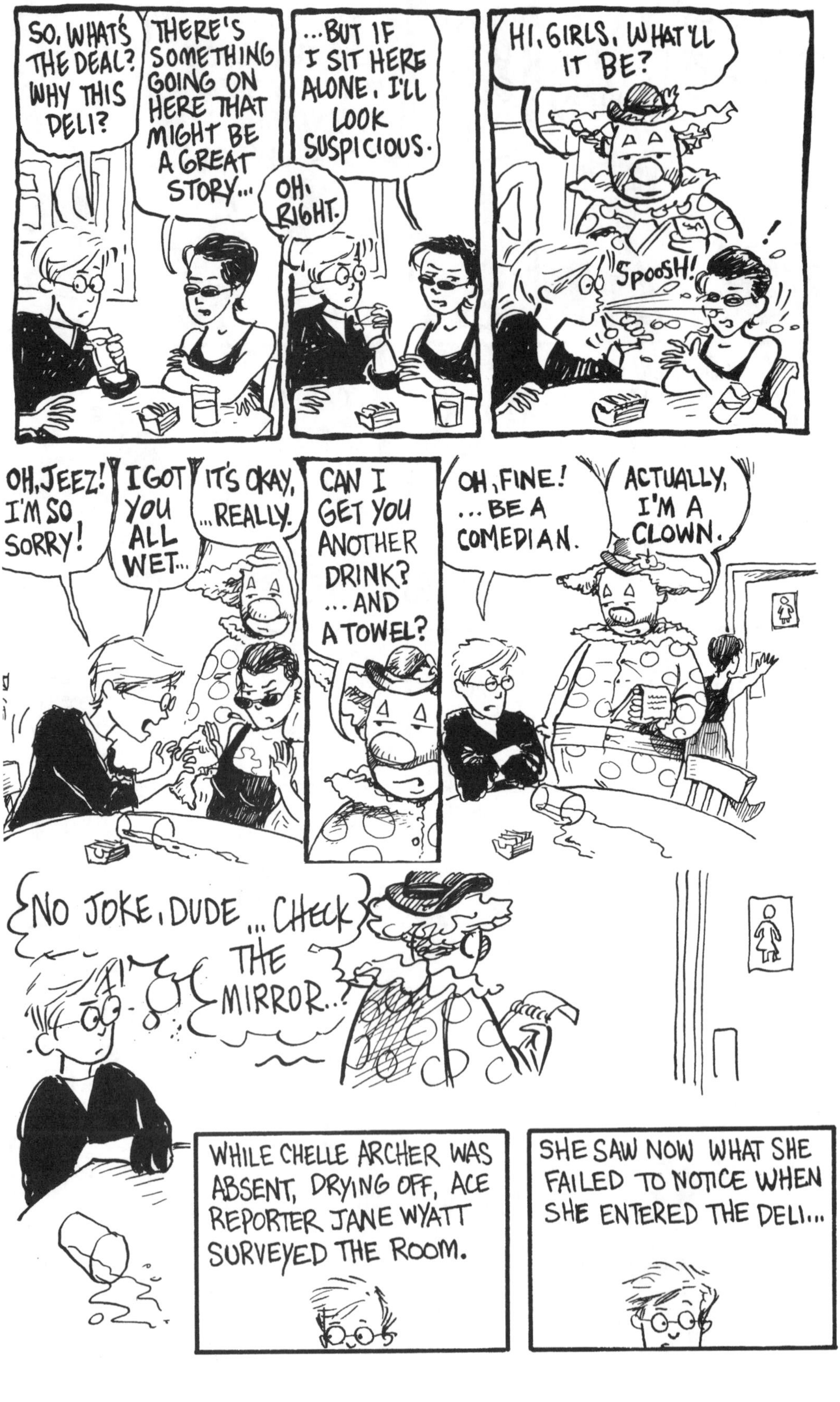
SO, WHAT'S THE DEAL? WHY THIS DELI?
THERE'S SOMETHING GOING ON HERE THAT MIGHT BE A GREAT STORY...
OH, RIGHT.
...BUT IF I SIT HERE ALONE, I'LL LOOK SUSPICIOUS.
HI, GIRLS. WHAT'LL IT BE?
SPOOSH!
OH, JEEZ! I'M SO SORRY!
I GOT YOU ALL WET...
IT'S OKAY, ...REALLY.
CAN I GET YOU ANOTHER DRINK? ...AND A TOWEL?
OH, FINE! ...BE A COMEDIAN.
ACTUALLY, I'M A CLOWN.
NO JOKE, DUDE ... CHECK THE MIRROR...
WHILE CHELLE ARCHER WAS ABSENT, DRYING OFF, ACE REPORTER JANE WYATT SURVEYED THE ROOM.
SHE SAW NOW WHAT SHE FAILED TO NOTICE WHEN SHE ENTERED THE DELI...

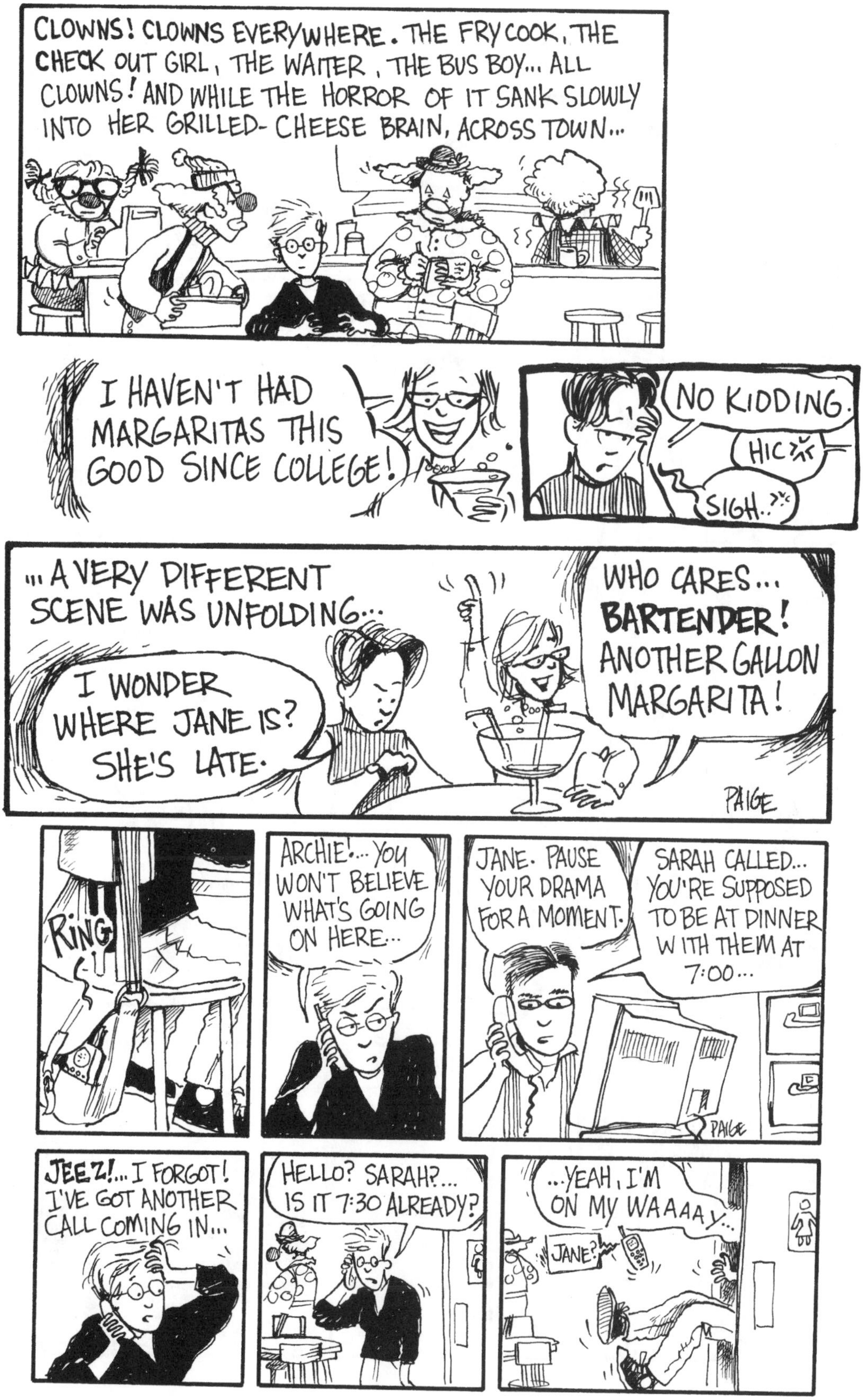
CLOWNS! CLOWNS EVERYWHERE. THE FRY COOK, THE CHECK OUT GIRL, THE WAITER, THE BUS BOY... ALL CLOWNS! AND WHILE THE HORROR OF IT SANK SLOWLY INTO HER GRILLED-CHEESE BRAIN, ACROSS TOWN...
I HAVEN'T HAD MARGARITAS THIS GOOD SINCE COLLEGE!
NO KIDDING.
HIC
SIGH..
...A VERY DIFFERENT SCENE WAS UNFOLDING...
I WONDER WHERE JANE IS? SHE'S LATE.
WHO CARES... BARTENDER! ANOTHER GALLON MARGARITA!
PAIGE
RING
ARCHIE!... YOU WON'T BELIEVE WHAT'S GOING ON HERE...
JANE. PAUSE YOUR DRAMA FOR A MOMENT.
SARAH CALLED... YOU'RE SUPPOSED TO BE AT DINNER WITH THEM AT 7:00...
PAIGE
JEEZ!... I FORGOT! I'VE GOT ANOTHER CALL COMING IN...
HELLO? SARAH?... IS IT 7:30 ALREADY?
...YEAH, I'M ON MY WAAAAY...
JANE?

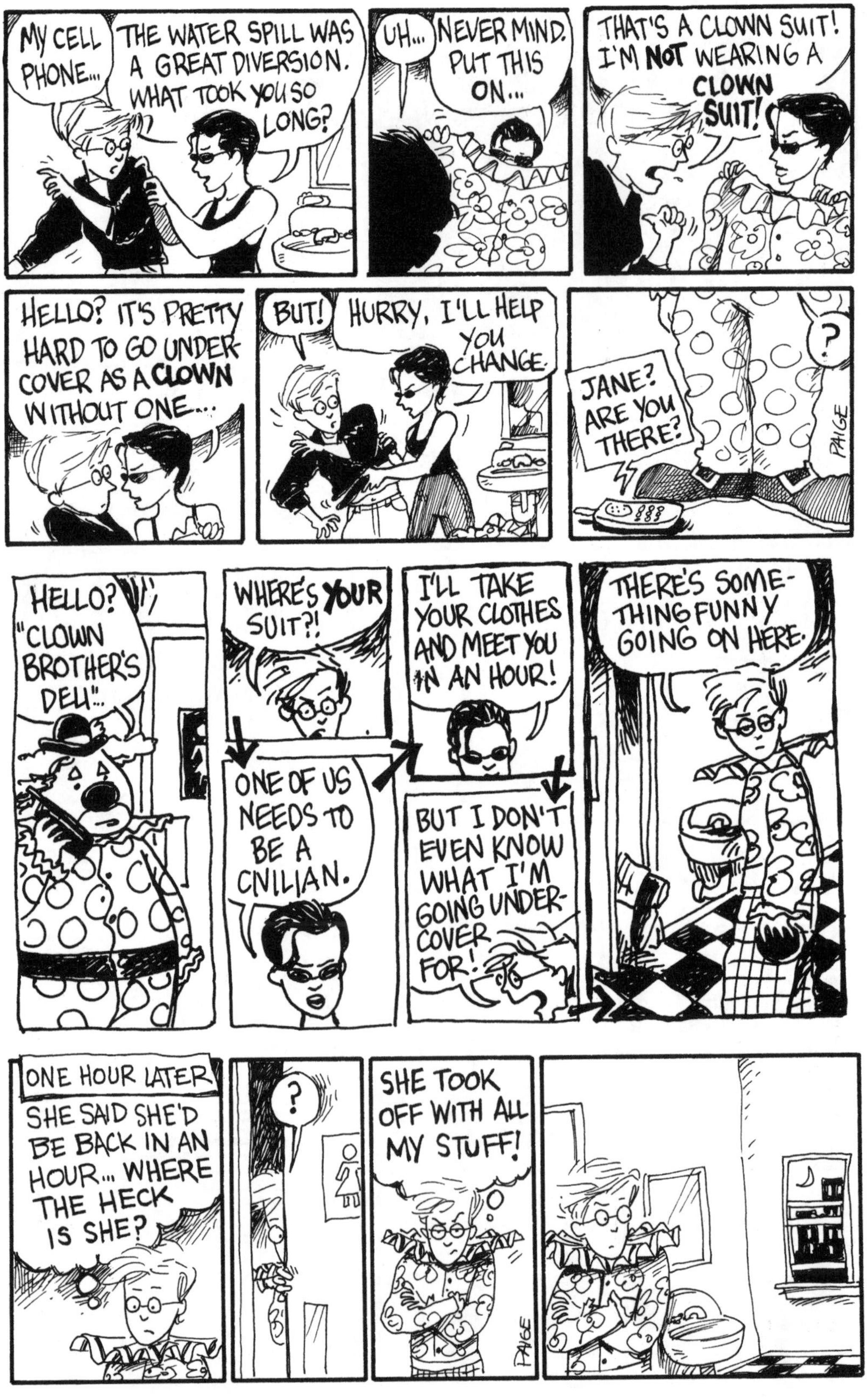
MY CELL PHONE...
THE WATER SPILL WAS A GREAT DIVERSION. WHAT TOOK YOU SO LONG?
UH...
NEVER MIND. PUT THIS ON...
THAT'S A CLOWN SUIT! I'M NOT WEARING A CLOWN SUIT!
HELLO? IT'S PRETTY HARD TO GO UNDER-COVER AS A CLOWN WITHOUT ONE...
BUT!
HURRY, I'LL HELP YOU CHANGE.
JANE? ARE YOU THERE?
?
PAIGE
HELLO? "CLOWN BROTHER'S DELI"...
WHERE'S YOUR SUIT?!
ONE OF US NEEDS TO BE A CIVILIAN.
I'LL TAKE YOUR CLOTHES AND MEET YOU IN AN HOUR!
BUT I DON'T EVEN KNOW WHAT I'M GOING UNDER-COVER FOR!
THERE'S SOME-THING FUNNY GOING ON HERE.
ONE HOUR LATER
SHE SAID SHE'D BE BACK IN AN HOUR... WHERE THE HECK IS SHE?
?
SHE TOOK OFF WITH ALL MY STUFF!
PAIGE

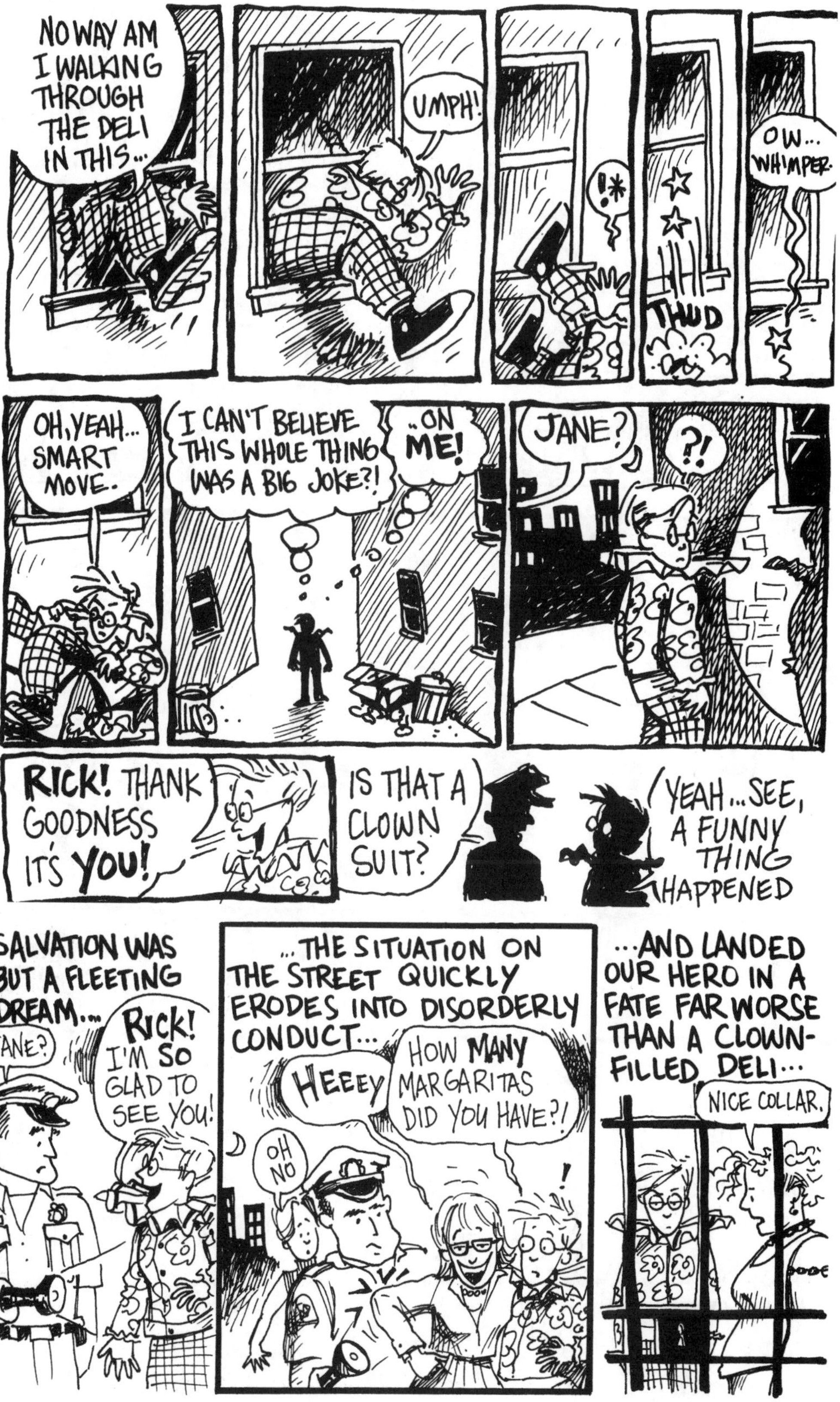
NO WAY AM I WALKING THROUGH THE DELI IN THIS...
UMPH!
!*
THUD
OW... WHIMPER
OH, YEAH... SMART MOVE.
I CAN'T BELIEVE THIS WHOLE THING WAS A BIG JOKE?!
..ON ME!
JANE?
?!
RICK! THANK GOODNESS IT'S YOU!
IS THAT A CLOWN SUIT?
YEAH... SEE, A FUNNY THING HAPPENED
SALVATION WAS BUT A FLEETING DREAM...
JANE?
RICK! I'M SO GLAD TO SEE YOU!
...THE SITUATION ON THE STREET QUICKLY ERODES INTO DISORDERLY CONDUCT...
HEEEY
HOW MANY MARGARITAS DID YOU HAVE?!
OH NO
!
...AND LANDED OUR HERO IN A FATE FAR WORSE THAN A CLOWN-FILLED DELI...
NICE COLLAR.

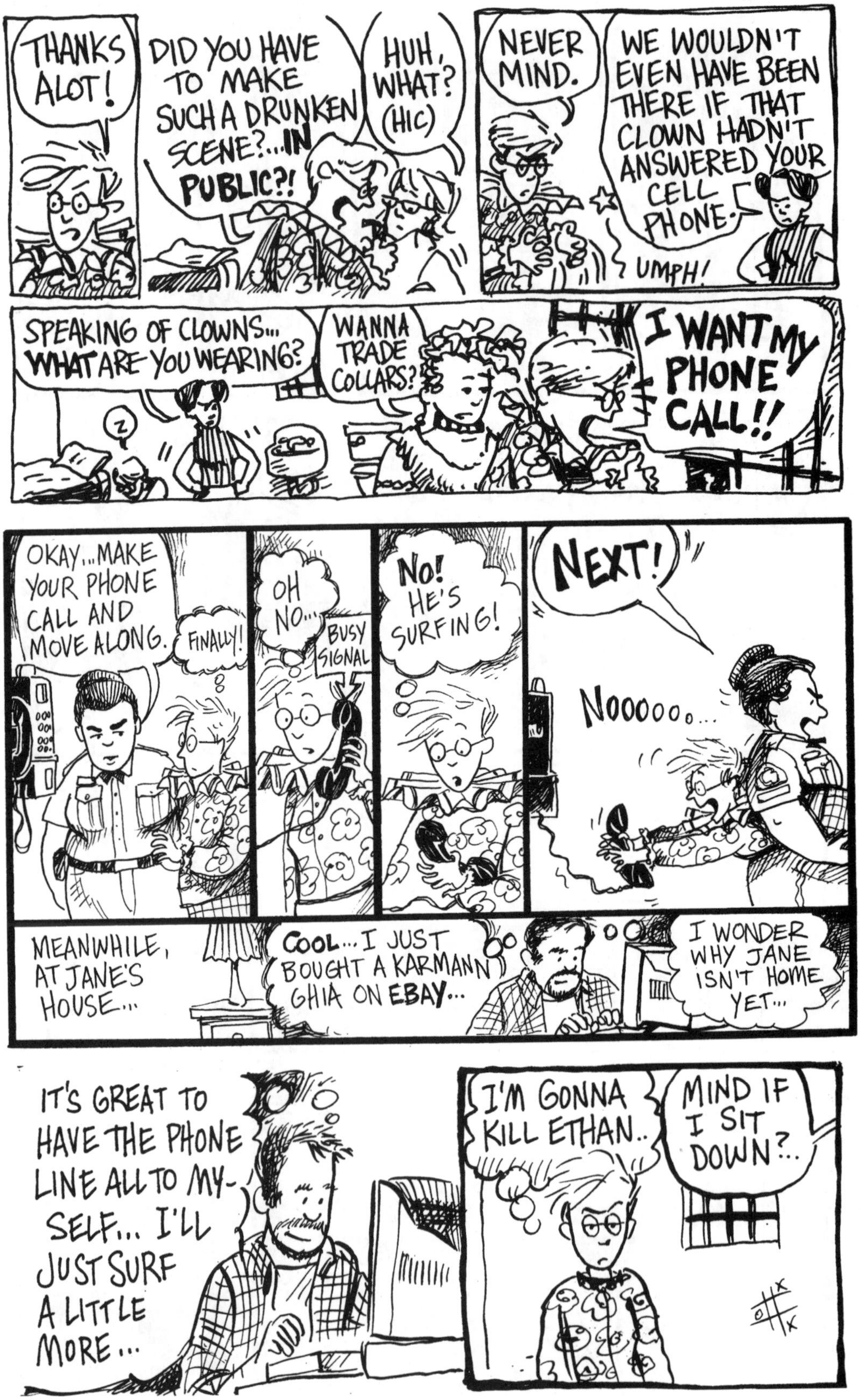
THANKS ALOT!
DID YOU HAVE TO MAKE SUCH A DRUNKEN SCENE?...IN PUBLIC?!
HUH, WHAT? (HIC)
NEVER MIND.
WE WOULDN'T EVEN HAVE BEEN THERE IF THAT CLOWN HADN'T ANSWERED YOUR CELL PHONE.
UMPH!
SPEAKING OF CLOWNS... WHAT ARE YOU WEARING?
Z
WANNA TRADE COLLARS?
I WANT MY PHONE CALL!!
OKAY...MAKE YOUR PHONE CALL AND MOVE ALONG.
FINALLY!
OH NO...
BUSY SIGNAL
NO! HE'S SURFING!
NEXT!
Nooooo...
MEANWHILE, AT JANE'S HOUSE...
COOL... I JUST BOUGHT A KARMANN GHIA ON EBAY...
I WONDER WHY JANE ISN'T HOME YET...
IT'S GREAT TO HAVE THE PHONE LINE ALL TO MY-SELF... I'LL JUST SURF A LITTLE MORE...
I'M GONNA KILL ETHAN..
MIND IF I SIT DOWN?..

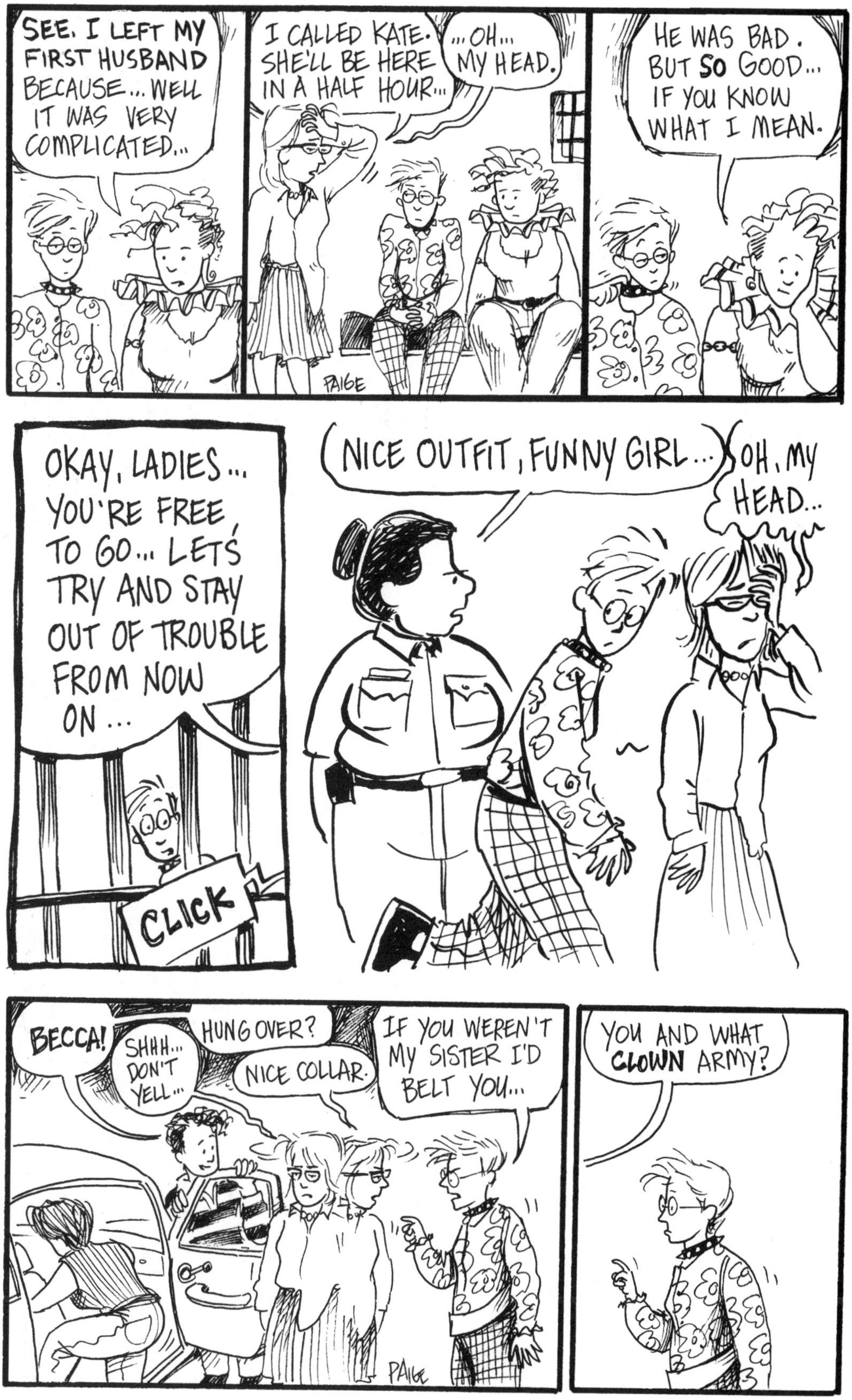

SEE. I LEFT MY FIRST HUSBAND BECAUSE... WELL IT WAS VERY COMPLICATED...
I CALLED KATE. SHE'LL BE HERE IN A HALF HOUR...
...OH... MY HEAD.
PAIGE
HE WAS BAD. BUT SO GOOD... IF YOU KNOW WHAT I MEAN.
OKAY, LADIES... YOU'RE FREE TO GO... LETS TRY AND STAY OUT OF TROUBLE FROM NOW ON...
CLICK
NICE OUTFIT, FUNNY GIRL...
OH, MY HEAD...
BECCA!
SHHH... DON'T YELL...
HUNG OVER?
NICE COLLAR.
IF YOU WEREN'T MY SISTER I'D BELT YOU...
PAIGE
YOU AND WHAT CLOWN ARMY?

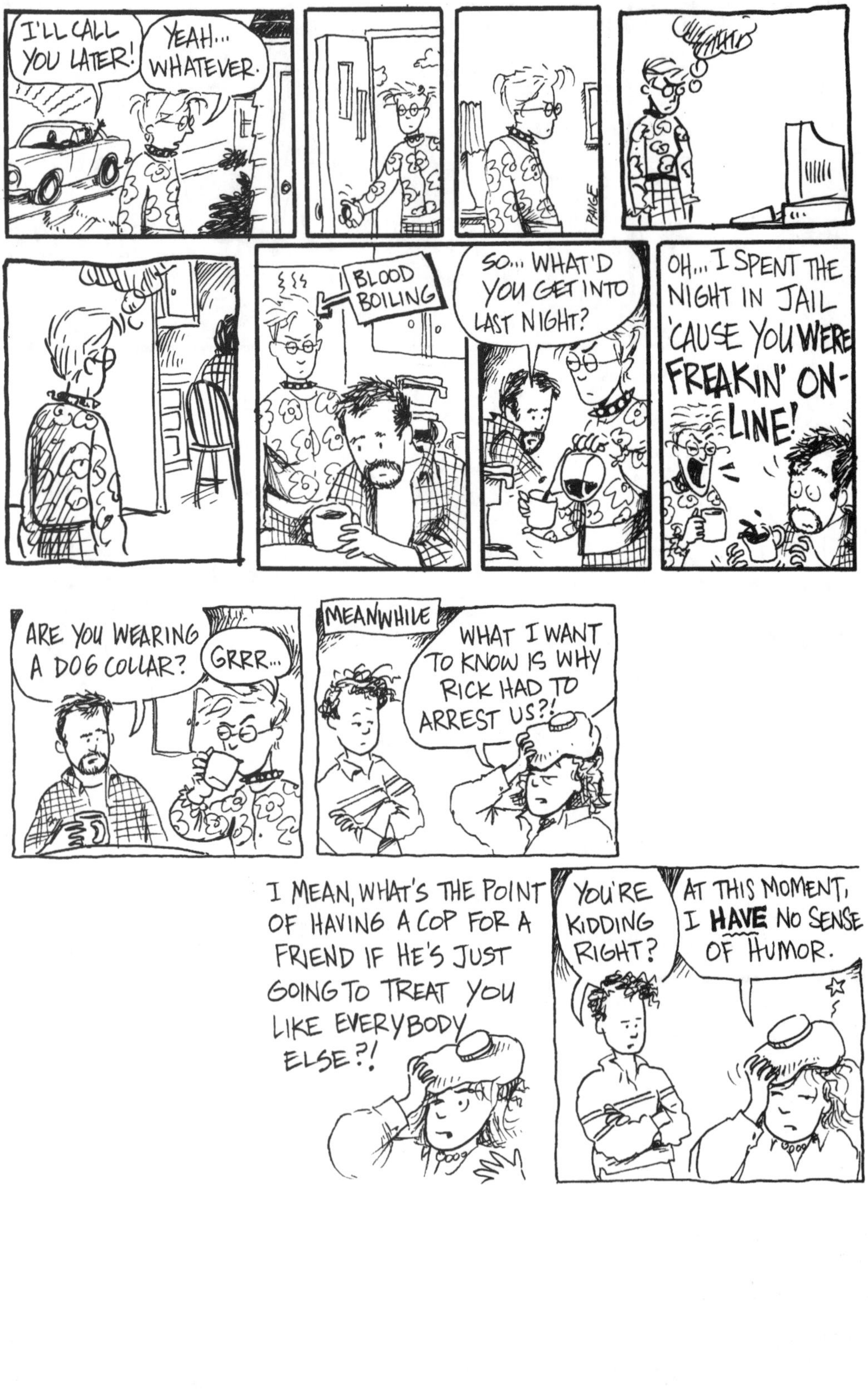
I'LL CALL YOU LATER!
YEAH... WHATEVER.
PAIGE
BLOOD BOILING
SO... WHAT'D YOU GET INTO LAST NIGHT?
OH... I SPENT THE NIGHT IN JAIL 'CAUSE YOU WERE FREAKIN' ON-LINE!
ARE YOU WEARING A DOG COLLAR?
GRRR...
MEANWHILE
WHAT I WANT TO KNOW IS WHY RICK HAD TO ARREST US?!
I MEAN, WHAT'S THE POINT OF HAVING A COP FOR A FRIEND IF HE'S JUST GOING TO TREAT YOU LIKE EVERYBODY ELSE?!
YOU'RE KIDDING RIGHT?
AT THIS MOMENT, I HAVE NO SENSE OF HUMOR.

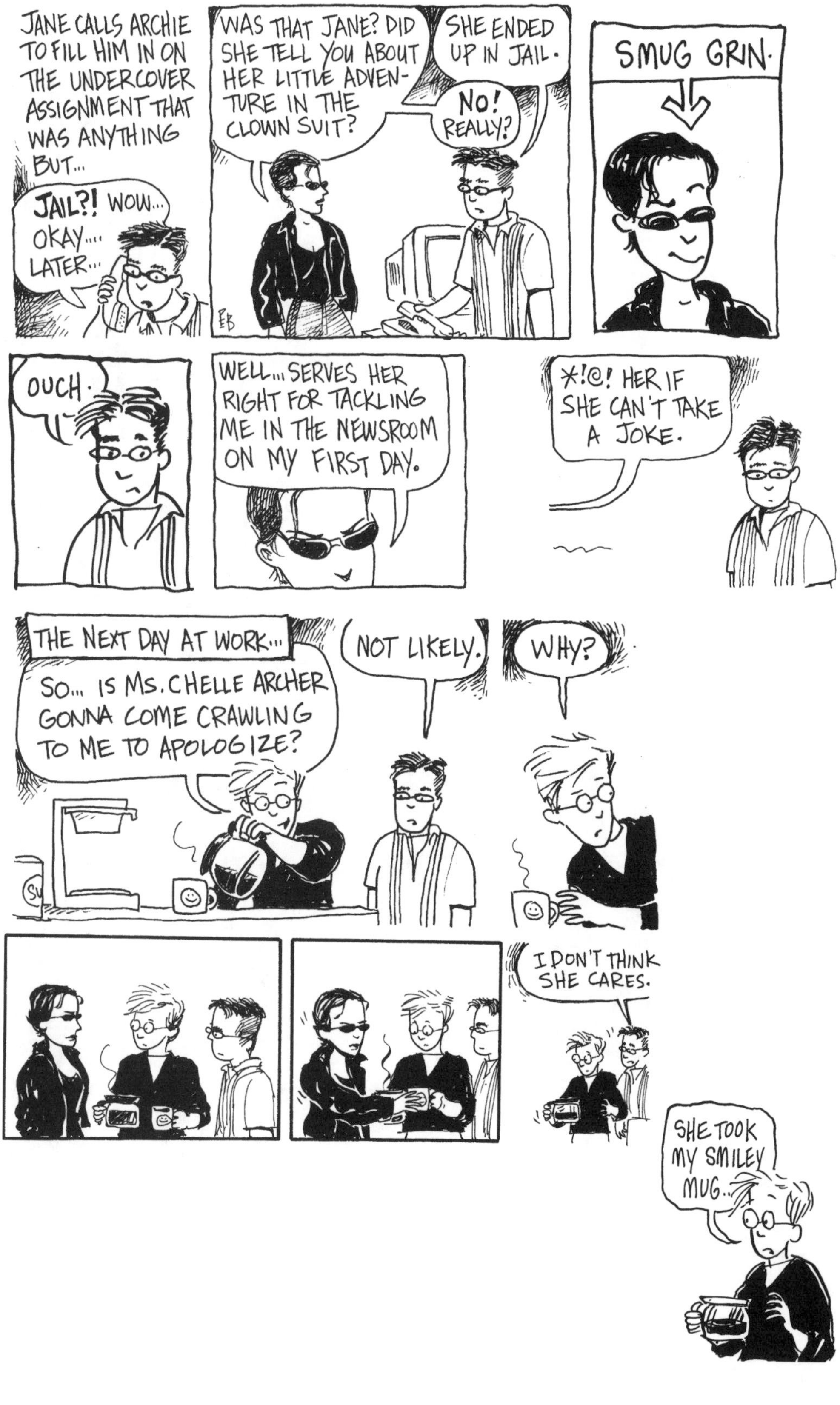
JANE CALLS ARCHIE TO FILL HIM IN ON THE UNDERCOVER ASSIGNMENT THAT WAS ANYTHING BUT...
JAIL?! WOW... OKAY.... LATER...
WAS THAT JANE? DID SHE TELL YOU ABOUT HER LITTLE ADVENTURE IN THE CLOWN SUIT?
SHE ENDED UP IN JAIL.
NO! REALLY?
SMUG GRIN.
OUCH.
WELL... SERVES HER RIGHT FOR TACKLING ME IN THE NEWSROOM ON MY FIRST DAY.
*!@! HER IF SHE CAN'T TAKE A JOKE.
THE NEXT DAY AT WORK...
SO... IS MS. CHELLE ARCHER GONNA COME CRAWLING TO ME TO APOLOGIZE?
NOT LIKELY.
WHY?
I DON'T THINK SHE CARES.
SHE TOOK MY SMILEY MUG...

Chapter 2

Goddess for a day

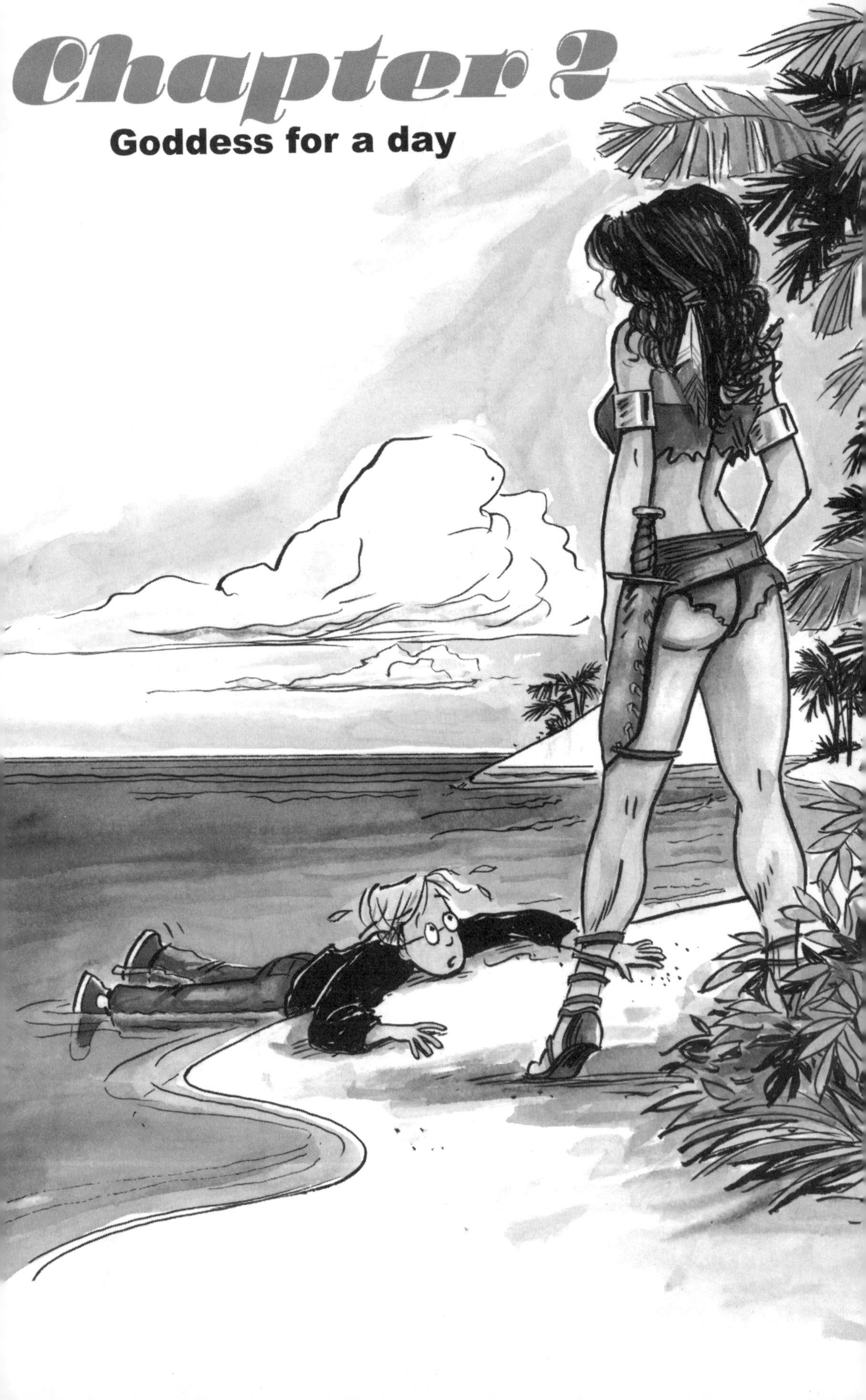

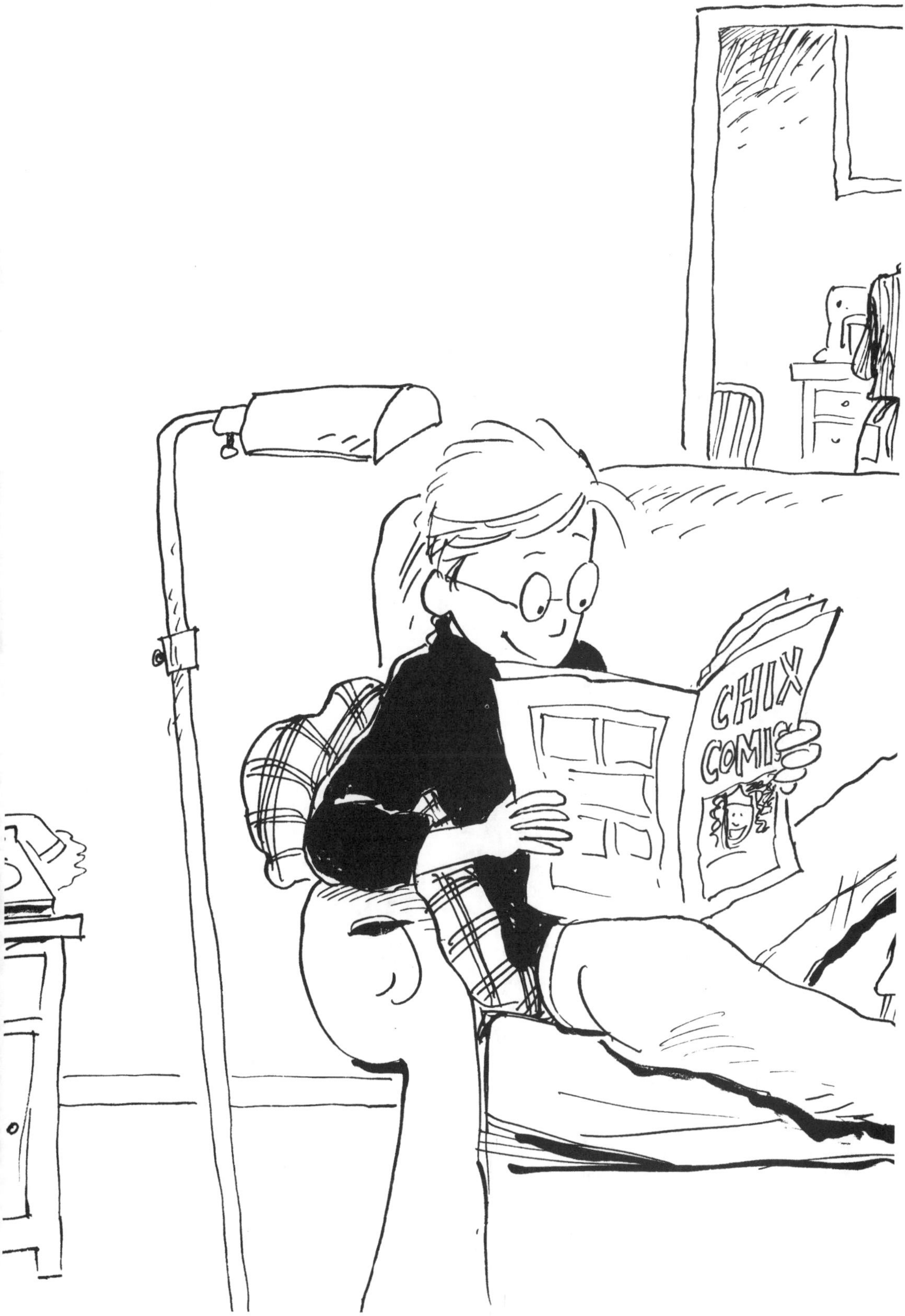
CHIX
COMIC

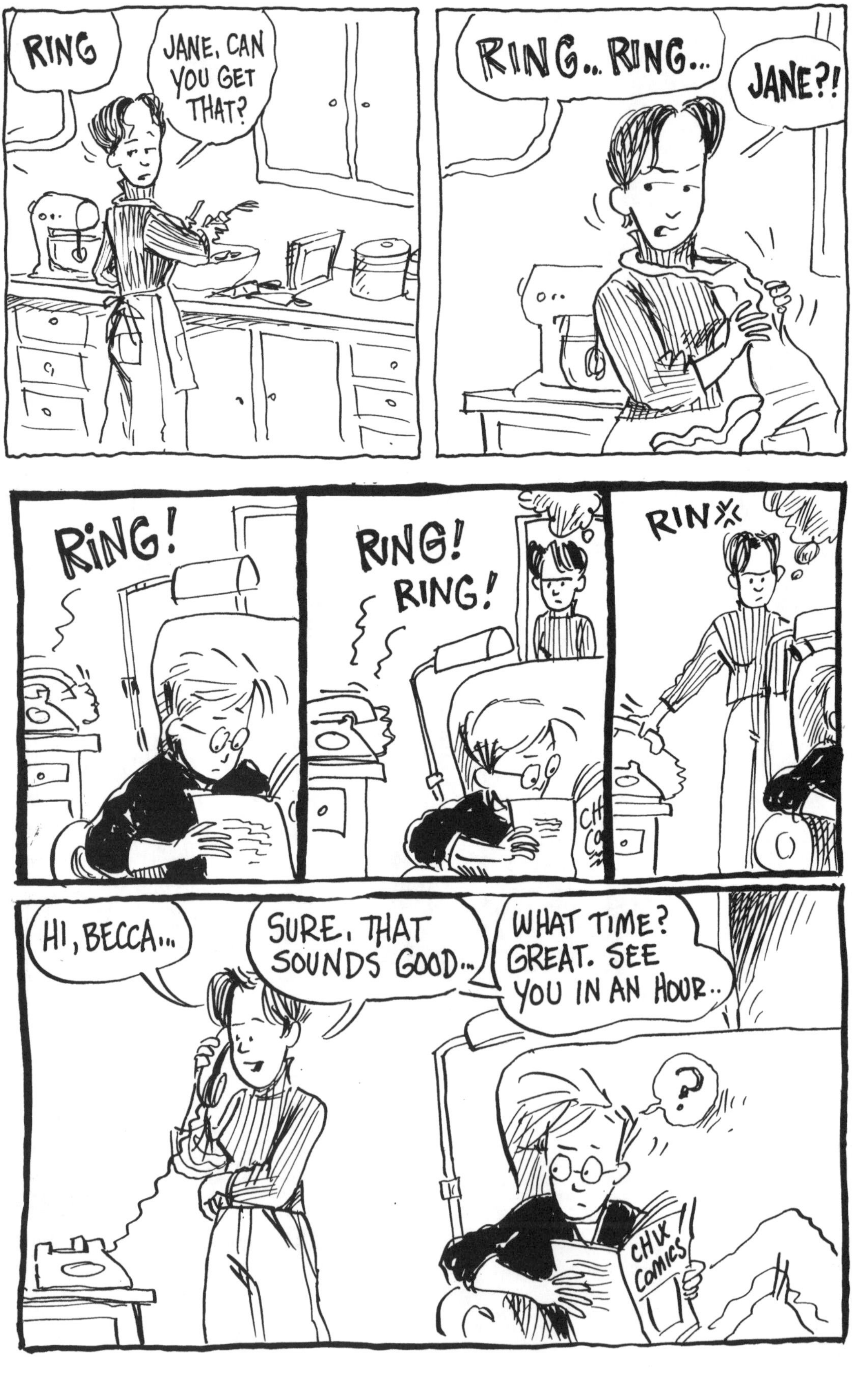
RING
JANE, CAN YOU GET THAT?
RING.. RING...
JANE?!
RING!
RING! RING!
RIN
HI, BECCA...
SURE. THAT SOUNDS GOOD...
WHAT TIME? GREAT. SEE YOU IN AN HOUR..
CHIX COMICS

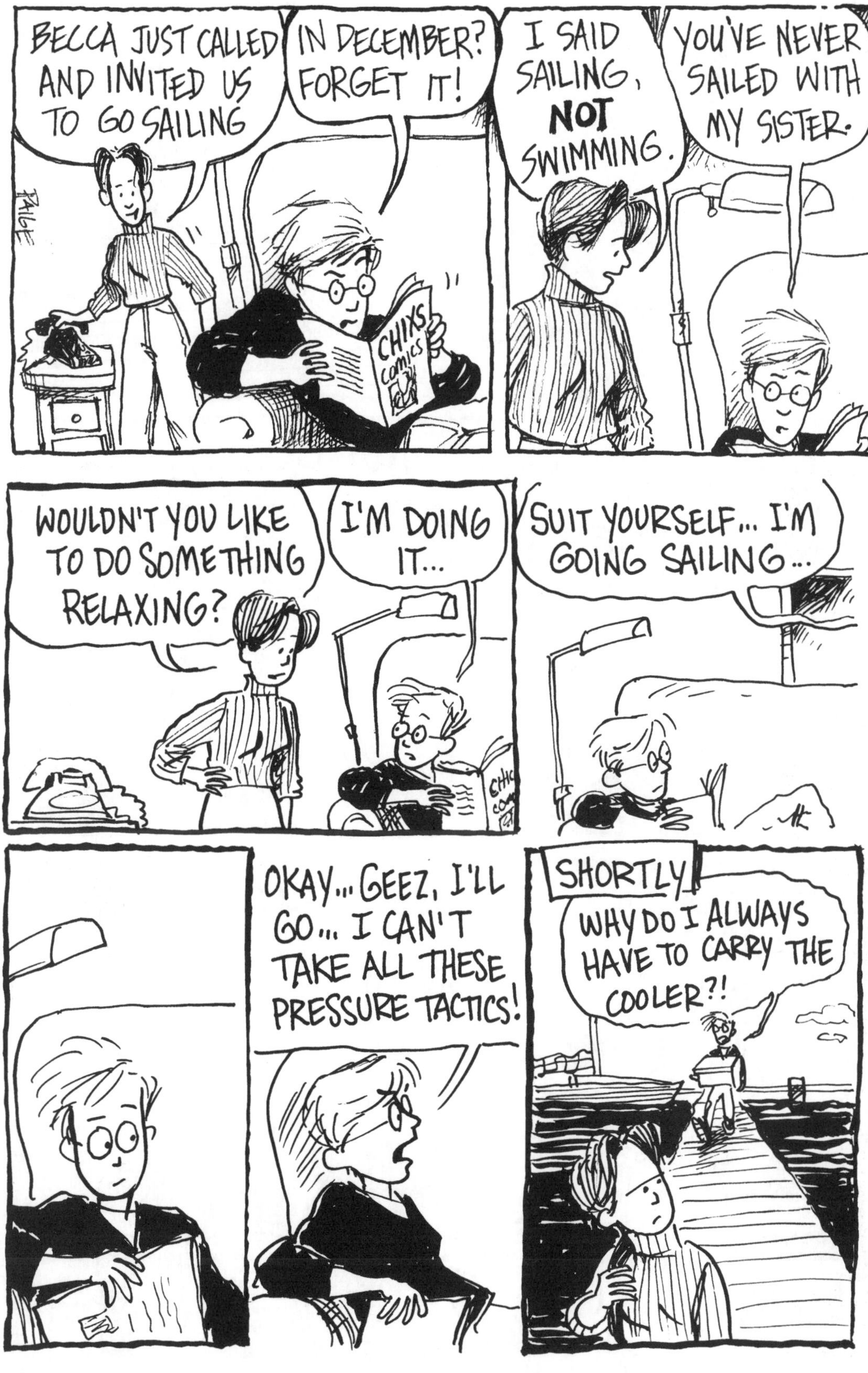
BECCA JUST CALLED AND INVITED US TO GO SAILING
IN DECEMBER? FORGET IT!
I SAID SAILING, **NOT** SWIMMING.
YOU'VE NEVER SAILED WITH MY SISTER.
WOULDN'T YOU LIKE TO DO SOMETHING RELAXING?
I'M DOING IT...
SUIT YOURSELF... I'M GOING SAILING...
OKAY... GEEZ, I'LL GO... I CAN'T TAKE ALL THESE PRESSURE TACTICS!
SHORTLY
WHY DO I ALWAYS HAVE TO CARRY THE COOLER?!

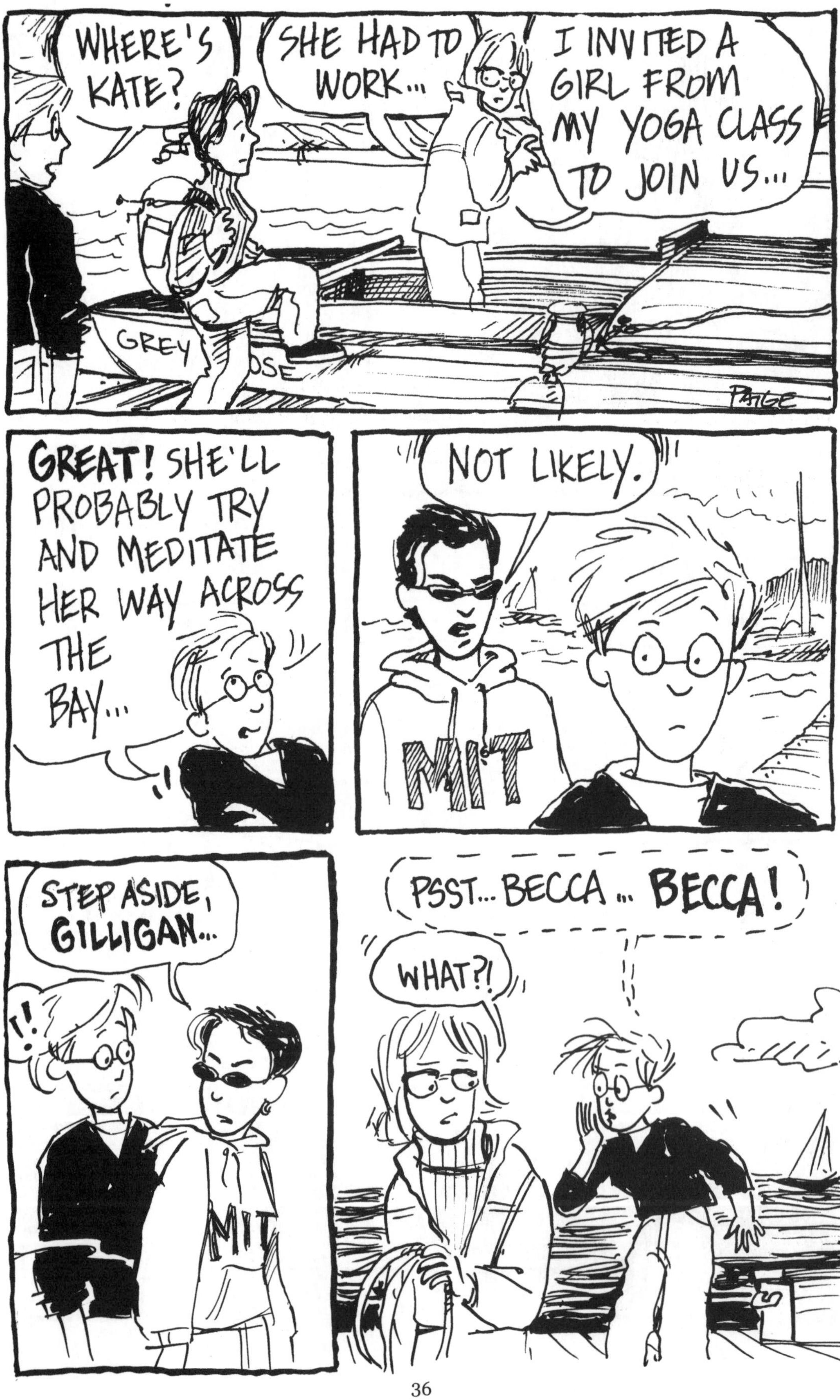
WHERE'S KATE?
SHE HAD TO WORK...
I INVITED A GIRL FROM MY YOGA CLASS TO JOIN US...
GREY
OSE
PAIGE
GREAT! SHE'LL PROBABLY TRY AND MEDITATE HER WAY ACROSS THE BAY...
NOT LIKELY.
MIT
STEP ASIDE, GILLIGAN...
MIT
PSST... BECCA ... BECCA!
WHAT?!

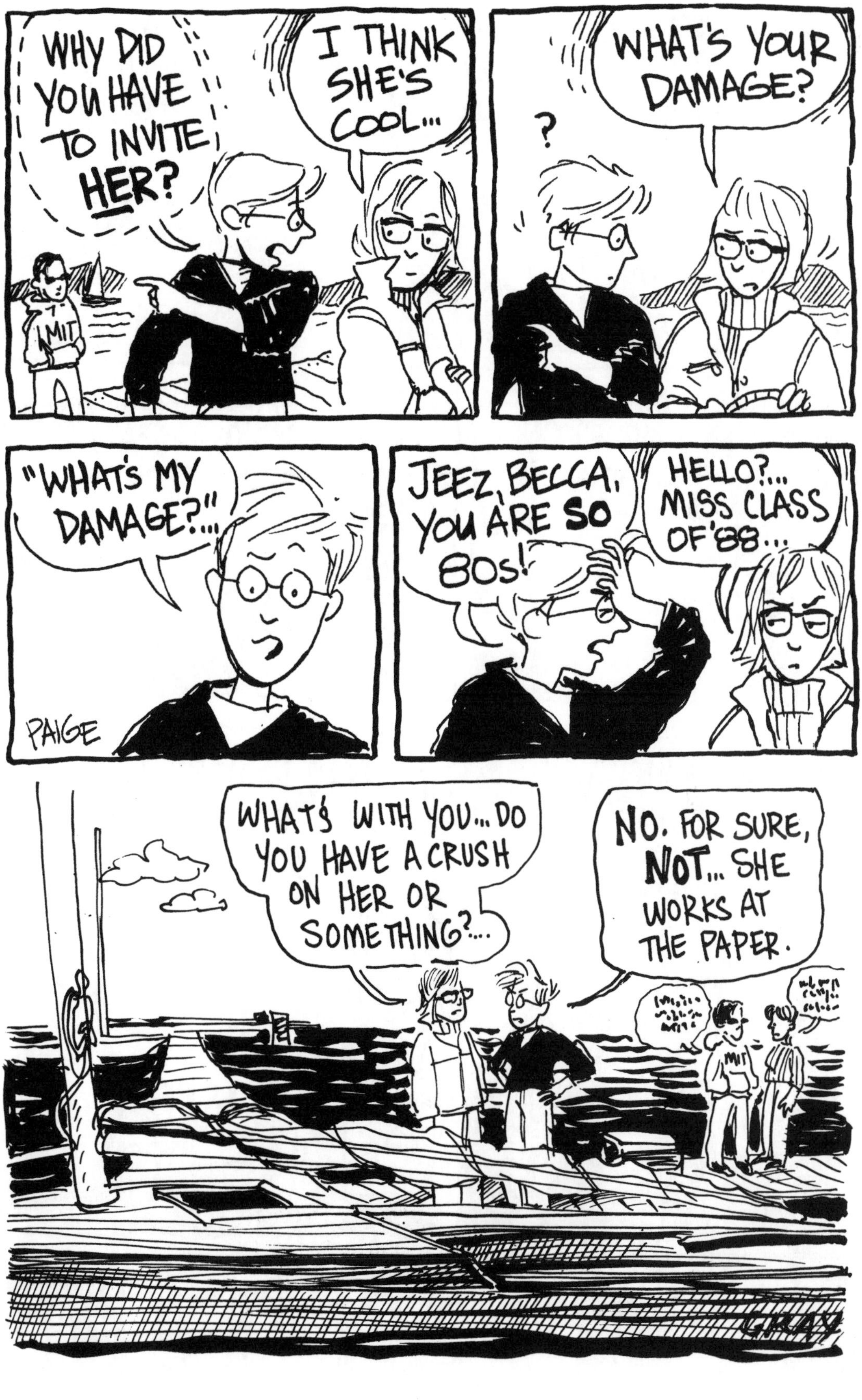
WHY DID YOU HAVE TO INVITE HER?
I THINK SHE'S COOL...
MIT
?
WHAT'S YOUR DAMAGE?
"WHAT'S MY DAMAGE?"...
PAIGE
JEEZ, BECCA, YOU ARE SO 80s!
HELLO?... MISS CLASS OF '88...
WHAT'S WITH YOU... DO YOU HAVE A CRUSH ON HER OR SOMETHING?...
NO. FOR SURE, NOT... SHE WORKS AT THE PAPER.
MIT
GRAY

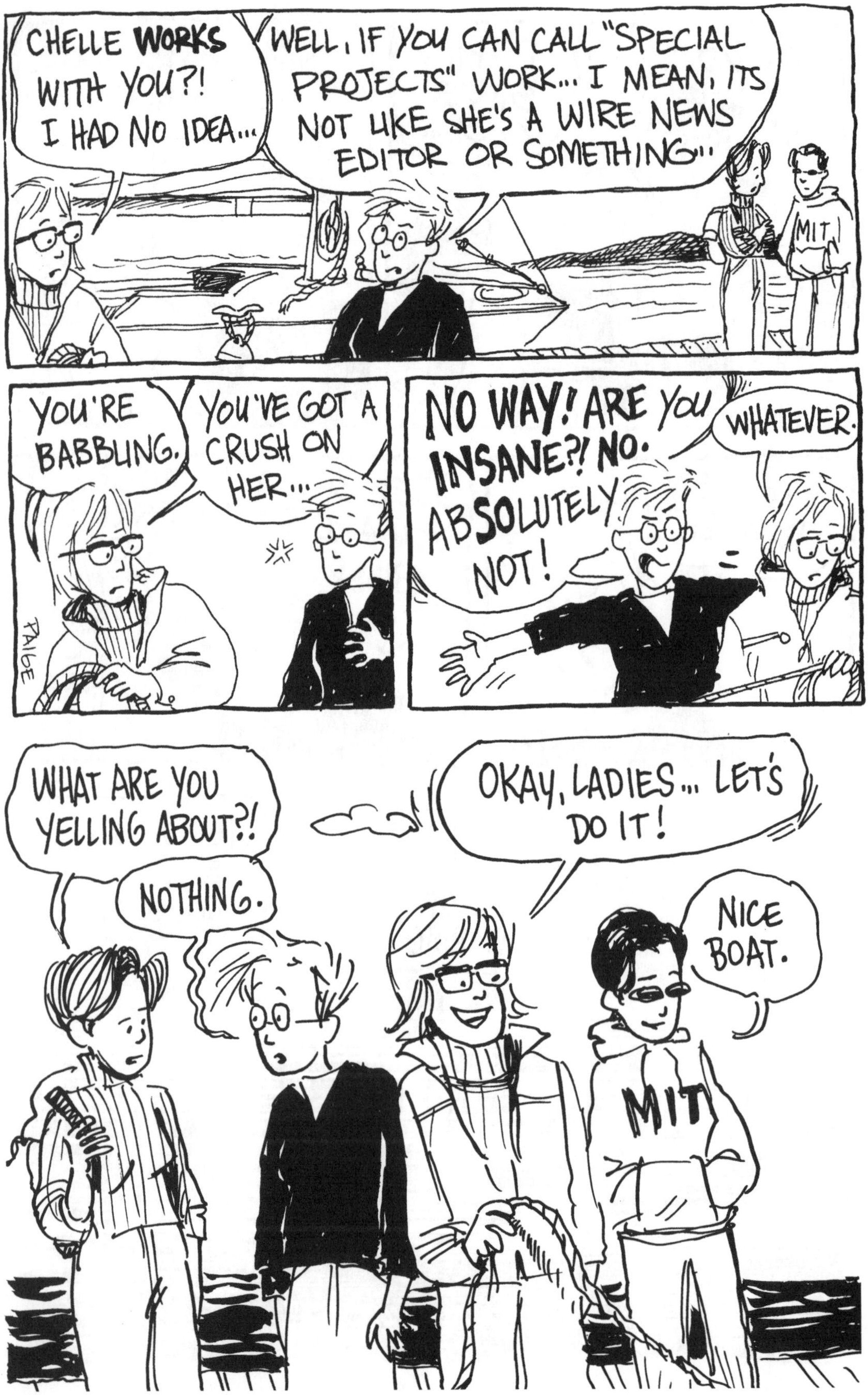
CHELLE WORKS WITH YOU?! I HAD NO IDEA...
WELL, IF YOU CAN CALL "SPECIAL PROJECTS" WORK... I MEAN, ITS NOT LIKE SHE'S A WIRE NEWS EDITOR OR SOMETHING...
MIT
YOU'RE BABBLING.
YOU'VE GOT A CRUSH ON HER...
PAIGE
NO WAY! ARE YOU INSANE?! NO. ABSOLUTELY NOT!
WHATEVER.
WHAT ARE YOU YELLING ABOUT?!
NOTHING.
OKAY, LADIES... LET'S DO IT!
NICE BOAT.
MIT

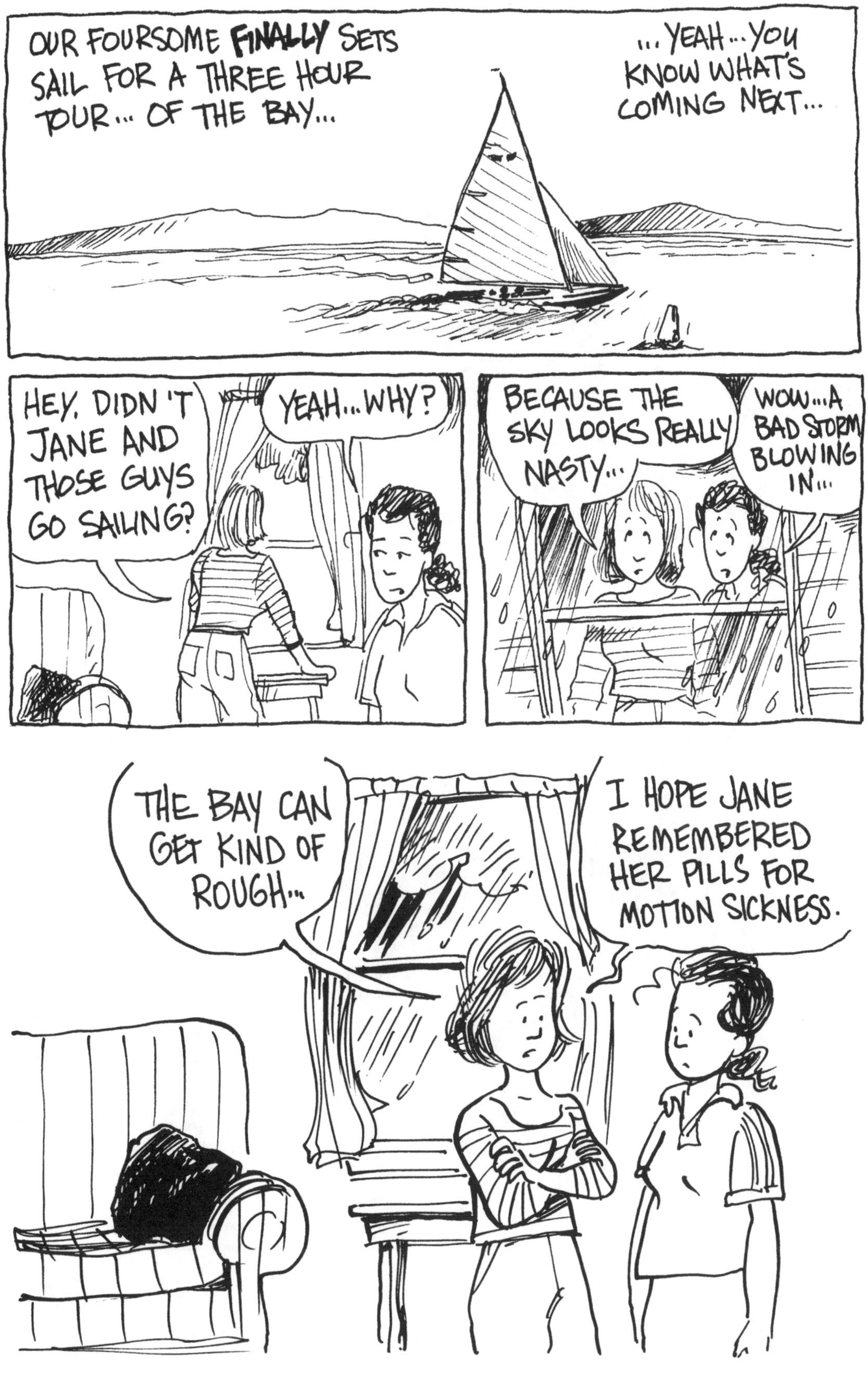
OUR FOURSOME FINALLY SETS SAIL FOR A THREE HOUR TOUR... OF THE BAY...
...YEAH...YOU KNOW WHAT'S COMING NEXT...
HEY, DIDN'T JANE AND THOSE GUYS GO SAILING?
YEAH...WHY?
BECAUSE THE SKY LOOKS REALLY NASTY...
WOW...A BAD STORM BLOWING IN...
THE BAY CAN GET KIND OF ROUGH...
I HOPE JANE REMEMBERED HER PILLS FOR MOTION SICKNESS.

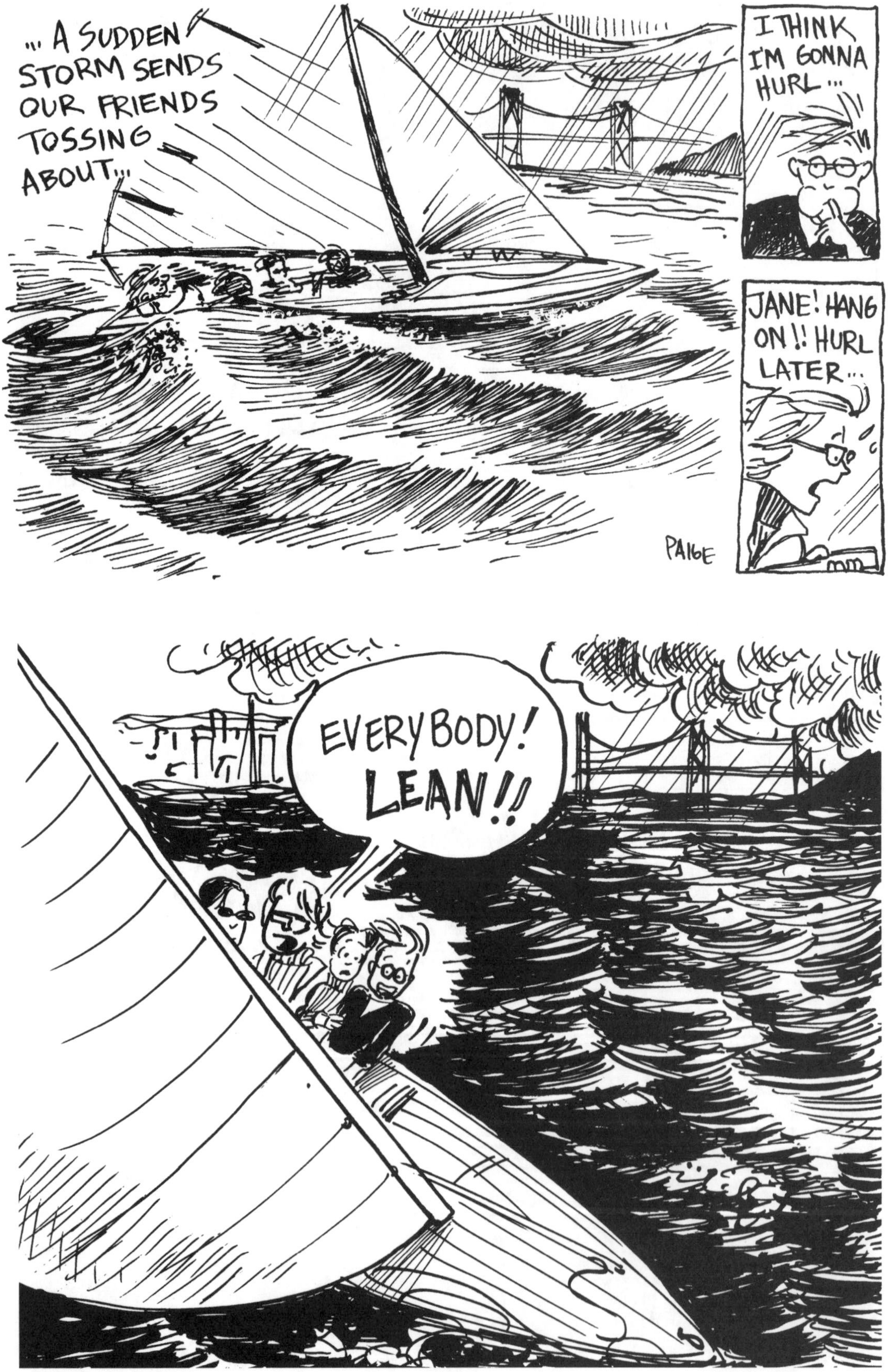
... A SUDDEN STORM SENDS OUR FRIENDS TOSSING ABOUT...
PAIGE
I THINK I'M GONNA HURL...
JANE! HANG ON!! HURL LATER...
EVERYBODY! LEAN!!

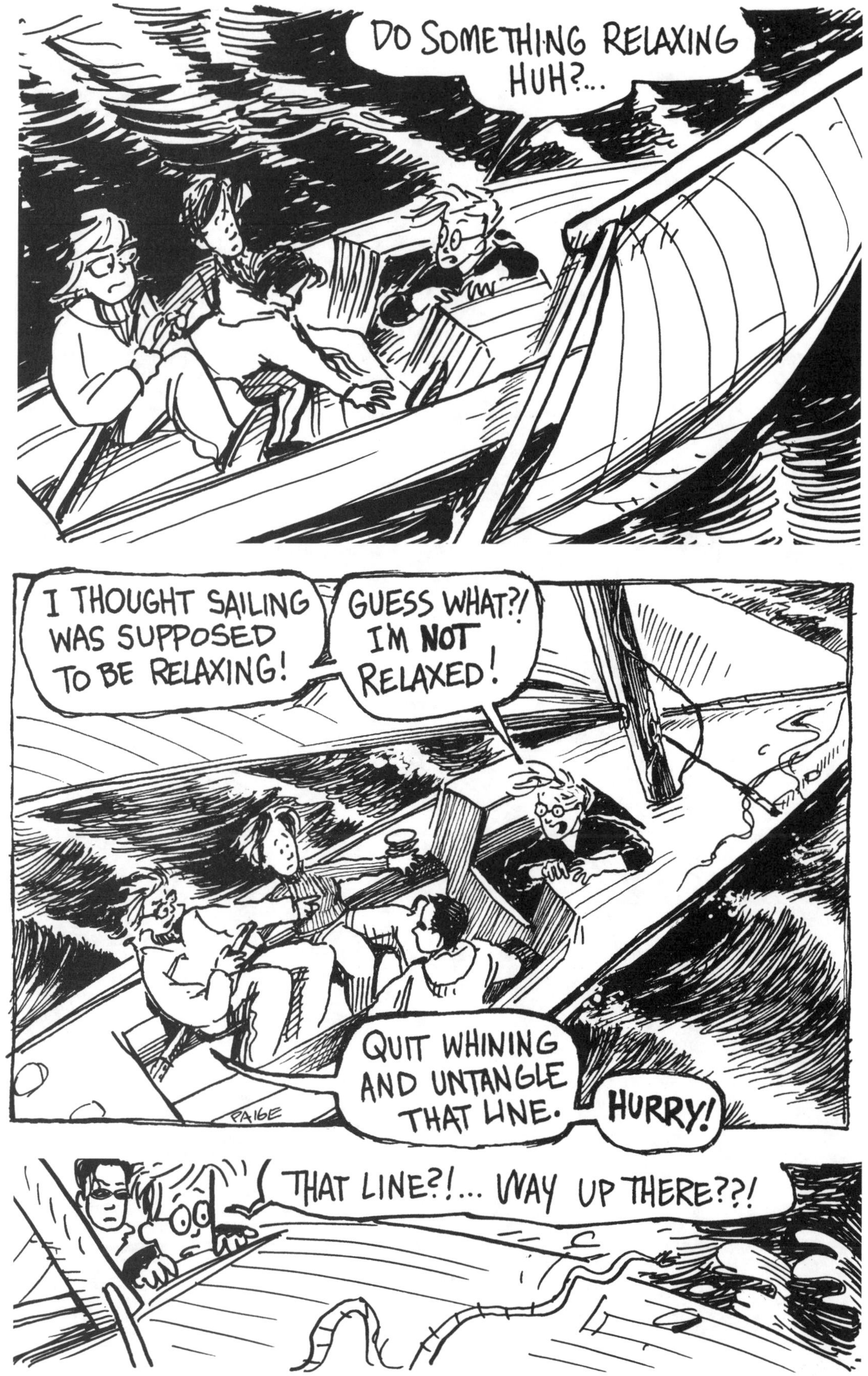
DO SOMETHING RELAXING HUH?...
I THOUGHT SAILING WAS SUPPOSED TO BE RELAXING!
GUESS WHAT?! I'M **NOT** RELAXED!
QUIT WHINING AND UNTANGLE THAT LINE.
HURRY!
PAIGE
THAT LINE?!... WAY UP THERE??!

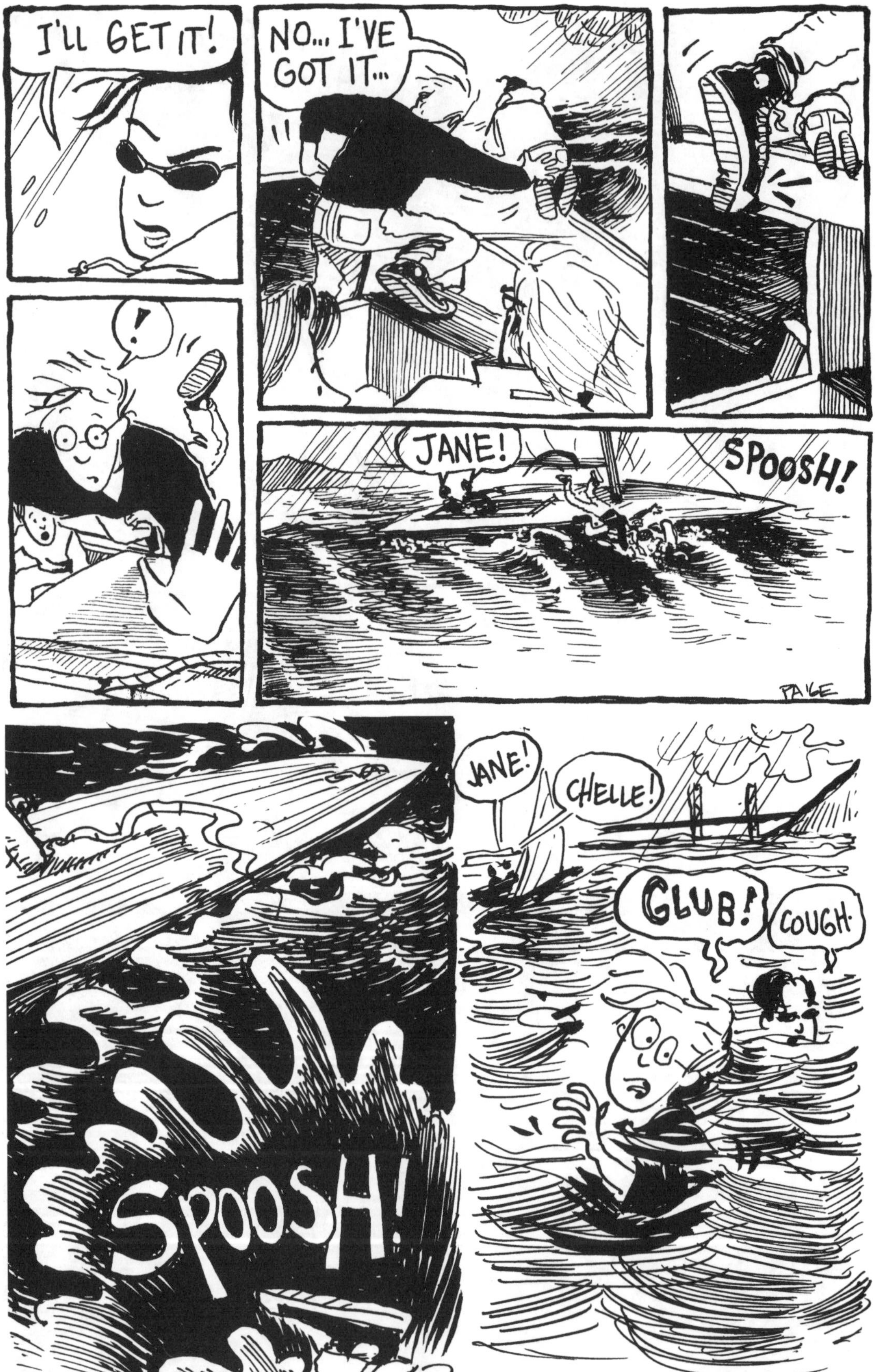
I'LL GET IT!
NO... I'VE GOT IT...
!
JANE!
SPOOSH!
PAIGE
SPOOSH!
JANE!
CHELLE!
GLUB!
COUGH·

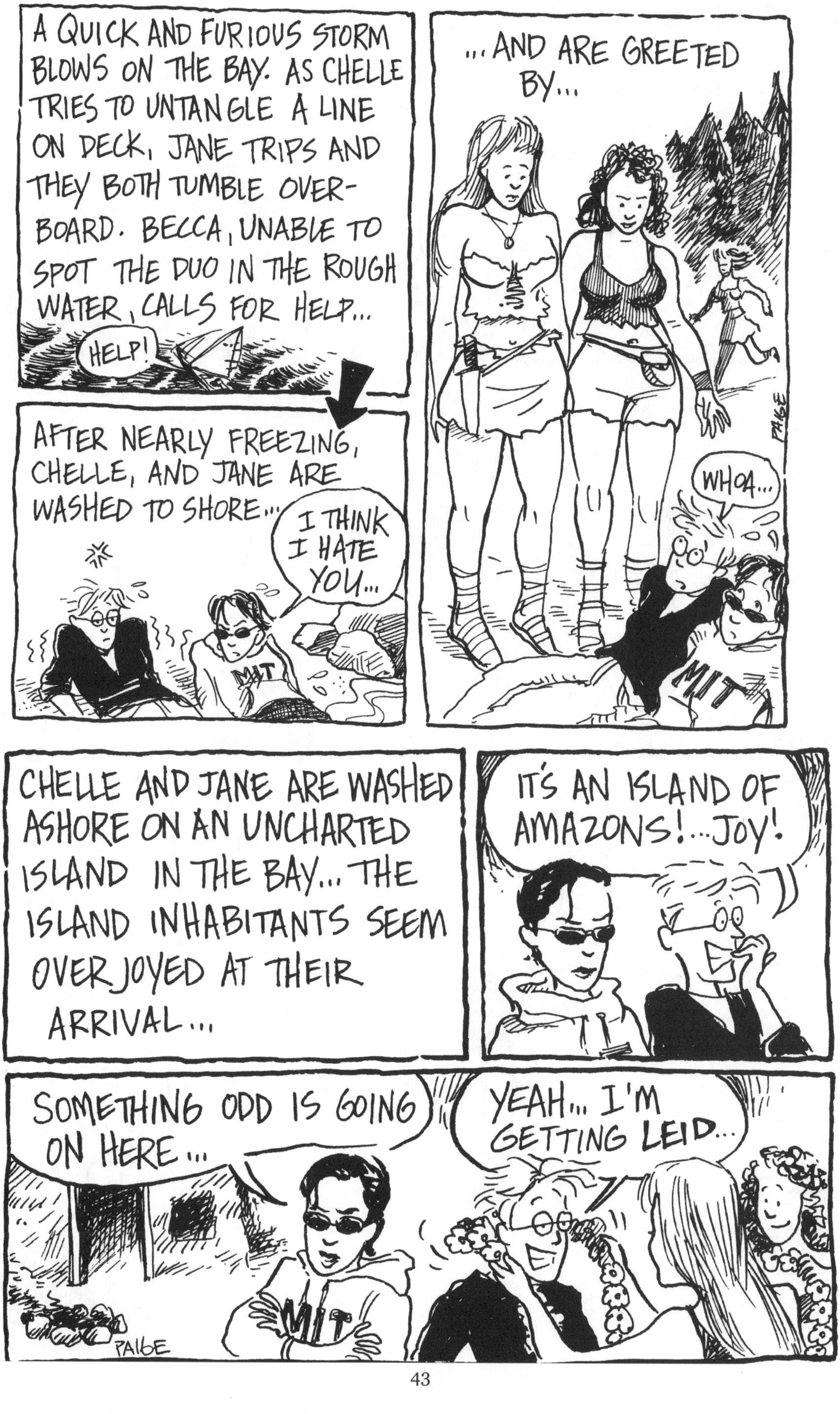
A QUICK AND FURIOUS STORM BLOWS ON THE BAY. AS CHELLE TRIES TO UNTANGLE A LINE ON DECK, JANE TRIPS AND THEY BOTH TUMBLE OVER-BOARD. BECCA, UNABLE TO SPOT THE DUO IN THE ROUGH WATER, CALLS FOR HELP...
HELP!
AFTER NEARLY FREEZING, CHELLE, AND JANE ARE WASHED TO SHORE...
I THINK I HATE YOU...
MIT
...AND ARE GREETED BY...
PAIGE
WHOA...
MIT
CHELLE AND JANE ARE WASHED ASHORE ON AN UNCHARTED ISLAND IN THE BAY... THE ISLAND INHABITANTS SEEM OVERJOYED AT THEIR ARRIVAL...
IT'S AN ISLAND OF AMAZONS!...JOY!
SOMETHING ODD IS GOING ON HERE...
YEAH... I'M GETTING LEID...
MIT
PAIGE

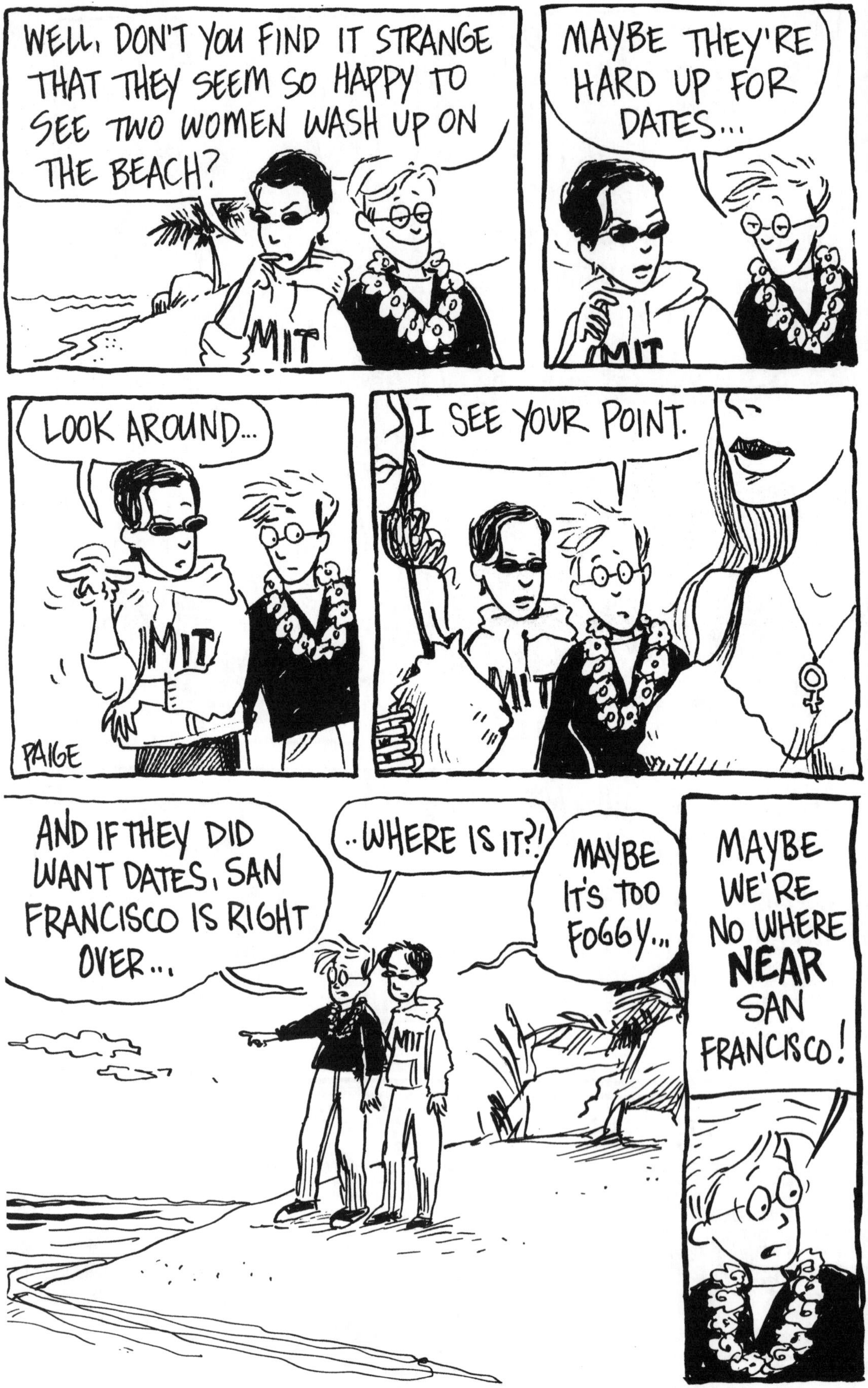

WELL, DON'T YOU FIND IT STRANGE THAT THEY SEEM SO HAPPY TO SEE TWO WOMEN WASH UP ON THE BEACH?
MIT
MAYBE THEY'RE HARD UP FOR DATES...
MIT
LOOK AROUND...
MIT
PAIGE
I SEE YOUR POINT.
MIT
AND IF THEY DID WANT DATES, SAN FRANCISCO IS RIGHT OVER...,
..WHERE IS IT?!
MAYBE IT'S TOO FOGGY...
MIT
MAYBE WE'RE NO WHERE **NEAR** SAN FRANCISCO!

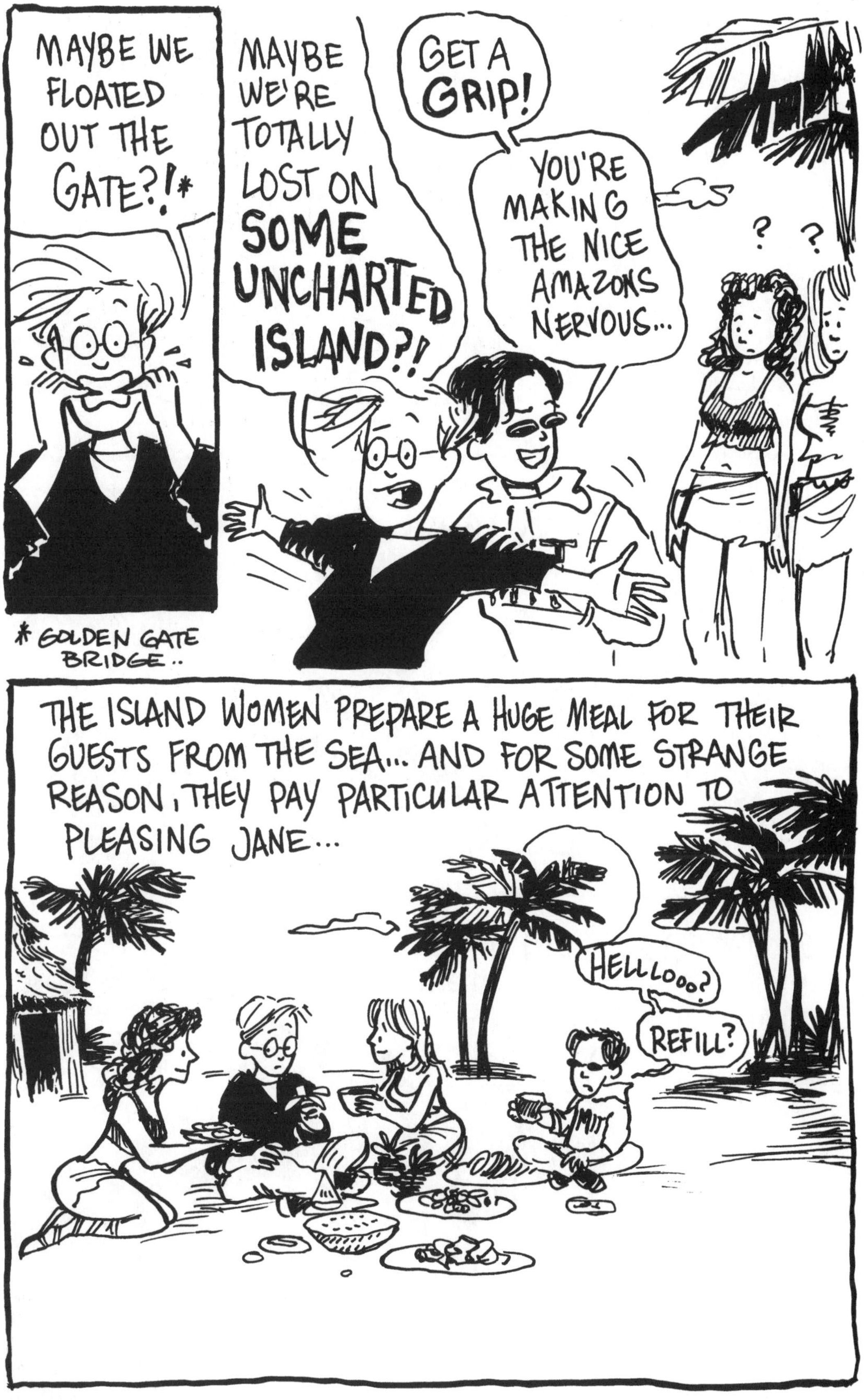
MAYBE WE FLOATED OUT THE GATE?!*
MAYBE WE'RE TOTALLY LOST ON SOME UNCHARTED ISLAND?!
GET A GRIP!
YOU'RE MAKING THE NICE AMAZONS NERVOUS...
? ?
* GOLDEN GATE BRIDGE..
THE ISLAND WOMEN PREPARE A HUGE MEAL FOR THEIR GUESTS FROM THE SEA... AND FOR SOME STRANGE REASON, THEY PAY PARTICULAR ATTENTION TO PLEASING JANE...
HELLLOOO?
REFILL?

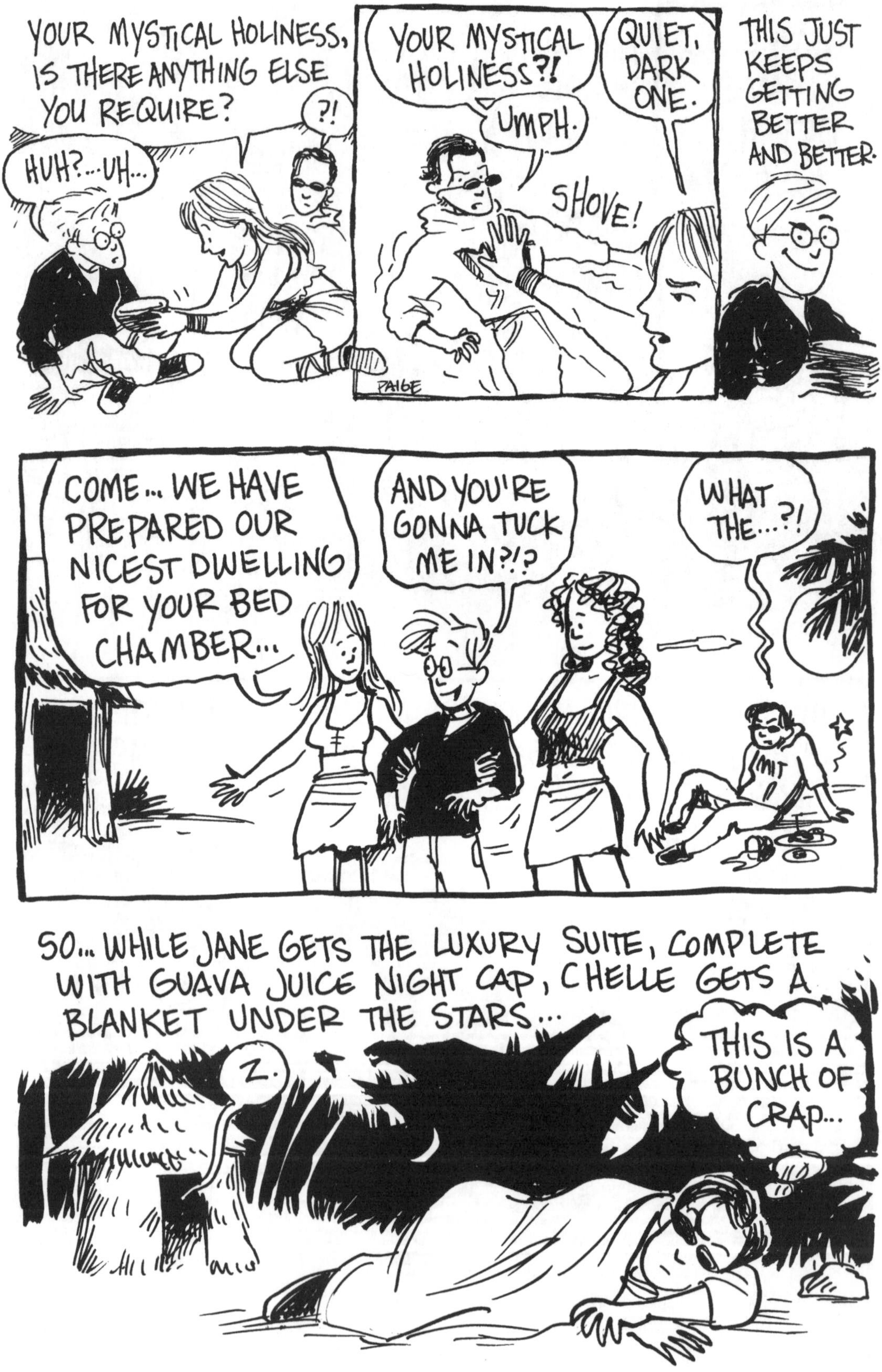
YOUR MYSTICAL HOLINESS, IS THERE ANYTHING ELSE YOU REQUIRE?
HUH?...UH...
?!
YOUR MYSTICAL HOLINESS?!
UMPH.
QUIET, DARK ONE.
SHOVE!
PAIGE
THIS JUST KEEPS GETTING BETTER AND BETTER.
COME... WE HAVE PREPARED OUR NICEST DWELLING FOR YOUR BED CHAMBER...
AND YOU'RE GONNA TUCK ME IN?!?
WHAT THE...?!
MIT
SO... WHILE JANE GETS THE LUXURY SUITE, COMPLETE WITH GUAVA JUICE NIGHT CAP, CHELLE GETS A BLANKET UNDER THE STARS...
Z.
THIS IS A BUNCH OF CRAP...

LATER, THAT NIGHT...

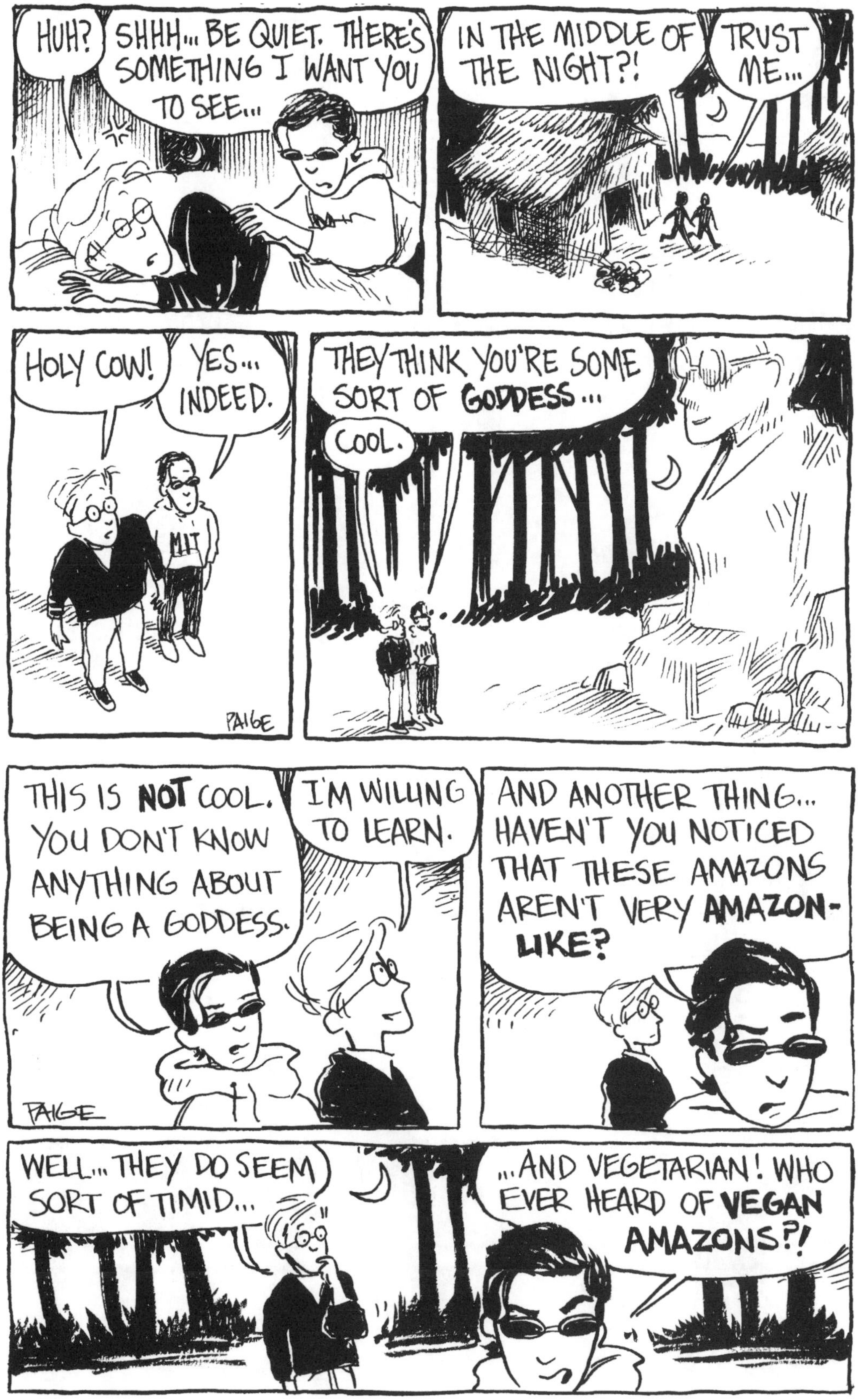
HUH?
SHHH... BE QUIET. THERE'S SOMETHING I WANT YOU TO SEE...
IN THE MIDDLE OF THE NIGHT?!
TRUST ME...
HOLY COW!
YES... INDEED.
MIT
PAIGE
THEY THINK YOU'RE SOME SORT OF GODDESS...
COOL.
THIS IS NOT COOL. YOU DON'T KNOW ANYTHING ABOUT BEING A GODDESS.
I'M WILLING TO LEARN.
PAIGE
AND ANOTHER THING... HAVEN'T YOU NOTICED THAT THESE AMAZONS AREN'T VERY AMAZON-LIKE?
WELL... THEY DO SEEM SORT OF TIMID...
...AND VEGETARIAN! WHO EVER HEARD OF VEGAN AMAZONS?!

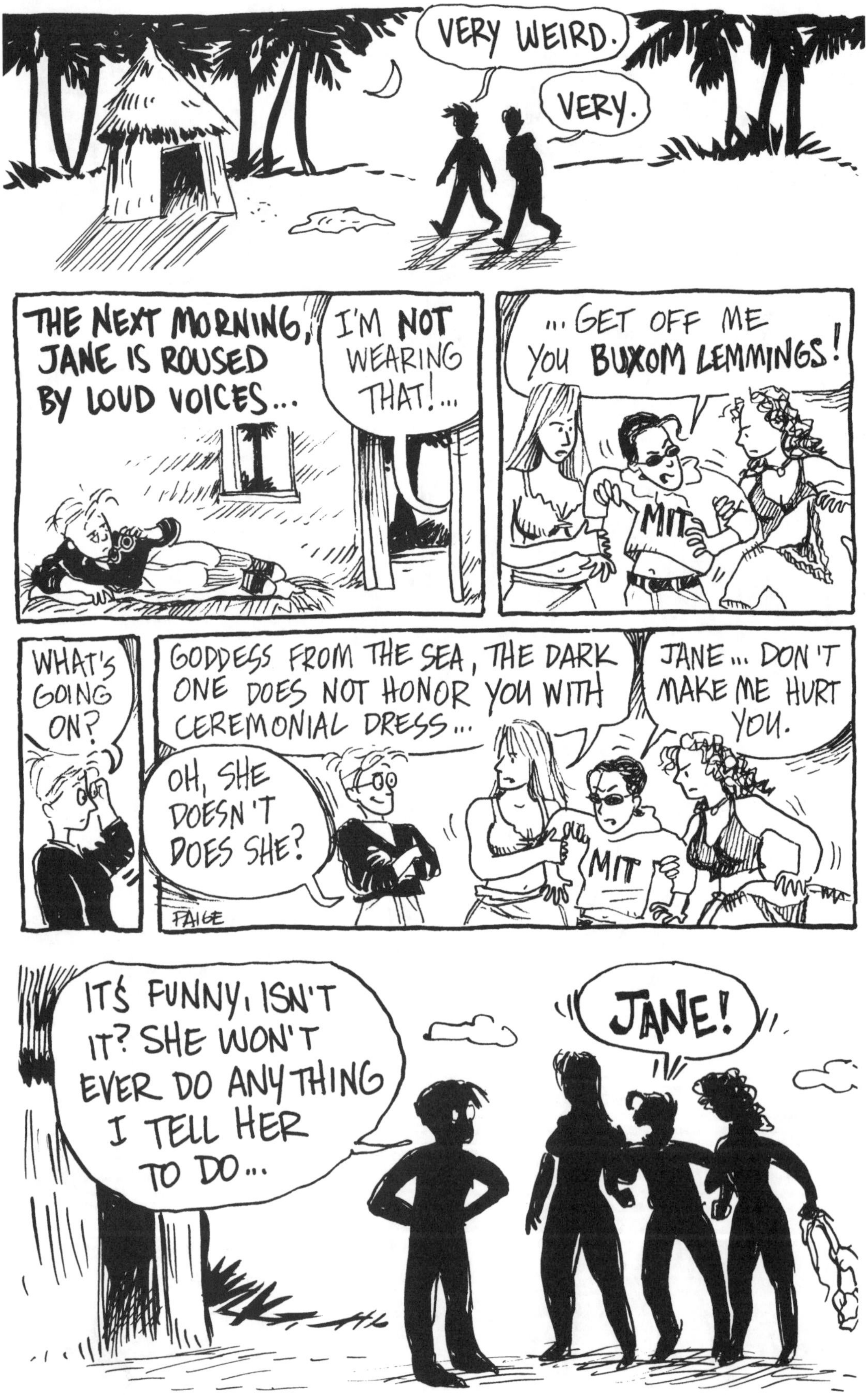
VERY WEIRD.
VERY.
THE NEXT MORNING, JANE IS ROUSED BY LOUD VOICES...
I'M NOT WEARING THAT!...
...GET OFF ME YOU BUXOM LEMMINGS!
MIT
WHAT'S GOING ON?
GODDESS FROM THE SEA, THE DARK ONE DOES NOT HONOR YOU WITH CEREMONIAL DRESS...
JANE... DON'T MAKE ME HURT YOU.
OH, SHE DOESN'T DOES SHE?
MIT
PAIGE
IT'S FUNNY, ISN'T IT? SHE WON'T EVER DO ANYTHING I TELL HER TO DO...
JANE!

SOOOO... WHAT EXACTLY **IS** THE CEREMONIAL GARB?...

IT DOESN'T MATTER, 'CAUSE I'M NOT WEARIN' IT!

QUIET!

CEREMONIAL GARB FOR WHAT?

THE WEDDING.

?!

CHELLE'S GETTING MARRIED?! ...TO WHOM?...

PAIGE

THE "PIT OF FIRE".

FIRE?

IT IS WRITTEN, WHEN THE GODDESS COMES FORTH FROM THE SEA SHE WILL BRING WITH HER THE SACRIFICIAL BRIDE TO PLEASE THE ISLAND SPIRITS.

I THOUGHT SACRIFICIAL BRIDES HAD TO BE VIRGINS?

JANE!

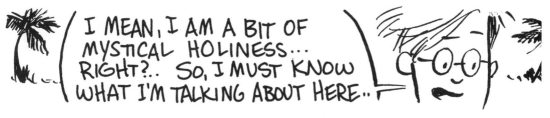

I MEAN, I AM A BIT OF MYSTICAL HOLINESS... RIGHT?.. SO, I MUST KNOW WHAT I'M TALKING ABOUT HERE..

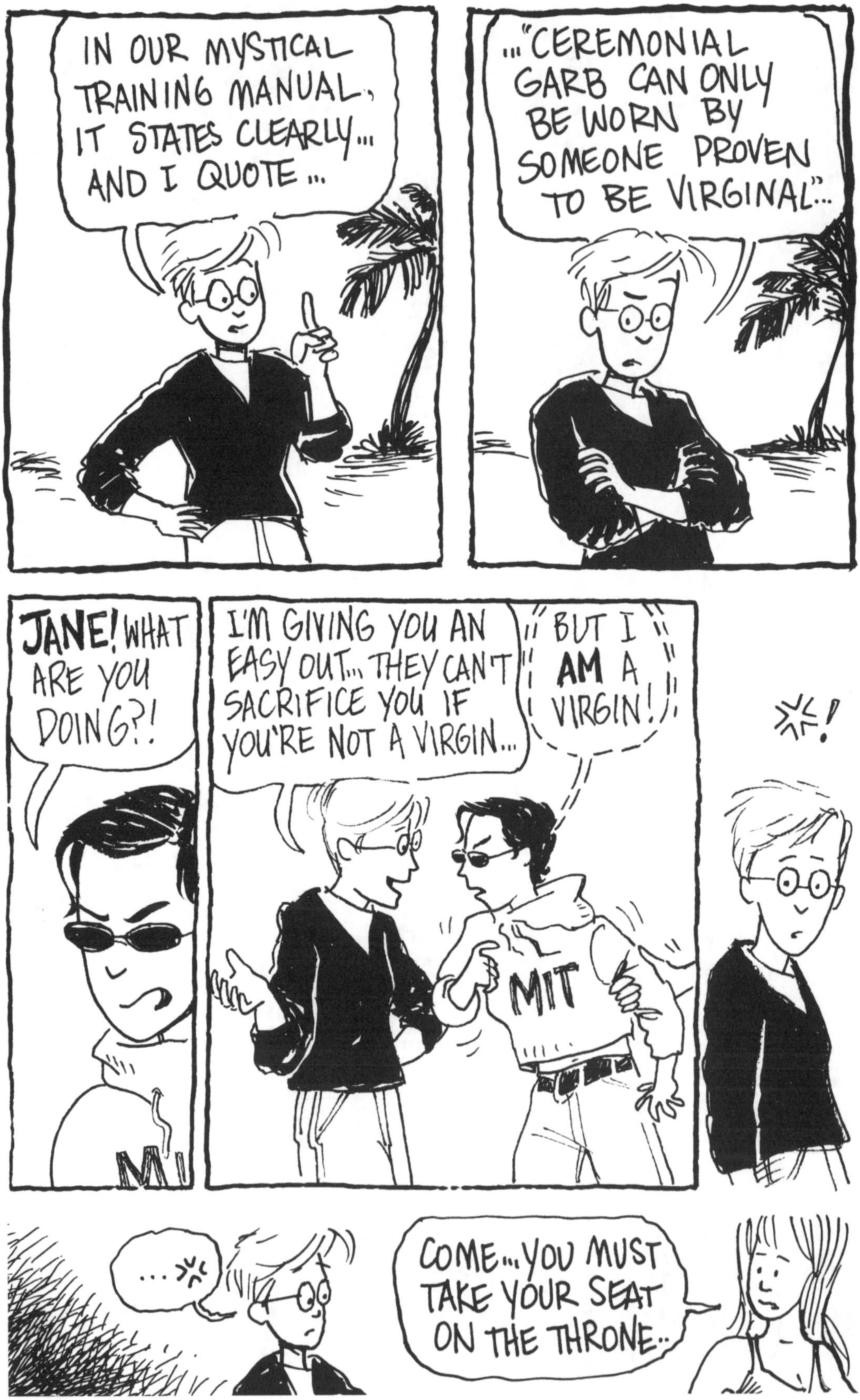

IN OUR MYSTICAL TRAINING MANUAL, IT STATES CLEARLY... AND I QUOTE...
..."CEREMONIAL GARB CAN ONLY BE WORN BY SOMEONE PROVEN TO BE VIRGINAL"...
JANE! WHAT ARE YOU DOING?!
I'M GIVING YOU AN EASY OUT... THEY CAN'T SACRIFICE YOU IF YOU'RE NOT A VIRGIN...
BUT I **AM** A VIRGIN!
MIT
!
...
COME... YOU MUST TAKE YOUR SEAT ON THE THRONE..

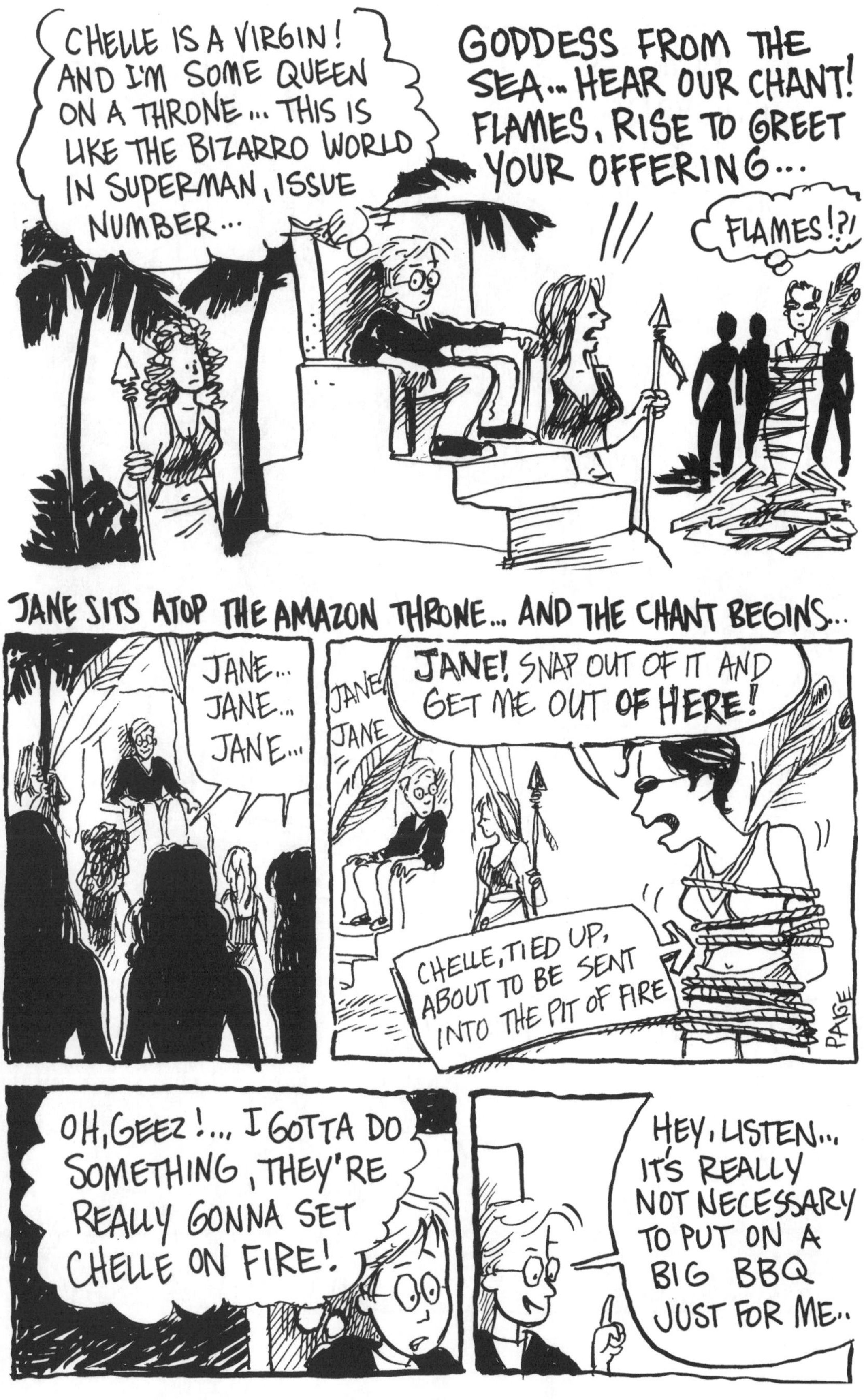
CHELLE IS A VIRGIN! AND I'M SOME QUEEN ON A THRONE... THIS IS LIKE THE BIZARRO WORLD IN SUPERMAN, ISSUE NUMBER...
GODDESS FROM THE SEA... HEAR OUR CHANT! FLAMES, RISE TO GREET YOUR OFFERING...
FLAMES!?!
JANE SITS ATOP THE AMAZON THRONE... AND THE CHANT BEGINS...
JANE... JANE... JANE...
JANE JANE
JANE! SNAP OUT OF IT AND GET ME OUT OF HERE!
CHELLE, TIED UP, ABOUT TO BE SENT INTO THE PIT OF FIRE
PAIGE
OH, GEEZ!... I GOTTA DO SOMETHING, THEY'RE REALLY GONNA SET CHELLE ON FIRE!
HEY, LISTEN... IT'S REALLY NOT NECESSARY TO PUT ON A BIG BBQ JUST FOR ME..

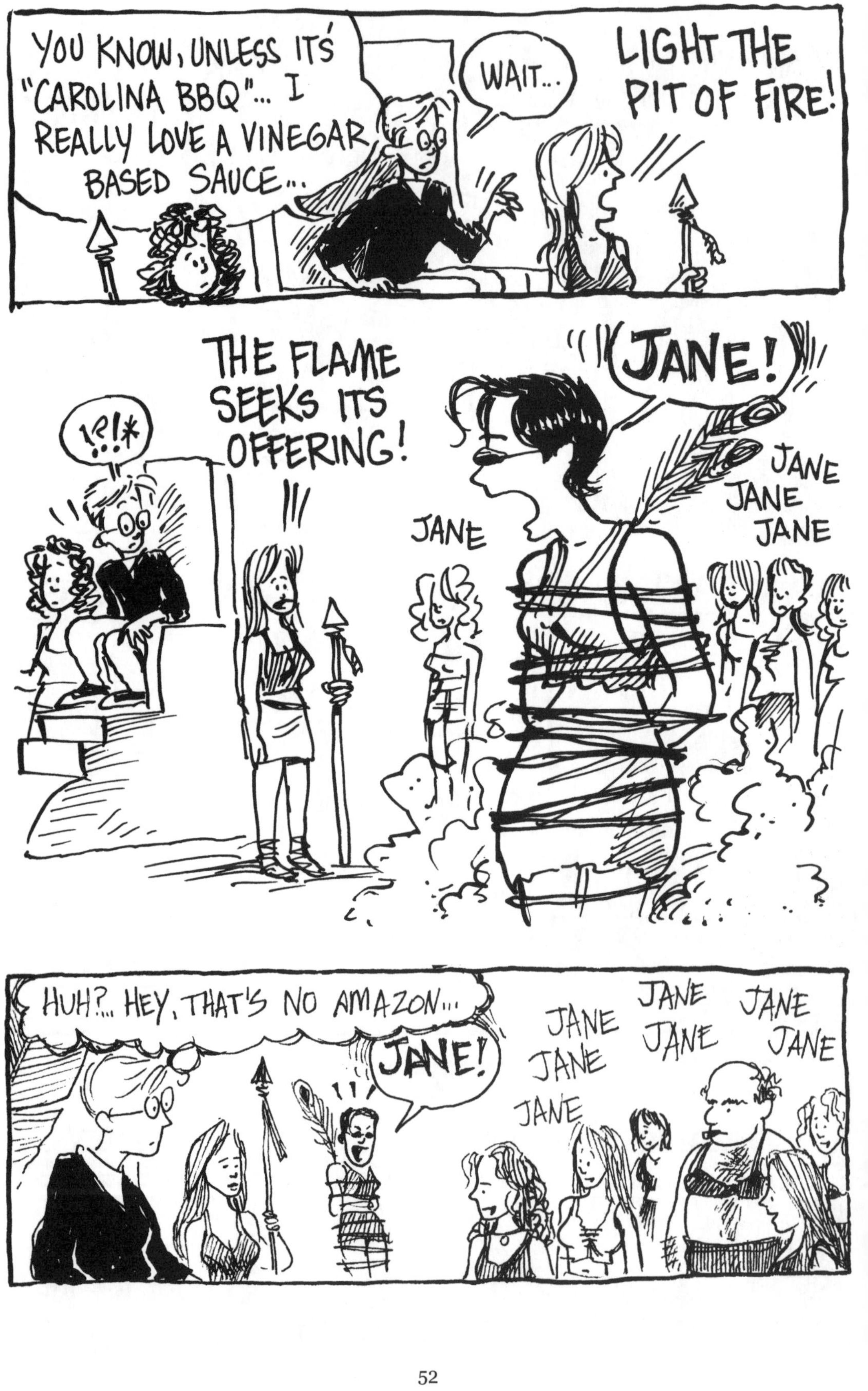
YOU KNOW, UNLESS IT'S "CAROLINA BBQ"... I REALLY LOVE A VINEGAR BASED SAUCE...
WAIT...
LIGHT THE PIT OF FIRE!
THE FLAME SEEKS ITS OFFERING!
!?!*
JANE!
JANE
JANE
JANE
JANE
HUH?... HEY, THAT'S NO AMAZON...
JANE!
JANE
JANE
JANE
JANE
JANE
JANE
JANE

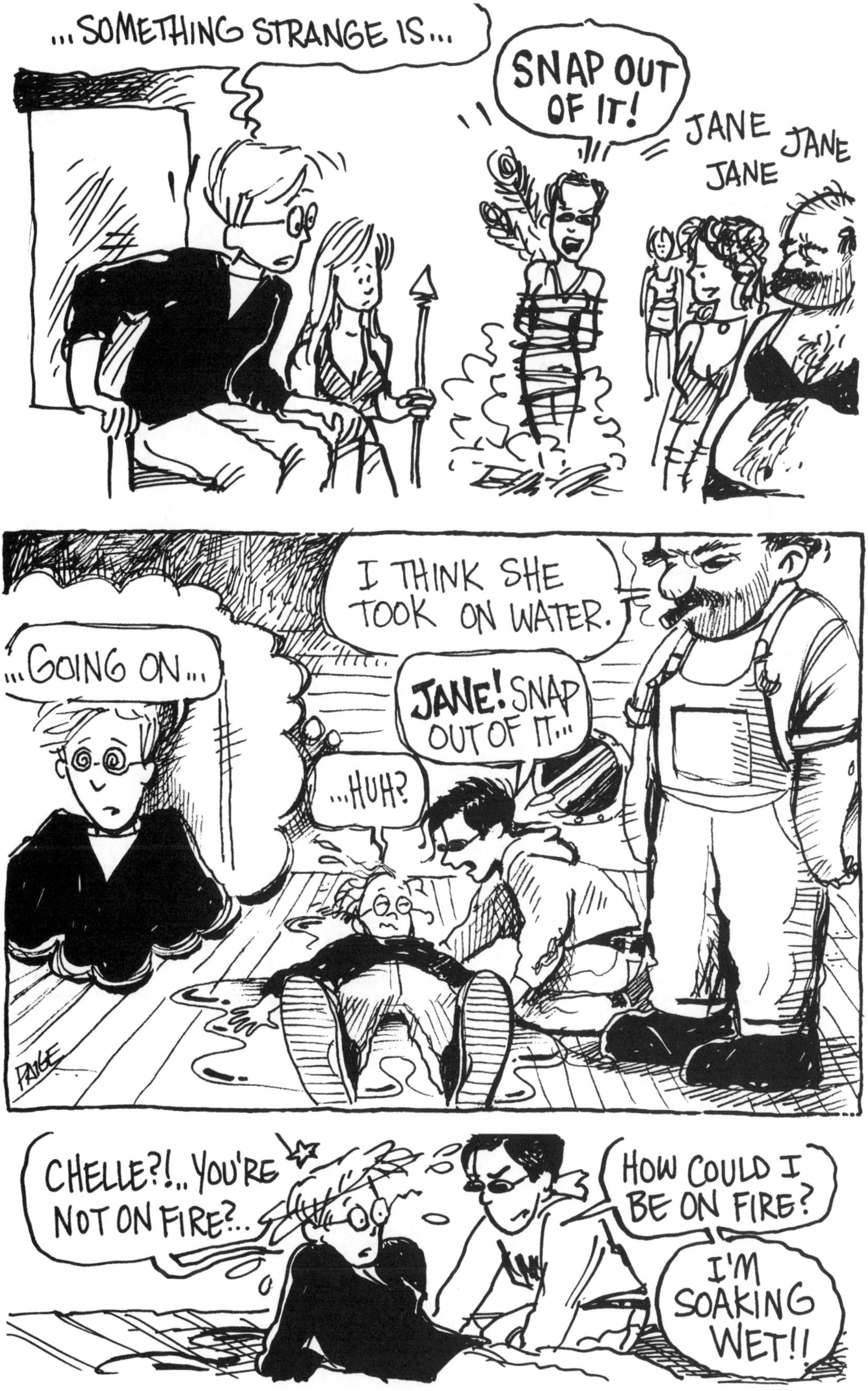
...SOMETHING STRANGE IS...
SNAP OUT OF IT!
JANE JANE JANE
...GOING ON...
I THINK SHE TOOK ON WATER.
JANE! SNAP OUT OF IT...
...HUH?
PAIGE
CHELLE?!.. YOU'RE NOT ON FIRE?..
HOW COULD I BE ON FIRE?
I'M SOAKING WET!!

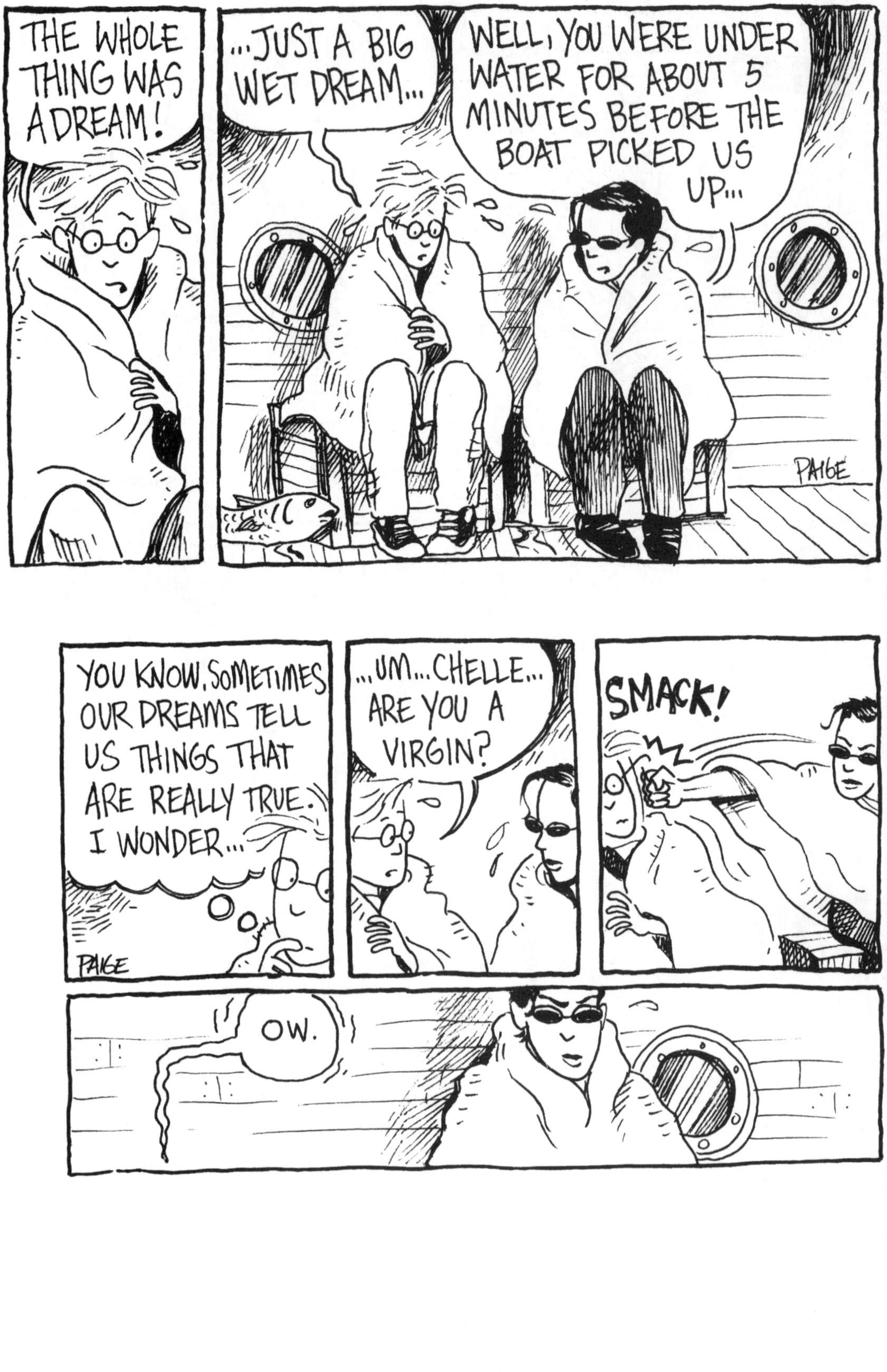
THE WHOLE THING WAS A DREAM!
...JUST A BIG WET DREAM...
WELL, YOU WERE UNDER WATER FOR ABOUT 5 MINUTES BEFORE THE BOAT PICKED US UP...
PAIGE
YOU KNOW, SOMETIMES OUR DREAMS TELL US THINGS THAT ARE REALLY TRUE. I WONDER...
PAIGE
...UM...CHELLE... ARE YOU A VIRGIN?
SMACK!
OW.

Chapter 3
Alien encounters

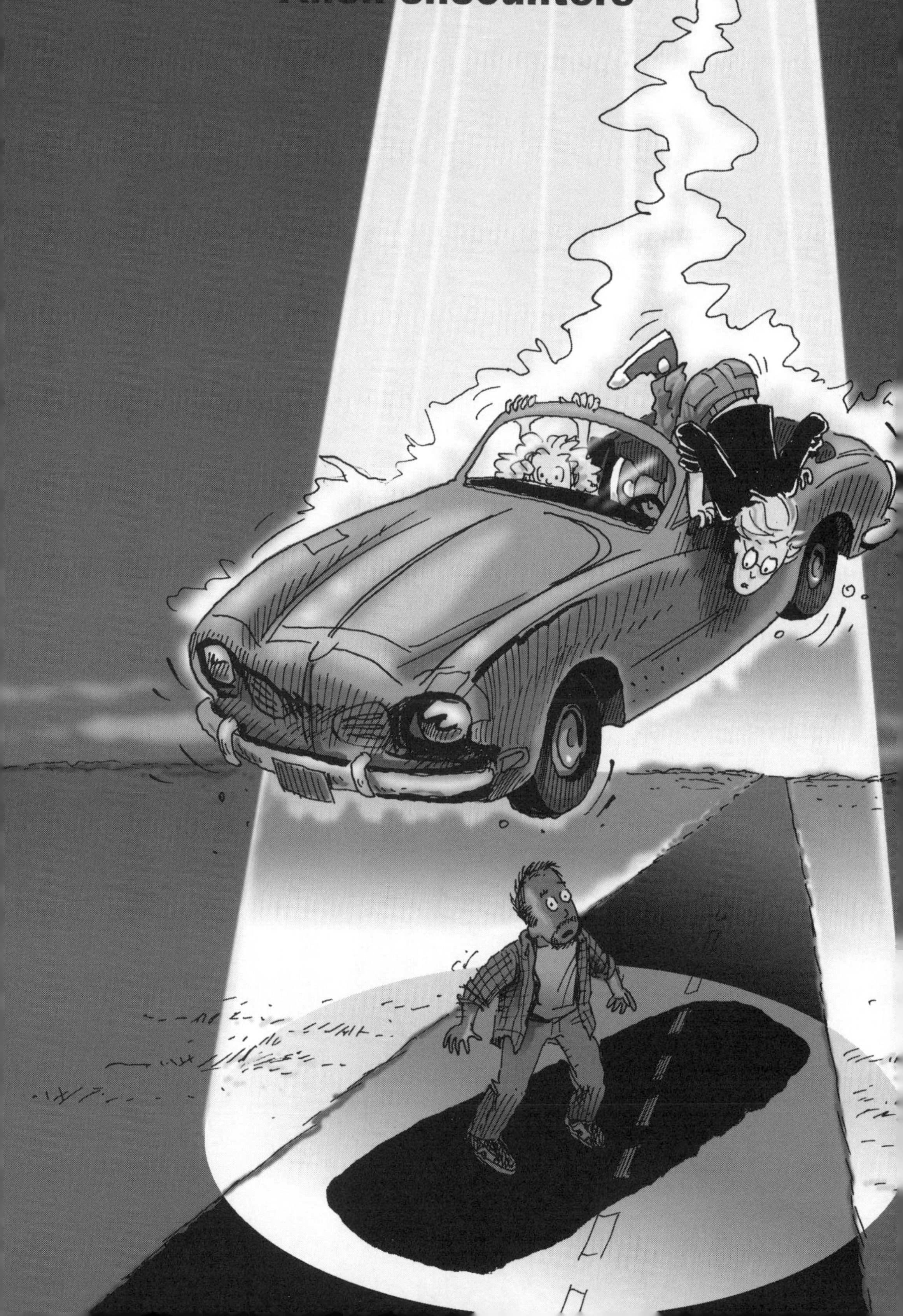

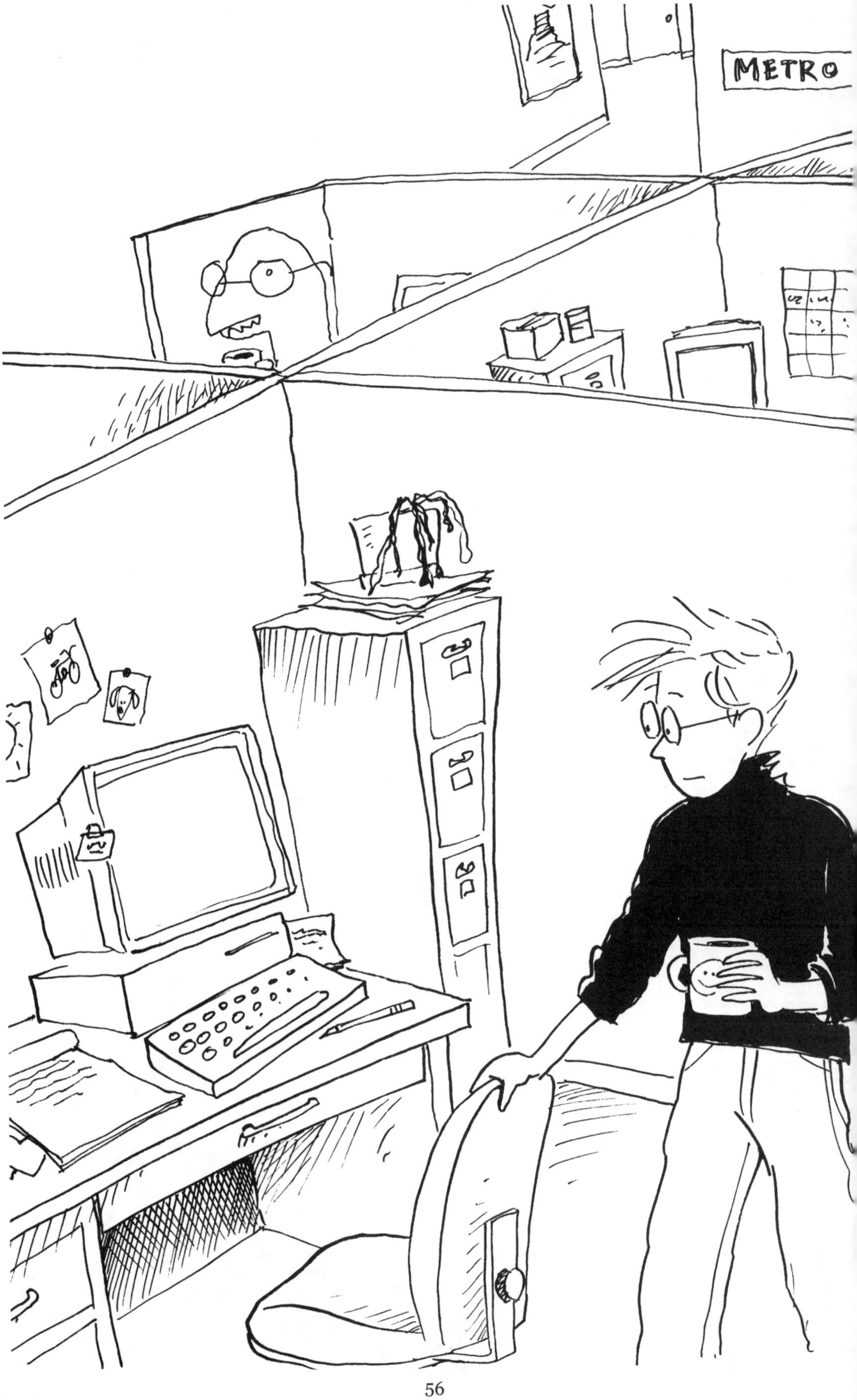
METRO

Jane begins her day, unaware that "community outreach" looms in her near future...

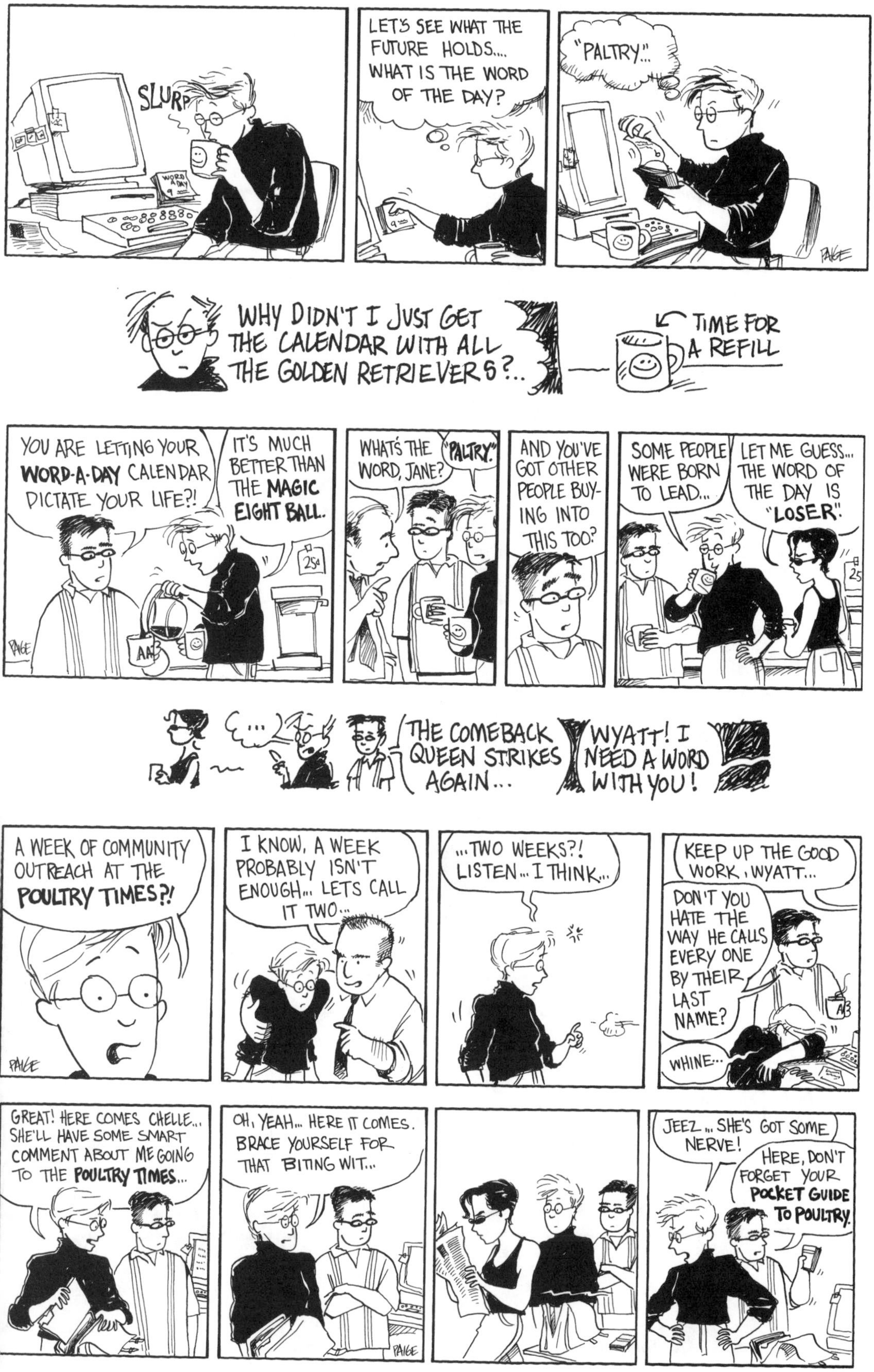

SLURP
LET'S SEE WHAT THE FUTURE HOLDS.... WHAT IS THE WORD OF THE DAY?
"PALTRY."
WHY DIDN'T I JUST GET THE CALENDAR WITH ALL THE GOLDEN RETRIEVERS?..
TIME FOR A REFILL
YOU ARE LETTING YOUR **WORD-A-DAY** CALENDAR DICTATE YOUR LIFE?!
IT'S MUCH BETTER THAN THE **MAGIC EIGHT BALL.**
WHAT'S THE WORD, JANE?
"PALTRY."
AND YOU'VE GOT OTHER PEOPLE BUYING INTO THIS TOO?
SOME PEOPLE WERE BORN TO LEAD...
LET ME GUESS... THE WORD OF THE DAY IS "**LOSER**".
THE COMEBACK QUEEN STRIKES AGAIN...
WYATT! I NEED A WORD WITH YOU!
A WEEK OF COMMUNITY OUTREACH AT THE **POULTRY TIMES?!**
I KNOW, A WEEK PROBABLY ISN'T ENOUGH... LETS CALL IT TWO...
...TWO WEEKS?! LISTEN... I THINK...
KEEP UP THE GOOD WORK, WYATT...
DON'T YOU HATE THE WAY HE CALLS EVERY ONE BY THEIR LAST NAME?
WHINE...
GREAT! HERE COMES CHELLE... SHE'LL HAVE SOME SMART COMMENT ABOUT ME GOING TO THE **POULTRY TIMES**...
OH, YEAH... HERE IT COMES. BRACE YOURSELF FOR THAT BITING WIT...
JEEZ... SHE'S GOT SOME NERVE!
HERE, DON'T FORGET YOUR **POCKET GUIDE TO POULTRY.**

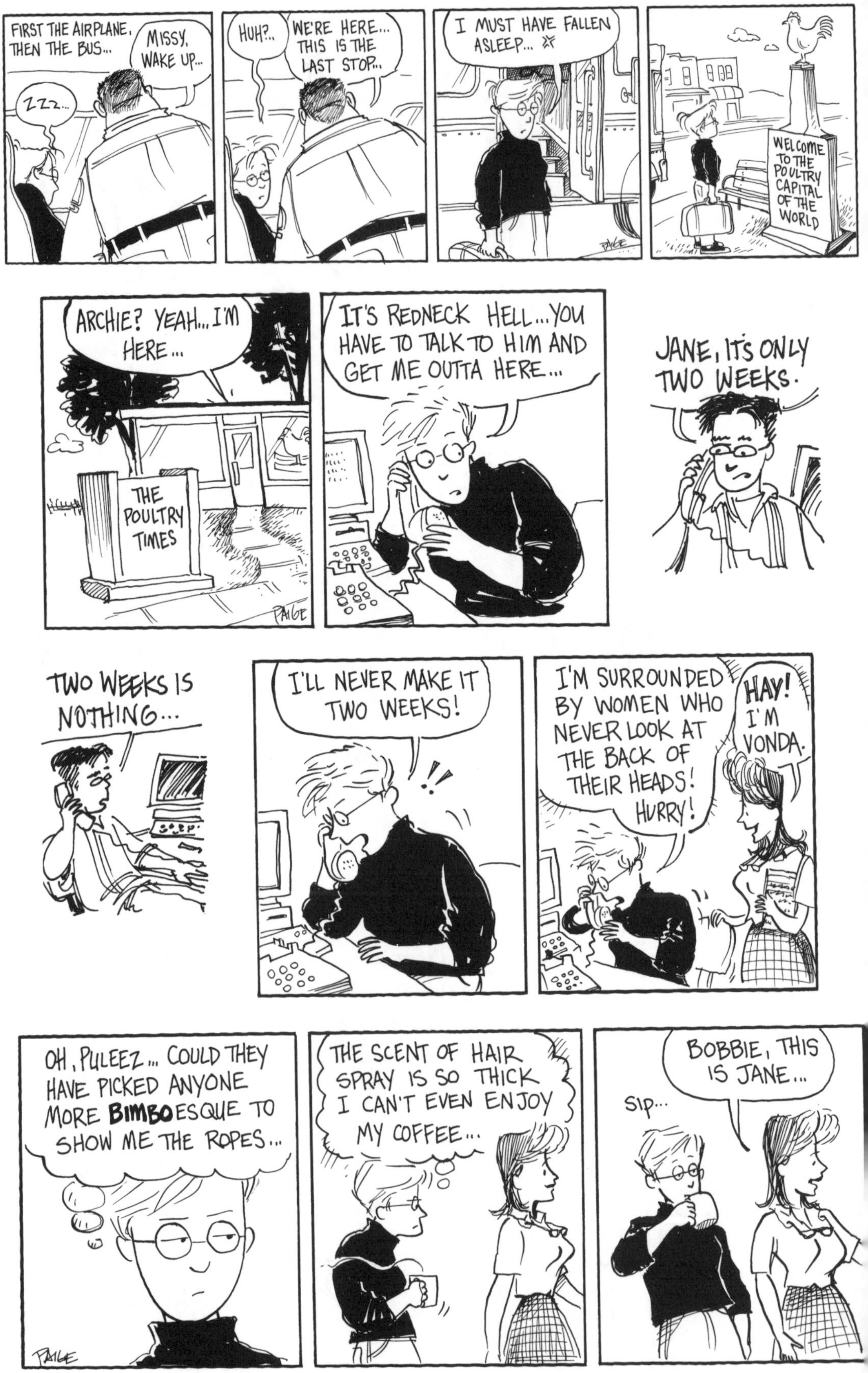
FIRST THE AIRPLANE, THEN THE BUS...
ZZZ...
MISSY, WAKE UP...
HUH?...
WE'RE HERE... THIS IS THE LAST STOP...
I MUST HAVE FALLEN ASLEEP...
WELCOME TO THE POULTRY CAPITAL OF THE WORLD
PAIGE
ARCHIE? YEAH... I'M HERE...
THE POULTRY TIMES
PAIGE
IT'S REDNECK HELL... YOU HAVE TO TALK TO HIM AND GET ME OUTTA HERE...
JANE, IT'S ONLY TWO WEEKS.
TWO WEEKS IS NOTHING...
I'LL NEVER MAKE IT TWO WEEKS!
!!
I'M SURROUNDED BY WOMEN WHO NEVER LOOK AT THE BACK OF THEIR HEADS! HURRY!
HAY! I'M VONDA.
OH, PULEEZ... COULD THEY HAVE PICKED ANYONE MORE BIMBOESQUE TO SHOW ME THE ROPES...
PAIGE
THE SCENT OF HAIR SPRAY IS SO THICK I CAN'T EVEN ENJOY MY COFFEE...
SIP...
BOBBIE, THIS IS JANE...

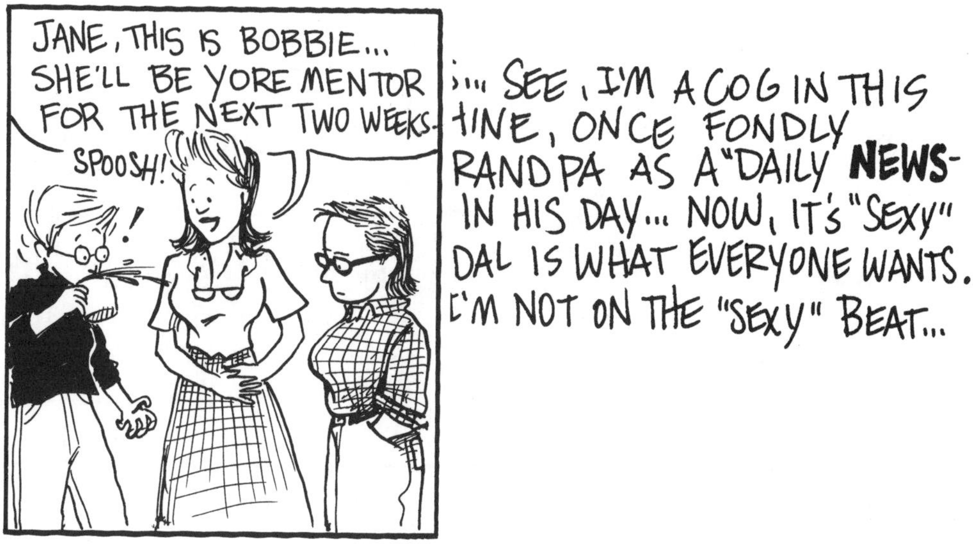
JANE, THIS IS BOBBIE... SHE'LL BE YORE MENTOR FOR THE NEXT TWO WEEKS.
SPOOSH!
!
... SEE, I'M A COG IN THIS
INE, ONCE FONDLY
RANDPA AS A "DAILY NEWS-
IN HIS DAY... NOW, IT'S "SEXY"
DAL IS WHAT EVERYONE WANTS.
I'M NOT ON THE "SEXY" BEAT...

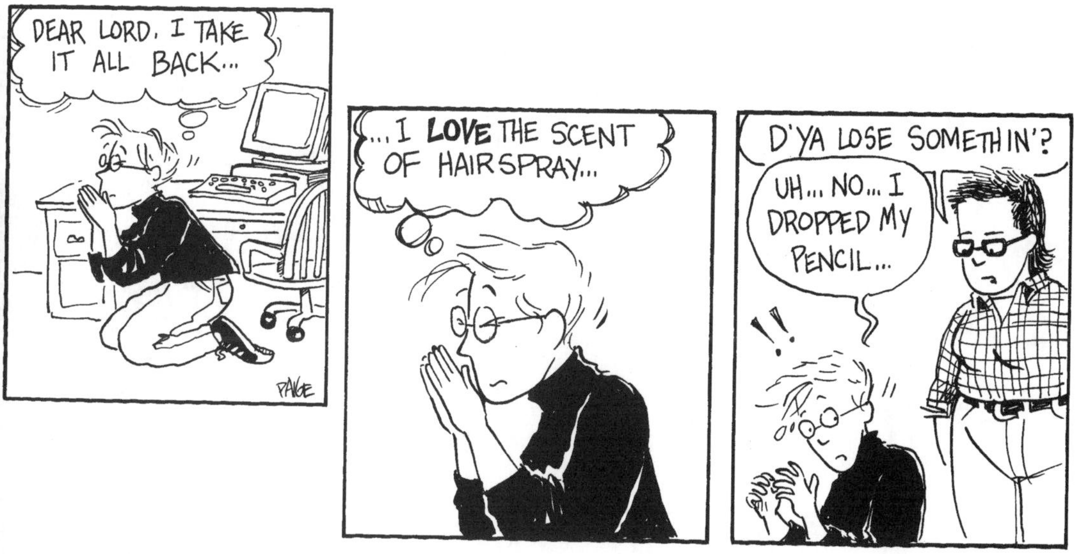
DEAR LORD, I TAKE IT ALL BACK...
...I **LOVE** THE SCENT OF HAIRSPRAY...
D'YA LOSE SOMETHIN'?
UH... NO... I DROPPED MY PENCIL...
!!

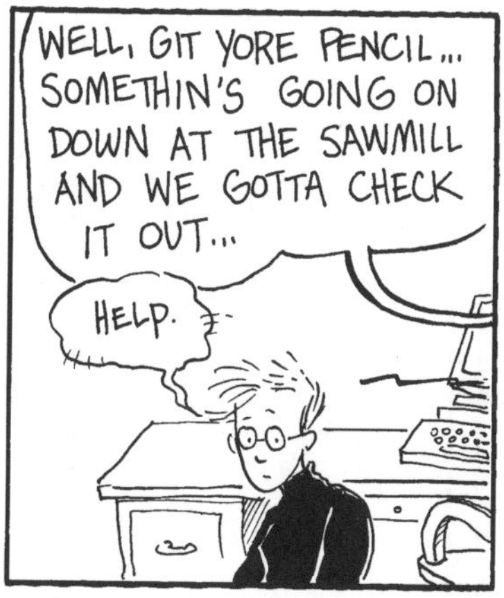
WELL, GIT YORE PENCIL... SOMETHIN'S GOING ON DOWN AT THE SAWMILL AND WE GOTTA CHECK IT OUT...
HELP.

A few moments later, in the parking lot at ***The Poultry Times...***

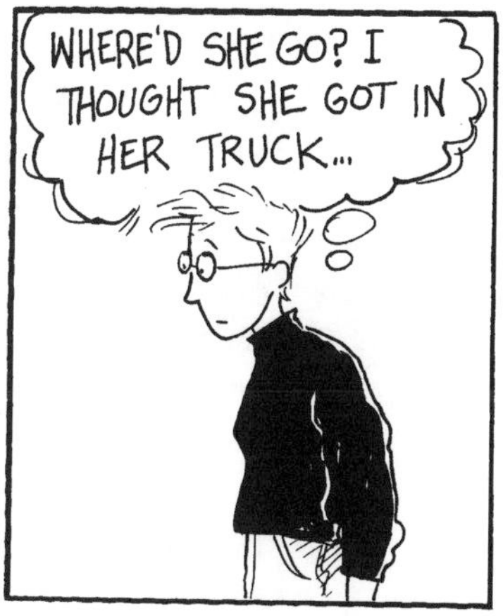
WHERE'D SHE GO? I THOUGHT SHE GOT IN HER TRUCK...

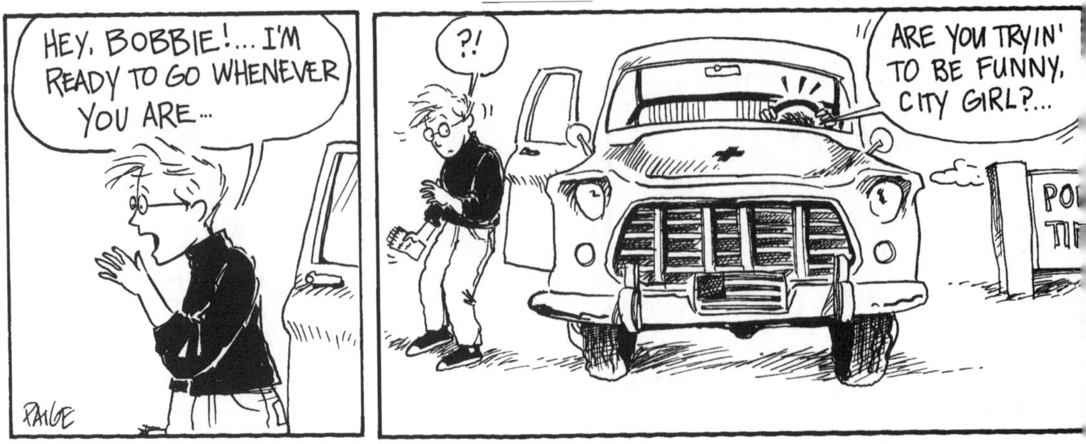
HEY, BOBBIE!... I'M READY TO GO WHENEVER YOU ARE...
?!
ARE YOU TRYIN' TO BE FUNNY, CITY GIRL?...

Jane soon discovers that Bobbie's view of the road is somewhat vertically challenged...

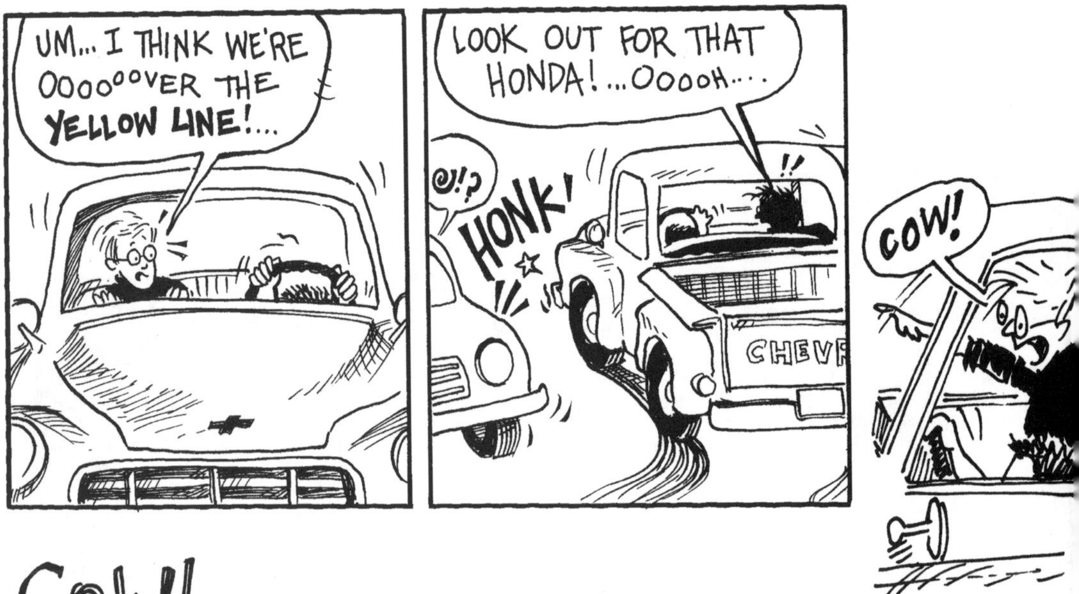
UM... I THINK WE'RE OOOOOOVER THE YELLOW LINE!...
LOOK OUT FOR THAT HONDA! ...OOOOH....
@!?
HONK!
!!
COW!

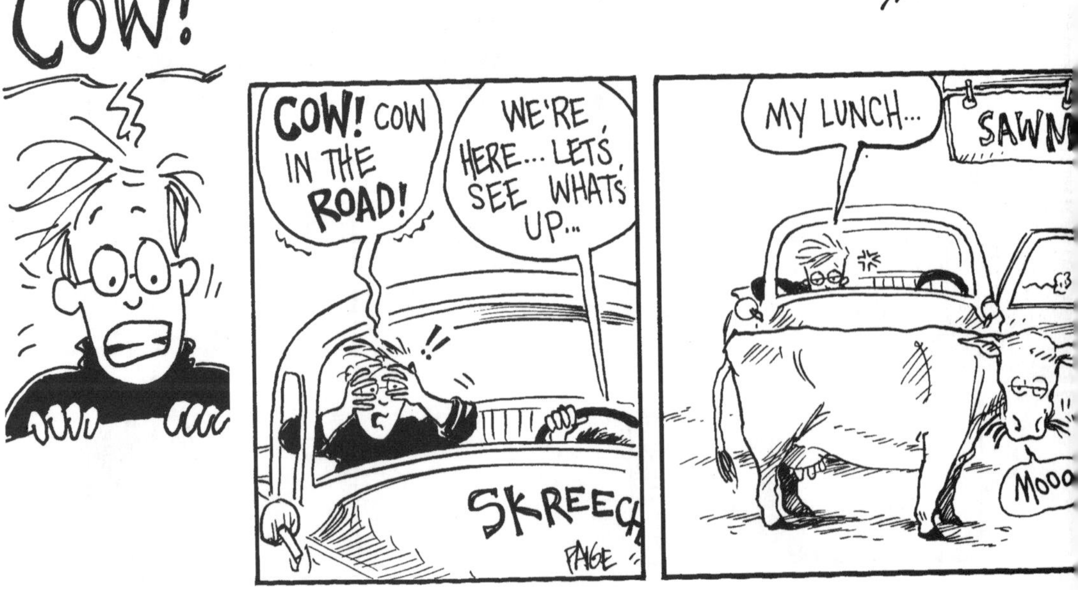
COW!
COW! COW IN THE ROAD!
WE'RE HERE... LETS SEE WHATS UP...
SKREECH
MY LUNCH...

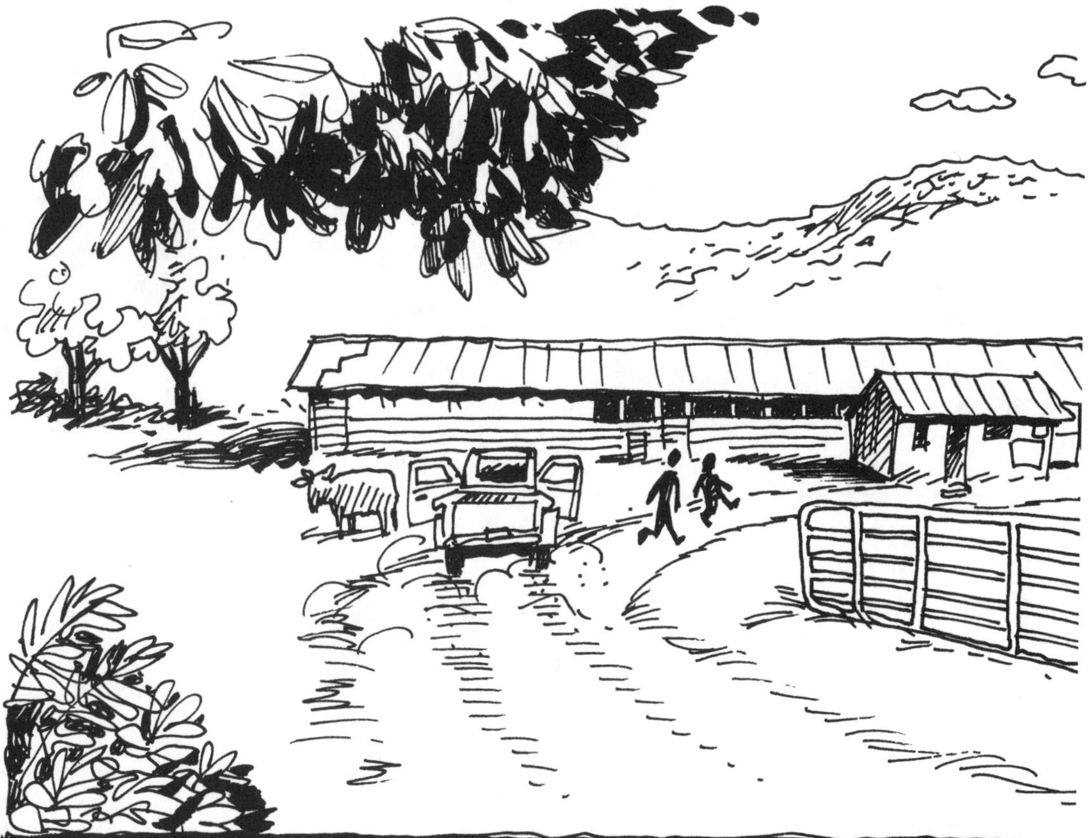

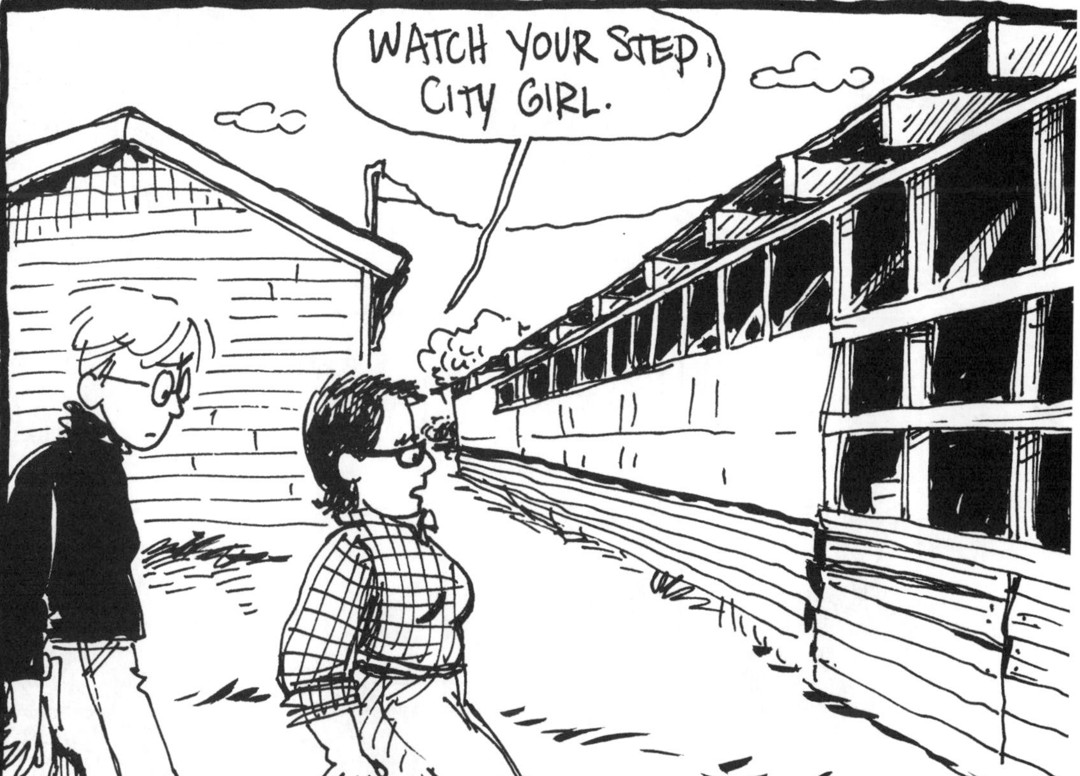
WATCH YOUR STEP, CITY GIRL.

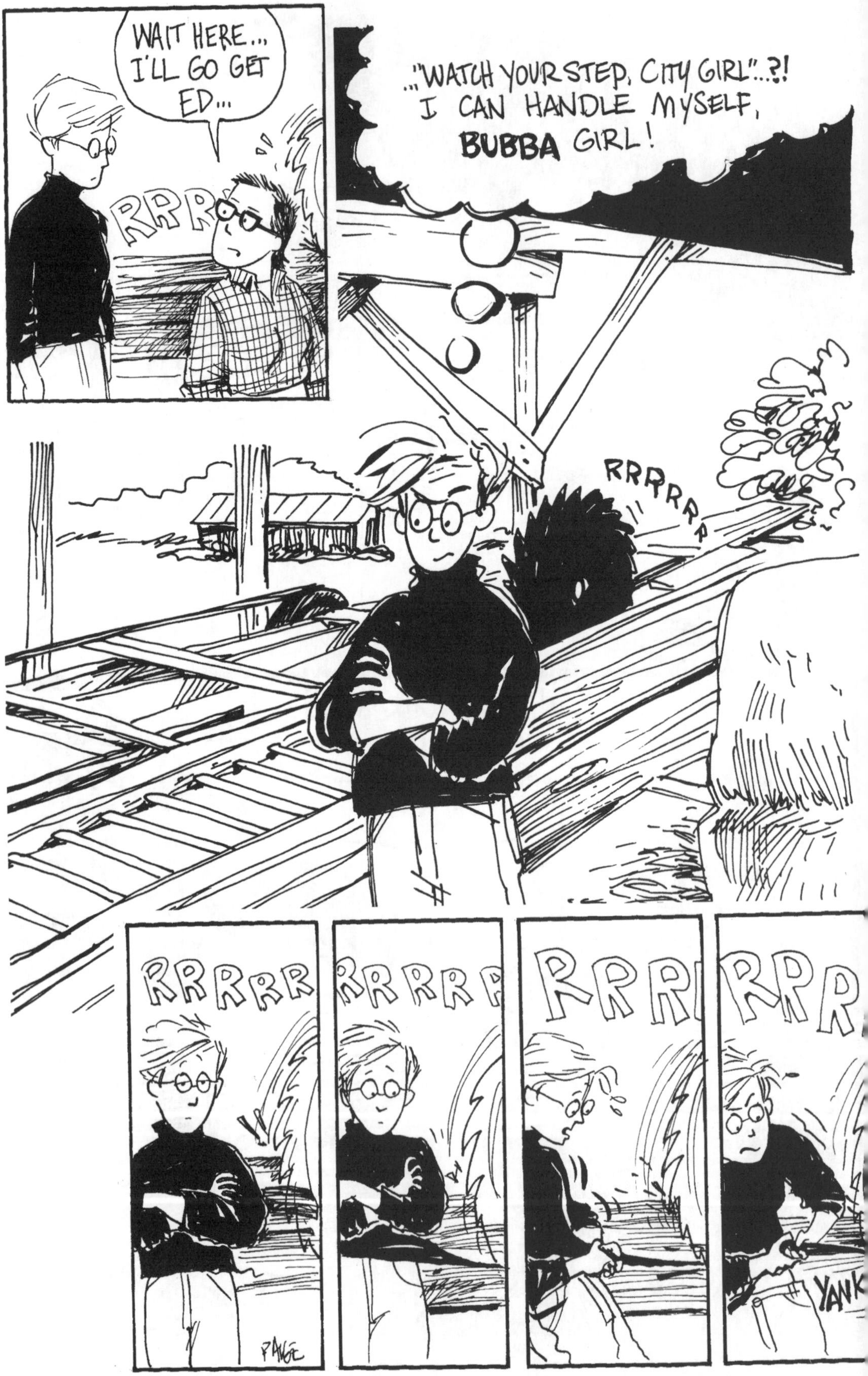
WAIT HERE... I'LL GO GET ED...
RRR
..."WATCH YOUR STEP, CITY GIRL"...?! I CAN HANDLE MYSELF, BUBBA GIRL!
RRRRRRR
RRRRR
PAIGE
RRRRR
RRR
RRR
YANK

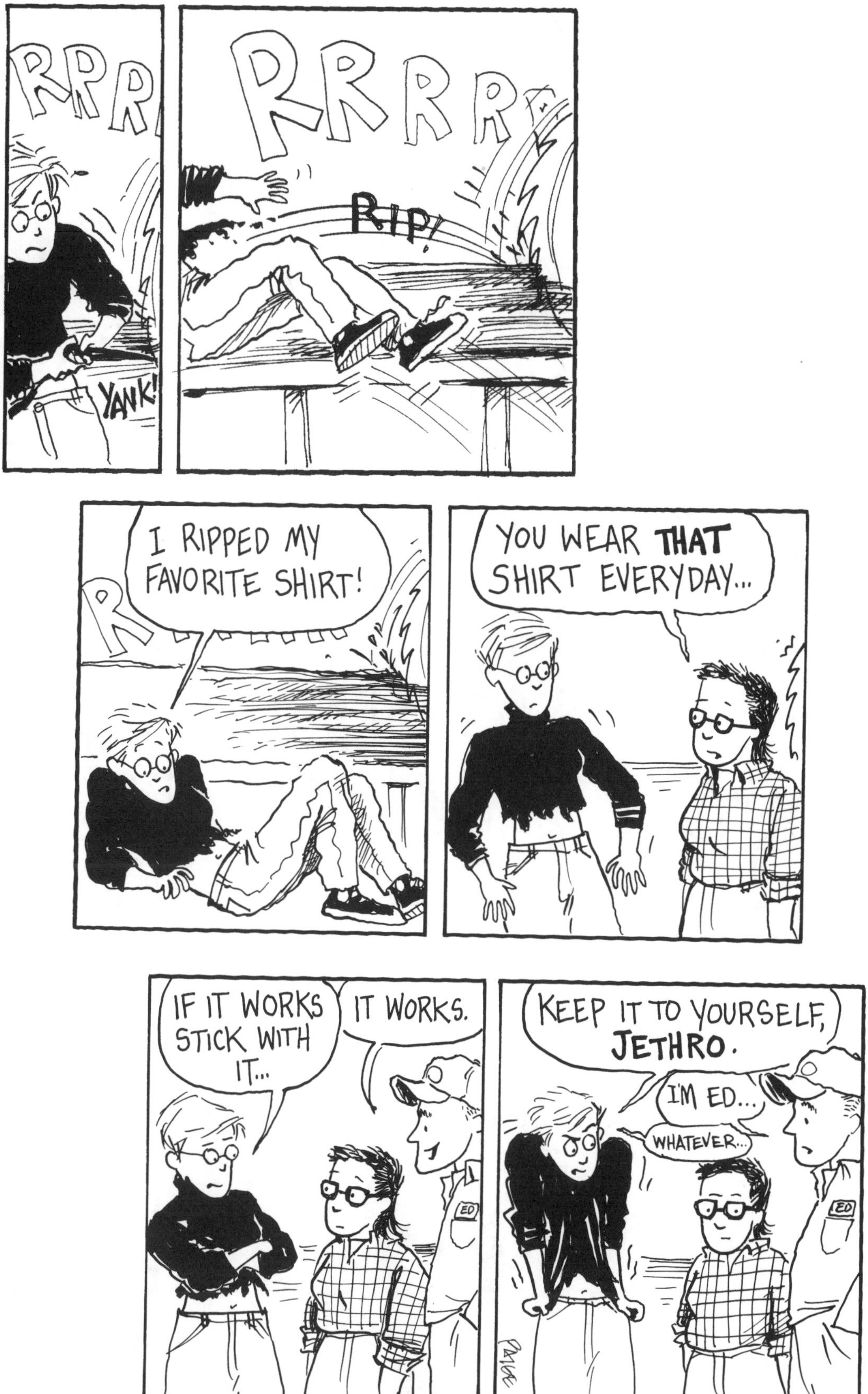
RRR
YANK!
RRRRR
RIP!
I RIPPED MY FAVORITE SHIRT!
R
YOU WEAR **THAT** SHIRT EVERYDAY...
IF IT WORKS STICK WITH IT...
IT WORKS.
ED
KEEP IT TO YOURSELF, **JETHRO**.
I'M ED...
WHATEVER...
ED

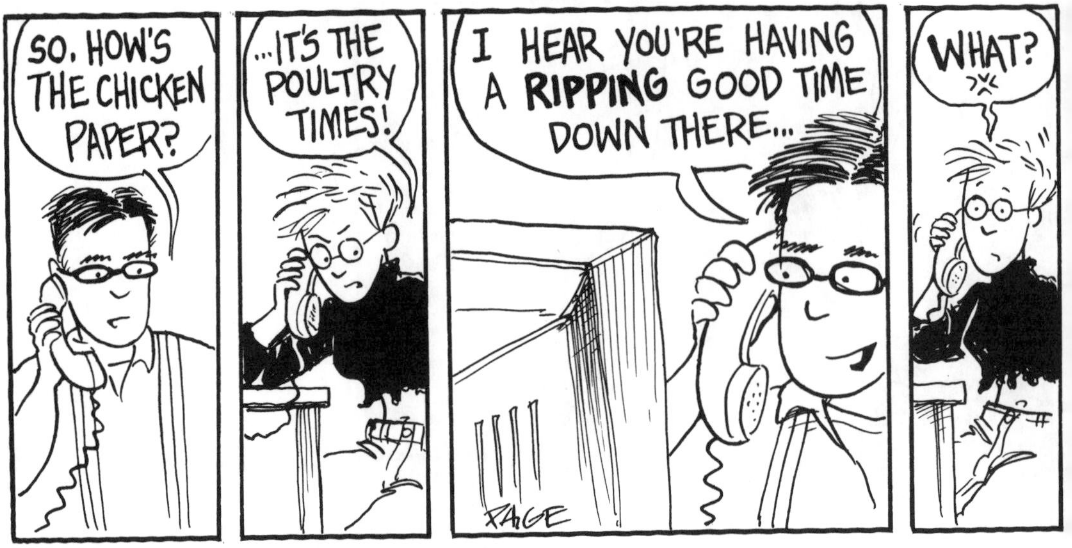
SO, HOW'S THE CHICKEN PAPER?
...IT'S THE POULTRY TIMES!
I HEAR YOU'RE HAVING A **RIPPING** GOOD TIME DOWN THERE...
WHAT?
PAGE

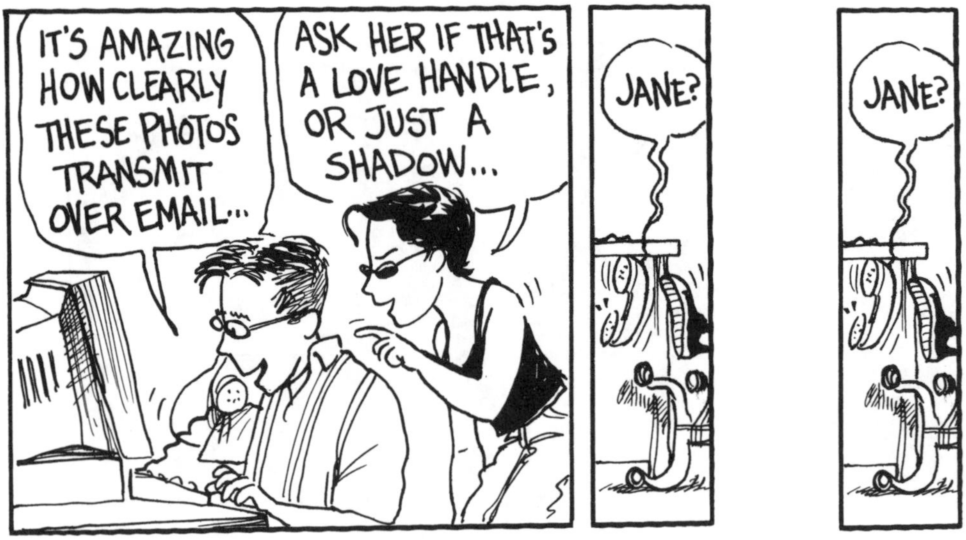
IT'S AMAZING HOW CLEARLY THESE PHOTOS TRANSMIT OVER EMAIL...
ASK HER IF THAT'S A LOVE HANDLE, OR JUST A SHADOW...
JANE?
JANE?

Later that night, Jane takes a private moment for self-reflection...

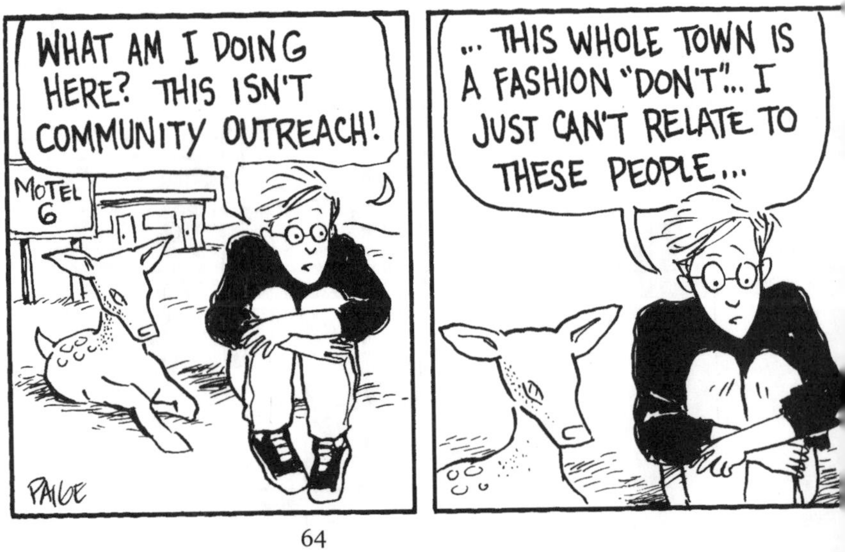
WHAT AM I DOING HERE? THIS ISN'T COMMUNITY OUTREACH!
MOTEL 6
... THIS WHOLE TOWN IS A FASHION "DON'T"... I JUST CAN'T RELATE TO THESE PEOPLE...
PAIGE

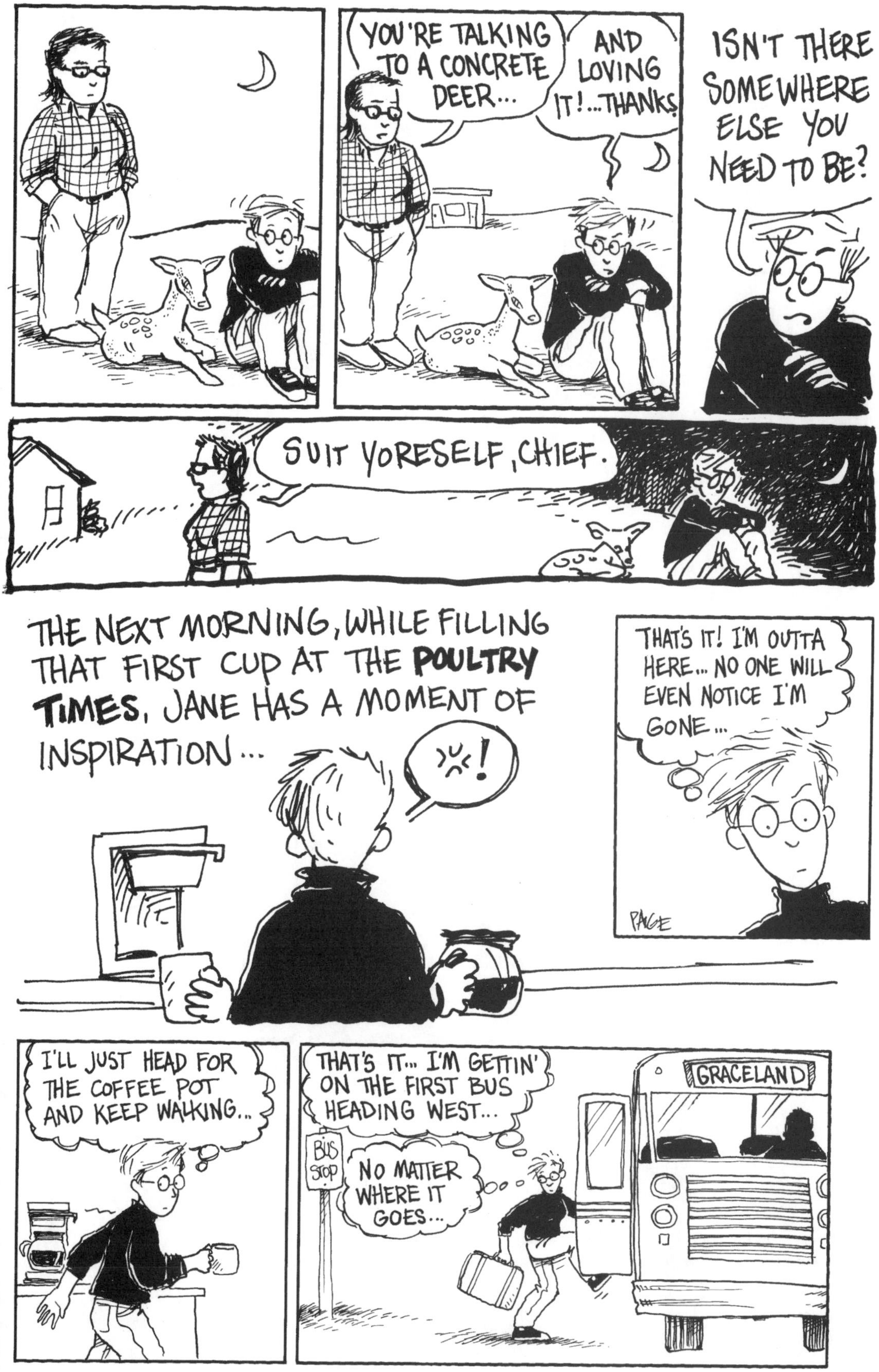

YOU'RE TALKING TO A CONCRETE DEER...
AND LOVING IT!...THANKS
ISN'T THERE SOMEWHERE ELSE YOU NEED TO BE?
SUIT YORESELF, CHIEF.
THE NEXT MORNING, WHILE FILLING THAT FIRST CUP AT THE **POULTRY TIMES**, JANE HAS A MOMENT OF INSPIRATION...
!
THAT'S IT! I'M OUTTA HERE... NO ONE WILL EVEN NOTICE I'M GONE...
PAGE
I'LL JUST HEAD FOR THE COFFEE POT AND KEEP WALKING...
THAT'S IT... I'M GETTIN' ON THE FIRST BUS HEADING WEST...
BUS STOP
NO MATTER WHERE IT GOES...
GRACELAND

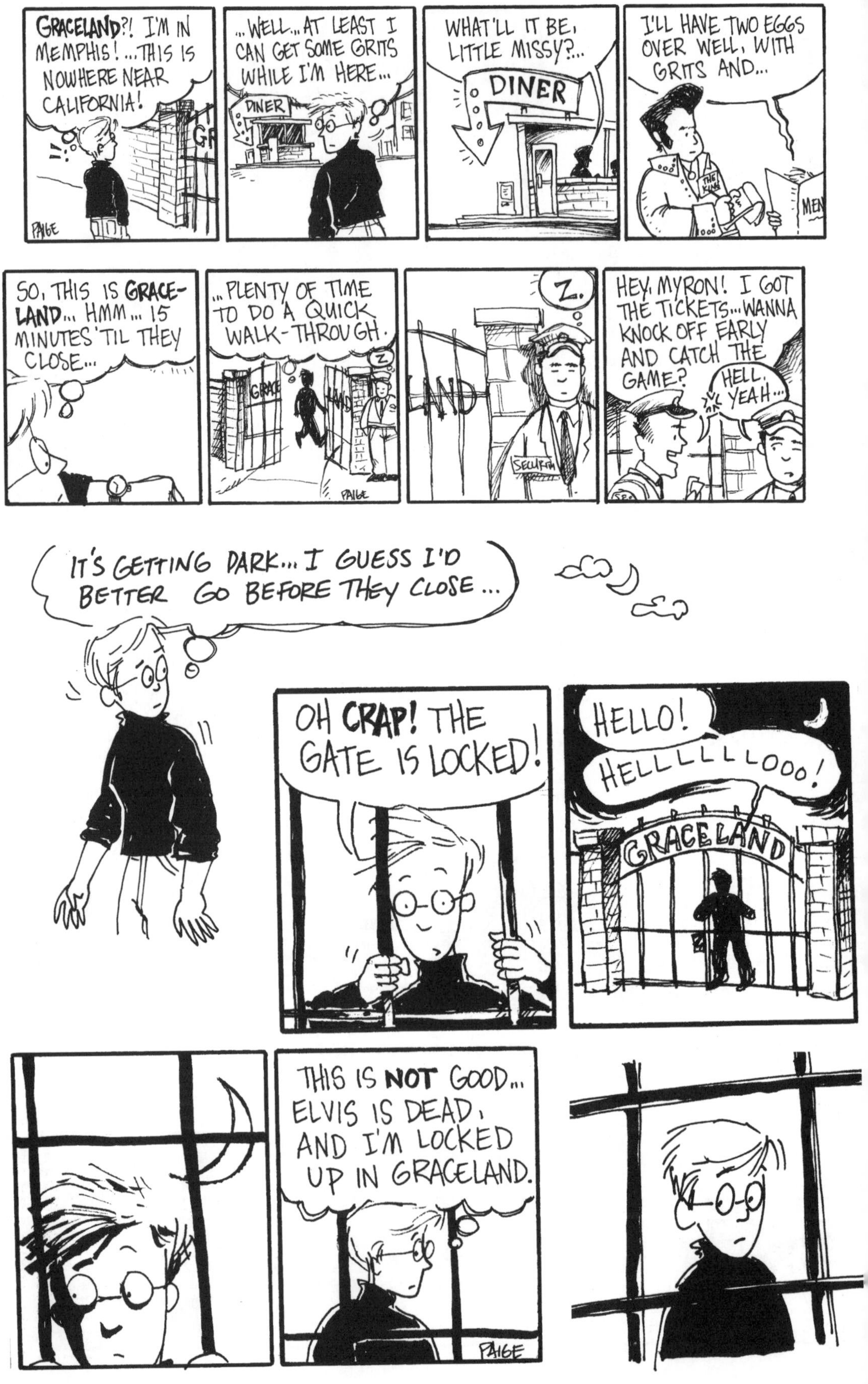
GRACELAND?! I'M IN MEMPHIS! ...THIS IS NOWHERE NEAR CALIFORNIA!
PAIGE
...WELL... AT LEAST I CAN GET SOME GRITS WHILE I'M HERE...
DINER
WHAT'LL IT BE, LITTLE MISSY?...
DINER
I'LL HAVE TWO EGGS OVER WELL, WITH GRITS AND...
THE KING
SO, THIS IS GRACELAND... HMM... 15 MINUTES 'TIL THEY CLOSE...
...PLENTY OF TIME TO DO A QUICK WALK-THROUGH.
Z
PAIGE
Z.
SECURITY
HEY, MYRON! I GOT THE TICKETS... WANNA KNOCK OFF EARLY AND CATCH THE GAME?
HELL, YEAH...
IT'S GETTING DARK... I GUESS I'D BETTER GO BEFORE THEY CLOSE...
OH CRAP! THE GATE IS LOCKED!
HELLO!
HELLLLLLLOOOO!
GRACELAND
THIS IS NOT GOOD... ELVIS IS DEAD, AND I'M LOCKED UP IN GRACELAND.
PAIGE

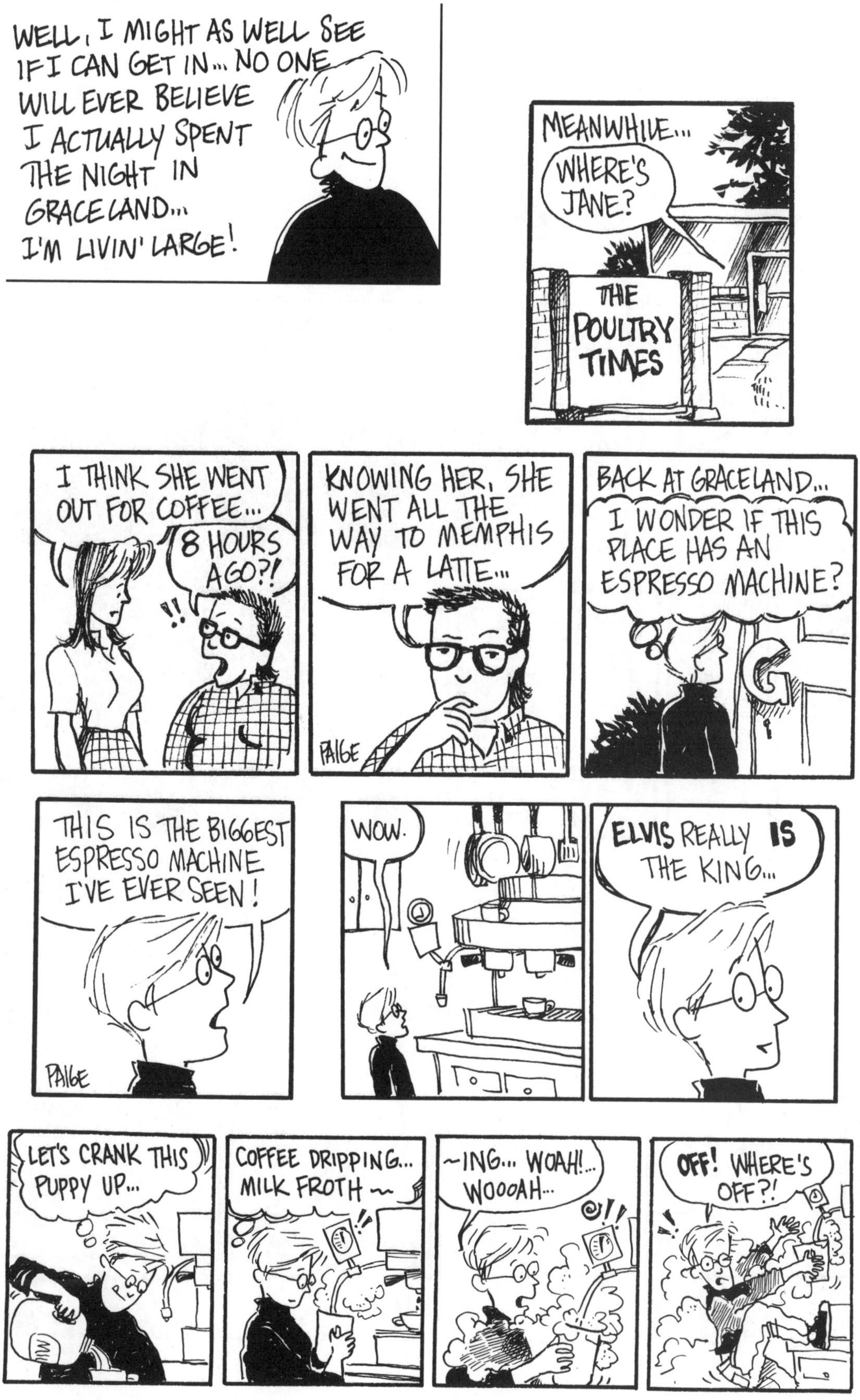
WELL, I MIGHT AS WELL SEE IF I CAN GET IN... NO ONE WILL EVER BELIEVE I ACTUALLY SPENT THE NIGHT IN GRACELAND... I'M LIVIN' LARGE!
MEANWHILE...
WHERE'S JANE?
THE POULTRY TIMES
I THINK SHE WENT OUT FOR COFFEE...
8 HOURS AGO?!
!!
KNOWING HER, SHE WENT ALL THE WAY TO MEMPHIS FOR A LATTE...
PAIGE
BACK AT GRACELAND...
I WONDER IF THIS PLACE HAS AN ESPRESSO MACHINE?
G
THIS IS THE BIGGEST ESPRESSO MACHINE I'VE EVER SEEN!
PAIGE
WOW.
ELVIS REALLY IS THE KING...
LET'S CRANK THIS PUPPY UP...
COFFEE DRIPPING... MILK FROTH ~~
~ING... WOAH!... WOOOAH...
OFF! WHERE'S OFF?!

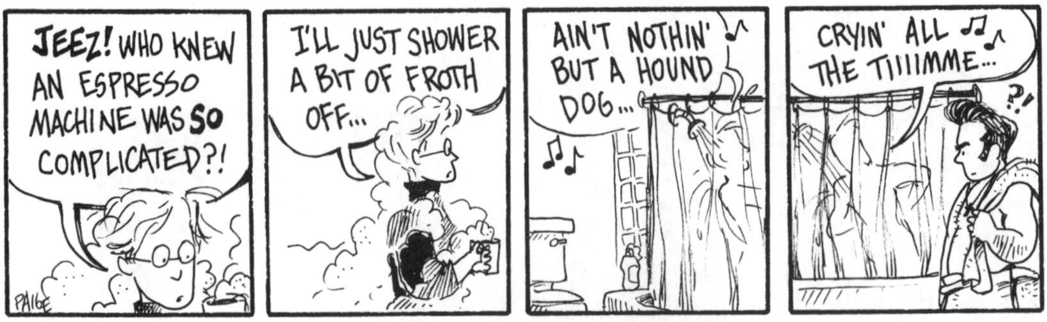
JEEZ! WHO KNEW AN ESPRESSO MACHINE WAS SO COMPLICATED?!
PAIGE
I'LL JUST SHOWER A BIT OF FROTH OFF...
AIN'T NOTHIN' BUT A HOUND DOG...
CRYIN' ALL THE TIIIIMME...
?!

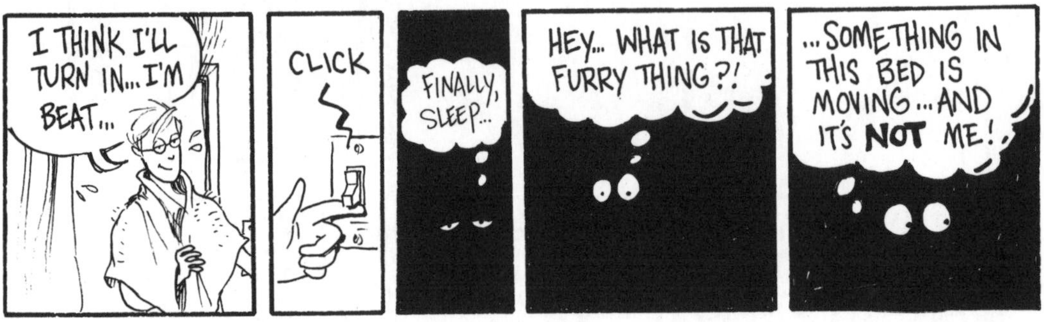
I THINK I'LL TURN IN... I'M BEAT...
CLICK
FINALLY, SLEEP...
HEY... WHAT IS THAT FURRY THING?!
...SOMETHING IN THIS BED IS MOVING... AND IT'S NOT ME!

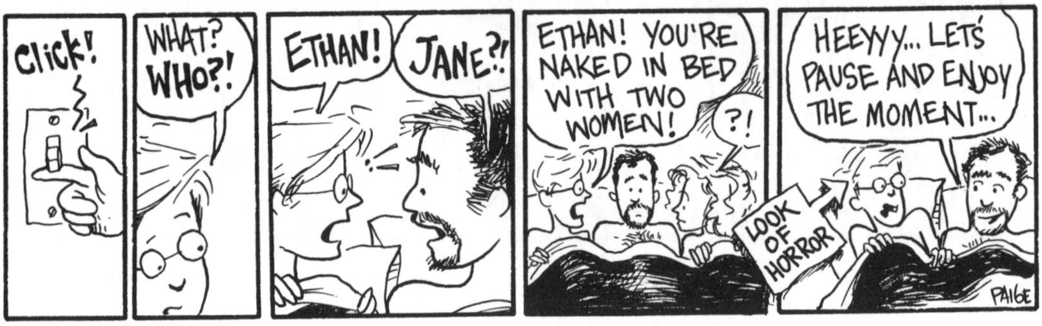
CLICK!
WHAT? WHO?!
ETHAN!
JANE?!
ETHAN! YOU'RE NAKED IN BED WITH TWO WOMEN!
?!
LOOK OF HORROR
HEEYYY... LETS PAUSE AND ENJOY THE MOMENT...
PAIGE

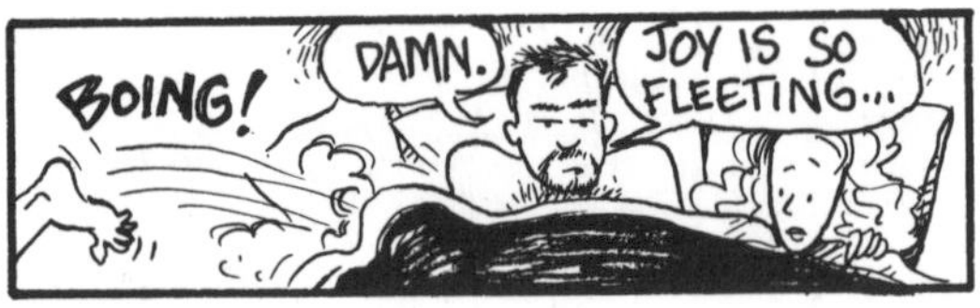
BOING!
DAMN.
JOY IS SO FLEETING...

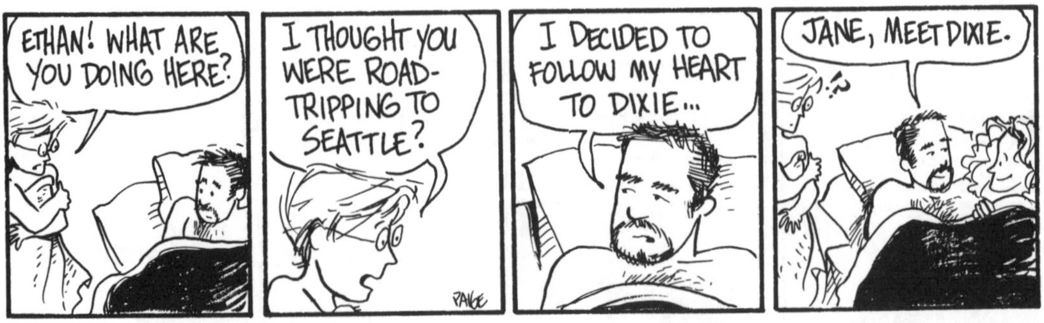
ETHAN! WHAT ARE YOU DOING HERE?
I THOUGHT YOU WERE ROAD-TRIPPING TO SEATTLE?
PAIGE
I DECIDED TO FOLLOW MY HEART TO DIXIE...
JANE, MEET DIXIE.

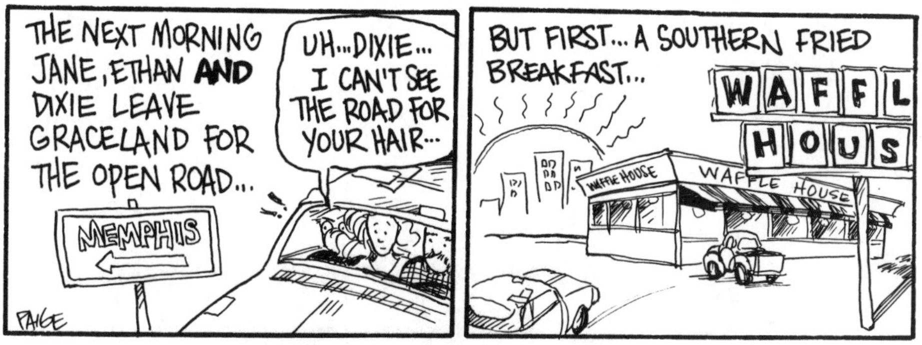
THE NEXT MORNING JANE, ETHAN **AND** DIXIE LEAVE GRACELAND FOR THE OPEN ROAD...
MEMPHIS
UH...DIXIE... I CAN'T SEE THE ROAD FOR YOUR HAIR...
PAIGE
BUT FIRST... A SOUTHERN FRIED BREAKFAST...
WAFFL
HOUS
WAFFLE HOUSE
WAFFLE HOUSE

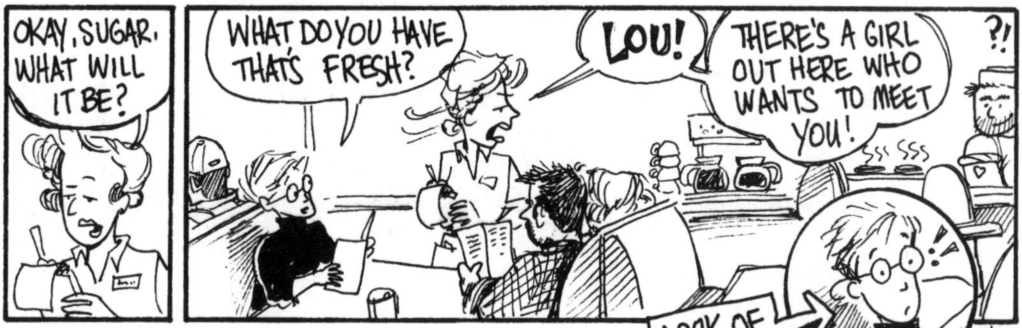
OKAY, SUGAR. WHAT WILL IT BE?
WHAT DO YOU HAVE THAT'S FRESH?
LOU!
THERE'S A GIRL OUT HERE WHO WANTS TO MEET YOU!
?!
PAIGE

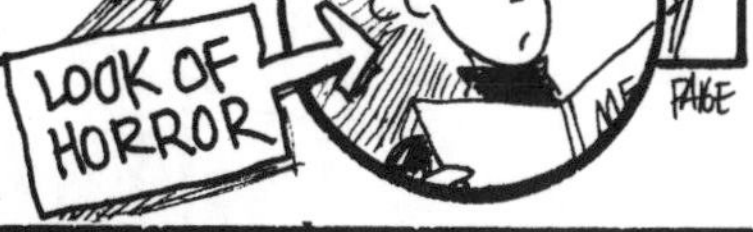
LOOK OF HORROR

Jane recovers and gets right to the point with Ethan...

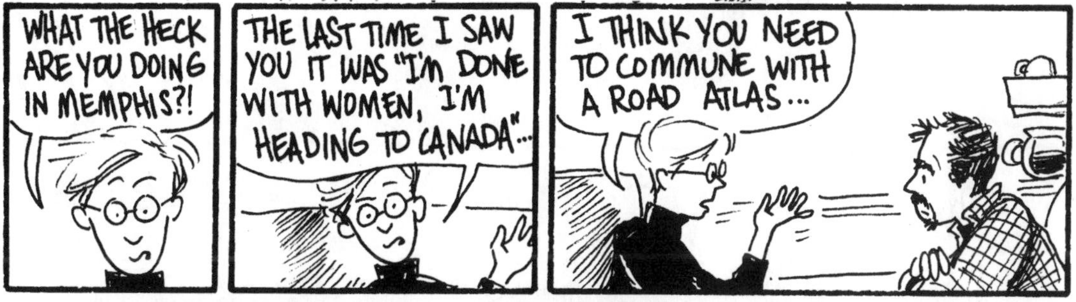
WHAT THE HECK ARE YOU DOING IN MEMPHIS?!
THE LAST TIME I SAW YOU IT WAS "I'M DONE WITH WOMEN, I'M HEADING TO CANADA"...
I THINK YOU NEED TO COMMUNE WITH A ROAD ATLAS...

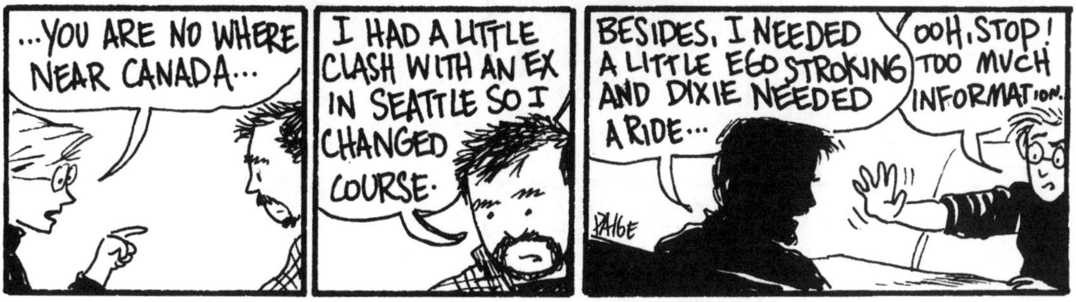
...YOU ARE NO WHERE NEAR CANADA...
I HAD A LITTLE CLASH WITH AN EX IN SEATTLE SO I CHANGED COURSE.
BESIDES, I NEEDED A LITTLE EGO STROKING AND DIXIE NEEDED A RIDE...
OOH, STOP! TOO MUCH INFORMATION.
PAIGE

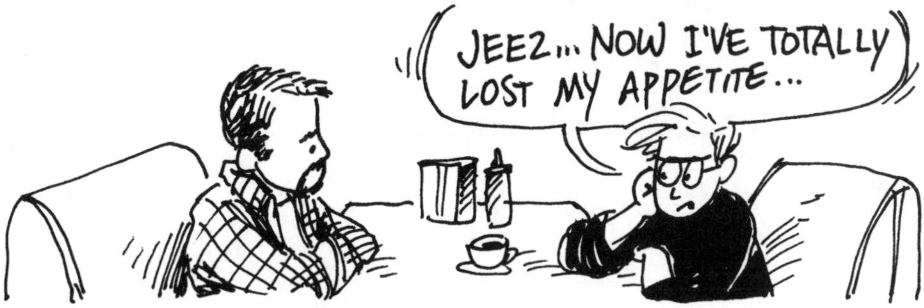
JEEZ... NOW I'VE TOTALLY LOST MY APPETITE...

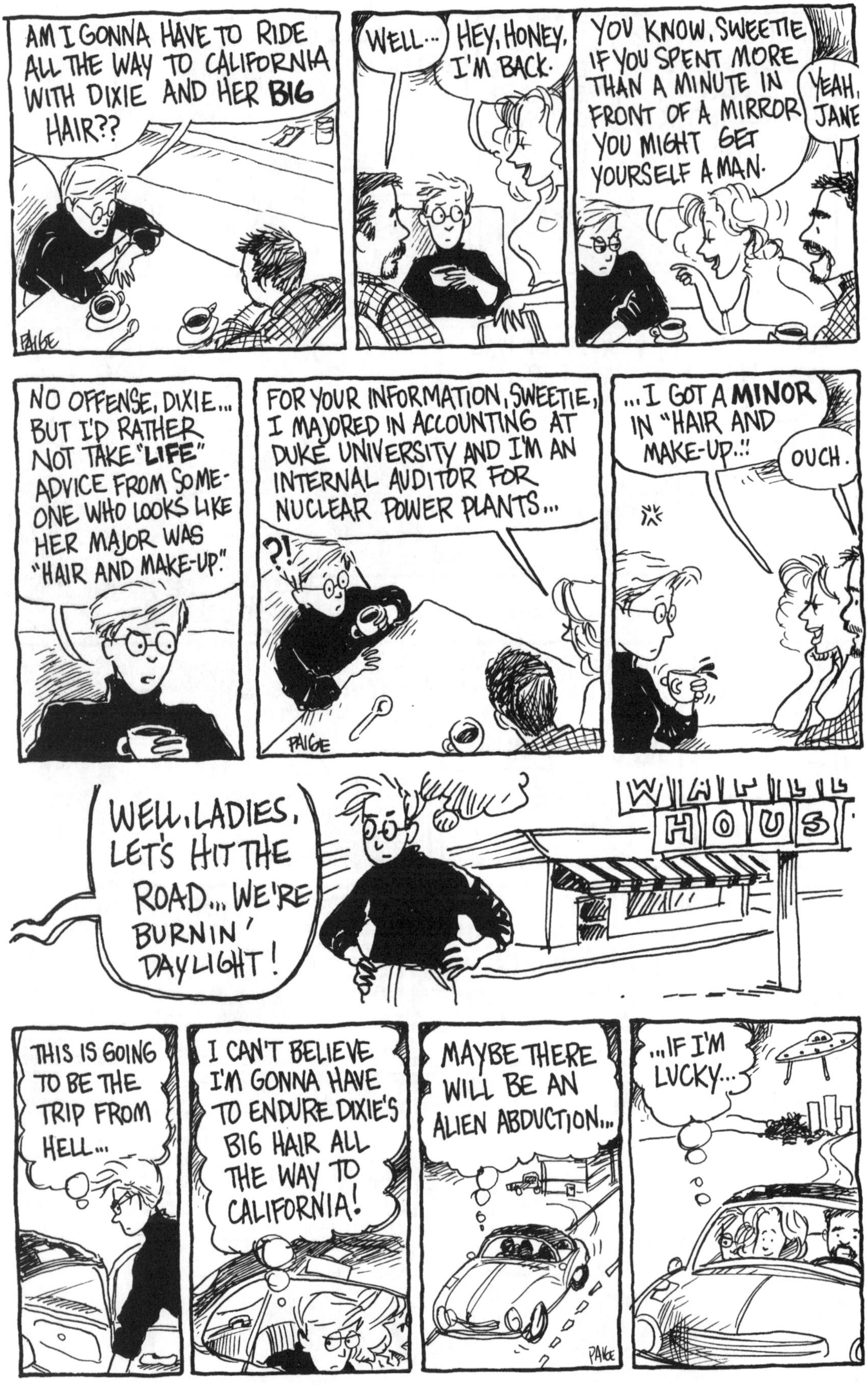
AM I GONNA HAVE TO RIDE ALL THE WAY TO CALIFORNIA WITH DIXIE AND HER **BIG** HAIR??
PAIGE
WELL...
HEY, HONEY, I'M BACK.
YOU KNOW, SWEETIE IF YOU SPENT MORE THAN A MINUTE IN FRONT OF A MIRROR YOU MIGHT GET YOURSELF A MAN.
YEAH, JANE
NO OFFENSE, DIXIE... BUT I'D RATHER NOT TAKE "**LIFE**" ADVICE FROM SOMEONE WHO LOOKS LIKE HER MAJOR WAS "HAIR AND MAKE-UP."
FOR YOUR INFORMATION, SWEETIE, I MAJORED IN ACCOUNTING AT DUKE UNIVERSITY AND I'M AN INTERNAL AUDITOR FOR NUCLEAR POWER PLANTS...
?!
PAIGE
...I GOT A **MINOR** IN "HAIR AND MAKE-UP..."
OUCH.
WELL, LADIES, LET'S HIT THE ROAD... WE'RE BURNIN' DAYLIGHT!
HOUS
THIS IS GOING TO BE THE TRIP FROM HELL...
I CAN'T BELIEVE I'M GONNA HAVE TO ENDURE DIXIE'S BIG HAIR ALL THE WAY TO CALIFORNIA!
MAYBE THERE WILL BE AN ALIEN ABDUCTION...
PAIGE
...IF I'M LUCKY...

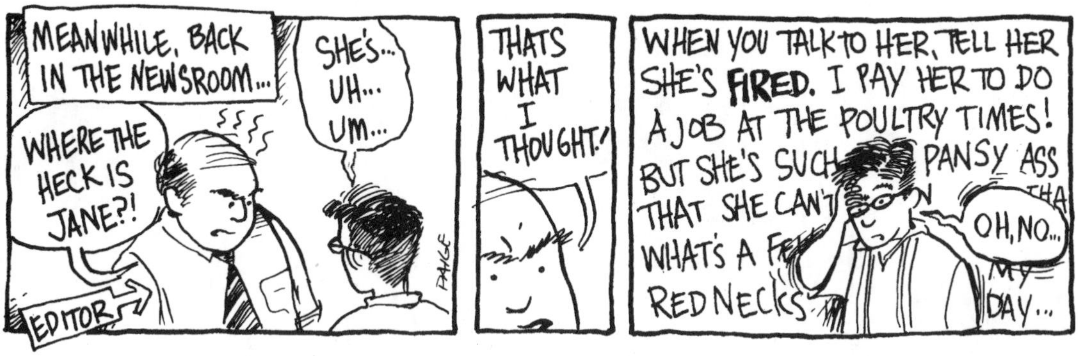
MEANWHILE, BACK IN THE NEWSROOM...
WHERE THE HECK IS JANE?!
EDITOR
SHE'S... UH... UM...
PAIGE
THATS WHAT I THOUGHT!
WHEN YOU TALK TO HER, TELL HER SHE'S FIRED. I PAY HER TO DO A JOB AT THE POULTRY TIMES! BUT SHE'S SUCH PANSY ASS THAT SHE CAN'T WHAT'S A REDNECKS DAY...
OH, NO...

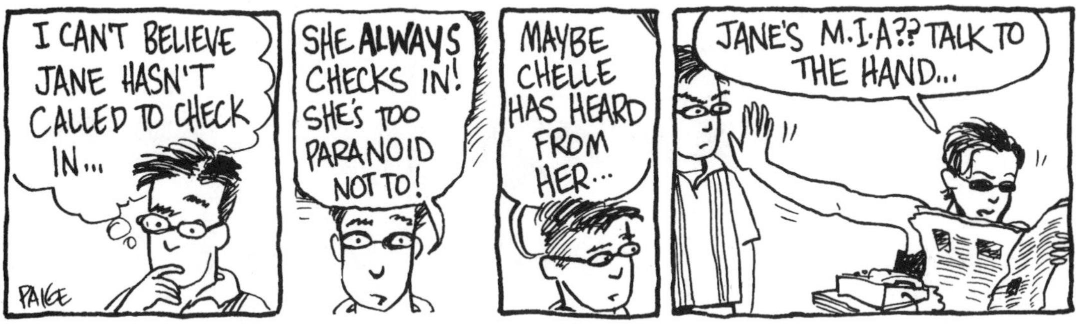
I CAN'T BELIEVE JANE HASN'T CALLED TO CHECK IN...
PAIGE
SHE ALWAYS CHECKS IN! SHE'S TOO PARANOID NOT TO!
MAYBE CHELLE HAS HEARD FROM HER...
JANE'S M.I.A?? TALK TO THE HAND...

Meanwhile, on the open road, our trio drives into the descending Oklahoma dusk...

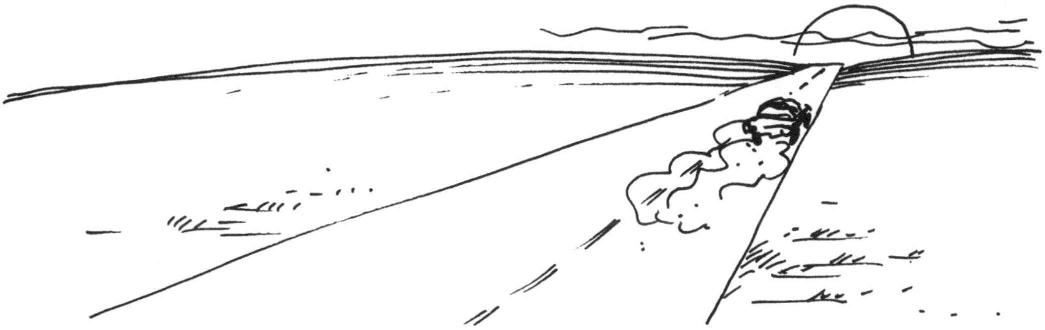

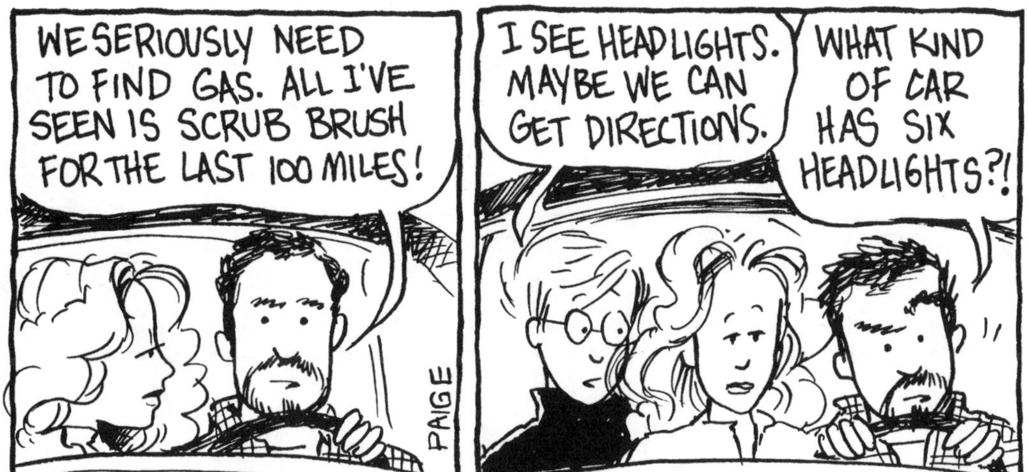
WE SERIOUSLY NEED TO FIND GAS. ALL I'VE SEEN IS SCRUB BRUSH FOR THE LAST 100 MILES!
PAIGE
I SEE HEADLIGHTS. MAYBE WE CAN GET DIRECTIONS.
WHAT KIND OF CAR HAS SIX HEADLIGHTS?!

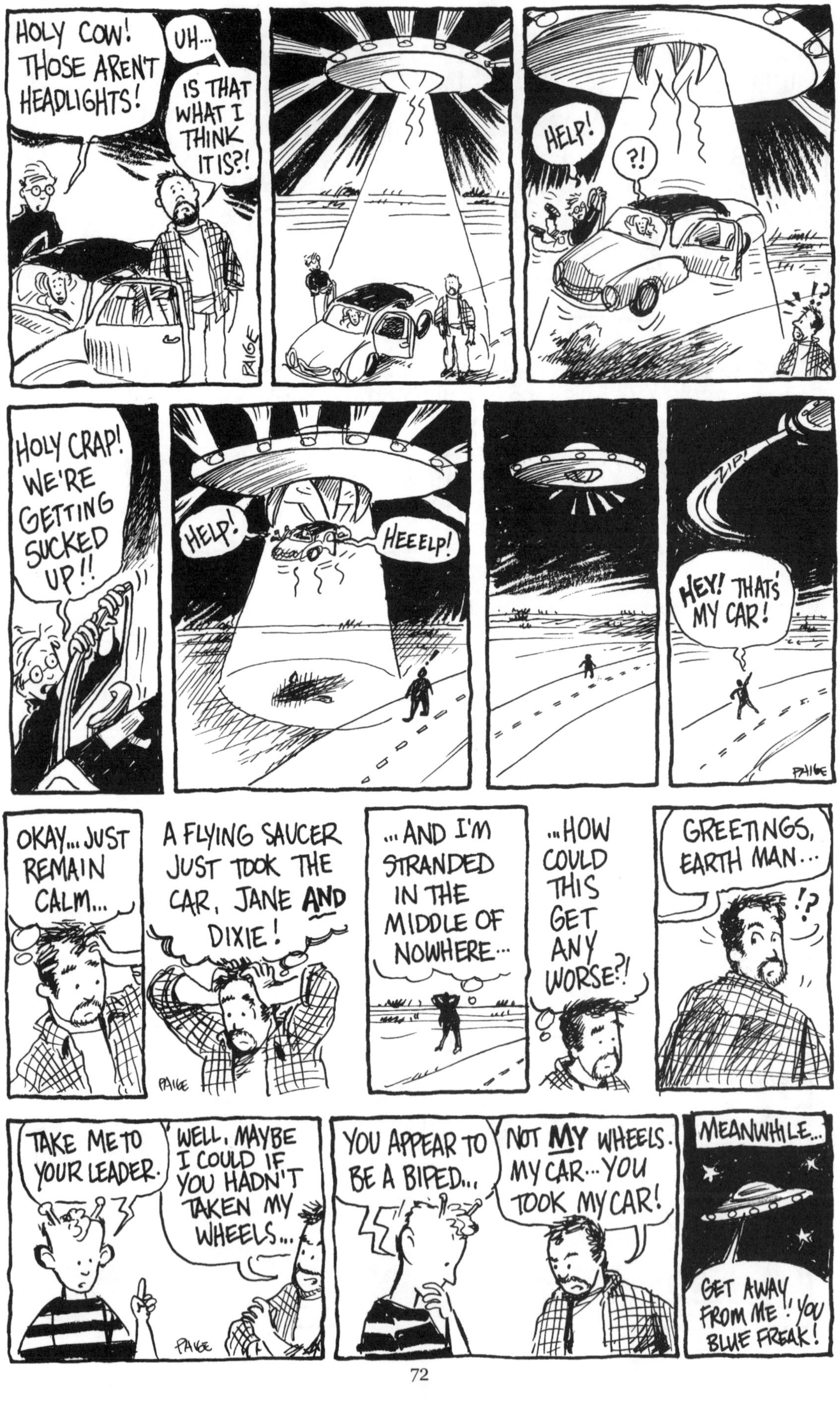
HOLY COW! THOSE AREN'T HEADLIGHTS!
UH...
IS THAT WHAT I THINK IT IS?!
PAIGE
HELP!
?!
!?
HOLY CRAP! WE'RE GETTING SUCKED UP!!
HELP!
HEEELP!
ZIP!
HEY! THAT'S MY CAR!
PAIGE
OKAY... JUST REMAIN CALM...
A FLYING SAUCER JUST TOOK THE CAR, JANE AND DIXIE!
PAIGE
...AND I'M STRANDED IN THE MIDDLE OF NOWHERE...
...HOW COULD THIS GET ANY WORSE?!
GREETINGS, EARTH MAN...
!?
TAKE ME TO YOUR LEADER.
WELL, MAYBE I COULD IF YOU HADN'T TAKEN MY WHEELS...
PAIGE
YOU APPEAR TO BE A BIPED...
NOT MY WHEELS. MY CAR... YOU TOOK MY CAR!
MEANWHILE...
GET AWAY FROM ME! YOU BLUE FREAK!

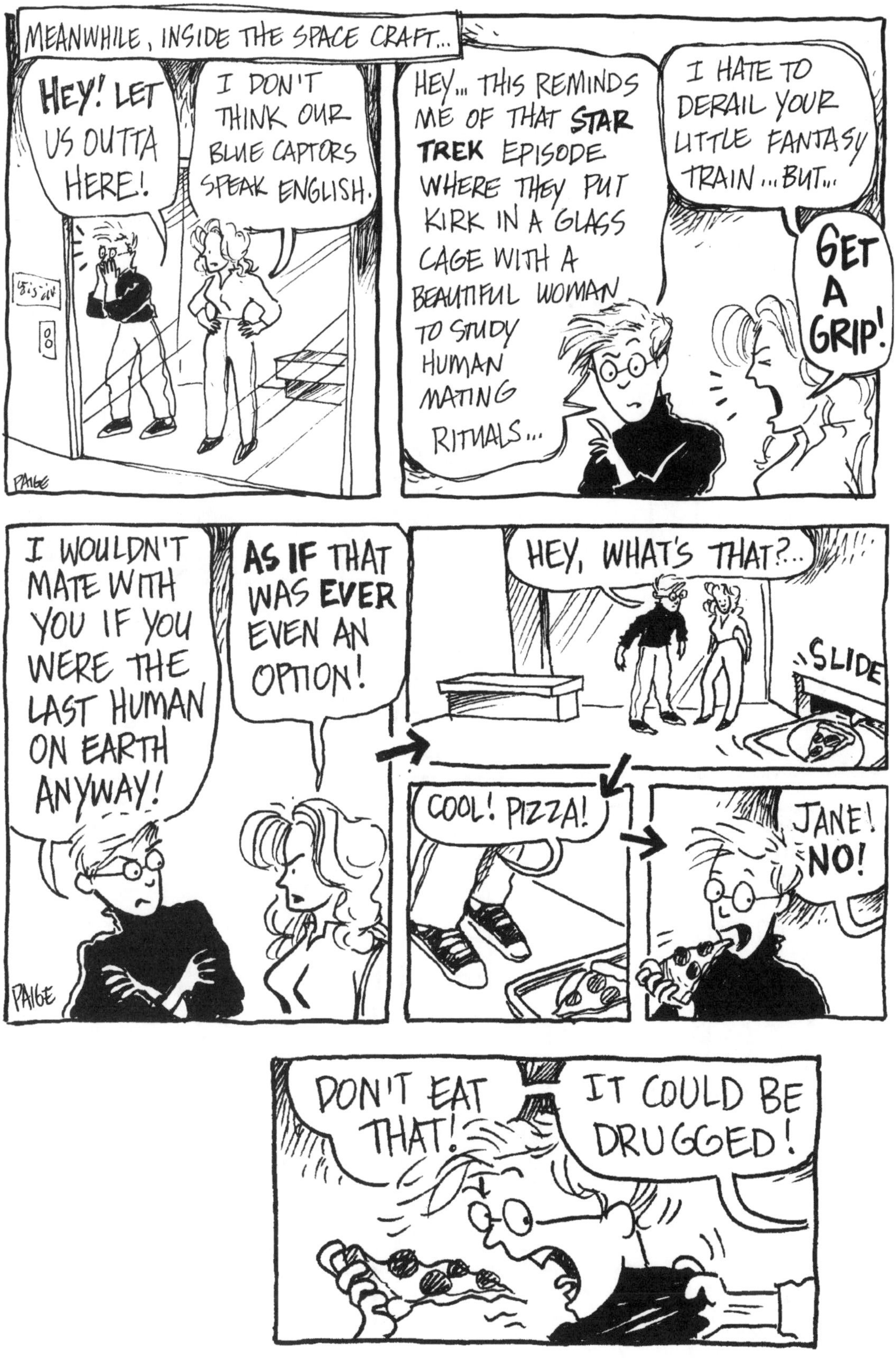
MEANWHILE, INSIDE THE SPACE CRAFT...
HEY! LET US OUTTA HERE!
I DON'T THINK OUR BLUE CAPTORS SPEAK ENGLISH.
PAIGE
HEY... THIS REMINDS ME OF THAT STAR TREK EPISODE WHERE THEY PUT KIRK IN A GLASS CAGE WITH A BEAUTIFUL WOMAN TO STUDY HUMAN MATING RITUALS...
I HATE TO DERAIL YOUR LITTLE FANTASY TRAIN ...BUT...
GET A GRIP!
I WOULDN'T MATE WITH YOU IF YOU WERE THE LAST HUMAN ON EARTH ANYWAY!
AS IF THAT WAS EVER EVEN AN OPTION!
PAIGE
HEY, WHAT'S THAT?...
SLIDE
COOL! PIZZA!
JANE! NO!
DON'T EAT THAT!
IT COULD BE DRUGGED!

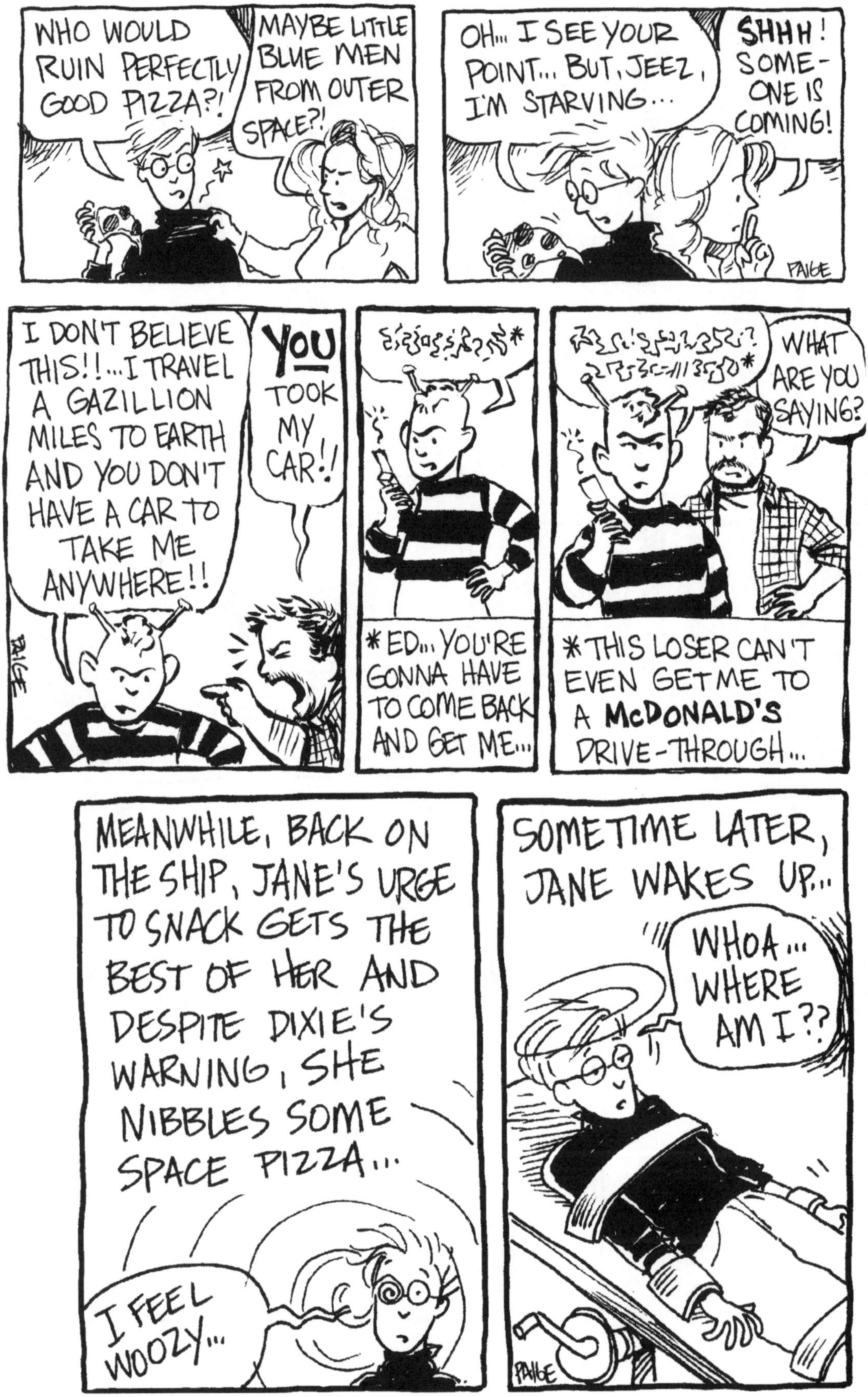
WHO WOULD RUIN PERFECTLY GOOD PIZZA?!
MAYBE LITTLE BLUE MEN FROM OUTER SPACE?!
OH... I SEE YOUR POINT... BUT, JEEZ, I'M STARVING...
SHHH! SOME-ONE IS COMING!
PAIGE
I DON'T BELIEVE THIS!!...I TRAVEL A GAZILLION MILES TO EARTH AND YOU DON'T HAVE A CAR TO TAKE ME ANYWHERE!!
YOU TOOK MY CAR!!
PAIGE
*ED... YOU'RE GONNA HAVE TO COME BACK AND GET ME...
WHAT ARE YOU SAYING?
*THIS LOSER CAN'T EVEN GET ME TO A McDONALD'S DRIVE-THROUGH...
MEANWHILE, BACK ON THE SHIP, JANE'S URGE TO SNACK GETS THE BEST OF HER AND DESPITE DIXIE'S WARNING, SHE NIBBLES SOME SPACE PIZZA...
I FEEL WOOZY...
SOMETIME LATER, JANE WAKES UP...
WHOA... WHERE AM I??
PAIGE

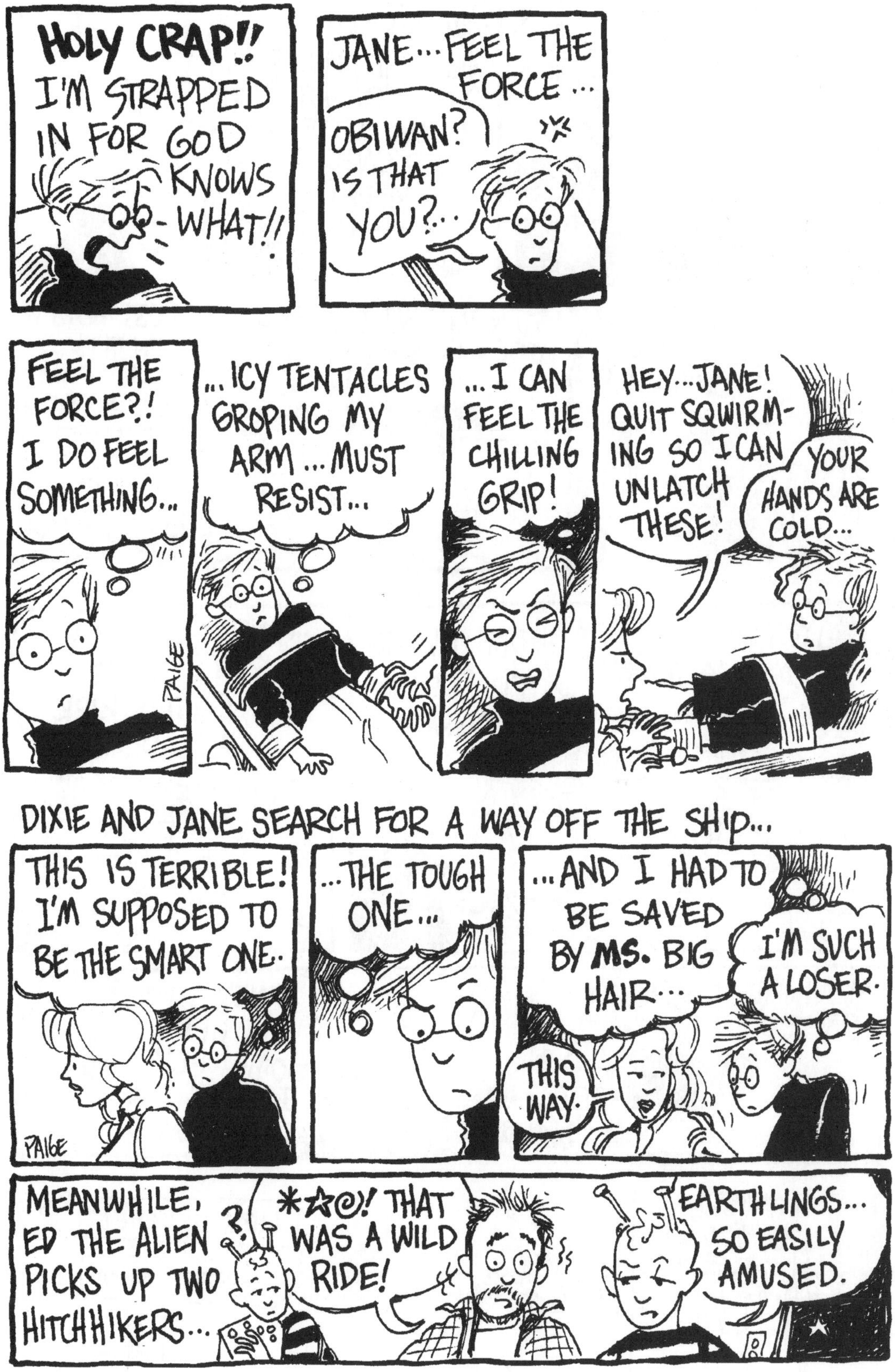
HOLY CRAP!! I'M STRAPPED IN FOR GOD KNOWS WHAT!!
JANE... FEEL THE FORCE...
OBIWAN? IS THAT YOU?...
FEEL THE FORCE?! I DO FEEL SOMETHING...
PAIGE
...ICY TENTACLES GROPING MY ARM ... MUST RESIST...
...I CAN FEEL THE CHILLING GRIP!
HEY...JANE! QUIT SQWIRMING SO I CAN UNLATCH THESE!
YOUR HANDS ARE COLD...
DIXIE AND JANE SEARCH FOR A WAY OFF THE SHIP...
THIS IS TERRIBLE! I'M SUPPOSED TO BE THE SMART ONE.
PAIGE
...THE TOUGH ONE...
...AND I HAD TO BE SAVED BY MS. BIG HAIR...
I'M SUCH A LOSER.
THIS WAY.
MEANWHILE, ED THE ALIEN PICKS UP TWO HITCHHIKERS...
*☆@! THAT WAS A WILD RIDE!
EARTHLINGS... SO EASILY AMUSED.

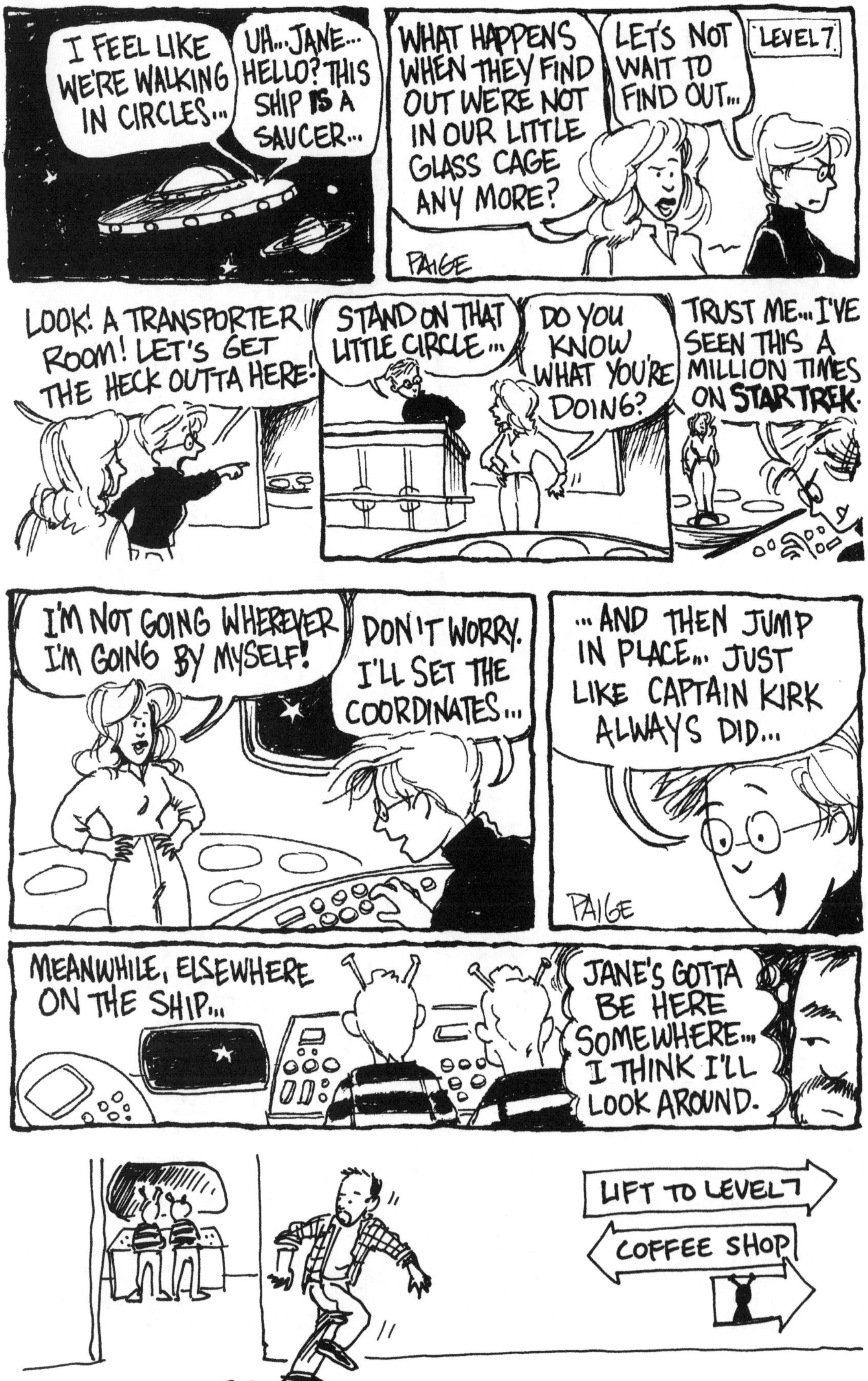
I FEEL LIKE WE'RE WALKING IN CIRCLES...
UH...JANE... HELLO? THIS SHIP IS A SAUCER...
WHAT HAPPENS WHEN THEY FIND OUT WE'RE NOT IN OUR LITTLE GLASS CAGE ANY MORE?
LET'S NOT WAIT TO FIND OUT...
LEVEL 7
PAIGE
LOOK! A TRANSPORTER ROOM! LET'S GET THE HECK OUTTA HERE!
STAND ON THAT LITTLE CIRCLE...
DO YOU KNOW WHAT YOU'RE DOING?
TRUST ME... I'VE SEEN THIS A MILLION TIMES ON STAR TREK.
I'M NOT GOING WHEREVER I'M GOING BY MYSELF!
DON'T WORRY. I'LL SET THE COORDINATES...
...AND THEN JUMP IN PLACE... JUST LIKE CAPTAIN KIRK ALWAYS DID...
PAIGE
MEANWHILE, ELSEWHERE ON THE SHIP...
JANE'S GOTTA BE HERE SOMEWHERE... I THINK I'LL LOOK AROUND.
LIFT TO LEVEL 7
COFFEE SHOP

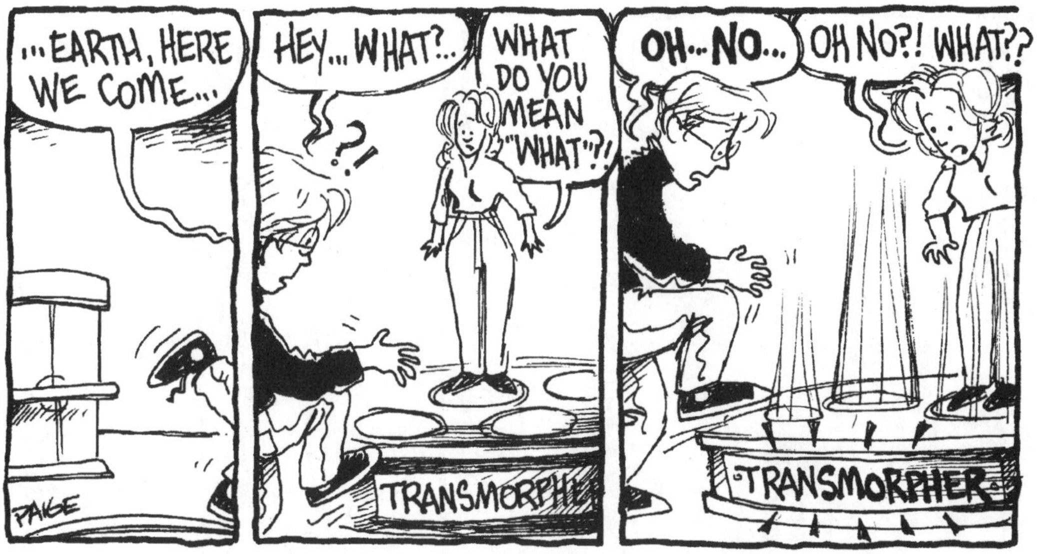
...EARTH, HERE WE COME...
PAIGE
HEY... WHAT?...
?!
WHAT DO YOU MEAN "WHAT"?!
TRANSMORPHE
OH.. NO...
OH NO?! WHAT??
TRANSMORPHER

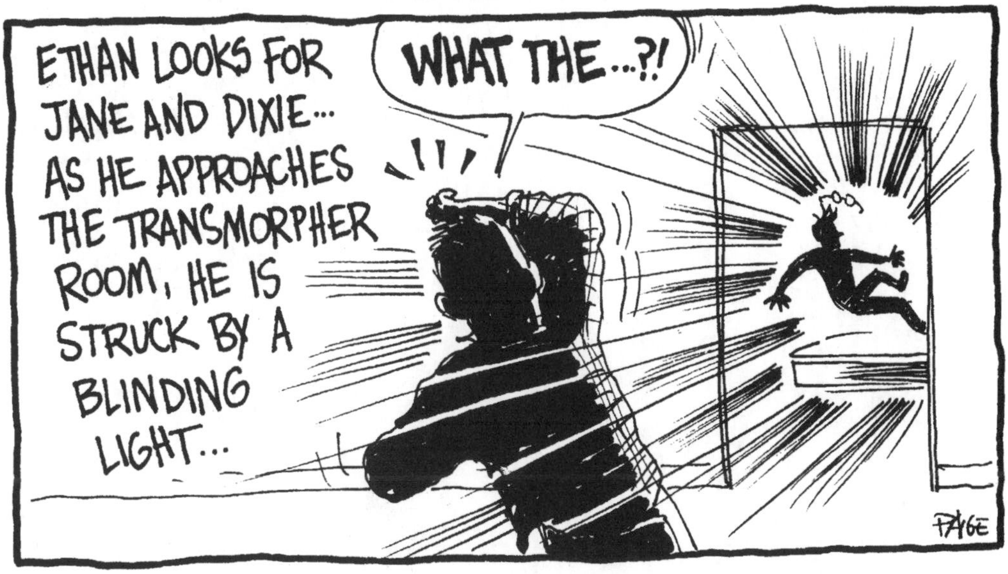
ETHAN LOOKS FOR JANE AND DIXIE... AS HE APPROACHES THE TRANSMORPHER ROOM, HE IS STRUCK BY A BLINDING LIGHT...
WHAT THE...?!
PAIGE

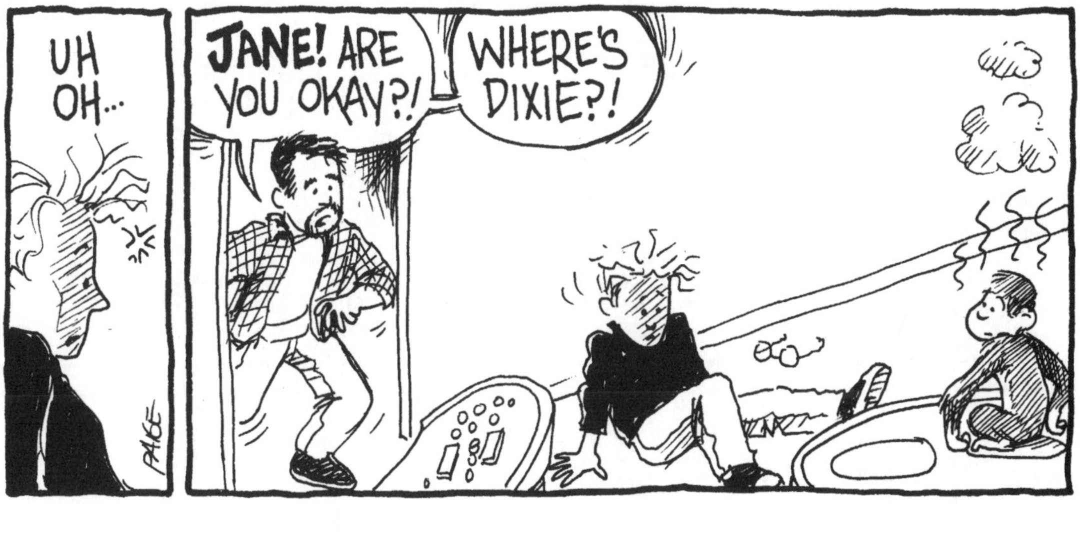
UH OH...
PAIGE
JANE! ARE YOU OKAY?!
WHERE'S DIXIE?!

Panel 1: YOU ARE UNBELIEVABLE! YOU... YOU...

Panel 2: YOU TURNED DIXIE INTO A CHMP!! GROAN

Panel 3: WELL...TECHNICALLY, SHE'S A MONKEY... GROAN ?

Panel 4: IT WAS PASSIVE AGGRESSIVE TRANSMORPHING ...THAT'S WHAT IT WAS... LOOK! A USERS MANUAL!

Panel 5: MAYBE THERE'S A WAY TO REVERSE THIS... WHY DIDN'T YOU READ THAT FIRST?!

Panel 6: NOBODY READS THE USERS MANUAL UNTIL THERE'S A PROBLEM.

Panel 7: WHAT'S IT SAY? UH... IT'S NOT GOOD...

Panel 8: IT SEEMS THE TRANSMORPHER CHANGES ANY PERSON INTO THEIR NEAREST DNA RELATIVE.

Panel 9: ...AND ONCE YOU LOSE A CHROMOSOME THERE'S NO GOING BACK... ?

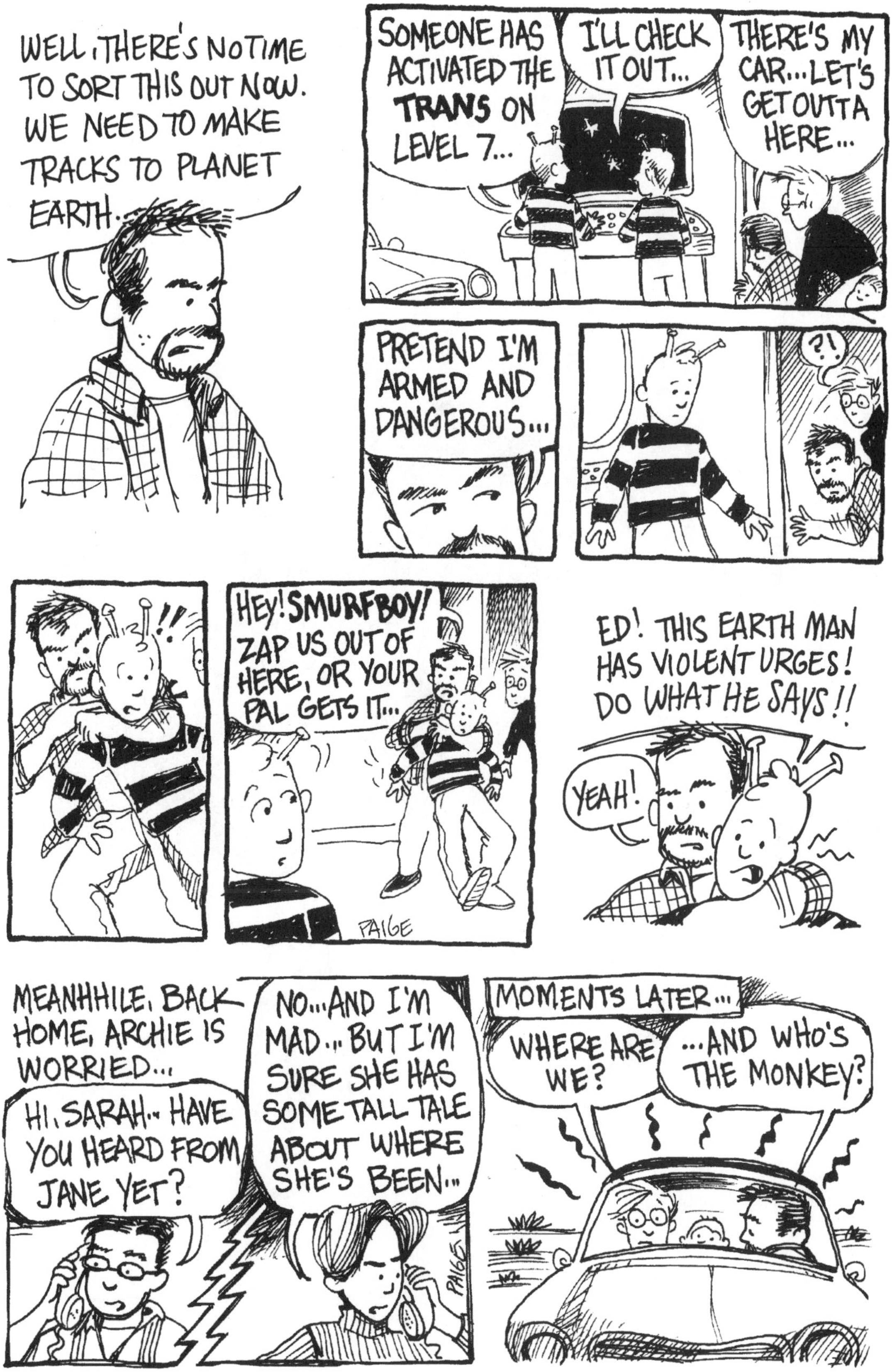
WELL, THERE'S NO TIME TO SORT THIS OUT NOW. WE NEED TO MAKE TRACKS TO PLANET EARTH.
SOMEONE HAS ACTIVATED THE **TRANS** ON LEVEL 7...
I'LL CHECK IT OUT...
THERE'S MY CAR... LET'S GET OUTTA HERE...
PRETEND I'M ARMED AND DANGEROUS...
?!
!!
HEY! **SMURFBOY!** ZAP US OUT OF HERE, OR YOUR PAL GETS IT...
PAIGE
ED! THIS EARTH MAN HAS VIOLENT URGES! DO WHAT HE SAYS!!
YEAH!
MEANWHILE, BACK HOME, ARCHIE IS WORRIED...
HI, SARAH.. HAVE YOU HEARD FROM JANE YET?
NO... AND I'M MAD... BUT I'M SURE SHE HAS SOME TALL TALE ABOUT WHERE SHE'S BEEN...
PAIGE
MOMENTS LATER...
WHERE ARE WE?
...AND WHO'S THE MONKEY?

Chapter 4
Wilderness retrograde

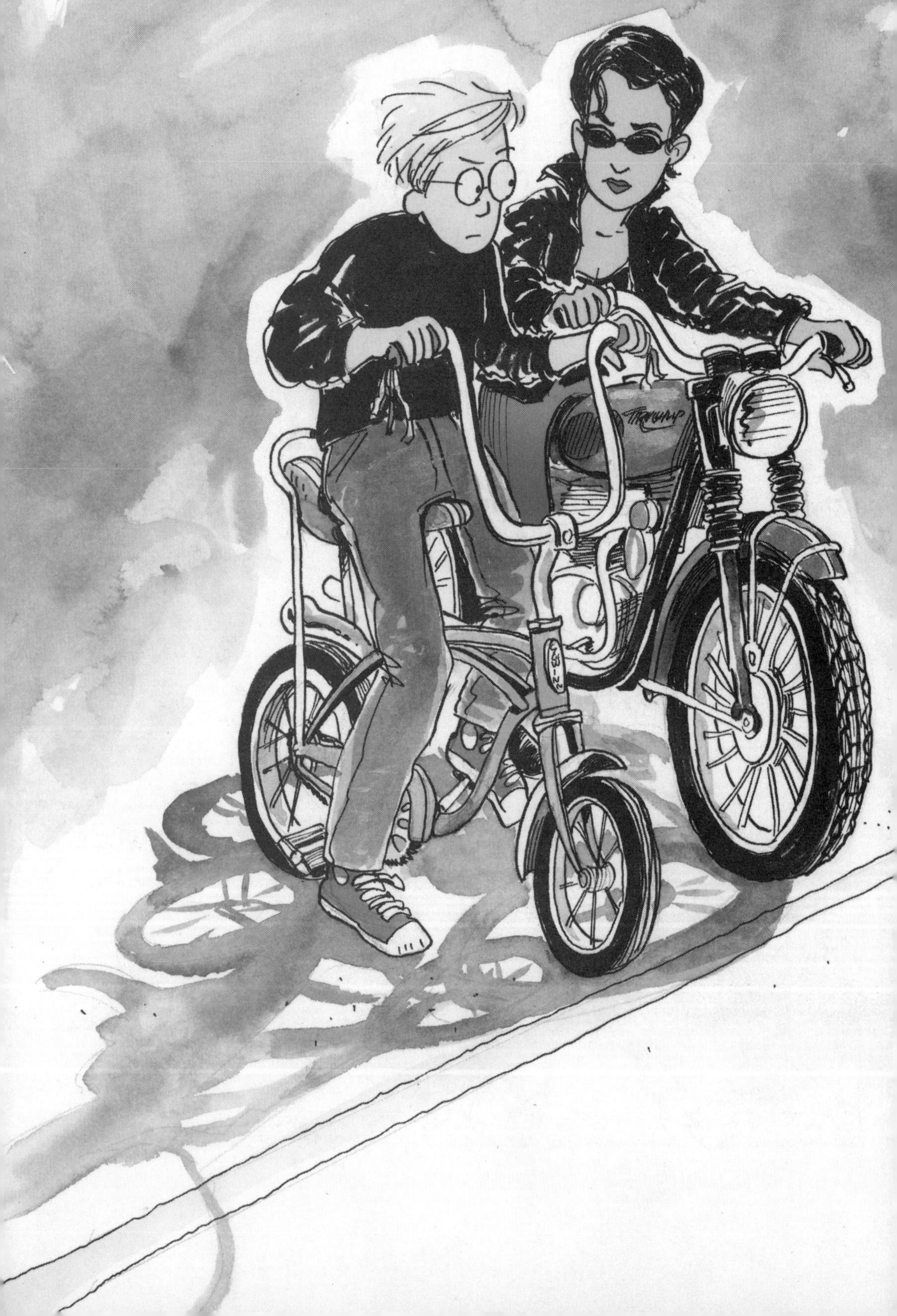

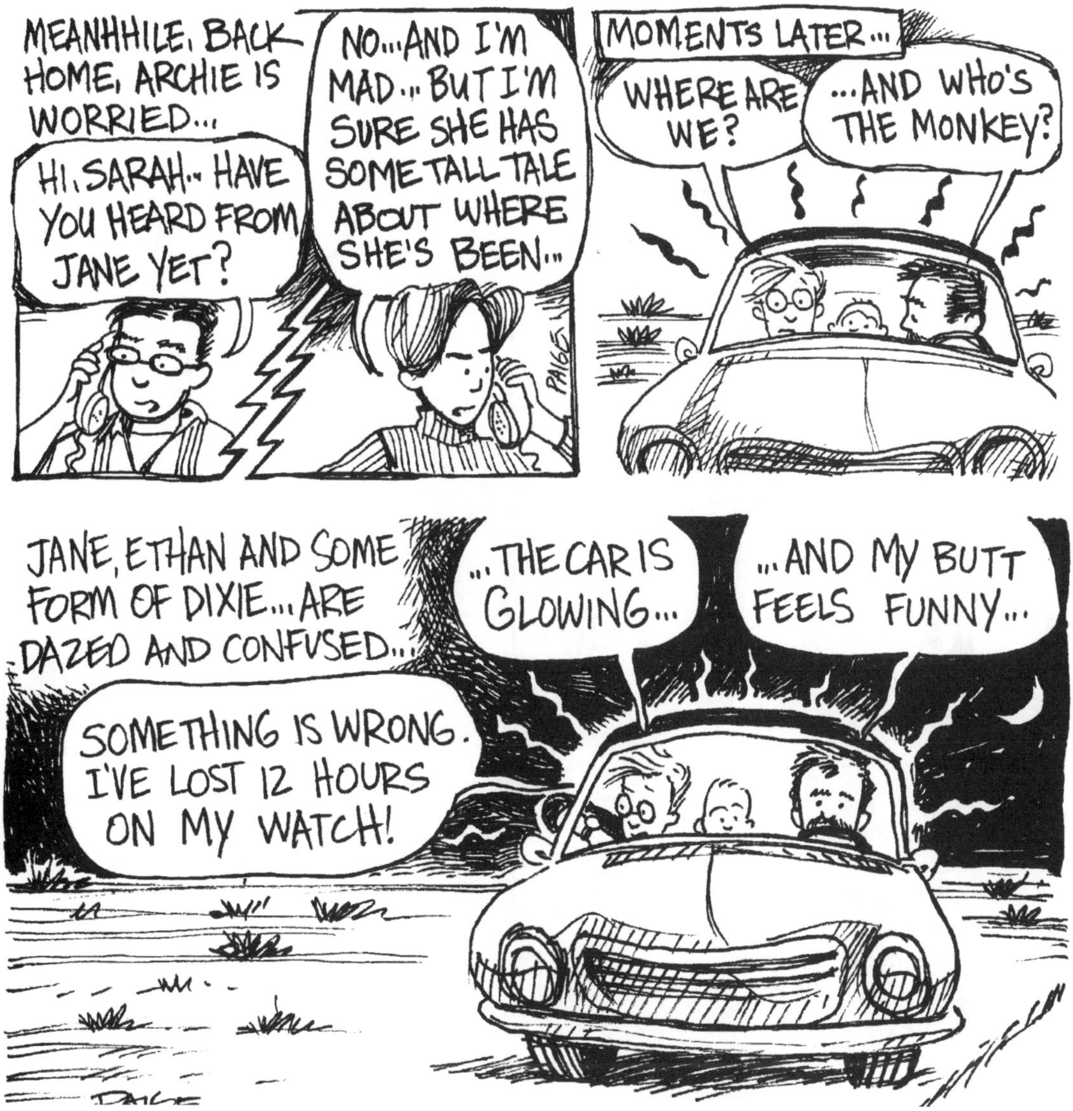
MEANHHILE, BACK HOME, ARCHIE IS WORRIED...
HI, SARAH.. HAVE YOU HEARD FROM JANE YET?
NO...AND I'M MAD... BUT I'M SURE SHE HAS SOME TALL TALE ABOUT WHERE SHE'S BEEN...
PAIGE
MOMENTS LATER...
WHERE ARE WE?
...AND WHO'S THE MONKEY?
JANE, ETHAN AND SOME FORM OF DIXIE...ARE DAZED AND CONFUSED...
...THE CAR IS GLOWING...
...AND MY BUTT FEELS FUNNY...
SOMETHING IS WRONG. I'VE LOST 12 HOURS ON MY WATCH!
PAIGE

After some deliberation, Ethan and Jane decide the best way to solve a problem is to feed it...

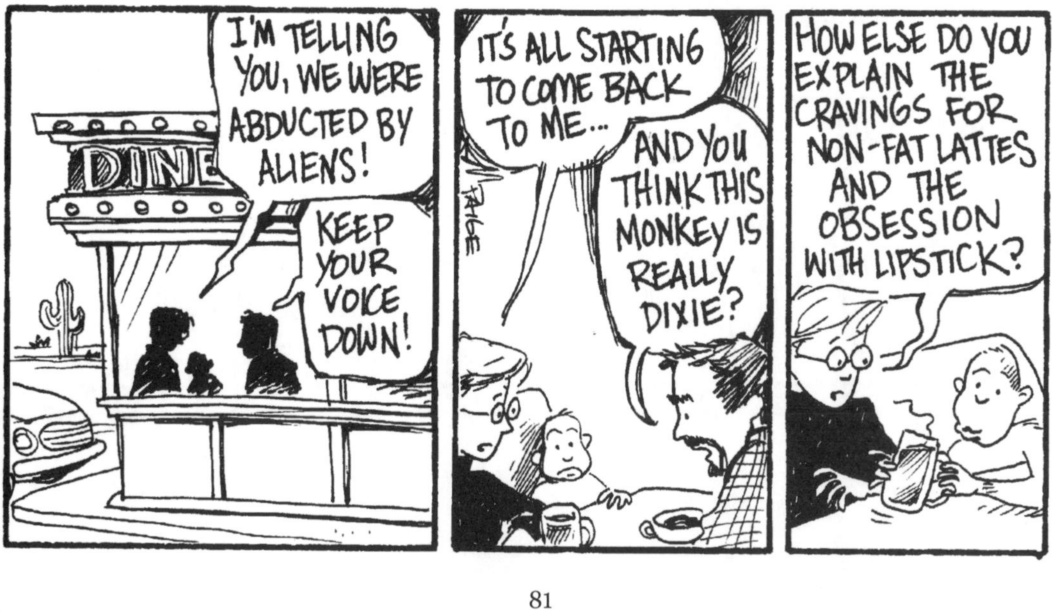
DINE
I'M TELLING YOU, WE WERE ABDUCTED BY ALIENS!
KEEP YOUR VOICE DOWN!
IT'S ALL STARTING TO COME BACK TO ME...
PAIGE
AND YOU THINK THIS MONKEY IS REALLY DIXIE?
HOW ELSE DO YOU EXPLAIN THE CRAVINGS FOR NON-FAT LATTES AND THE OBSESSION WITH LIPSTICK?

... before hitting the highway again, Jane decides to check in with Archie, at the newspaper...

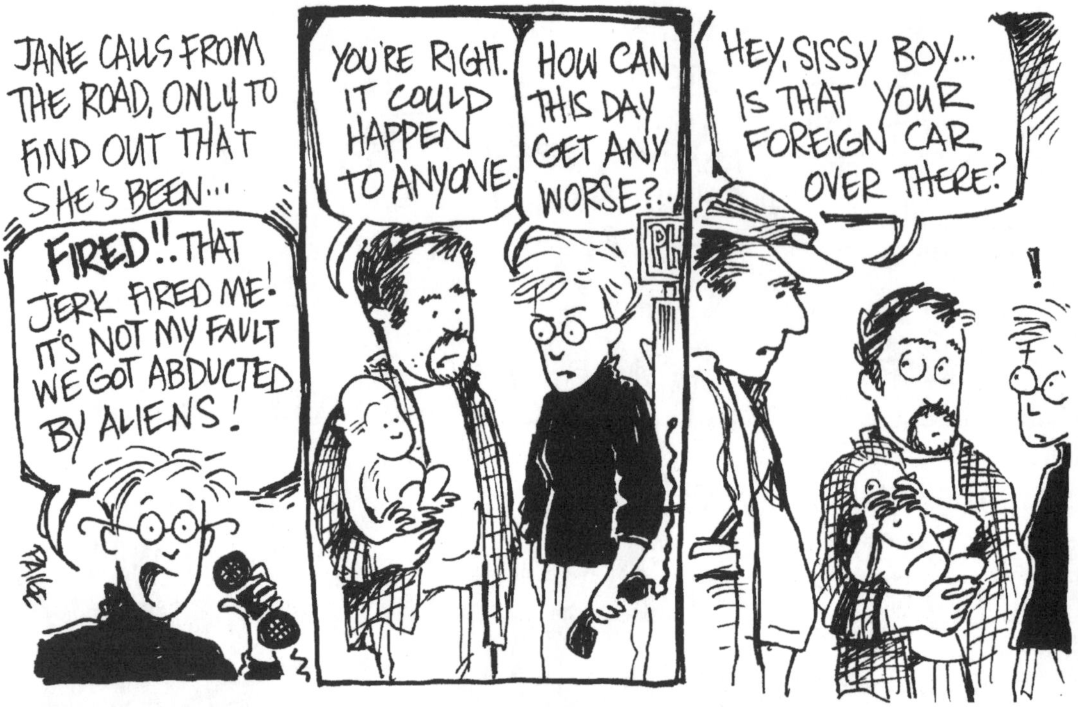

JANE CALLS FROM THE ROAD, ONLY TO FIND OUT THAT SHE'S BEEN...
FIRED!! THAT JERK FIRED ME! IT'S NOT MY FAULT WE GOT ABDUCTED BY ALIENS!
PAIGE
YOU'RE RIGHT. IT COULD HAPPEN TO ANYONE.
HOW CAN THIS DAY GET ANY WORSE?..
HEY, SISSY BOY... IS THAT YOUR FOREIGN CAR OVER THERE?
!

... Unfortunately, our friends suffer one setback after another.

Being abducted by space aliens was an exciting side trip for Jane, but it was hell for her career. While circling the planet with a woman soon to become a chimp, Jane was fired from her job at the newspaper. Not only that, by the time Jane made it back to California, Sarah was so annoyed by her M.I.A. status that she plunked Jane's belongings into a box and left them on the front lawn. Granted, the box only contained a few Indigo Girls CDs and a pair of Valentine boxer shorts... oh, and a slightly wilted New Year's Eve party hat... but still, that's gotta hurt.

It didn't hurt nearly as much as what happened next!

With proximity and a vintage Triumph in her possession, Chelle seizes this opening to make a move on Sarah!

How can Jane compete with all that coolness?!

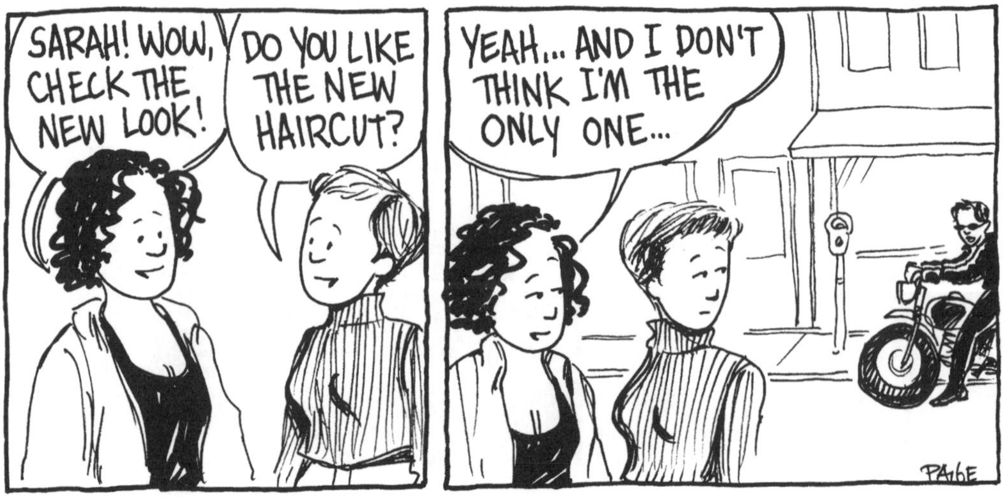

SARAH! WOW, CHECK THE NEW LOOK!
DO YOU LIKE THE NEW HAIRCUT?
YEAH... AND I DON'T THINK I'M THE ONLY ONE...
PAIGE

Being generally uninformed and victim of a carefree, type "B" personality, Jane decides to let things cool off with Sarah a bit. She mistakenly assumes that once Sarah has calmed down all will return to normal. Unfortunately, inertia is not necessarily the key to romance...

HMM... THAT LOOKED LIKE SARAH...
...WITH CHELLE...
NO. WAY.
HERE'S YOUR LATTE.
HEY... WHAT'S SARAH DOING ON THE BACK OF CHELLE'S BIKE?
NEW
VAROOO
PAIGE

THERE'S NO WAY SARAH WAS ON THAT BIKE.
I HATE TO TELL YOU BUT... IT WAS SARAH.
BUT IT'S ONLY BEEN LIKE 24 HOURS SINCE WE BROKE UP!
I'M SORRY, BUT IF CHELLE RODE UP ON THAT BIKE 24 HOURS AFTER MY BREAK-UP I'D GO FOR A RIDE.
WHERE ARE YOU GOING?
TO APPLY FOR THAT JOB AT THE QUICKI-MART...
COME BY LATER FOR A SLUSHIE...
PAIGE

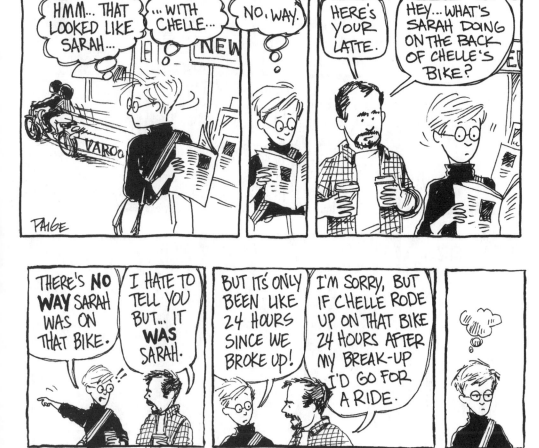

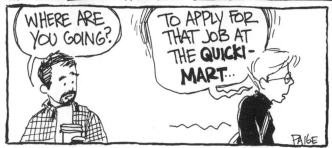

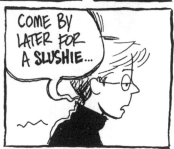

Jane decides her low checking account balance requires drastic economical measures. She applies for a night job at the corner Quicki-Mart. "How bad could it be?" she figured... flexible hours, low stress and ample snackage at every turn.

Her friends couldn't believe that Jane had chosen this new, downwardly-mobile career path. One by one they stopped into the Q.M. to see this fiasco for themselves.

Dorrie was first on the scene. (Shown sometimes with halftone screens and sometimes without, depending on deadline restrictions.) She tried to offer some sort of moral support for her pal Jane.

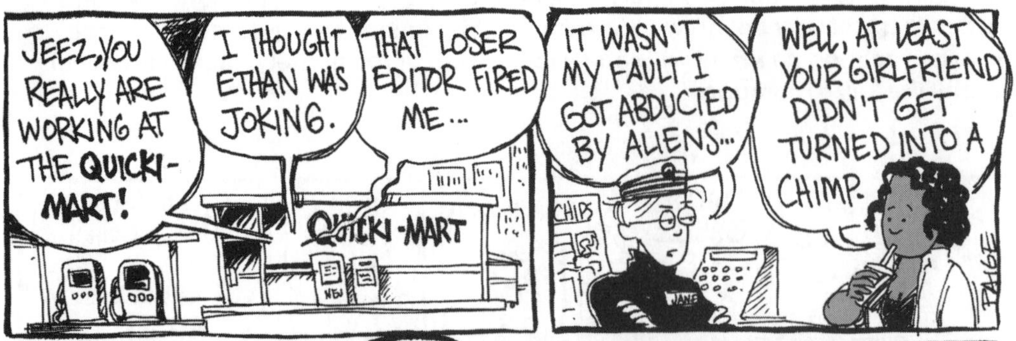
JEEZ, YOU REALLY ARE WORKING AT THE QUICKI-MART!
I THOUGHT ETHAN WAS JOKING.
THAT LOSER EDITOR FIRED ME...
QUICKI-MART
IT WASN'T MY FAULT I GOT ABDUCTED BY ALIENS...
WELL, AT LEAST YOUR GIRLFRIEND DIDN'T GET TURNED INTO A CHIMP.
CHIPS
JANE
PAIGE

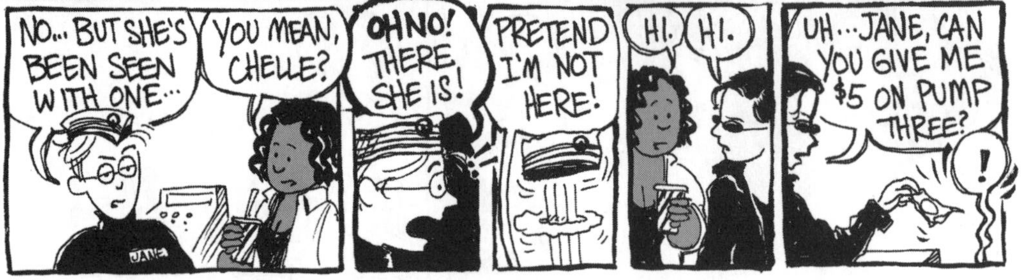
NO... BUT SHE'S BEEN SEEN WITH ONE...
YOU MEAN, CHELLE?
OH NO! THERE SHE IS!
PRETEND I'M NOT HERE!
HI.
HI.
UH... JANE, CAN YOU GIVE ME $5 ON PUMP THREE?
!
JANE

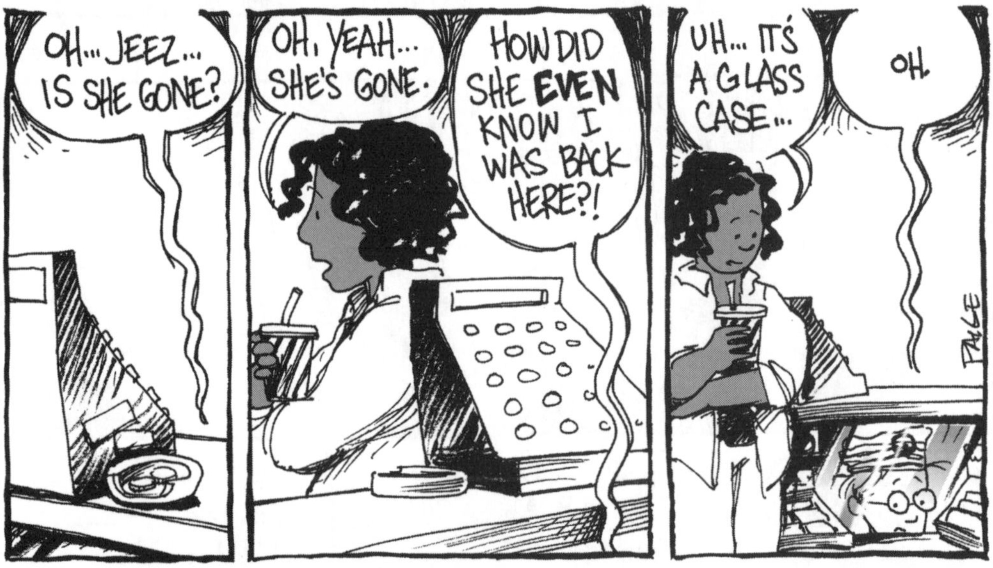
OH... JEEZ... IS SHE GONE?
OH, YEAH... SHE'S GONE.
HOW DID SHE EVEN KNOW I WAS BACK HERE?!
UH... IT'S A GLASS CASE...
OH.
PAIGE

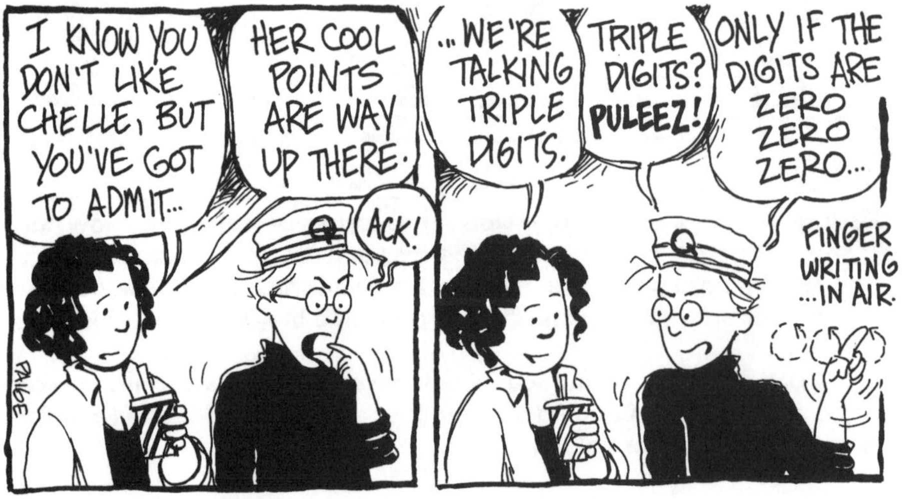
I KNOW YOU DON'T LIKE CHELLE, BUT YOU'VE GOT TO ADMIT...
HER COOL POINTS ARE WAY UP THERE.
ACK!
...WE'RE TALKING TRIPLE DIGITS.
TRIPLE DIGITS? PULEEZ!
ONLY IF THE DIGITS ARE ZERO ZERO ZERO...
FINGER WRITING ...IN AIR.
PAIGE

Jane wasn't the only one having an issue with downward mobility. Mia and Dorothy had hit a rough spot while Jane and Ethan were away. It had something to do with an ex-Hooter's girl, turned massage therapist, named Inga... but it's probably not worth going into here.

As Pride week approached, skeletons were falling out of closets all around...

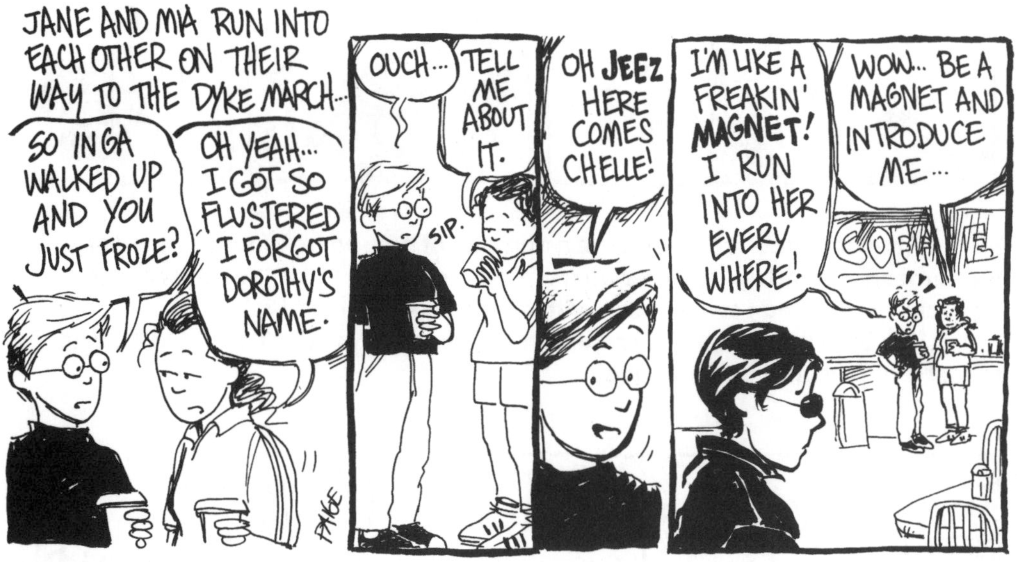
JANE AND MIA RUN INTO EACH OTHER ON THEIR WAY TO THE DYKE MARCH...
SO INGA WALKED UP AND YOU JUST FROZE?
OH YEAH... I GOT SO FLUSTERED I FORGOT DOROTHY'S NAME.
PAIGE
OUCH...
TELL ME ABOUT IT.
SIP.
OH JEEZ HERE COMES CHELLE!
I'M LIKE A FREAKIN' MAGNET! I RUN INTO HER EVERY WHERE!
WOW... BE A MAGNET AND INTRODUCE ME...

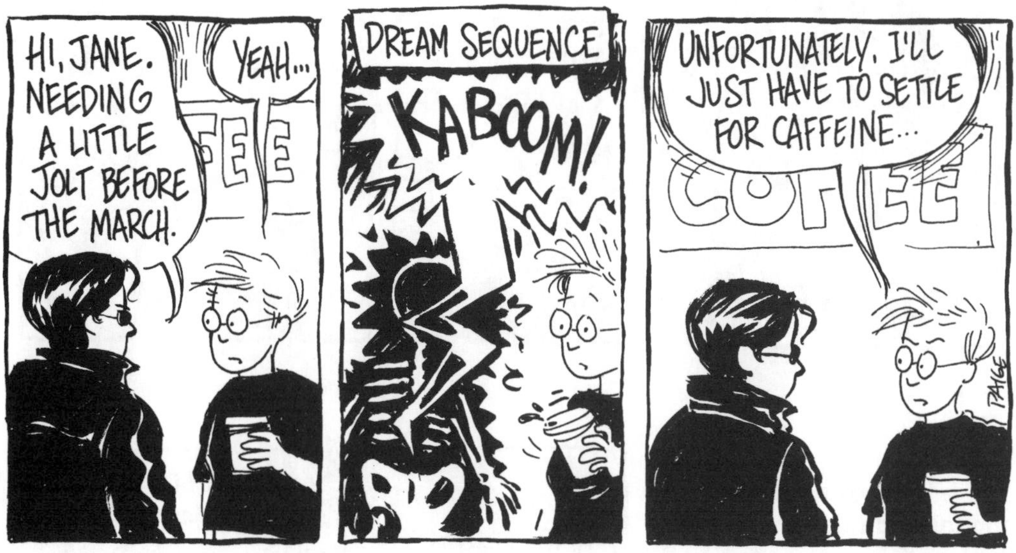
HI, JANE. NEEDING A LITTLE JOLT BEFORE THE MARCH.
YEAH...
DREAM SEQUENCE
KABOOM!
UNFORTUNATELY, I'LL JUST HAVE TO SETTLE FOR CAFFEINE...
COFFEE
PAIGE

A few moments later, Jane and Mia run into Ethan... coffee in tow...

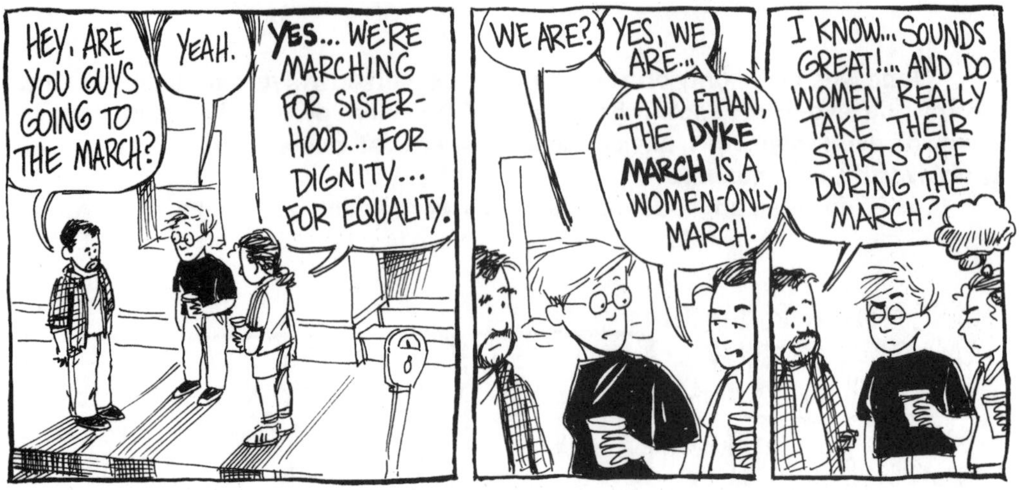
HEY, ARE YOU GUYS GOING TO THE MARCH?
YEAH.
YES... WE'RE MARCHING FOR SISTER-HOOD... FOR DIGNITY... FOR EQUALITY.
WE ARE?
YES, WE ARE...
...AND ETHAN, THE DYKE MARCH IS A WOMEN-ONLY MARCH.
I KNOW... SOUNDS GREAT!... AND DO WOMEN REALLY TAKE THEIR SHIRTS OFF DURING THE MARCH?

Then it happened... Jane got a glimpse of her worse nightmare... her ex and her nemesis, cozied up together on a vintage motorcycle for the parade. Jane was in shock!... until Ethan swooped in with a little dose of "reality."

At some point, Jane will realize that friends who aren't afraid to be brutally honest is a rare gift... but not today...

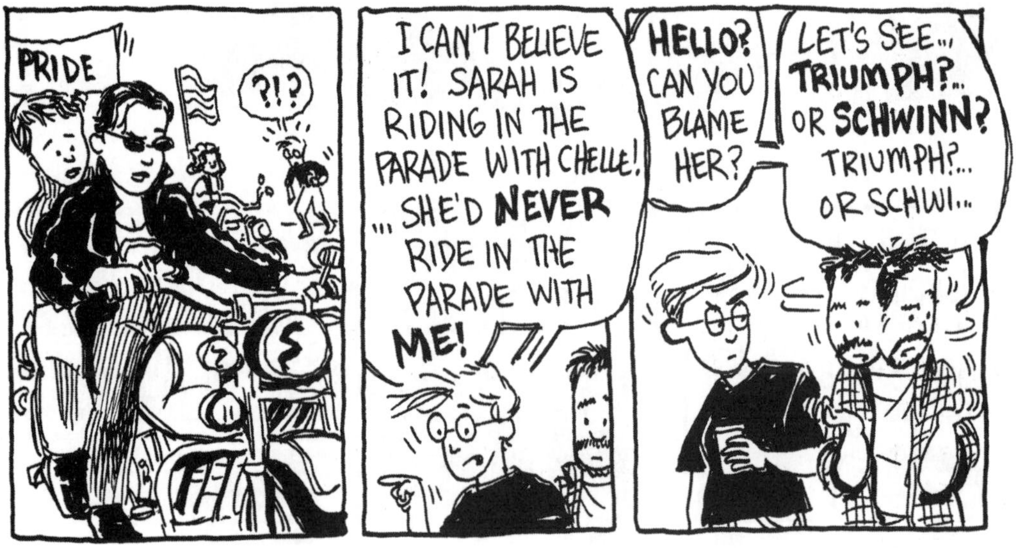
PRIDE
?!?
I CAN'T BELIEVE IT! SARAH IS RIDING IN THE PARADE WITH CHELLE! ...SHE'D NEVER RIDE IN THE PARADE WITH ME!
HELLO? CAN YOU BLAME HER?
LET'S SEE... TRIUMPH?... OR SCHWINN? TRIUMPH?... OR SCHWI...

A week or so passes... and Jane comes up with a brilliant idea.

It all started with a failed lunch date...

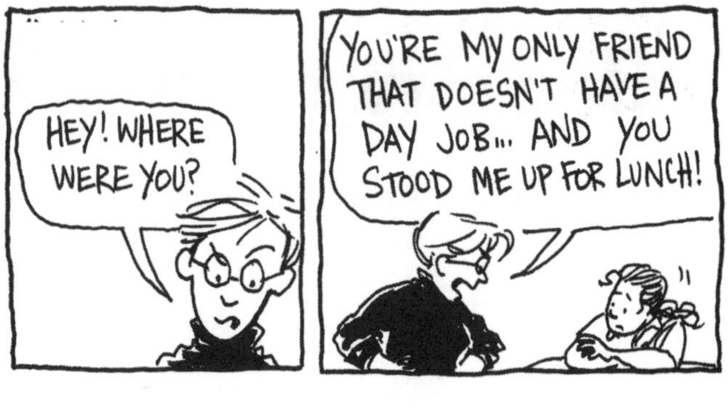
HEY! WHERE WERE YOU?
YOU'RE MY ONLY FRIEND THAT DOESN'T HAVE A DAY JOB... AND YOU STOOD ME UP FOR LUNCH!

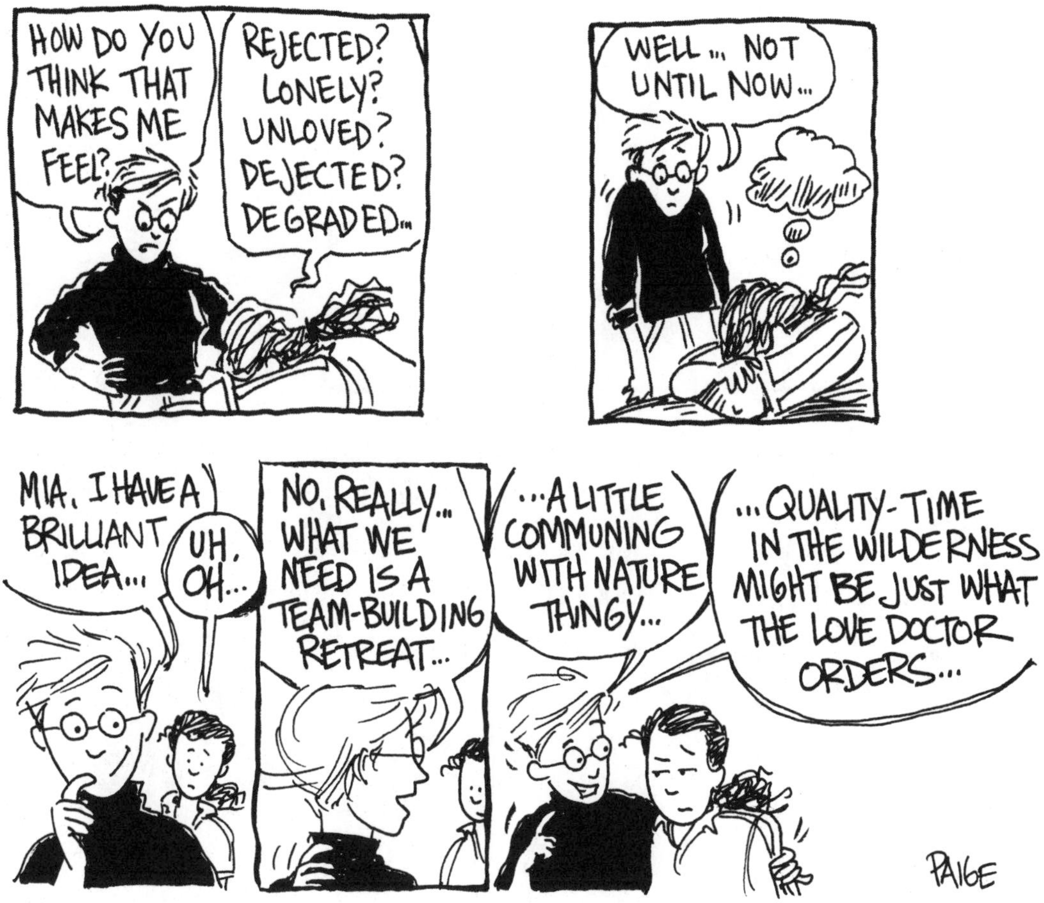
HOW DO YOU THINK THAT MAKES ME FEEL?
REJECTED? LONELY? UNLOVED? DEJECTED? DEGRADED...
WELL... NOT UNTIL NOW...
MIA, I HAVE A BRILLIANT IDEA...
UH, OH...
NO, REALLY... WHAT WE NEED IS A TEAM-BUILDING RETREAT...
...A LITTLE COMMUNING WITH NATURE THINGY...
...QUALITY-TIME IN THE WILDERNESS MIGHT BE JUST WHAT THE LOVE DOCTOR ORDERS...
PAIGE

Jane shares her "master plan" with Ethan... he was underwhelmed...

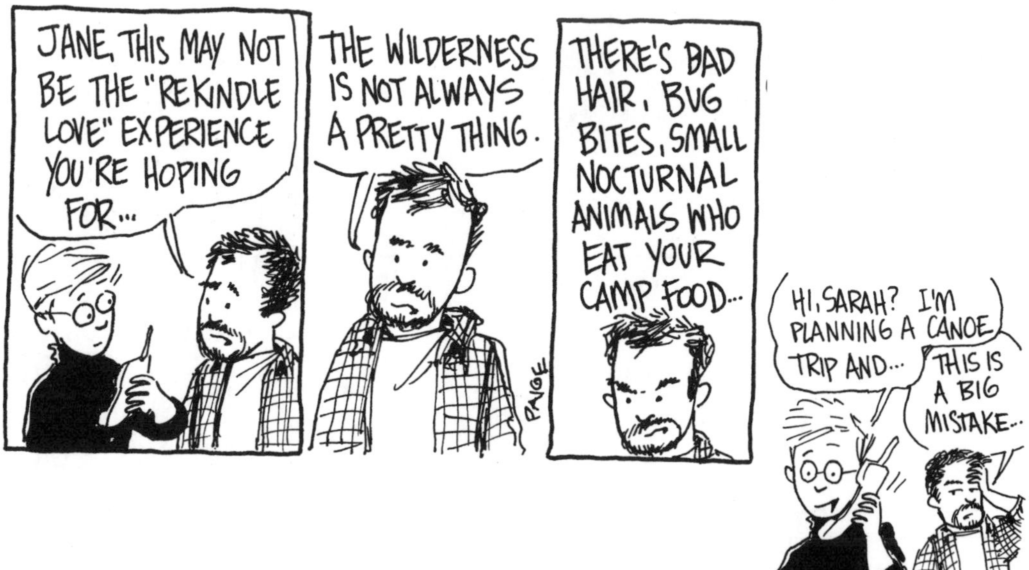
JANE, THIS MAY NOT BE THE "REKINDLE LOVE" EXPERIENCE YOU'RE HOPING FOR...
THE WILDERNESS IS NOT ALWAYS A PRETTY THING.
PAIGE
THERE'S BAD HAIR, BUG BITES, SMALL NOCTURNAL ANIMALS WHO EAT YOUR CAMP FOOD...
HI, SARAH? I'M PLANNING A CANOE TRIP AND...
THIS IS A BIG MISTAKE...

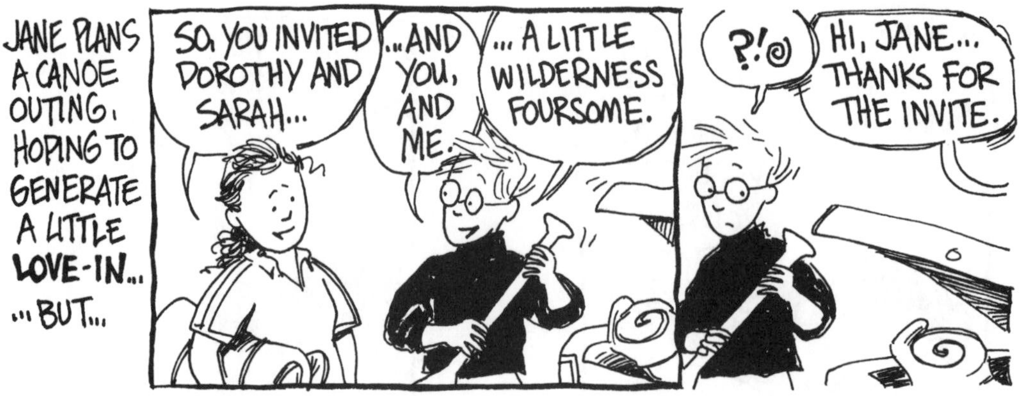
JANE PLANS A CANOE OUTING, HOPING TO GENERATE A LITTLE LOVE-IN... ...BUT...
SO, YOU INVITED DOROTHY AND SARAH...
...AND YOU, AND ME...
...A LITTLE WILDERNESS FOURSOME.
?!
HI, JANE... THANKS FOR THE INVITE.

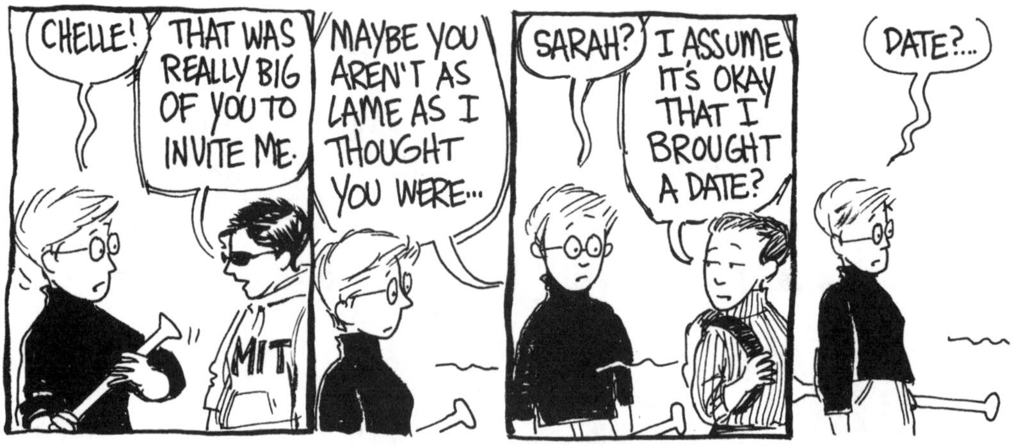
CHELLE!
THAT WAS REALLY BIG OF YOU TO INVITE ME.
MIT
MAYBE YOU AREN'T AS LAME AS I THOUGHT YOU WERE...
SARAH?
I ASSUME IT'S OKAY THAT I BROUGHT A DATE?
DATE?...

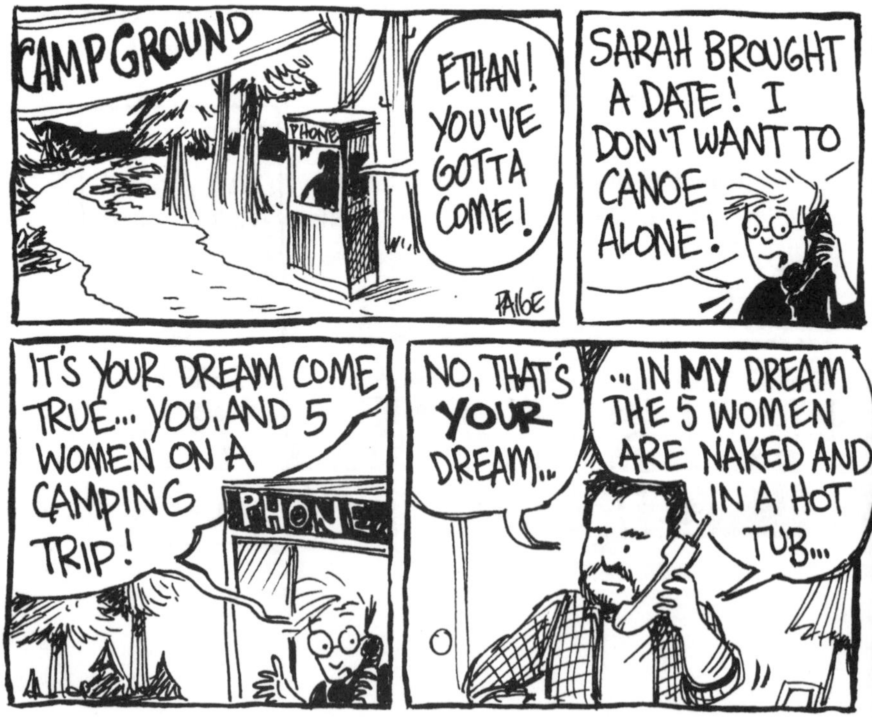
CAMPGROUND
PHONE
ETHAN! YOU'VE GOTTA COME!
PAIGE
SARAH BROUGHT A DATE! I DON'T WANT TO CANOE ALONE!
IT'S YOUR DREAM COME TRUE... YOU, AND 5 WOMEN ON A CAMPING TRIP!
PHONE
NO, THAT'S YOUR DREAM...
...IN MY DREAM THE 5 WOMEN ARE NAKED AND IN A HOT TUB...

... despite his unrequited dream, Ethan shows up to help Jane out...

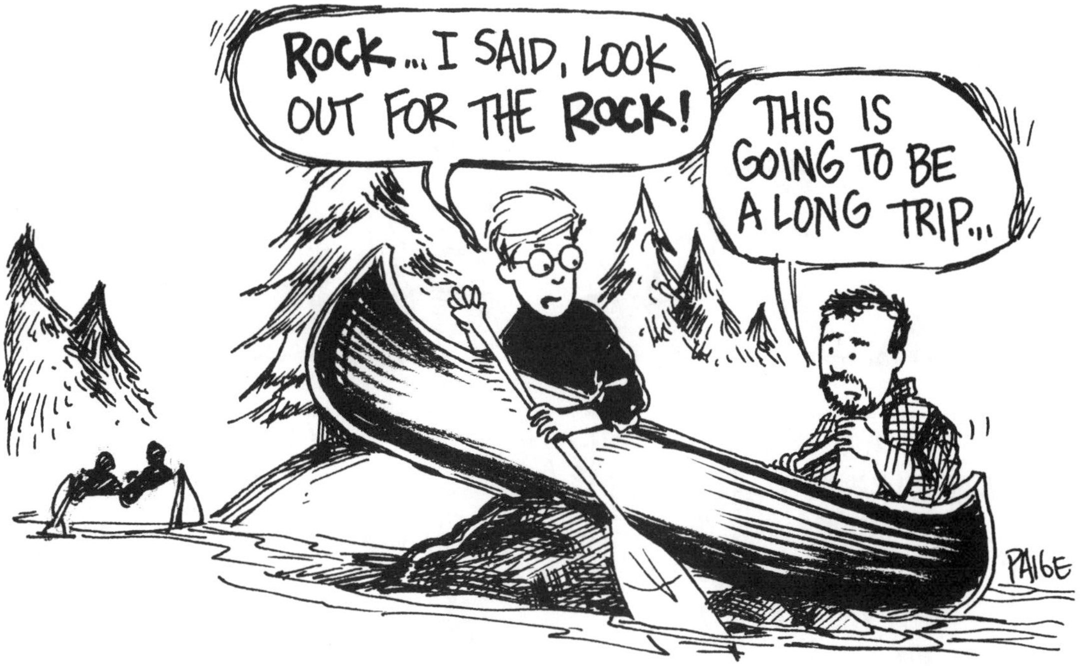
ROCK... I SAID, LOOK OUT FOR THE ROCK!
THIS IS GOING TO BE A LONG TRIP...
PAIGE

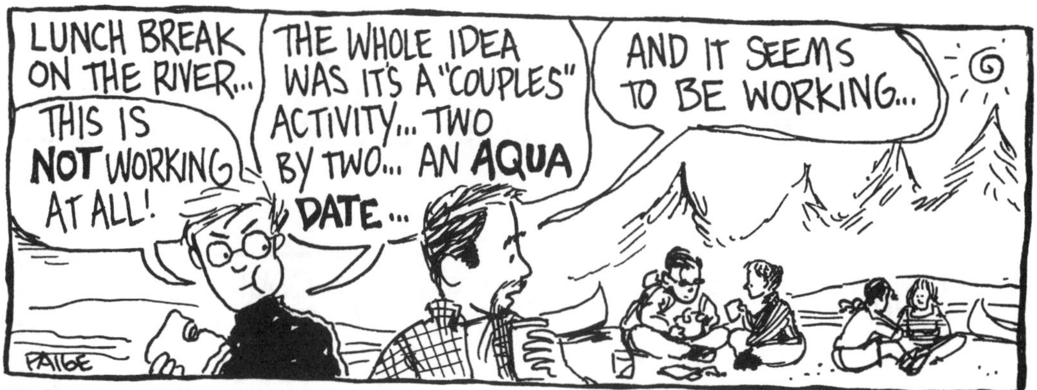
LUNCH BREAK ON THE RIVER...
THIS IS NOT WORKING AT ALL!
THE WHOLE IDEA WAS IT'S A "COUPLES" ACTIVITY... TWO BY TWO... AN AQUA DATE...
AND IT SEEMS TO BE WORKING...
PAIGE

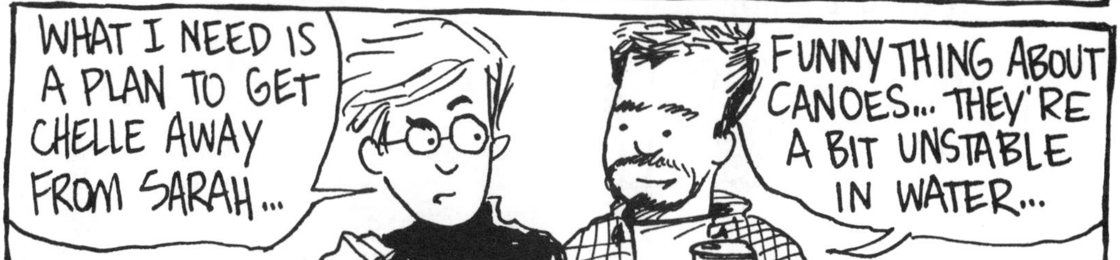
WHAT I NEED IS A PLAN TO GET CHELLE AWAY FROM SARAH...
FUNNY THING ABOUT CANOES... THEY'RE A BIT UNSTABLE IN WATER...

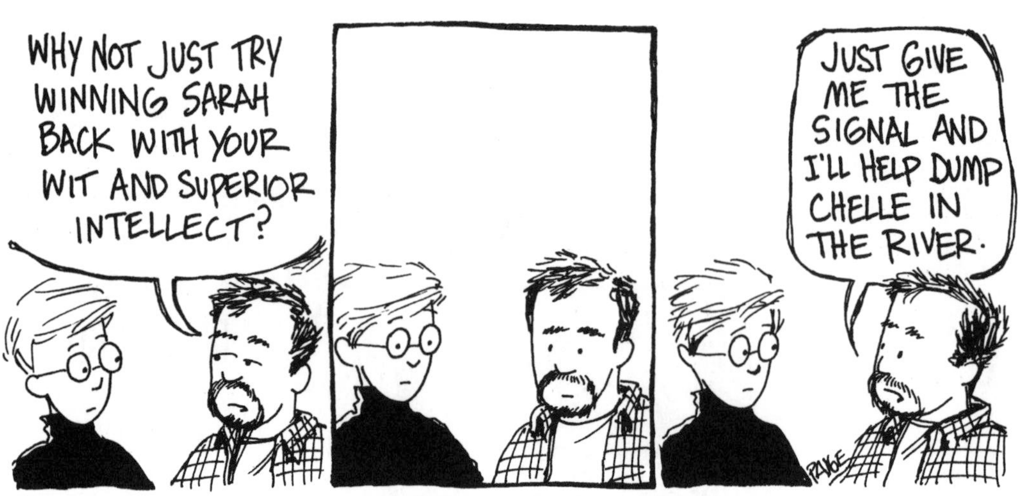
WHY NOT JUST TRY WINNING SARAH BACK WITH YOUR WIT AND SUPERIOR INTELLECT?
JUST GIVE ME THE SIGNAL AND I'LL HELP DUMP CHELLE IN THE RIVER.
PAIGE

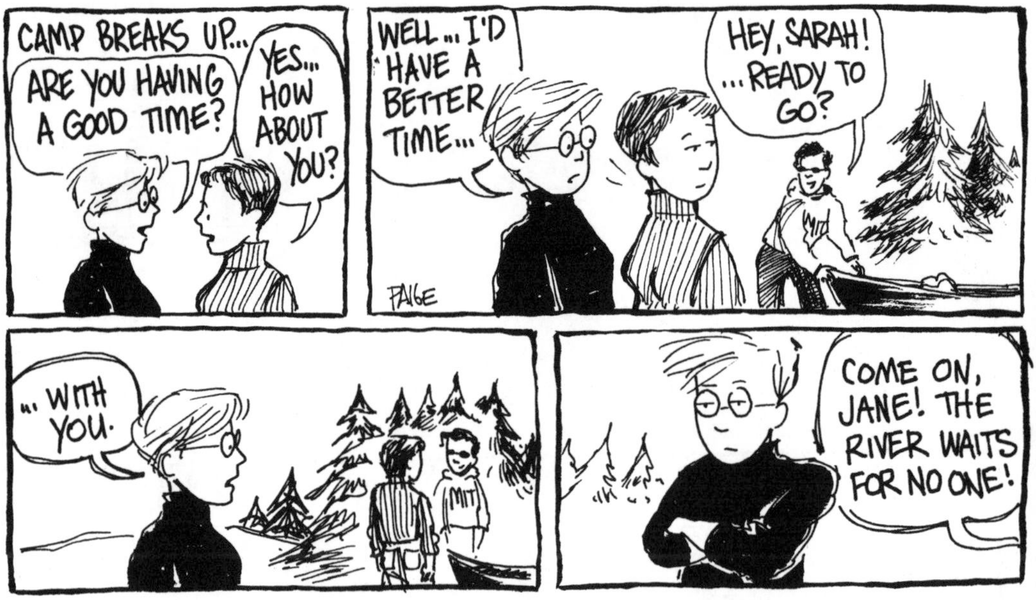
CAMP BREAKS UP...
ARE YOU HAVING A GOOD TIME?
YES... HOW ABOUT YOU?
WELL... I'D HAVE A BETTER TIME...
HEY, SARAH! ...READY TO GO?
PAIGE
MIT
... WITH YOU.
MIT
COME ON, JANE! THE RIVER WAITS FOR NO ONE!

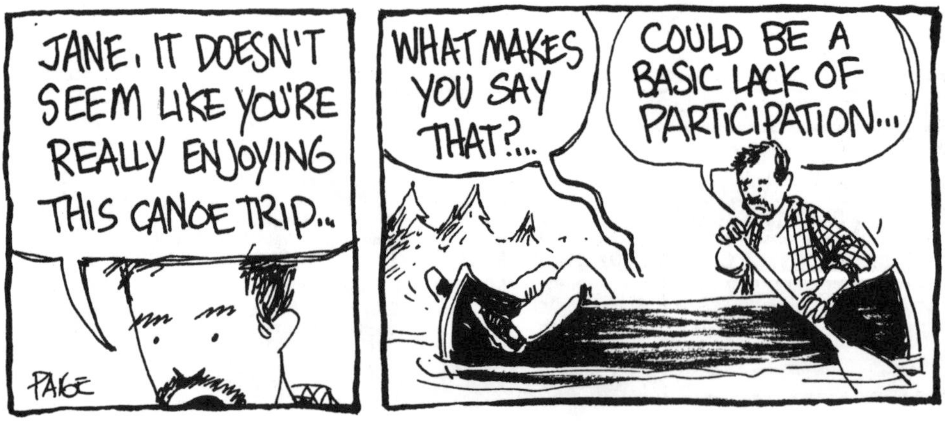
JANE, IT DOESN'T SEEM LIKE YOU'RE REALLY ENJOYING THIS CANOE TRIP...
PAIGE
WHAT MAKES YOU SAY THAT?...
COULD BE A BASIC LACK OF PARTICIPATION...

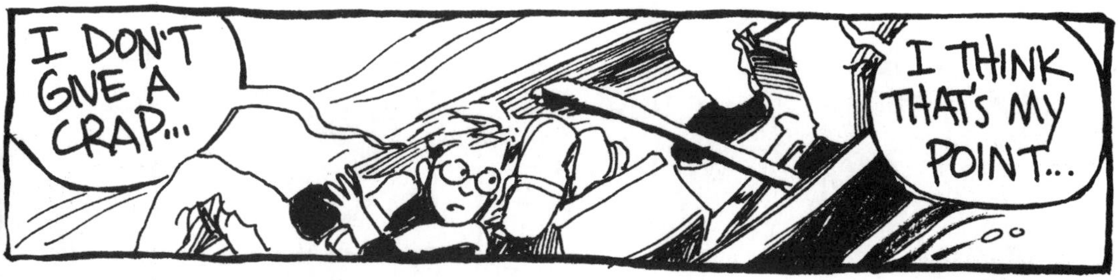
I DON'T GIVE A CRAP...
I THINK THAT'S MY POINT...

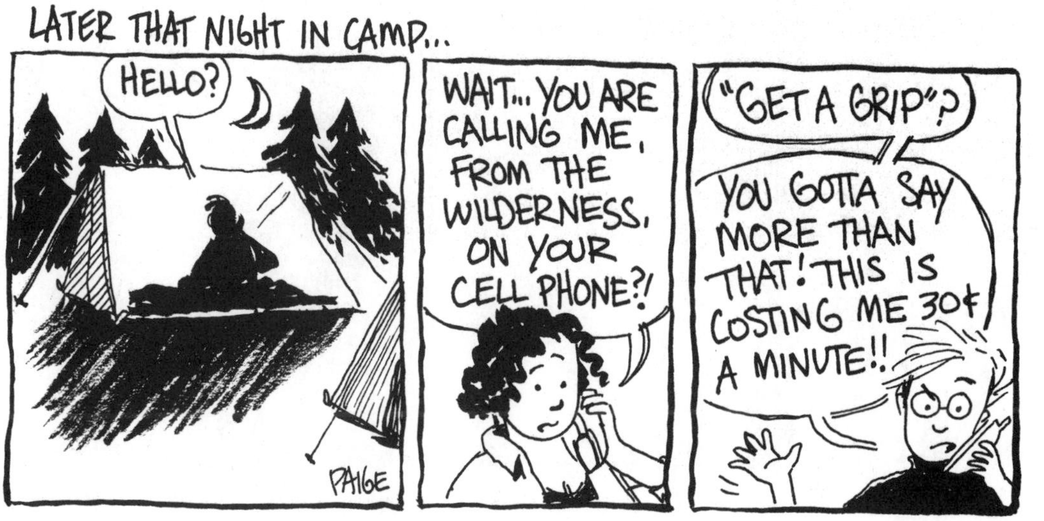
LATER THAT NIGHT IN CAMP...
HELLO?
PAIGE
WAIT... YOU ARE CALLING ME, FROM THE WILDERNESS, ON YOUR CELL PHONE?!
"GET A GRIP"?
YOU GOTTA SAY MORE THAN THAT! THIS IS COSTING ME 30¢ A MINUTE!!

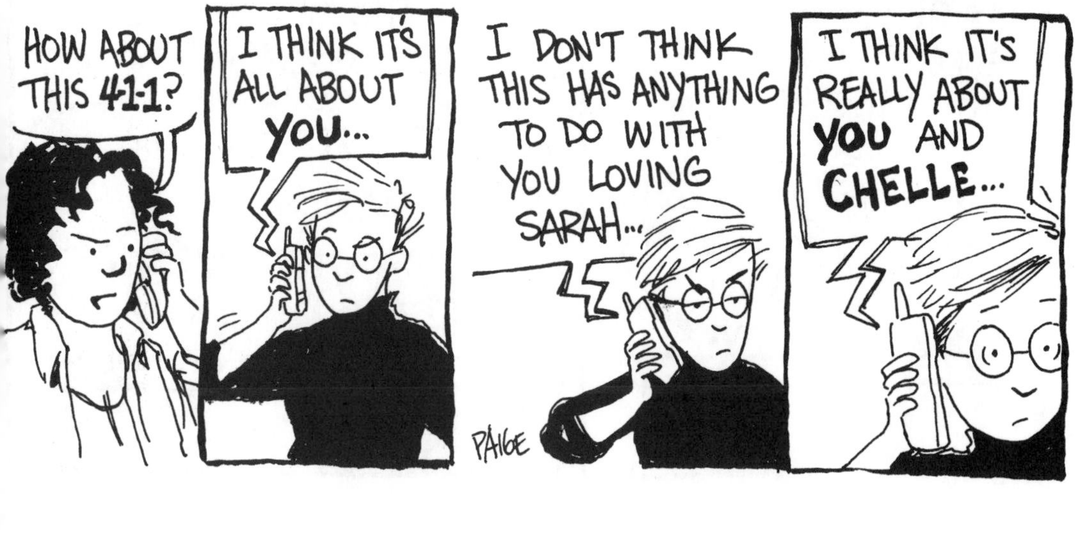
HOW ABOUT THIS 411?
I THINK IT'S ALL ABOUT **YOU**...
I DON'T THINK THIS HAS ANYTHING TO DO WITH YOU LOVING SARAH...
PAIGE
I THINK IT'S REALLY ABOUT **YOU** AND **CHELLE**...

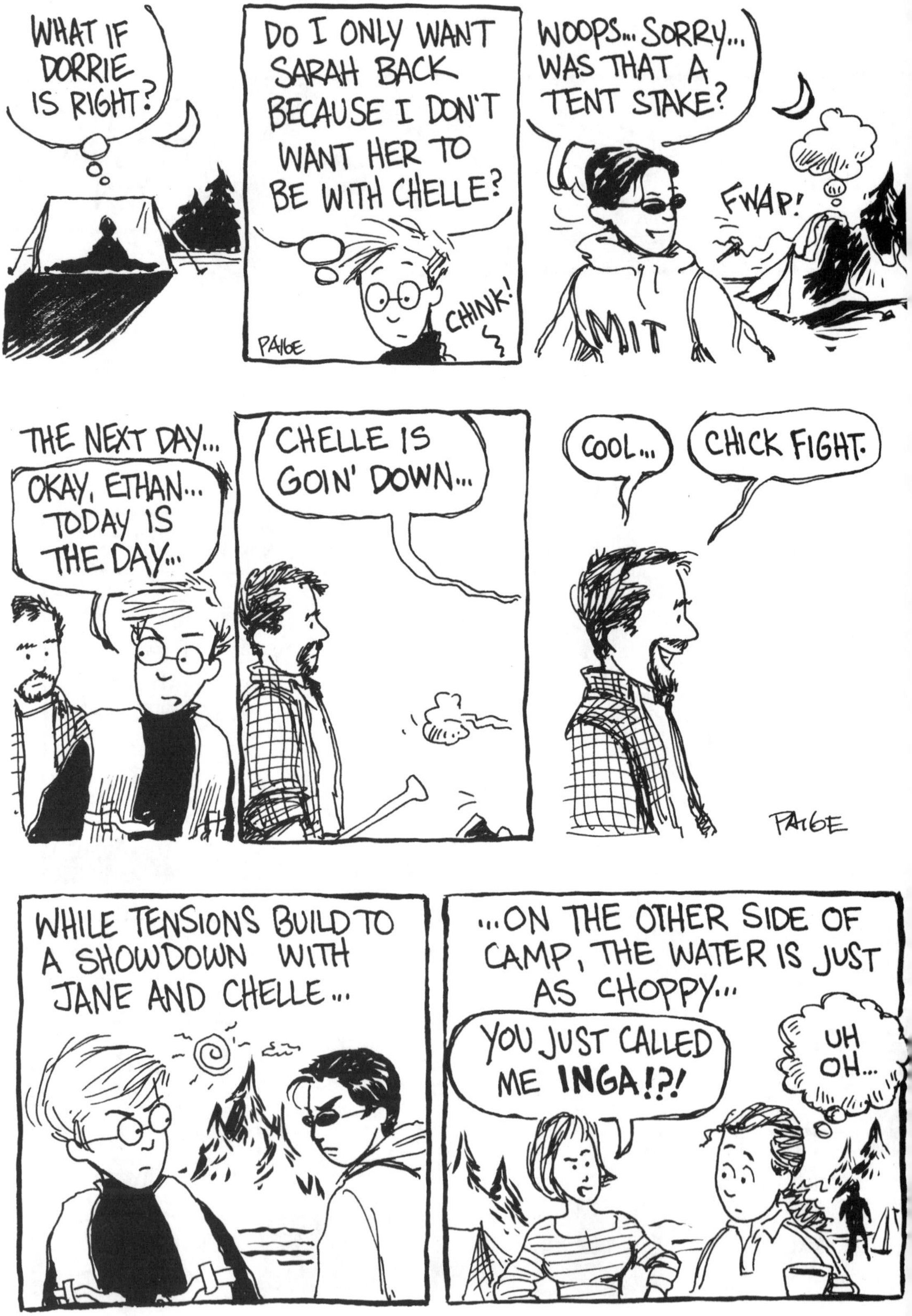
WHAT IF DORRIE IS RIGHT?
DO I ONLY WANT SARAH BACK BECAUSE I DON'T WANT HER TO BE WITH CHELLE?
CHINK!
PAIGE
WOOPS... SORRY... WAS THAT A TENT STAKE?
FWAP!
MIT
THE NEXT DAY...
OKAY, ETHAN... TODAY IS THE DAY...
CHELLE IS GOIN' DOWN...
COOL...
CHICK FIGHT.
PAIGE
WHILE TENSIONS BUILD TO A SHOWDOWN WITH JANE AND CHELLE...
...ON THE OTHER SIDE OF CAMP, THE WATER IS JUST AS CHOPPY...
YOU JUST CALLED ME **INGA!?!**
UH OH...

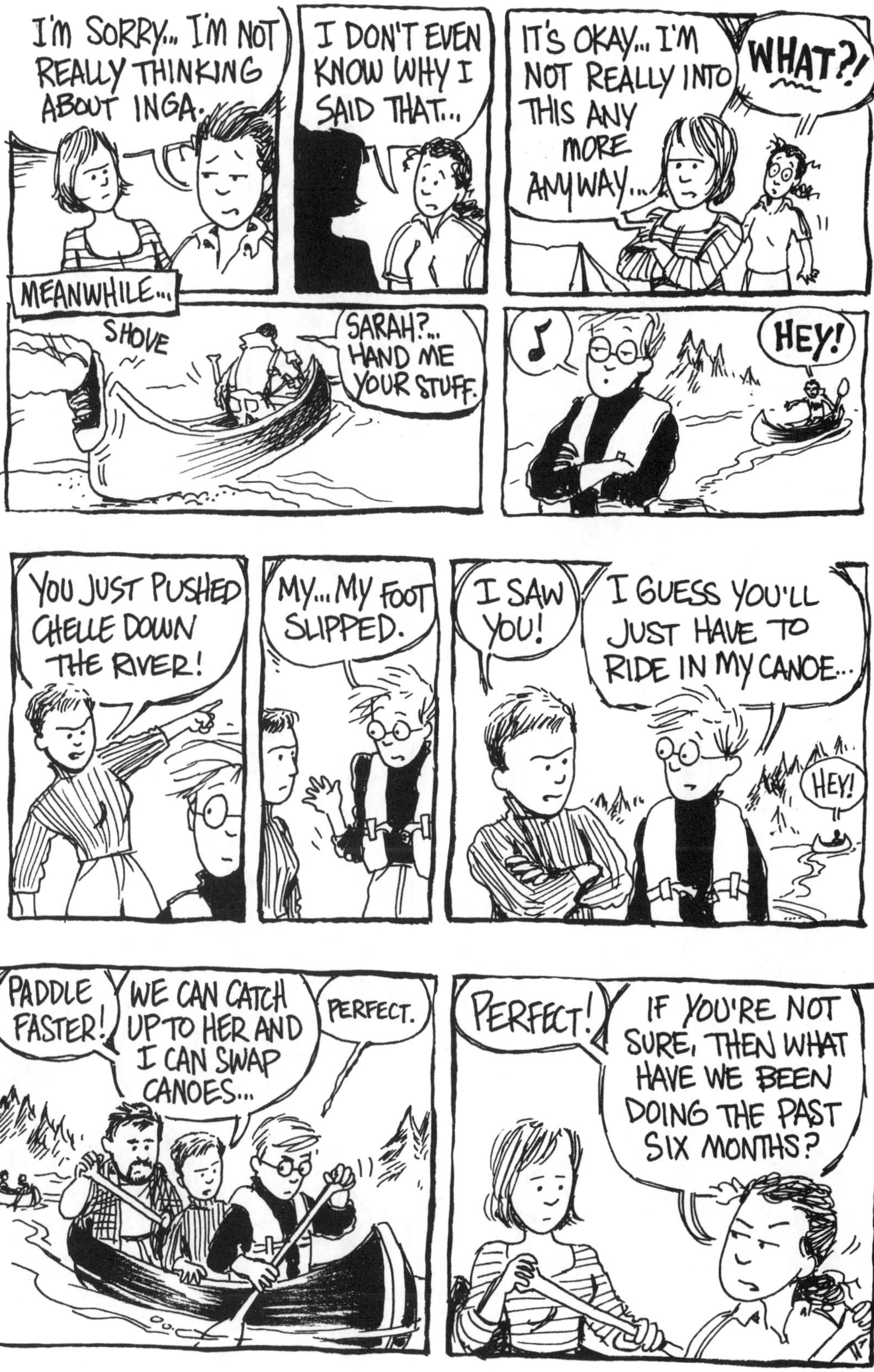
I'M SORRY... I'M NOT REALLY THINKING ABOUT INGA.
I DON'T EVEN KNOW WHY I SAID THAT...
IT'S OKAY... I'M NOT REALLY INTO THIS ANY MORE ANYWAY...
WHAT?!
MEANWHILE...
SHOVE
SARAH?... HAND ME YOUR STUFF.
HEY!
YOU JUST PUSHED CHELLE DOWN THE RIVER!
MY... MY FOOT SLIPPED.
I SAW YOU!
I GUESS YOU'LL JUST HAVE TO RIDE IN MY CANOE...
HEY!
PADDLE FASTER!
WE CAN CATCH UP TO HER AND I CAN SWAP CANOES...
PERFECT.
PERFECT!
IF YOU'RE NOT SURE, THEN WHAT HAVE WE BEEN DOING THE PAST SIX MONTHS?

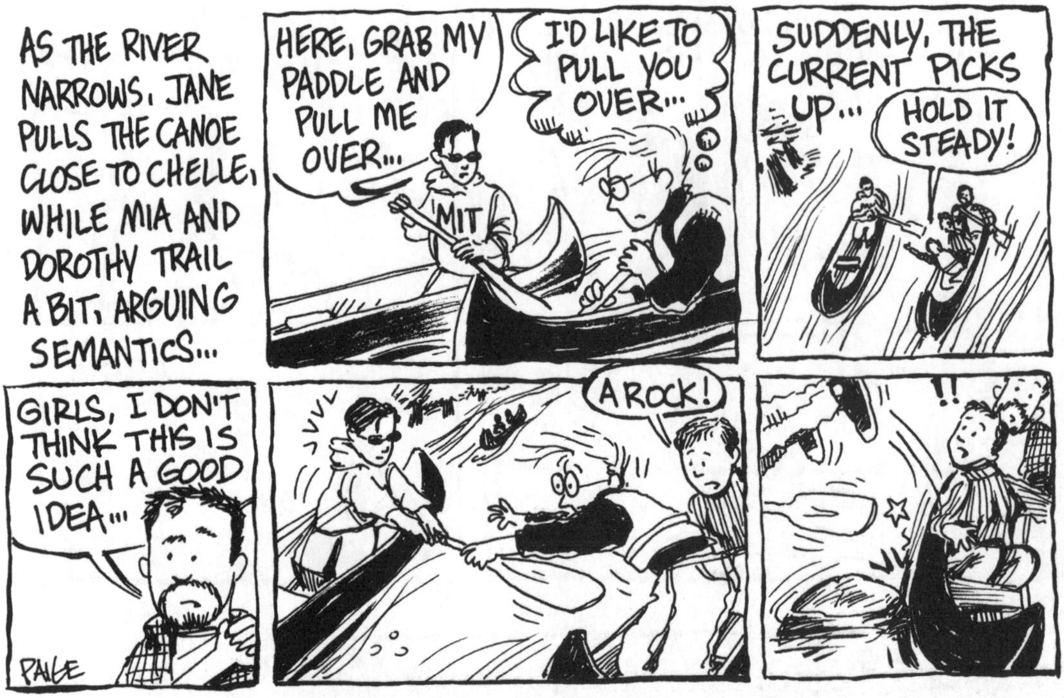
AS THE RIVER NARROWS, JANE PULLS THE CANOE CLOSE TO CHELLE, WHILE MIA AND DOROTHY TRAIL A BIT, ARGUING SEMANTICS...
HERE, GRAB MY PADDLE AND PULL ME OVER...
I'D LIKE TO PULL YOU OVER...
MIT
SUDDENLY, THE CURRENT PICKS UP...
HOLD IT STEADY!
GIRLS, I DON'T THINK THIS IS SUCH A GOOD IDEA...
PAIGE
A ROCK!

Jane is thrown from the boat and manages to cling to the side of Chelle's nearby canoe...

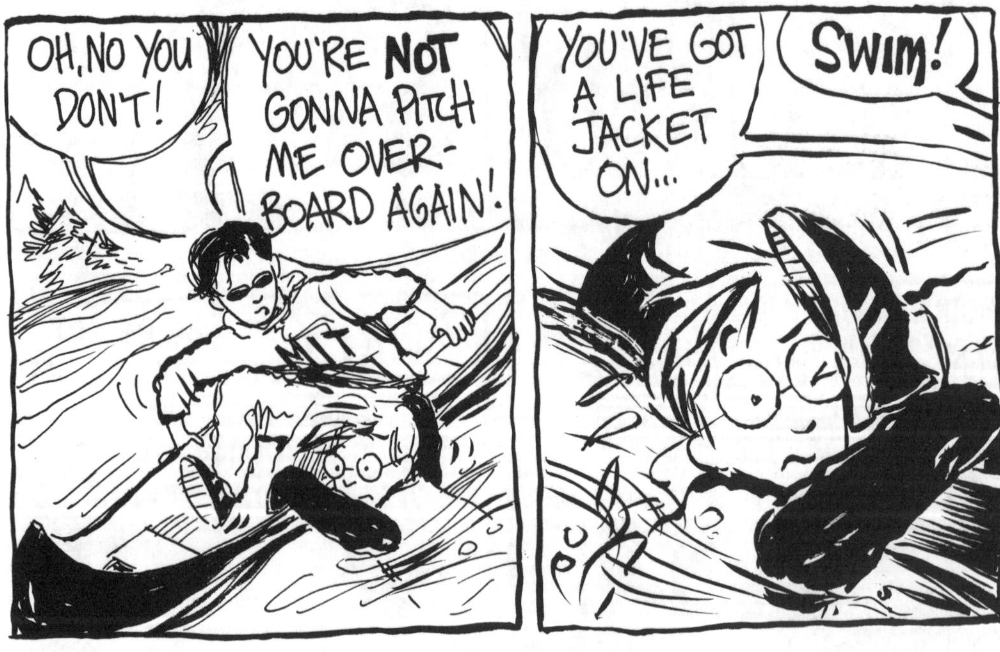
OH, NO YOU DON'T!
YOU'RE **NOT** GONNA PITCH ME OVER-BOARD AGAIN!
MIT
YOU'VE GOT A LIFE JACKET ON...
SWIM!

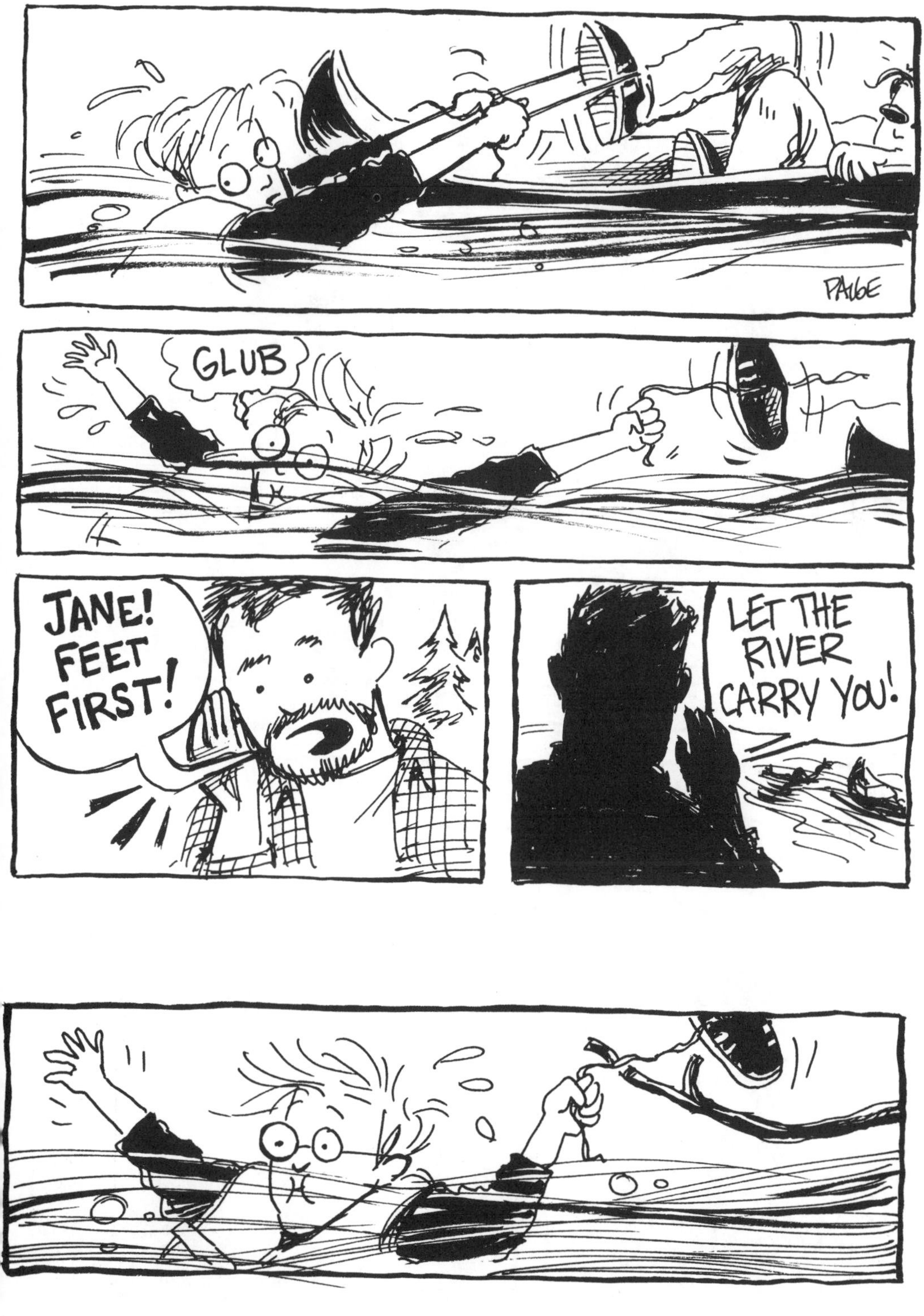
PAIGE
GLUB
JANE! FEET FIRST!
LET THE RIVER CARRY YOU!

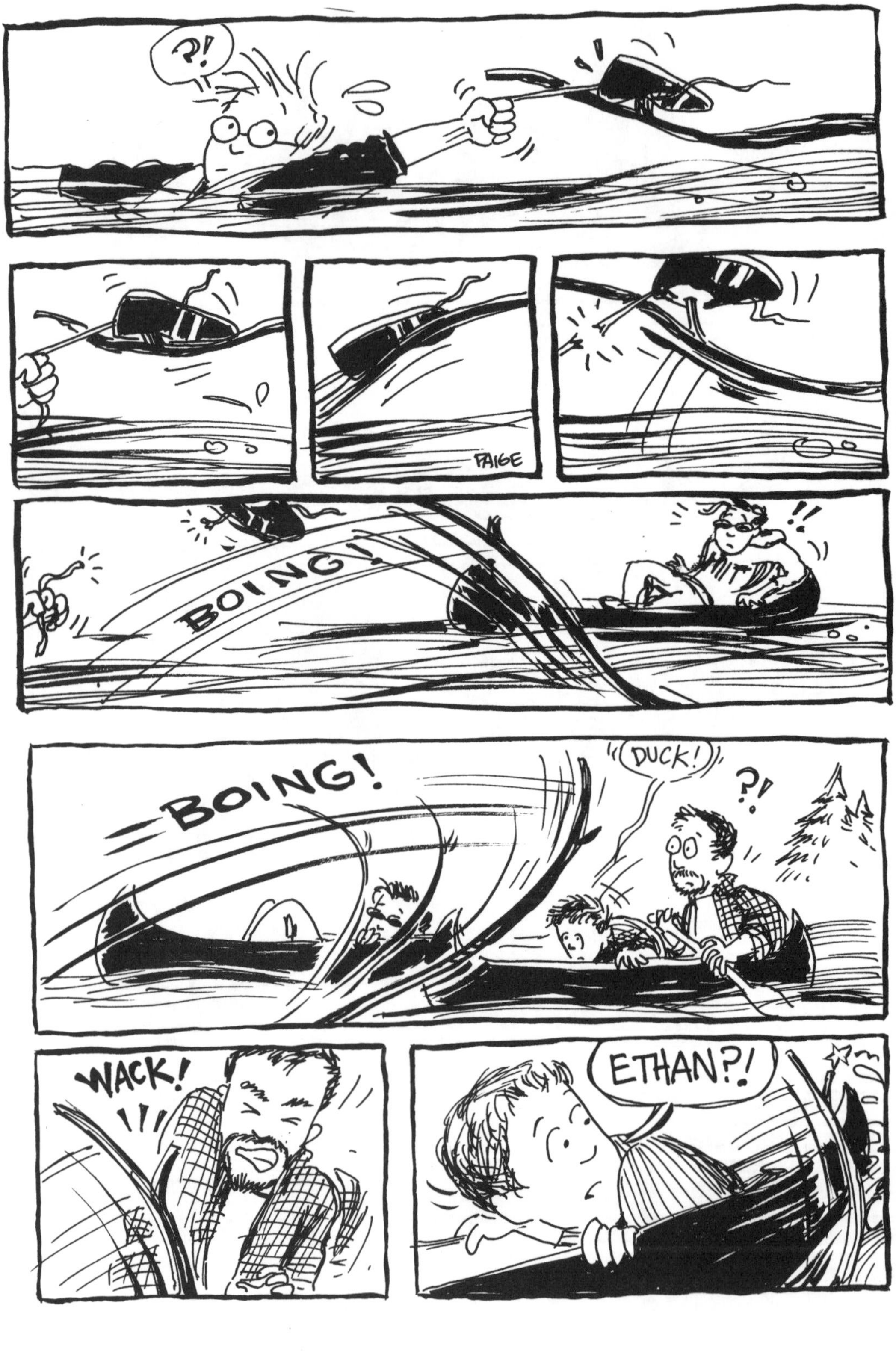
?!
PAIGE
BOING!
!!
BOING!
DUCK!
?!
WACK!
ETHAN?!

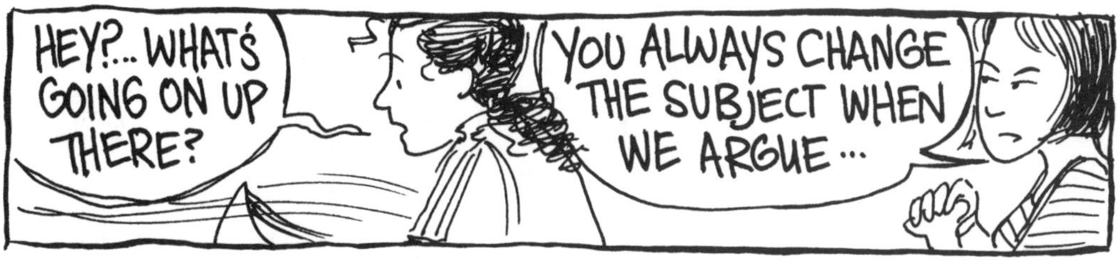
HEY?... WHAT'S GOING ON UP THERE?
YOU ALWAYS CHANGE THE SUBJECT WHEN WE ARGUE...

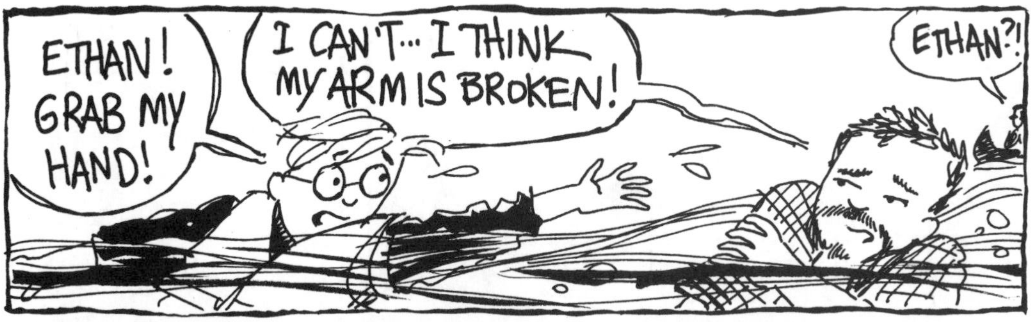
ETHAN! GRAB MY HAND!
I CAN'T... I THINK MY ARM IS BROKEN!
ETHAN?!

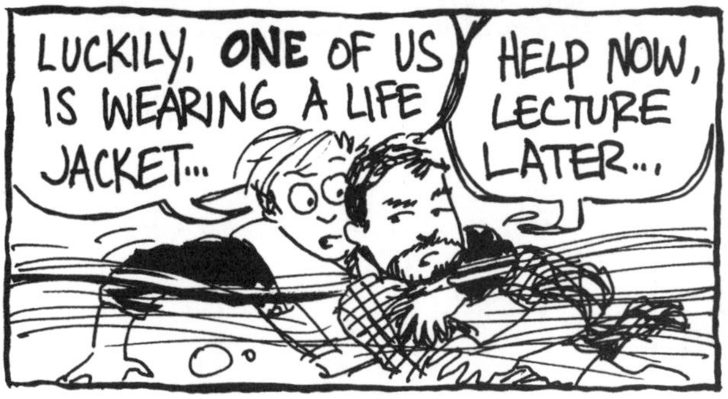
LUCKILY, **ONE** OF US IS WEARING A LIFE JACKET...
HELP NOW, LECTURE LATER...

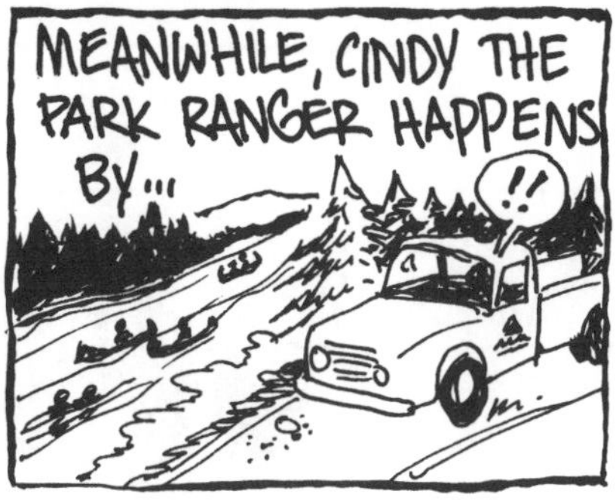
MEANWHILE, CINDY THE PARK RANGER HAPPENS BY...
!!

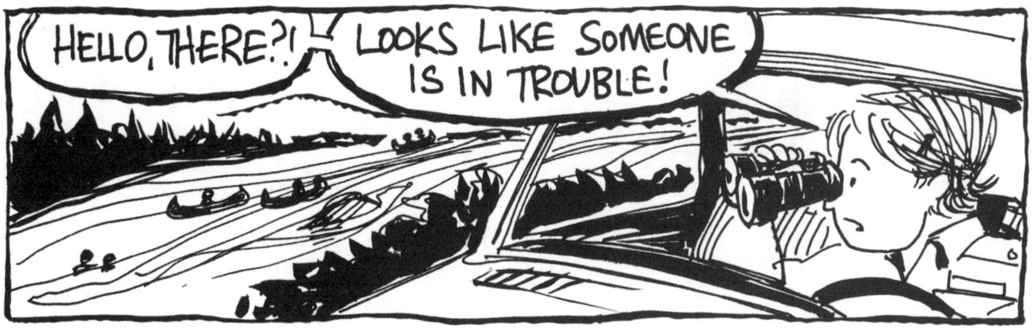
HELLO, THERE?!
LOOKS LIKE SOMEONE IS IN TROUBLE!

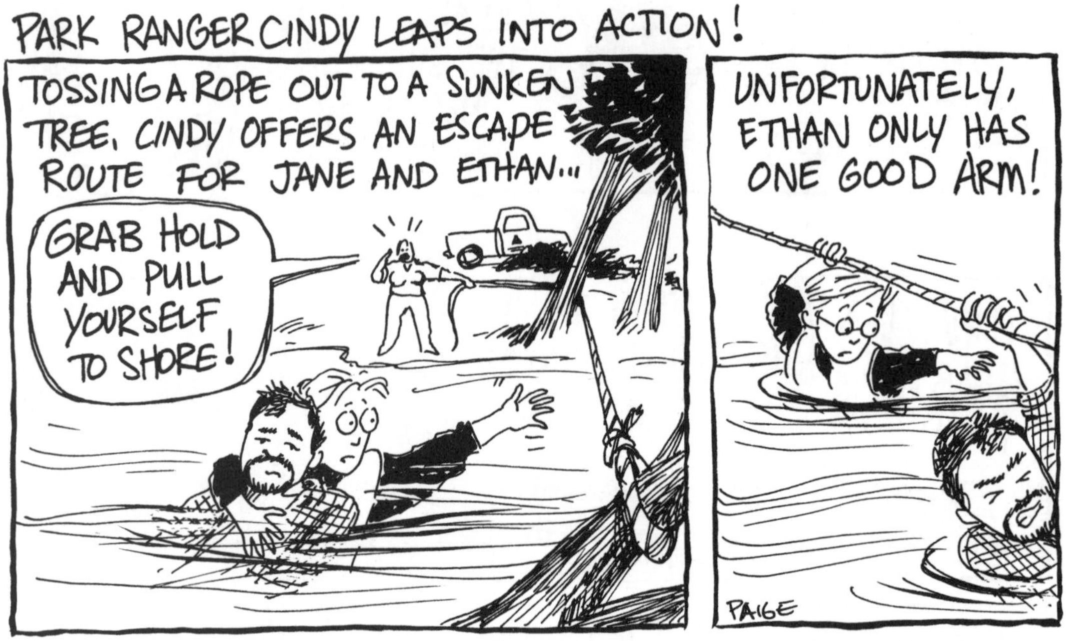
PARK RANGER CINDY LEAPS INTO ACTION!
TOSSING A ROPE OUT TO A SUNKEN TREE, CINDY OFFERS AN ESCAPE ROUTE FOR JANE AND ETHAN...
GRAB HOLD AND PULL YOURSELF TO SHORE!
UNFORTUNATELY, ETHAN ONLY HAS ONE GOOD ARM!
PAIGE

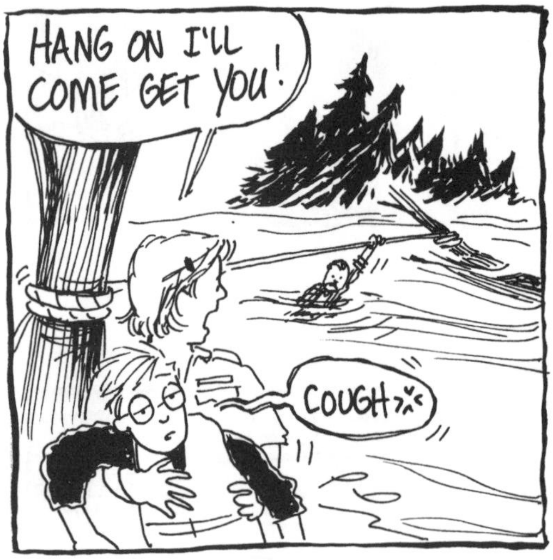
HANG ON I'LL COME GET YOU!
COUGH

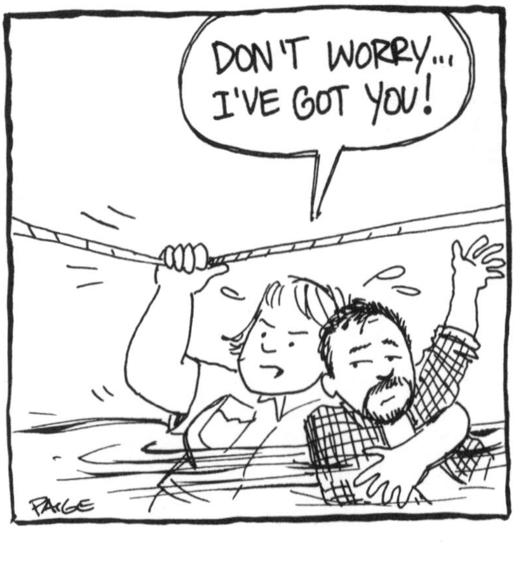
DON'T WORRY... I'VE GOT YOU!
PAIGE

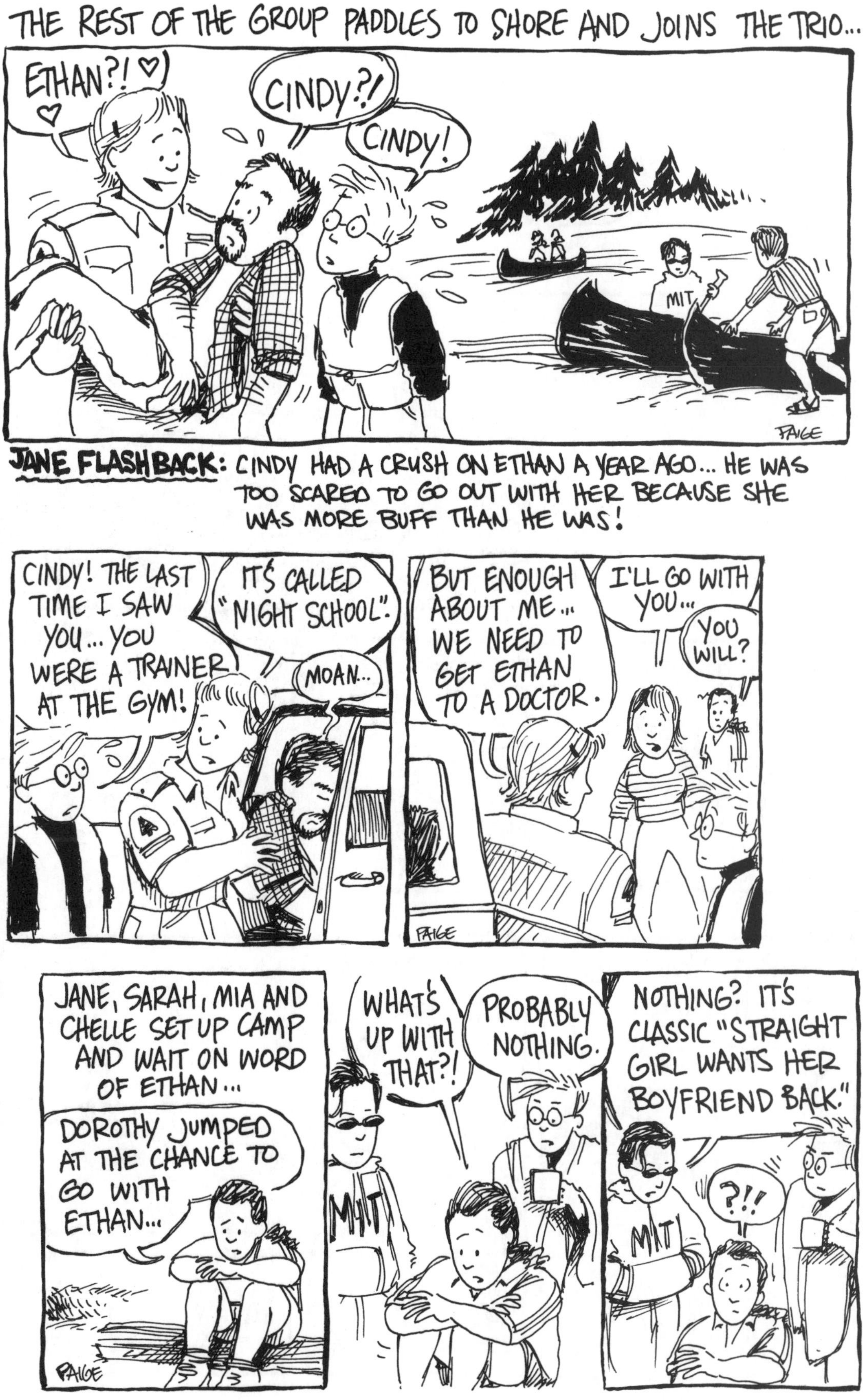
THE REST OF THE GROUP PADDLES TO SHORE AND JOINS THE TRIO...
ETHAN?!
CINDY?!
CINDY!
MIT
PAIGE
JANE FLASHBACK: CINDY HAD A CRUSH ON ETHAN A YEAR AGO... HE WAS TOO SCARED TO GO OUT WITH HER BECAUSE SHE WAS MORE BUFF THAN HE WAS!
CINDY! THE LAST TIME I SAW YOU... YOU WERE A TRAINER AT THE GYM!
IT'S CALLED "NIGHT SCHOOL".
MOAN...
BUT ENOUGH ABOUT ME... WE NEED TO GET ETHAN TO A DOCTOR.
I'LL GO WITH YOU...
YOU WILL?
PAIGE
JANE, SARAH, MIA AND CHELLE SET UP CAMP AND WAIT ON WORD OF ETHAN...
DOROTHY JUMPED AT THE CHANCE TO GO WITH ETHAN...
PAIGE
WHAT'S UP WITH THAT?!
PROBABLY NOTHING.
MIT
NOTHING? IT'S CLASSIC "STRAIGHT GIRL WANTS HER BOYFRIEND BACK."
?!!
MIT

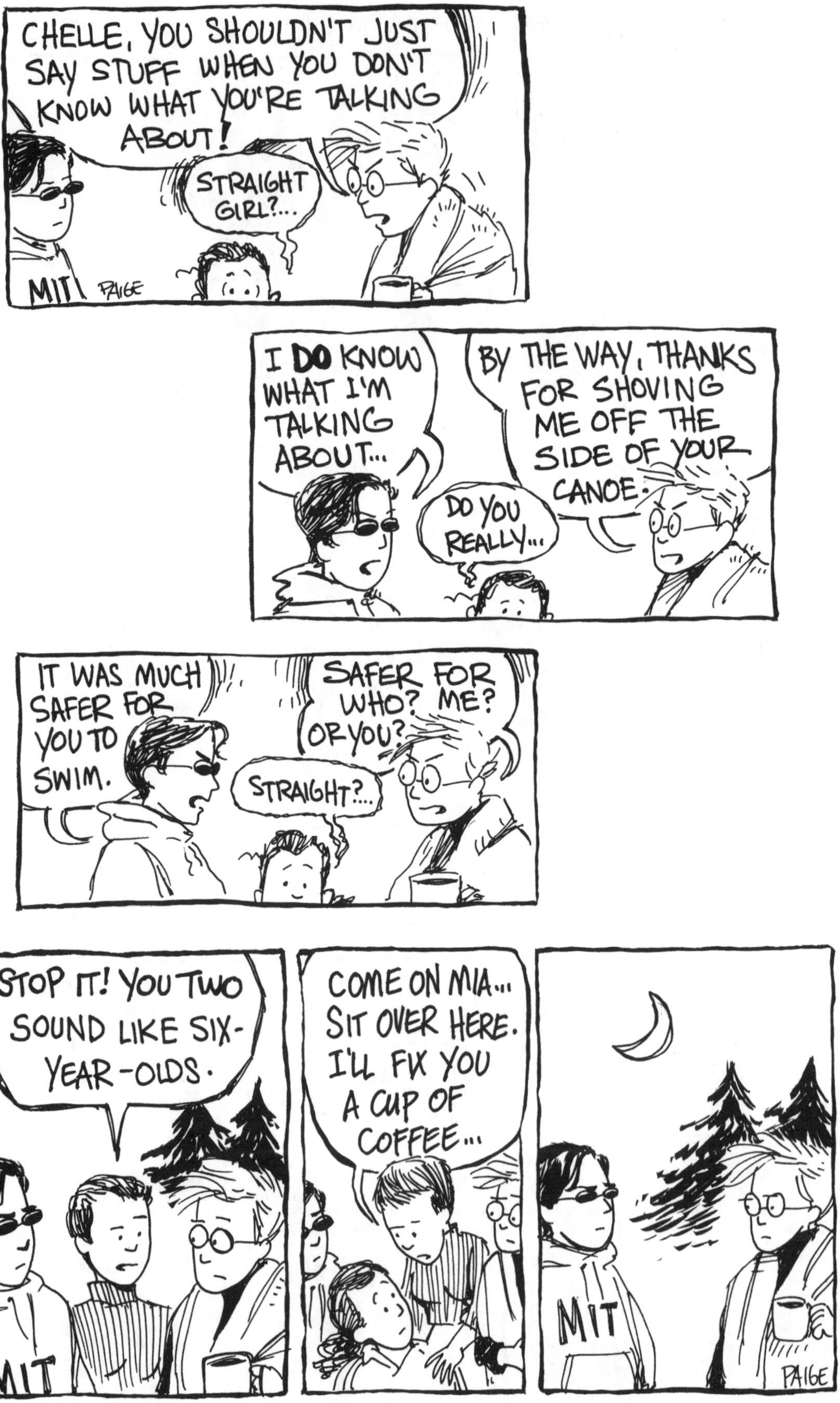
CHELLE, YOU SHOULDN'T JUST SAY STUFF WHEN YOU DON'T KNOW WHAT YOU'RE TALKING ABOUT!
STRAIGHT GIRL?...
MIT
PAIGE
I **DO** KNOW WHAT I'M TALKING ABOUT...
BY THE WAY, THANKS FOR SHOVING ME OFF THE SIDE OF YOUR CANOE.
DO YOU REALLY...
IT WAS MUCH SAFER FOR YOU TO SWIM.
SAFER FOR WHO? ME? OR YOU?
STRAIGHT?...
STOP IT! YOU TWO SOUND LIKE SIX-YEAR-OLDS.
MIT
COME ON MIA... SIT OVER HERE. I'LL FIX YOU A CUP OF COFFEE...
MIT
PAIGE

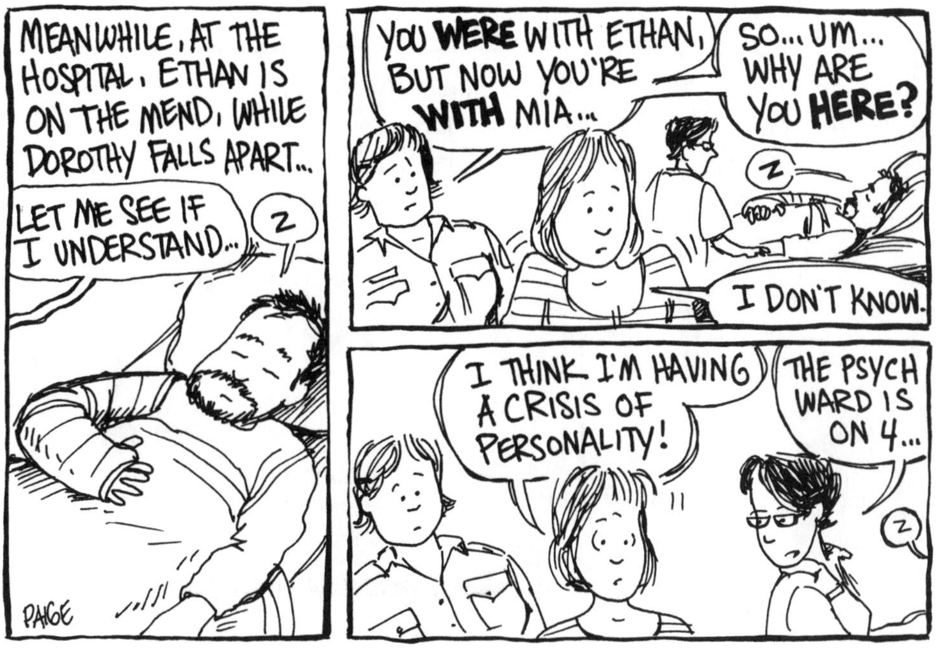
MEANWHILE, AT THE HOSPITAL, ETHAN IS ON THE MEND, WHILE DOROTHY FALLS APART...
LET ME SEE IF I UNDERSTAND...
Z
YOU WERE WITH ETHAN, BUT NOW YOU'RE WITH MIA...
SO... UM... WHY ARE YOU HERE?
Z
I DON'T KNOW.
I THINK I'M HAVING A CRISIS OF PERSONALITY!
THE PSYCH WARD IS ON 4...
Z
PAIGE

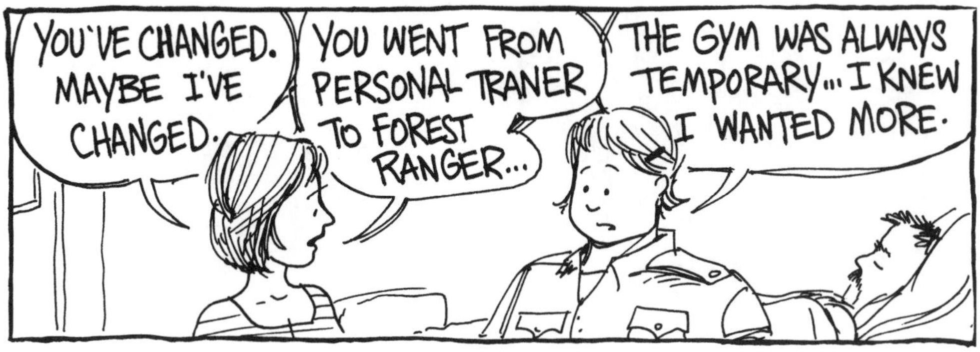
YOU'VE CHANGED. MAYBE I'VE CHANGED.
YOU WENT FROM PERSONAL TRANER TO FOREST RANGER...
THE GYM WAS ALWAYS TEMPORARY... I KNEW I WANTED MORE.

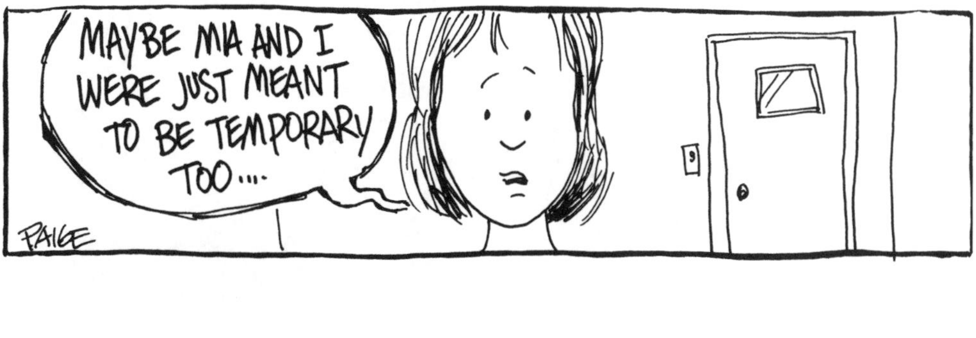
MAYBE MIA AND I WERE JUST MEANT TO BE TEMPORARY TOO....
PAIGE

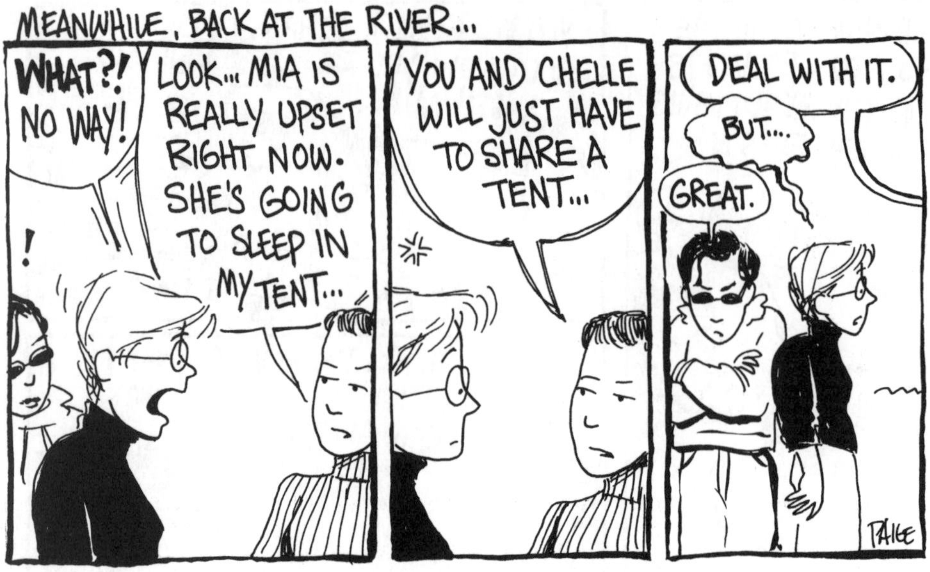
MEANWHILE, BACK AT THE RIVER...
WHAT?! NO WAY!
LOOK... MIA IS REALLY UPSET RIGHT NOW. SHE'S GOING TO SLEEP IN MY TENT...
!
YOU AND CHELLE WILL JUST HAVE TO SHARE A TENT...
DEAL WITH IT.
BUT...
GREAT.
PAIGE

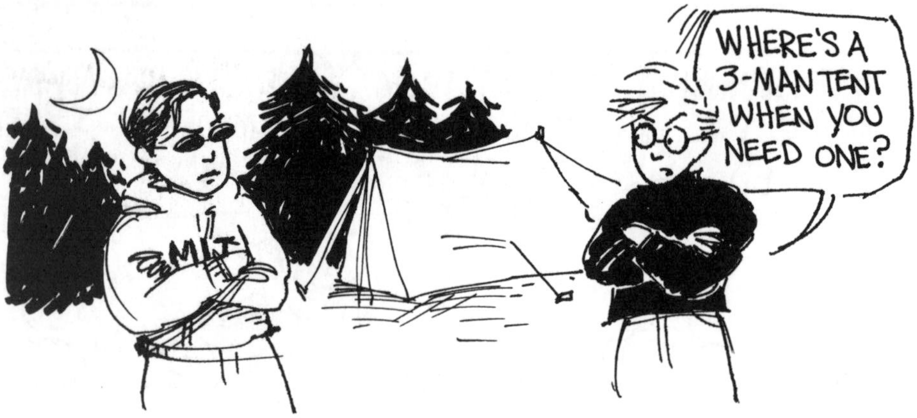
WHERE'S A 3-MAN TENT WHEN YOU NEED ONE?
MIT

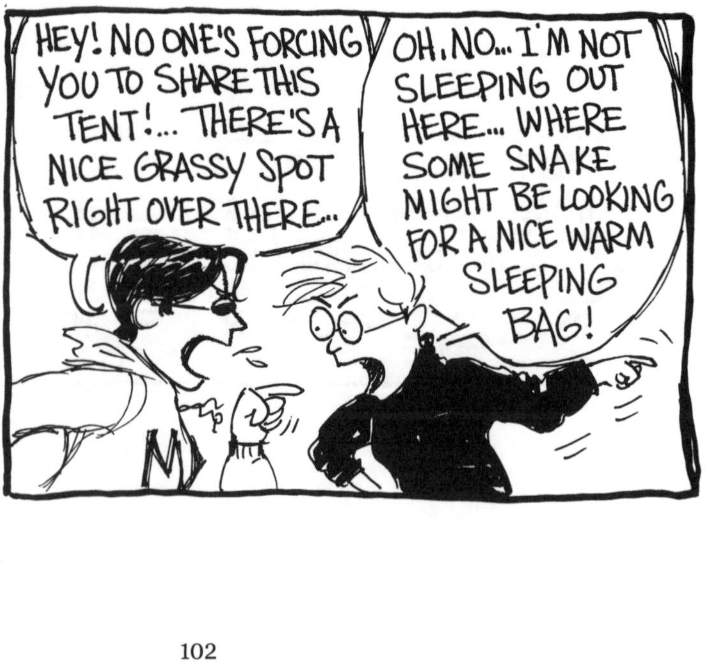
HEY! NO ONE'S FORCING YOU TO SHARE THIS TENT!... THERE'S A NICE GRASSY SPOT RIGHT OVER THERE...
OH, NO... I'M NOT SLEEPING OUT HERE... WHERE SOME SNAKE MIGHT BE LOOKING FOR A NICE WARM SLEEPING BAG!

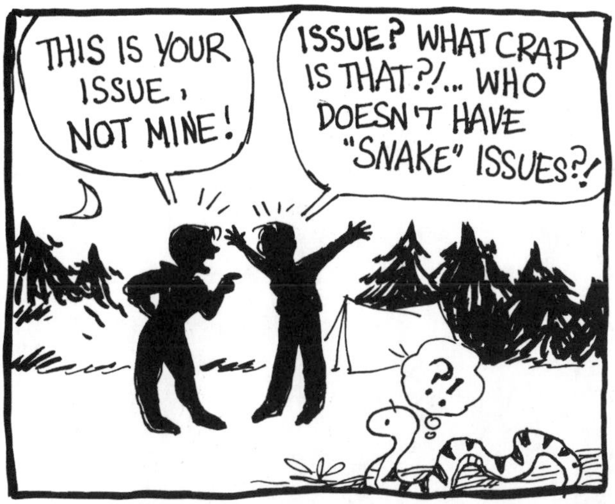
THIS IS YOUR ISSUE, NOT MINE!
ISSUE? WHAT CRAP IS THAT?!... WHO DOESN'T HAVE "SNAKE" ISSUES?!
?!

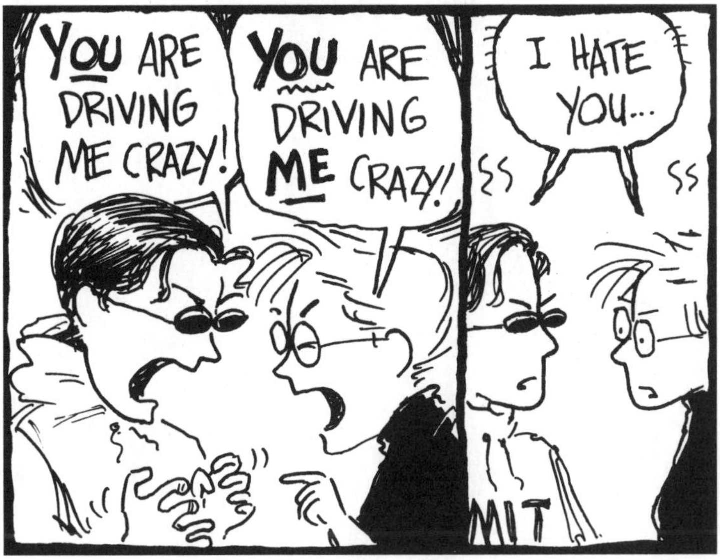
YOU ARE DRIVING ME CRAZY!
YOU ARE DRIVING ME CRAZY!
I HATE YOU...
MIT

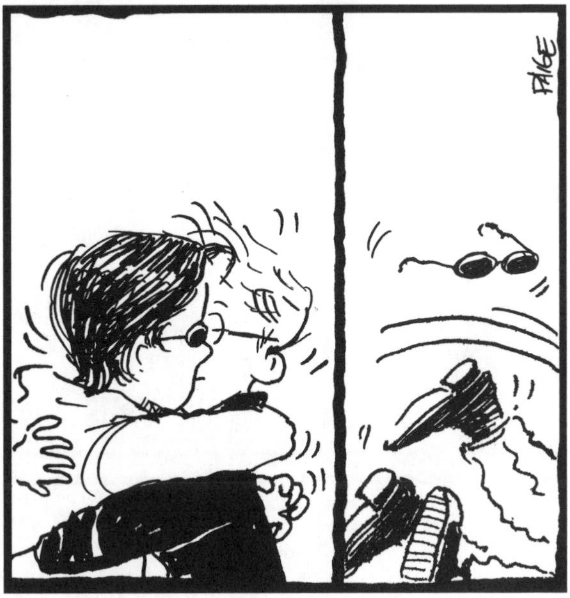
PAIGE

Chapter 5
Group therapy potluck

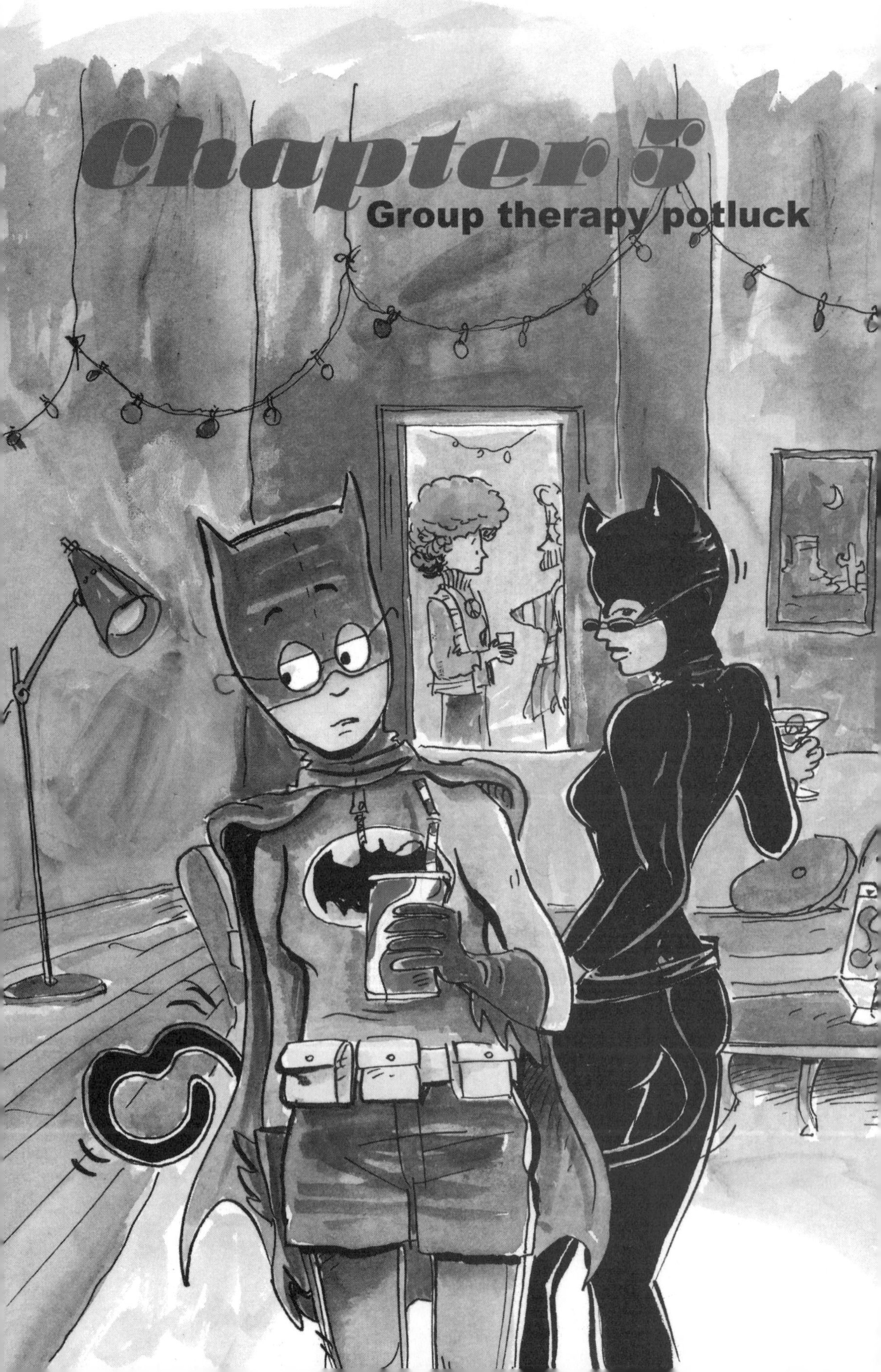

...Ethan suffered a fractured arm during his body surf down the river.
Dorothy decides to ride with Cindy as she transports Ethan to the emergency room, leaving Mia to draw her own conclusions about what exactly all of this means.
Mia isn't too happy about this turn of romantic events, but Ethan is...

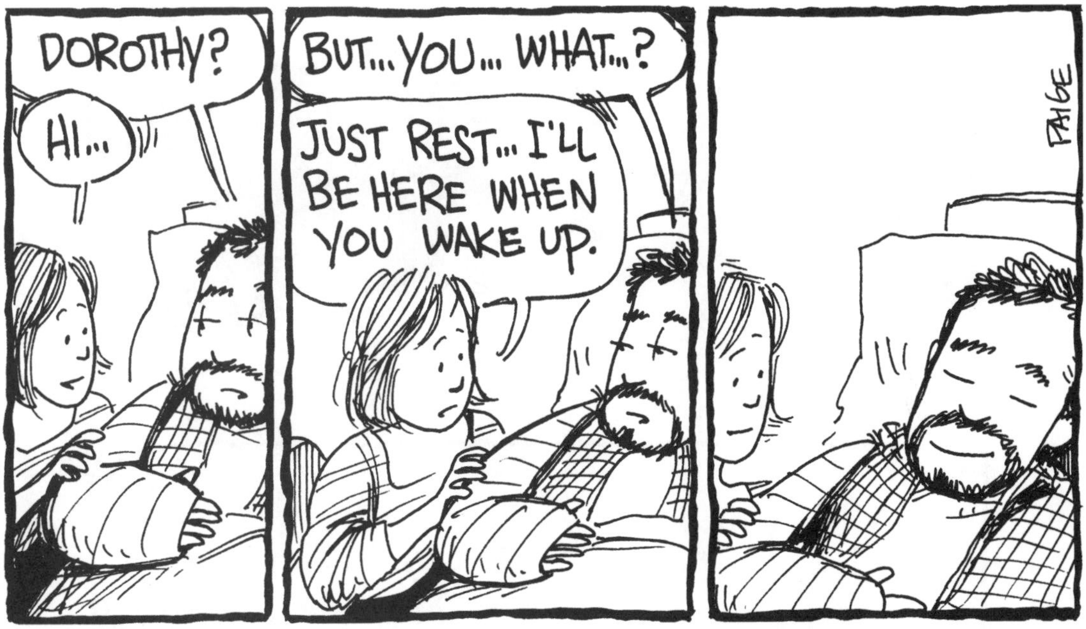
DOROTHY?
HI...
BUT... YOU... WHAT...?
JUST REST... I'LL BE HERE WHEN YOU WAKE UP.
PAIGE

...Meanwhile, Jane and Chelle wake up from a surprisingly cozy night together.

Back in camp, it's the morning after...

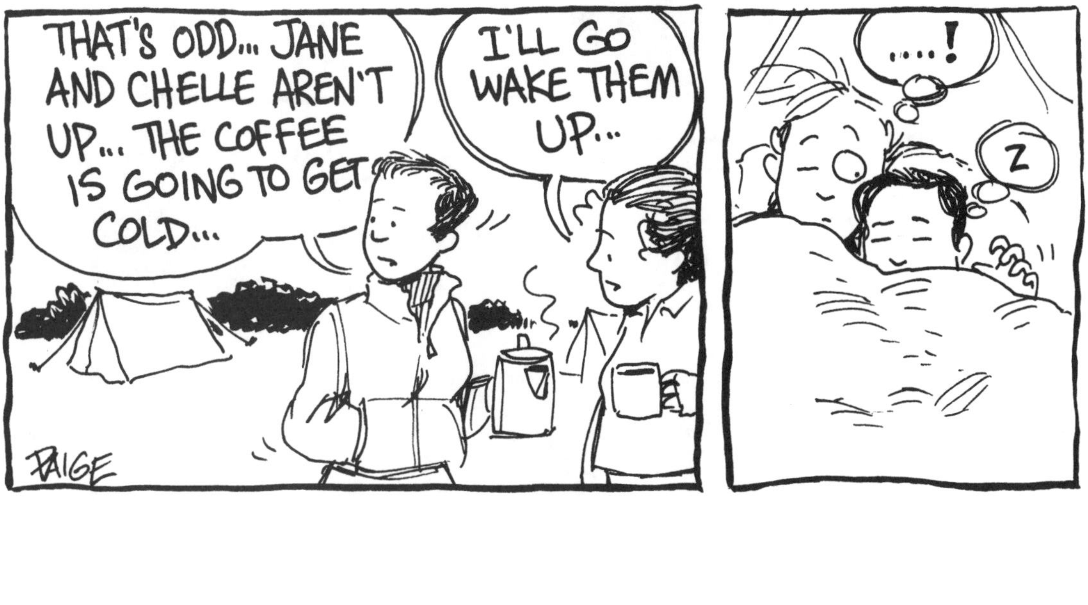
THAT'S ODD... JANE AND CHELLE AREN'T UP... THE COFFEE IS GOING TO GET COLD...
I'LL GO WAKE THEM UP...
PAIGE
....!
Z

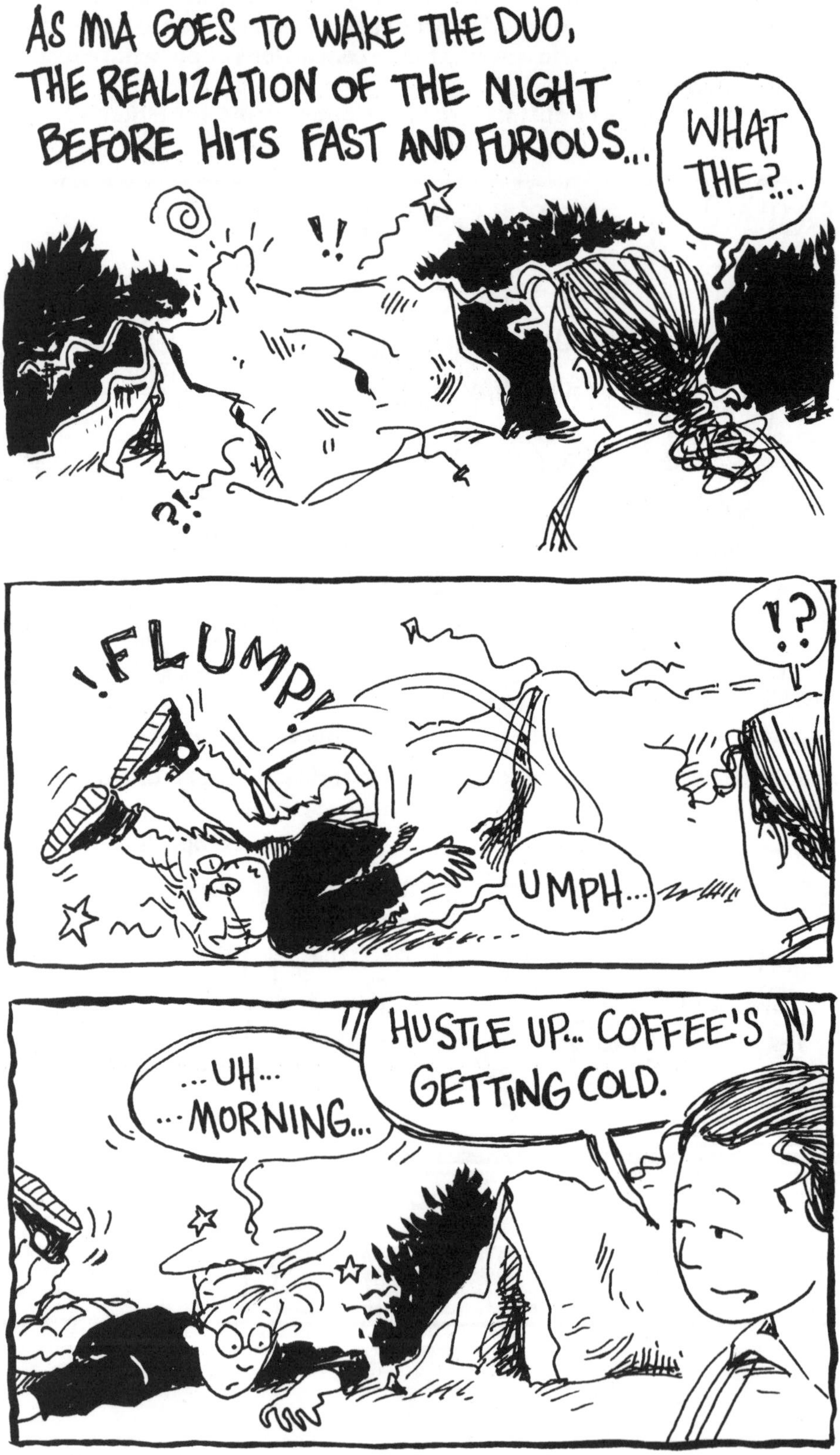
AS MIA GOES TO WAKE THE DUO, THE REALIZATION OF THE NIGHT BEFORE HITS FAST AND FURIOUS...
WHAT THE?...
!!
?!
!FLUMP!
!?
UMPH...
...UH... ...MORNING...
HUSTLE UP... COFFEE'S GETTING COLD.

Chelle and Jane are a bit Dazed and Confused... They gravitate toward the camp-fire hoping coffee will provide them with a bit of "morning after" clarity...

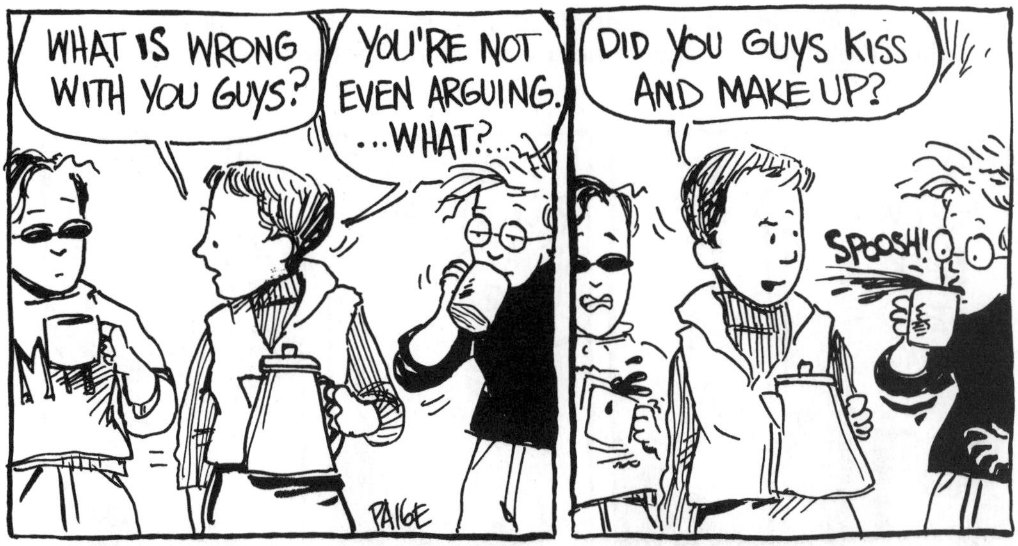

WHAT IS WRONG WITH YOU GUYS?
YOU'RE NOT EVEN ARGUING. ...WHAT?...
PAIGE
DID YOU GUYS KISS AND MAKE UP?
SPOOSH!

...Sarah walks off, puzzled... and Chelle gives Jane a little dose of her own reality...

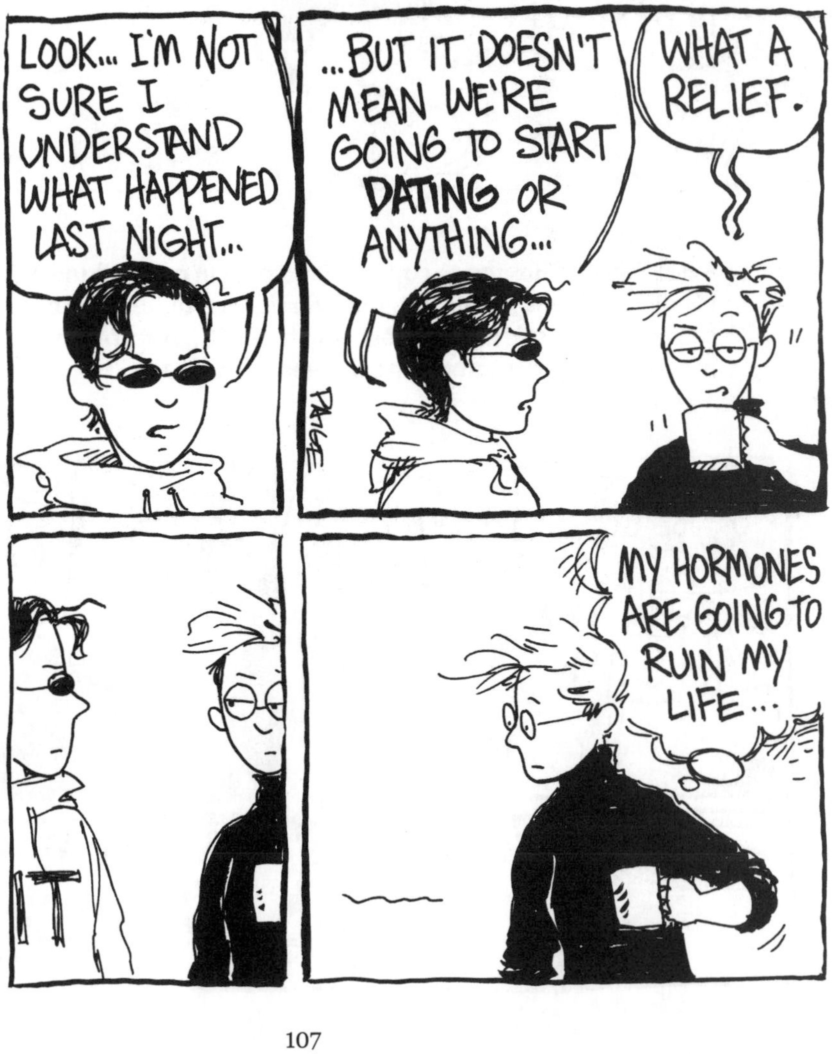

LOOK... I'M NOT SURE I UNDERSTAND WHAT HAPPENED LAST NIGHT...
PAIGE
...BUT IT DOESN'T MEAN WE'RE GOING TO START DATING OR ANYTHING...
WHAT A RELIEF.
MY HORMONES ARE GOING TO RUIN MY LIFE...

Park ranger, Cindy, picks up the somewhat sullen foursome on the river bank and takes them back to city life... finally... It's a long ride... Five women on a bench seat provides a little too much togetherness for the ride home.

After Cindy drops Jane off, Jane decides to check in with Dorrie about the chimp... or should we say, the chimp that once was, Dixie...

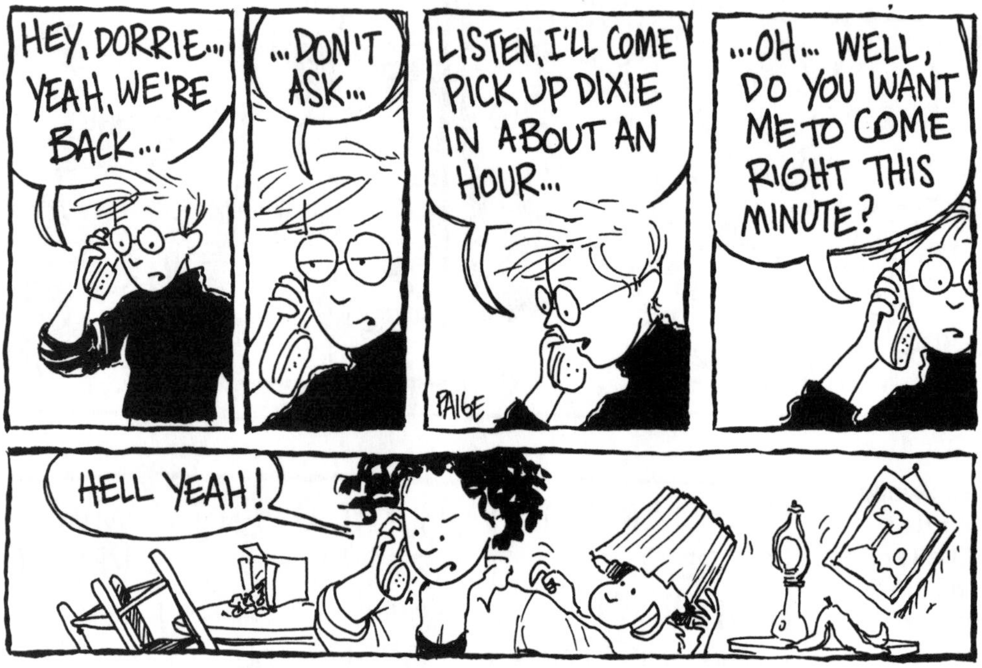
HEY, DORRIE... YEAH, WE'RE BACK...
...DON'T ASK...
LISTEN, I'LL COME PICK UP DIXIE IN ABOUT AN HOUR...
PAIGE
...OH... WELL, DO YOU WANT ME TO COME RIGHT THIS MINUTE?
HELL YEAH!

Since Ethan is having to cope with an arm in a cast, Jane offers to pick up his ex-girlfriend, turned chimp. Dorrie was unlucky enough to get to pet sit... maybe that's not the best way to put it... but you know what we mean... moments later, Jane arrives to rescue Dorrie...

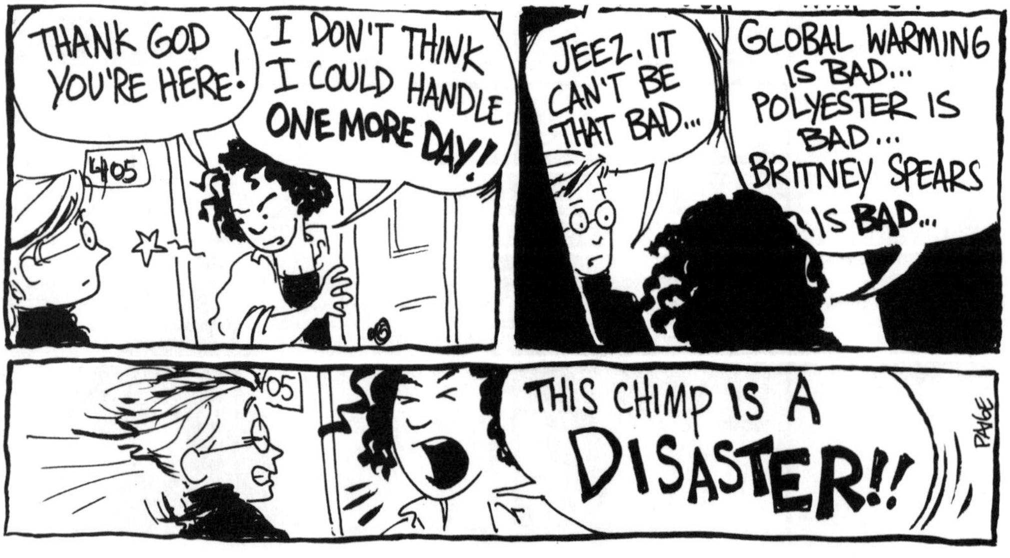
THANK GOD YOU'RE HERE!
I DON'T THINK I COULD HANDLE ONE MORE DAY!
405
JEEZ, IT CAN'T BE THAT BAD...
GLOBAL WARMING IS BAD... POLYESTER IS BAD... BRITNEY SPEARS IS BAD...
THIS CHIMP IS A DISASTER!!
PAIGE

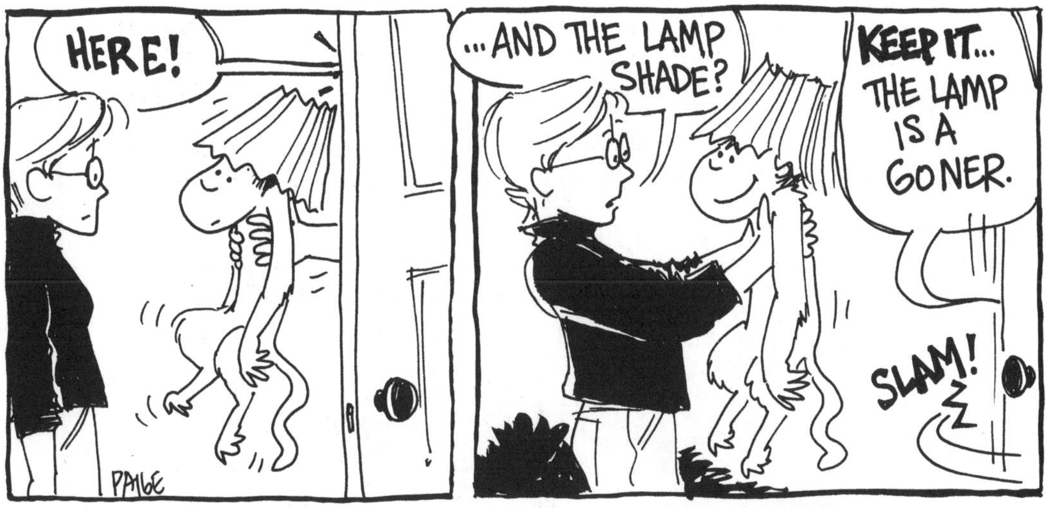
HERE!
PAIGE
...AND THE LAMP SHADE?
KEEP IT... THE LAMP IS A GONER.
SLAM!

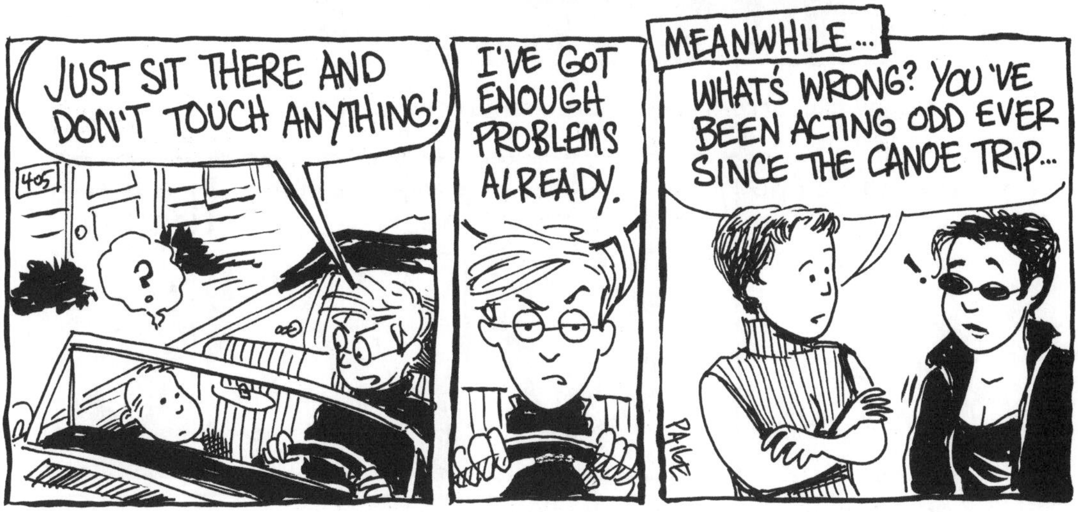
JUST SIT THERE AND DON'T TOUCH ANYTHING!
405
?
I'VE GOT ENOUGH PROBLEMS ALREADY.
MEANWHILE...
WHAT'S WRONG? YOU'VE BEEN ACTING ODD EVER SINCE THE CANOE TRIP...
!
PAIGE

Later, back at Jane's...

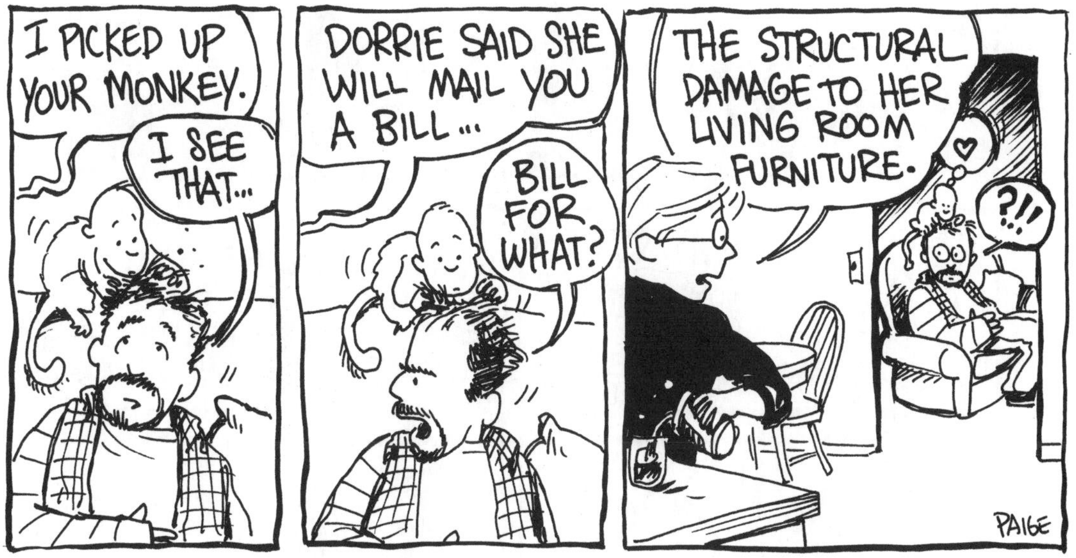
I PICKED UP YOUR MONKEY.
I SEE THAT...
DORRIE SAID SHE WILL MAIL YOU A BILL...
BILL FOR WHAT?
THE STRUCTURAL DAMAGE TO HER LIVING ROOM FURNITURE.
?!!
PAIGE

Later, that same day, Mia decides to confront Dorothy about her recent change of heart...

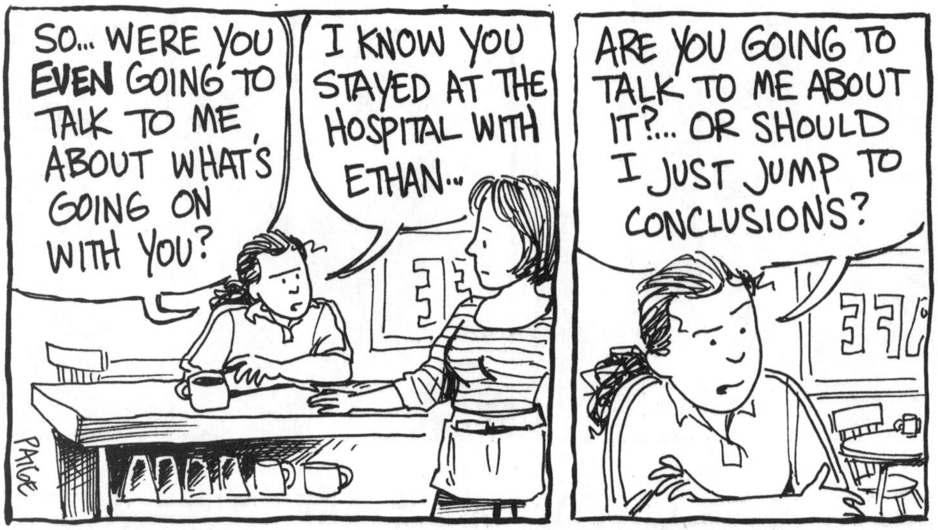
SO... WERE YOU EVEN GOING TO TALK TO ME ABOUT WHAT'S GOING ON WITH YOU?
I KNOW YOU STAYED AT THE HOSPITAL WITH ETHAN...
PAIGE
ARE YOU GOING TO TALK TO ME ABOUT IT?... OR SHOULD I JUST JUMP TO CONCLUSIONS?

Meanwhile, across town, more drama comes to light...

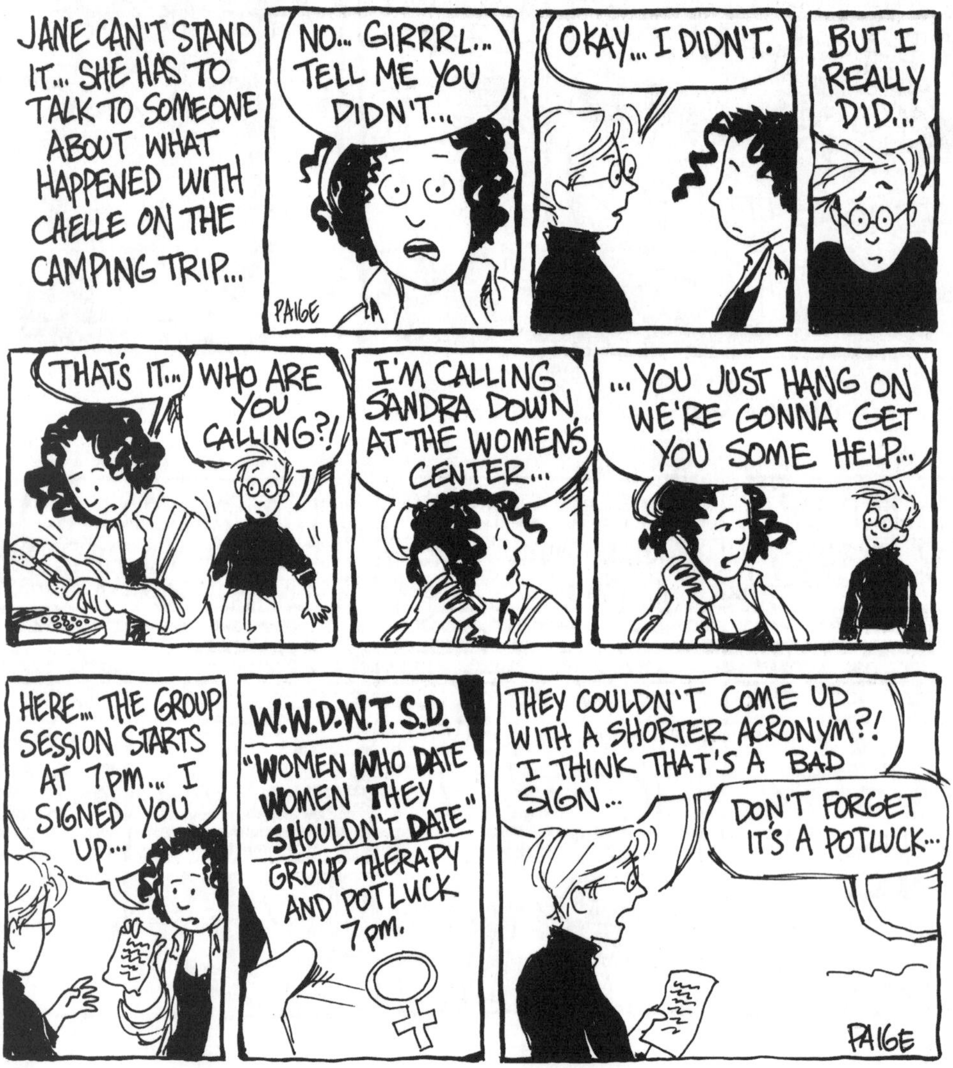
JANE CAN'T STAND IT... SHE HAS TO TALK TO SOMEONE ABOUT WHAT HAPPENED WITH CAELLE ON THE CAMPING TRIP...
NO... GIRRRL... TELL ME YOU DIDN'T...
PAIGE
OKAY... I DIDN'T.
BUT I REALLY DID...
THAT'S IT...
WHO ARE YOU CALLING?!
I'M CALLING SANDRA DOWN AT THE WOMEN'S CENTER...
...YOU JUST HANG ON WE'RE GONNA GET YOU SOME HELP...
HERE... THE GROUP SESSION STARTS AT 7pm... I SIGNED YOU UP...
W.W.D.W.T.S.D.
"WOMEN WHO DATE WOMEN THEY SHOULDN'T DATE"
GROUP THERAPY AND POTLUCK 7pm.
THEY COULDN'T COME UP WITH A SHORTER ACRONYM?! I THINK THAT'S A BAD SIGN...
DON'T FORGET IT'S A POTLUCK...
PAIGE

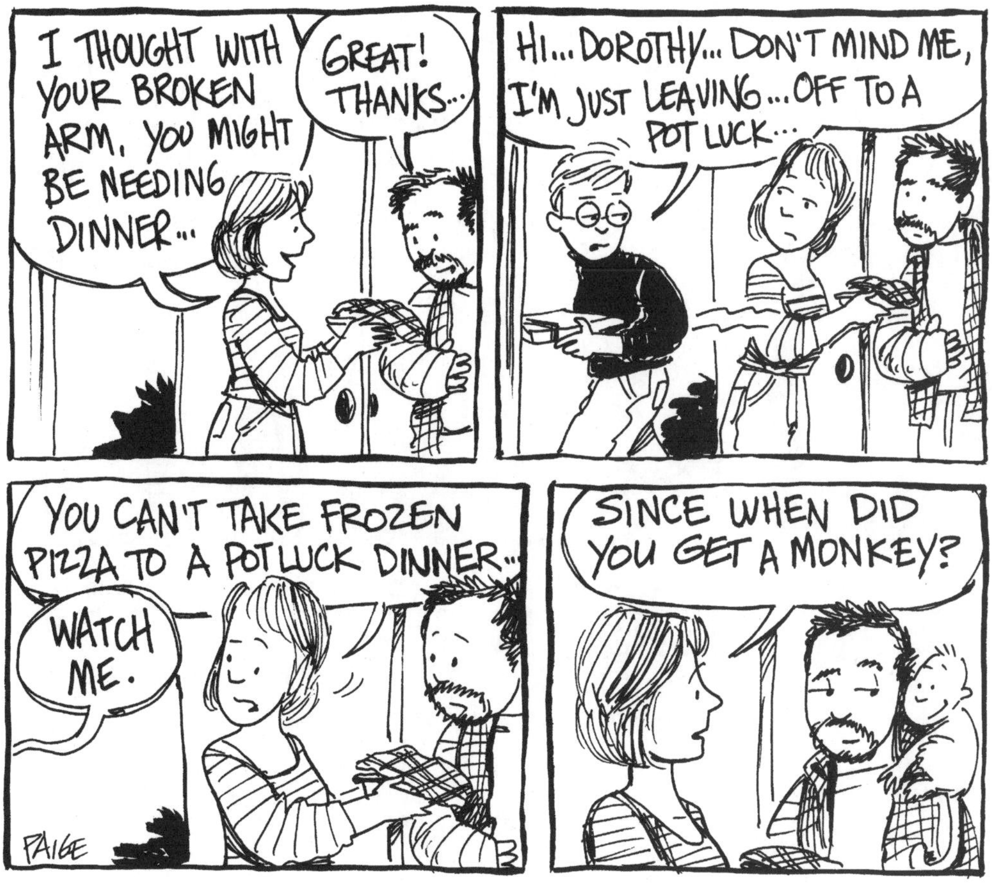
I THOUGHT WITH YOUR BROKEN ARM, YOU MIGHT BE NEEDING DINNER...
GREAT! THANKS...
HI... DOROTHY... DON'T MIND ME, I'M JUST LEAVING... OFF TO A POT LUCK...
YOU CAN'T TAKE FROZEN PIZZA TO A POT LUCK DINNER...
WATCH ME.
PAIGE
SINCE WHEN DID YOU GET A MONKEY?

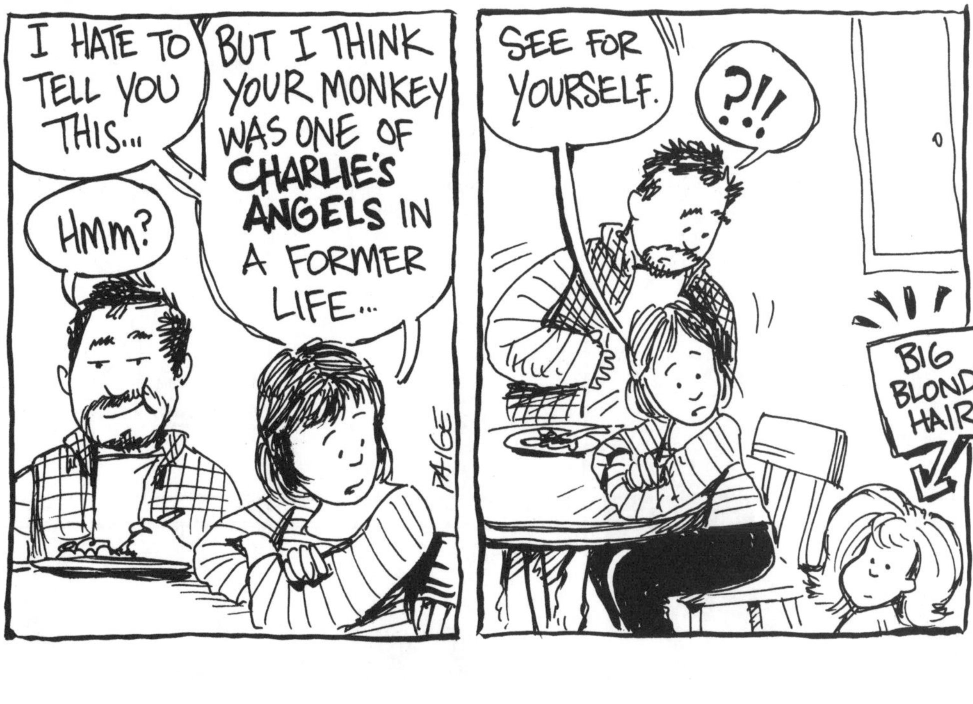
I HATE TO TELL YOU THIS...
BUT I THINK YOUR MONKEY WAS ONE OF CHARLIE'S ANGELS IN A FORMER LIFE...
Hmm?
PAIGE
SEE FOR YOURSELF.
?!!
BIG BLONDE HAIR!!

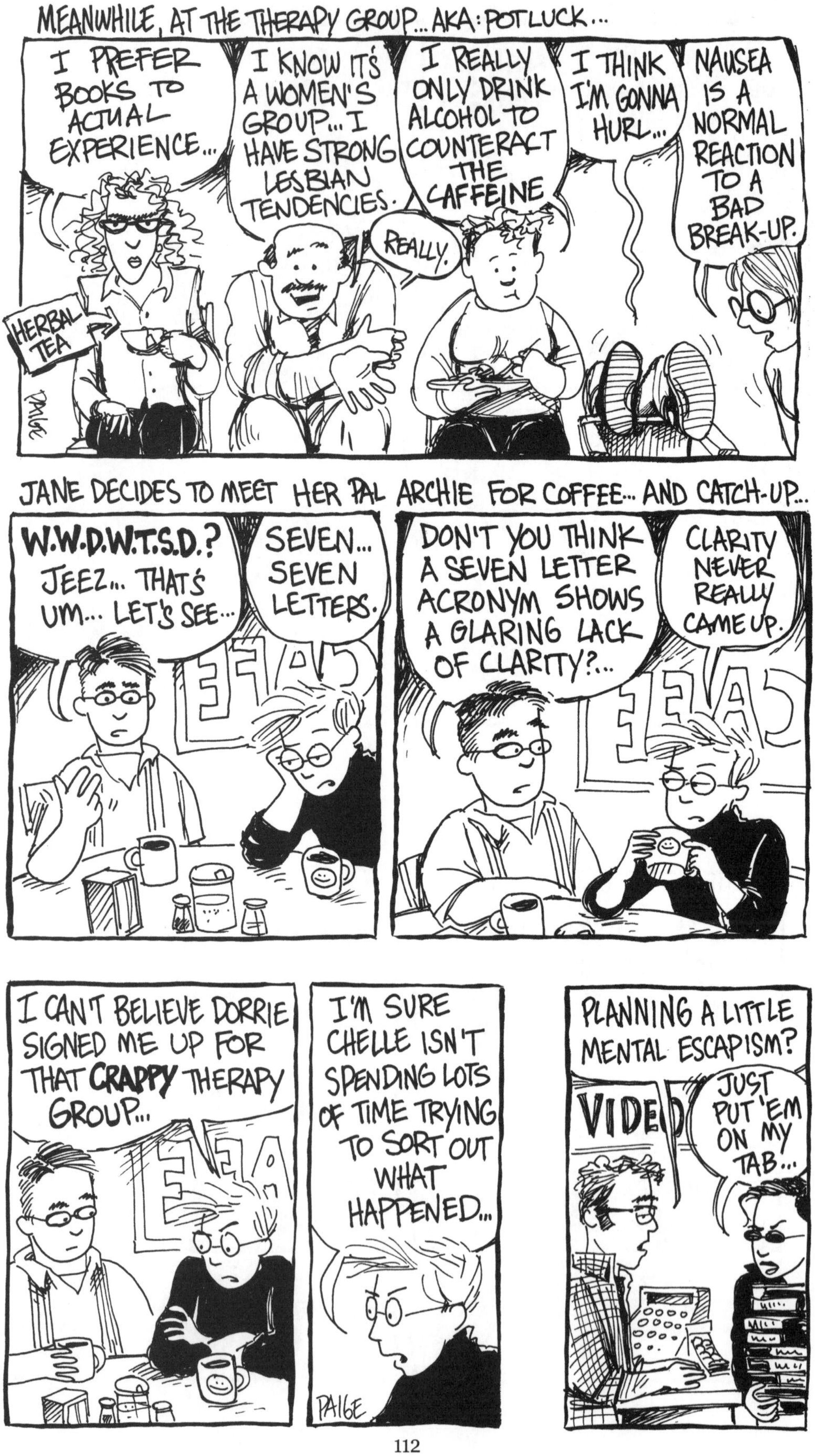
MEANWHILE, AT THE THERAPY GROUP... AKA: POTLUCK...
I PREFER BOOKS TO ACTUAL EXPERIENCE...
HERBAL TEA
I KNOW IT'S A WOMEN'S GROUP... I HAVE STRONG LESBIAN TENDENCIES.
REALLY.
I REALLY ONLY DRINK ALCOHOL TO COUNTERACT THE CAFFEINE
I THINK I'M GONNA HURL...
NAUSEA IS A NORMAL REACTION TO A BAD BREAK-UP.
PAIGE
JANE DECIDES TO MEET HER PAL ARCHIE FOR COFFEE... AND CATCH-UP...
W.W.D.W.T.S.D.? JEEZ... THAT'S UM... LET'S SEE...
SEVEN... SEVEN LETTERS.
DON'T YOU THINK A SEVEN LETTER ACRONYM SHOWS A GLARING LACK OF CLARITY?...
CLARITY NEVER REALLY CAME UP.
I CAN'T BELIEVE DORRIE SIGNED ME UP FOR THAT CRAPPY THERAPY GROUP...
I'M SURE CHELLE ISN'T SPENDING LOTS OF TIME TRYING TO SORT OUT WHAT HAPPENED...
PAIGE
PLANNING A LITTLE MENTAL ESCAPISM?
VIDE
JUST PUT 'EM ON MY TAB...

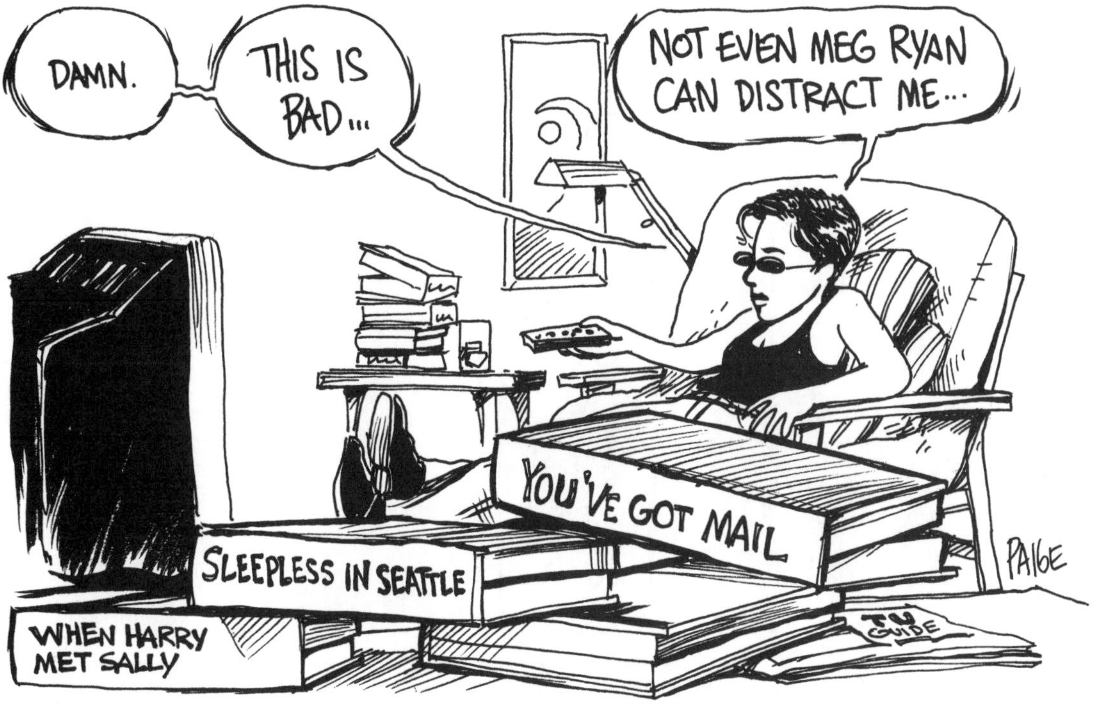
DAMN.
THIS IS BAD...
NOT EVEN MEG RYAN CAN DISTRACT ME...
YOU'VE GOT MAIL
SLEEPLESS IN SEATTLE
WHEN HARRY MET SALLY
TV GUIDE
PAIGE

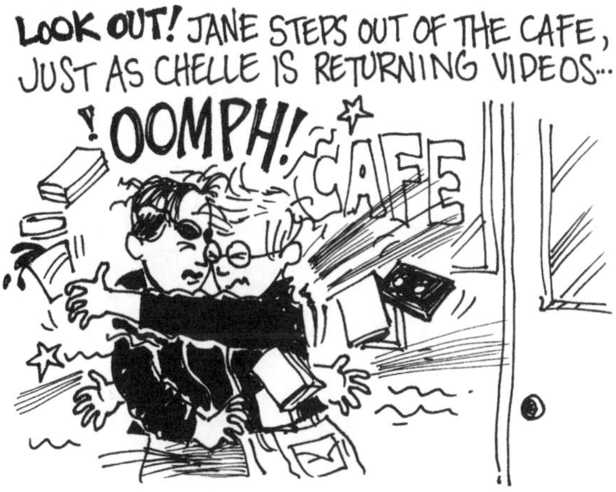
LOOK OUT! JANE STEPS OUT OF THE CAFE, JUST AS CHELLE IS RETURNING VIDEOS...
!OOMPH!
CAFE

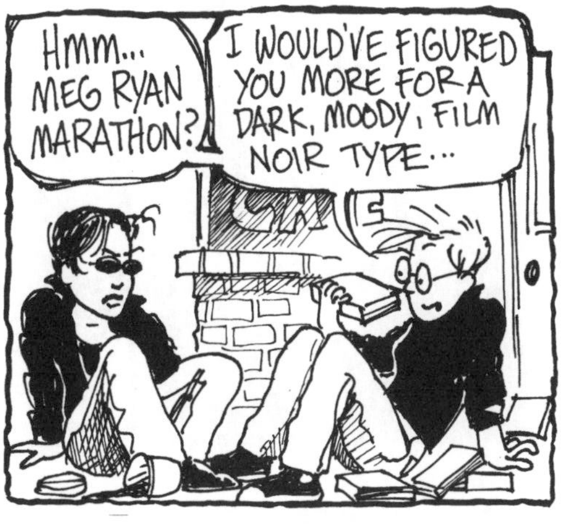
Hmm... MEG RYAN MARATHON?
I WOULD'VE FIGURED YOU MORE FOR A DARK, MOODY, FILM NOIR TYPE...

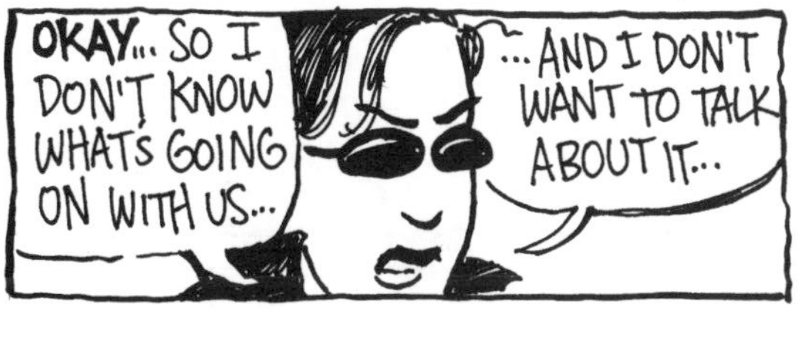
OKAY... SO I DON'T KNOW WHATS GOING ON WITH US...
...AND I DON'T WANT TO TALK ABOUT IT...

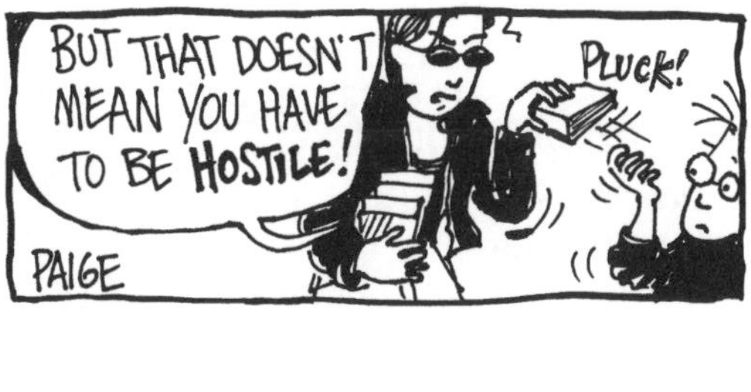
BUT THAT DOESN'T MEAN YOU HAVE TO BE HOSTILE!
PLUCK!
PAIGE

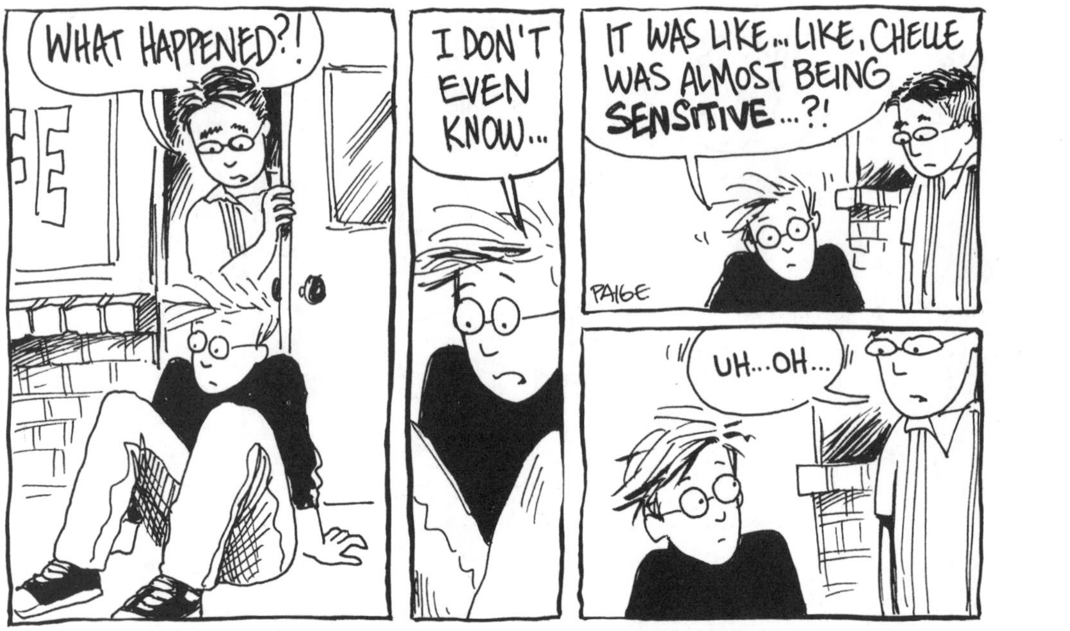
WHAT HAPPENED?!
I DON'T EVEN KNOW...
IT WAS LIKE... LIKE, CHELLE WAS ALMOST BEING **SENSITIVE**...?!
PAIGE
UH...OH...

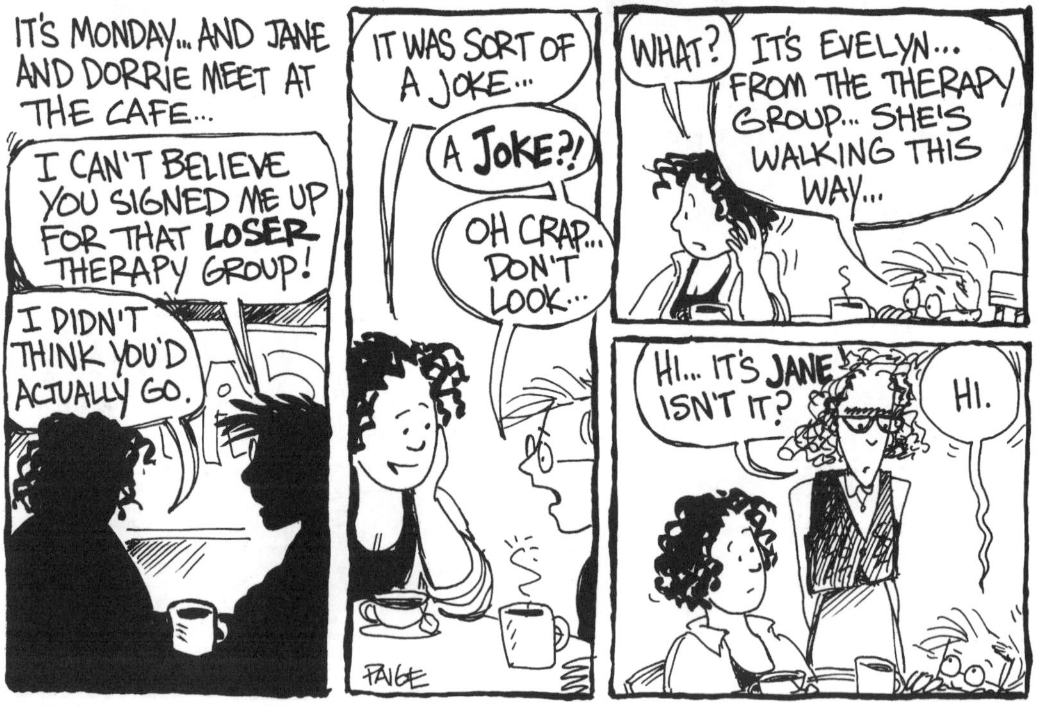
IT'S MONDAY... AND JANE AND DORRIE MEET AT THE CAFE...
I CAN'T BELIEVE YOU SIGNED ME UP FOR THAT **LOSER** THERAPY GROUP!
I DIDN'T THINK YOU'D ACTUALLY GO.
IT WAS SORT OF A JOKE...
A **JOKE**?!
OH CRAP... DON'T LOOK...
PAIGE
WHAT?
IT'S EVELYN... FROM THE THERAPY GROUP... SHE'S WALKING THIS WAY...
HI... IT'S **JANE** ISN'T IT?
HI.

True to form, Jane can't seem to escape uncomfortable social meetings. She's forced to samll talk with Evelyn for at least three minutes... just long enough for a spark to generate for Dorrie... Can you say "speed dating?"

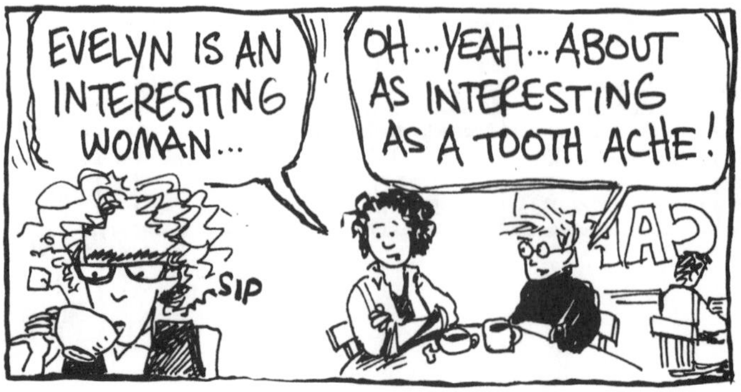
EVELYN IS AN INTERESTING WOMAN...
OH...YEAH...ABOUT AS INTERESTING AS A TOOTH ACHE!
SIP

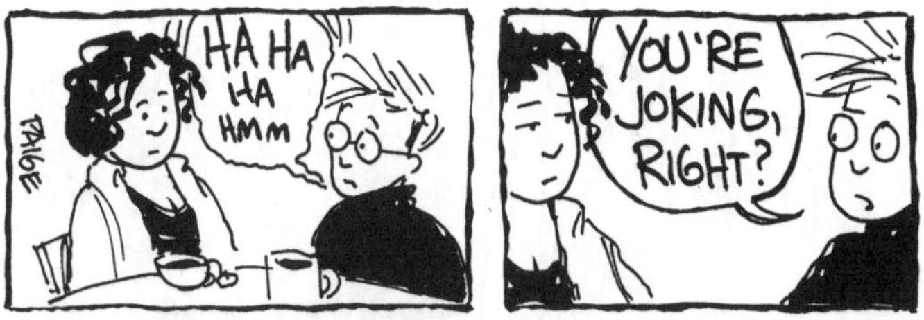
PAIGE
HA HA HA HMM
YOU'RE JOKING, RIGHT?

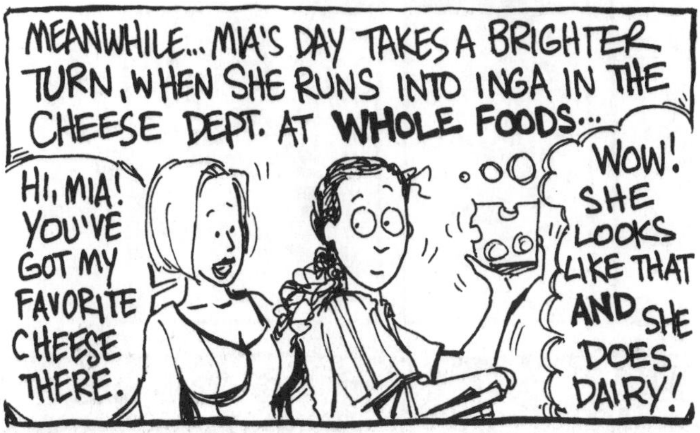
MEANWHILE... MIA'S DAY TAKES A BRIGHTER TURN, WHEN SHE RUNS INTO INGA IN THE CHEESE DEPT. AT WHOLE FOODS...
HI, MIA! YOU'VE GOT MY FAVORITE CHEESE THERE.
WOW! SHE LOOKS LIKE THAT AND SHE DOES DAIRY!

Remember Inga? She's who got Mia into so much trouble with Dorothy on the canoe trip. How did all that start anyway? Who is Inga? How about a little flash-back?...

It all started because Dorothy talked Mia into a mud bath at a spa... only Mia wasn't into the whole group nudity factor...

Flashback... roll tape!

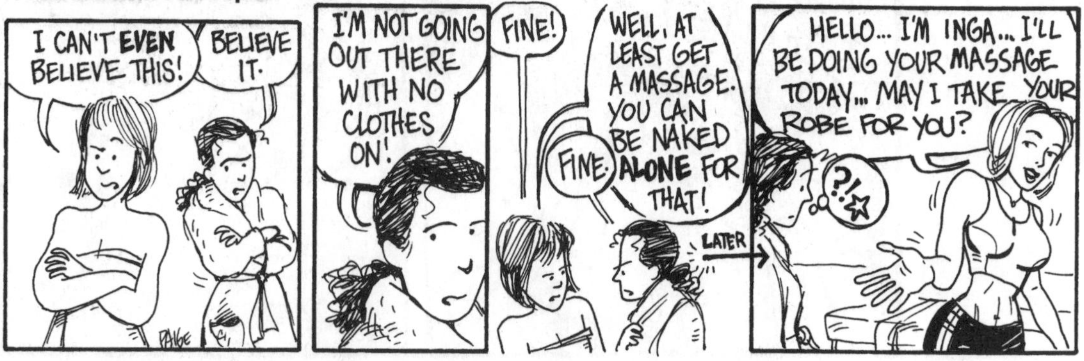
I CAN'T EVEN BELIEVE THIS!
BELIEVE IT.
PAIGE
I'M NOT GOING OUT THERE WITH NO CLOTHES ON!
FINE!
WELL, AT LEAST GET A MASSAGE. YOU CAN BE NAKED ALONE FOR THAT!
FINE.
LATER
HELLO... I'M INGA... I'LL BE DOING YOUR MASSAGE TODAY... MAY I TAKE YOUR ROBE FOR YOU?
?!☆

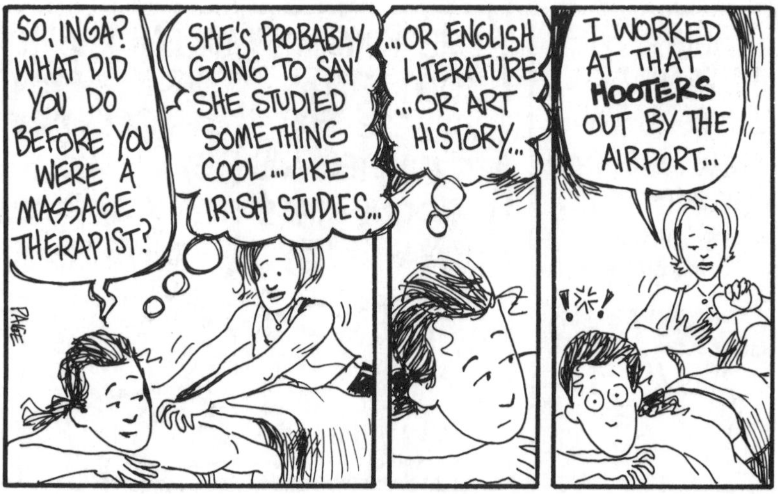
SO, INGA? WHAT DID YOU DO BEFORE YOU WERE A MASSAGE THERAPIST?
SHE'S PROBABLY GOING TO SAY SHE STUDIED SOMETHING COOL... LIKE IRISH STUDIES...
...OR ENGLISH LITERATURE ...OR ART HISTORY...
PAIGE
I WORKED AT THAT HOOTERS OUT BY THE AIRPORT...
!※!

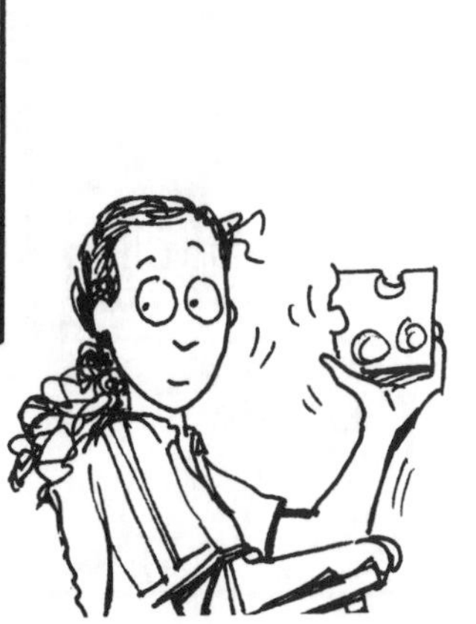

We now rejoin our story, where Mia's romantic imagination has caught up with her at the cheese counter...

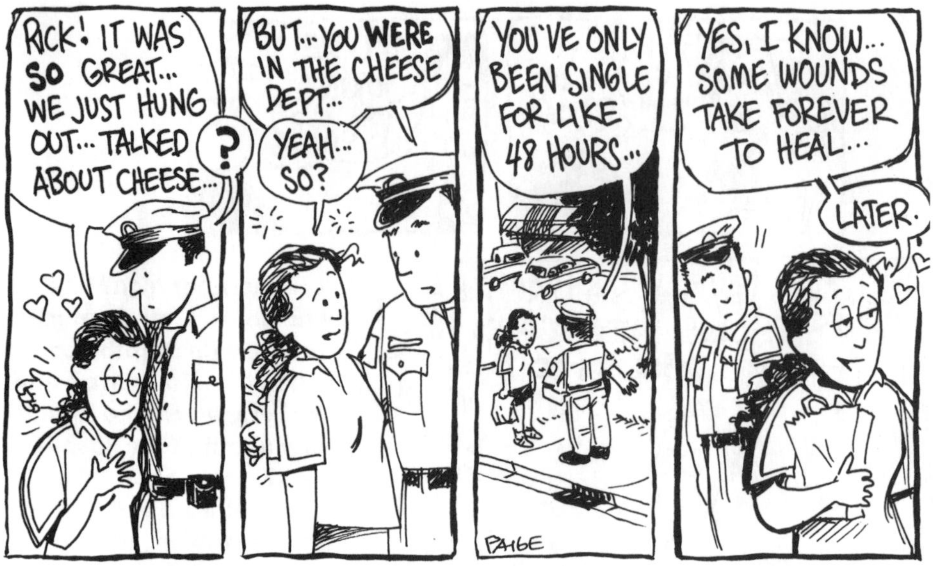
RICK! IT WAS SO GREAT... WE JUST HUNG OUT... TALKED ABOUT CHEESE...
?
BUT... YOU WERE IN THE CHEESE DEPT...
YEAH... SO?
YOU'VE ONLY BEEN SINGLE FOR LIKE 48 HOURS...
PAIGE
YES, I KNOW... SOME WOUNDS TAKE FOREVER TO HEAL...
LATER.

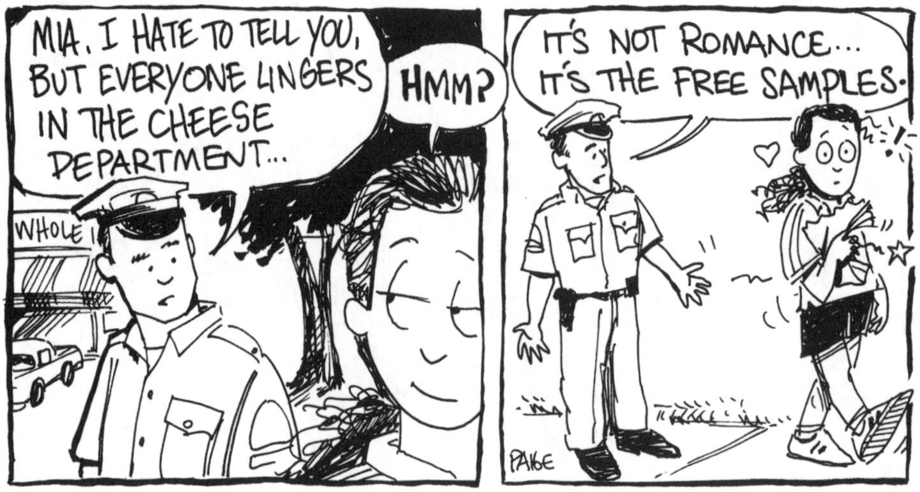
MIA, I HATE TO TELL YOU, BUT EVERYONE LINGERS IN THE CHEESE DEPARTMENT...
HMM?
WHOLE
IT'S NOT ROMANCE... IT'S THE FREE SAMPLES.
PAIGE

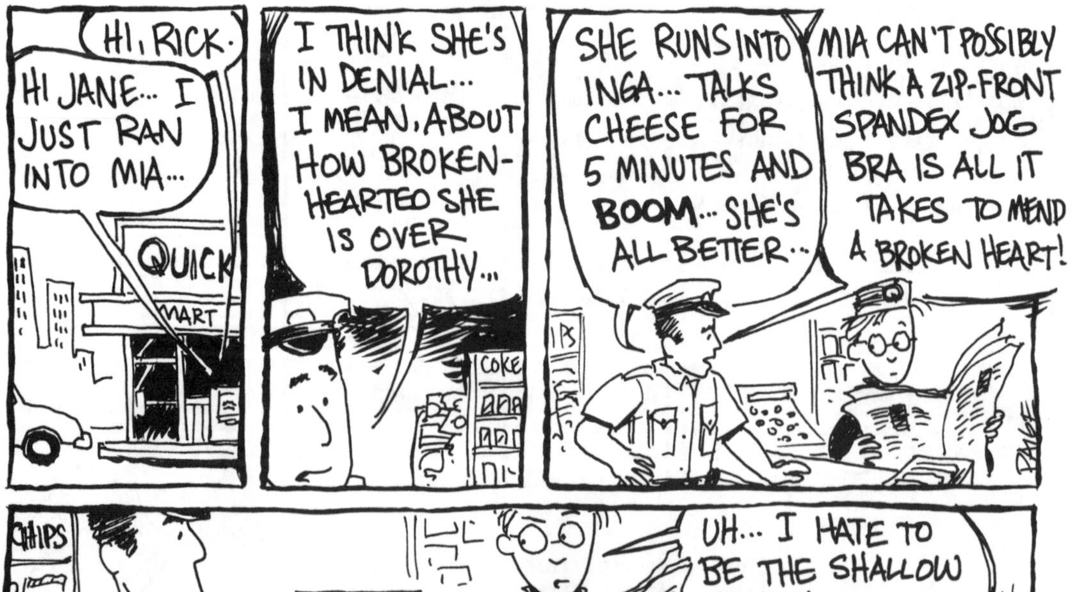
HI, RICK.
HI JANE... I JUST RAN INTO MIA...
QUICK
MART
I THINK SHE'S IN DENIAL... I MEAN, ABOUT HOW BROKEN-HEARTED SHE IS OVER DOROTHY...
COKE
SHE RUNS INTO INGA... TALKS CHEESE FOR 5 MINUTES AND BOOM... SHE'S ALL BETTER...
MIA CAN'T POSSIBLY THINK A ZIP-FRONT SPANDEX JOG BRA IS ALL IT TAKES TO MEND A BROKEN HEART!

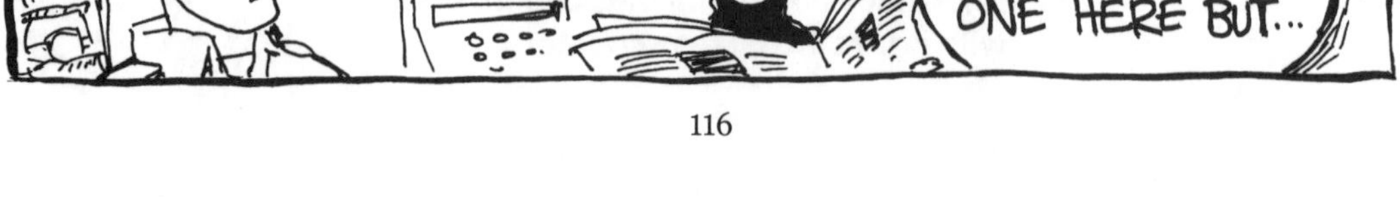
CHIPS
UH... I HATE TO BE THE SHALLOW ONE HERE BUT...

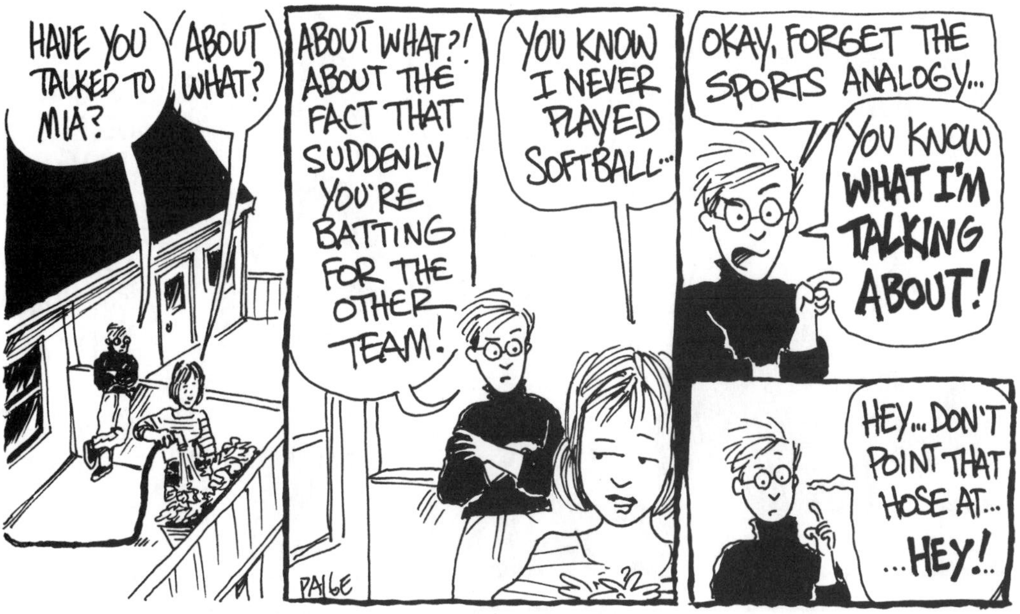
HAVE YOU TALKED TO MIA?
ABOUT WHAT?
ABOUT WHAT?! ABOUT THE FACT THAT SUDDENLY YOU'RE BATTING FOR THE OTHER TEAM!
YOU KNOW I NEVER PLAYED SOFTBALL...
OKAY, FORGET THE SPORTS ANALOGY...
YOU KNOW **WHAT I'M TALKING ABOUT!**
HEY... DON'T POINT THAT HOSE AT...
...**HEY!**..
PAIGE

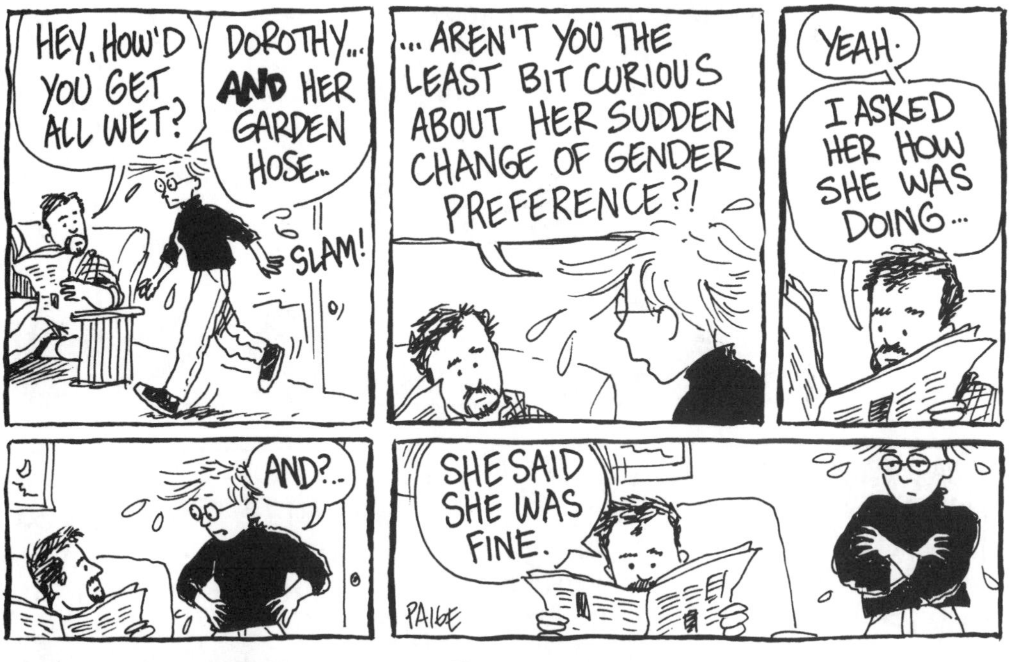
HEY, HOW'D YOU GET ALL WET?
DOROTHY... **AND** HER GARDEN HOSE..
SLAM!
... AREN'T YOU THE LEAST BIT CURIOUS ABOUT HER SUDDEN CHANGE OF GENDER PREFERENCE?!
YEAH.
I ASKED HER HOW SHE WAS DOING...
AND?..
SHE SAID SHE WAS FINE.
PAIGE

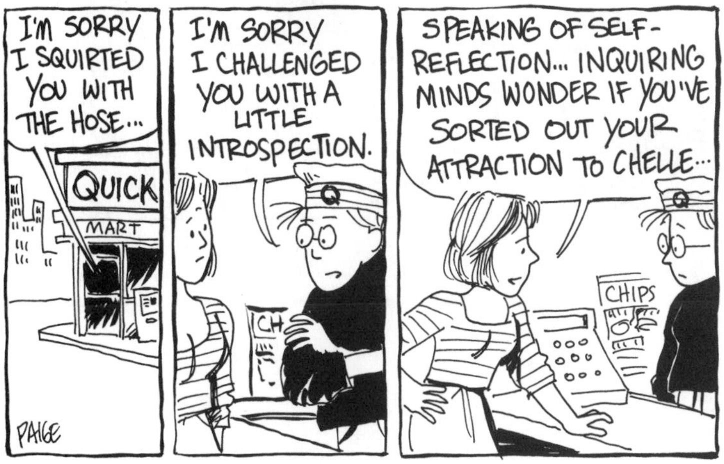
I'M SORRY I SQUIRTED YOU WITH THE HOSE...
QUICK
MART
PAIGE
I'M SORRY I CHALLENGED YOU WITH A LITTLE INTROSPECTION.
SPEAKING OF SELF-REFLECTION... INQUIRING MINDS WONDER IF YOU'VE SORTED OUT YOUR ATTRACTION TO CHELLE...
CHIPS

Luckily, Jane was at the end of her shift... so she didn't have to self-reflect in public... she could save it for the drive home...

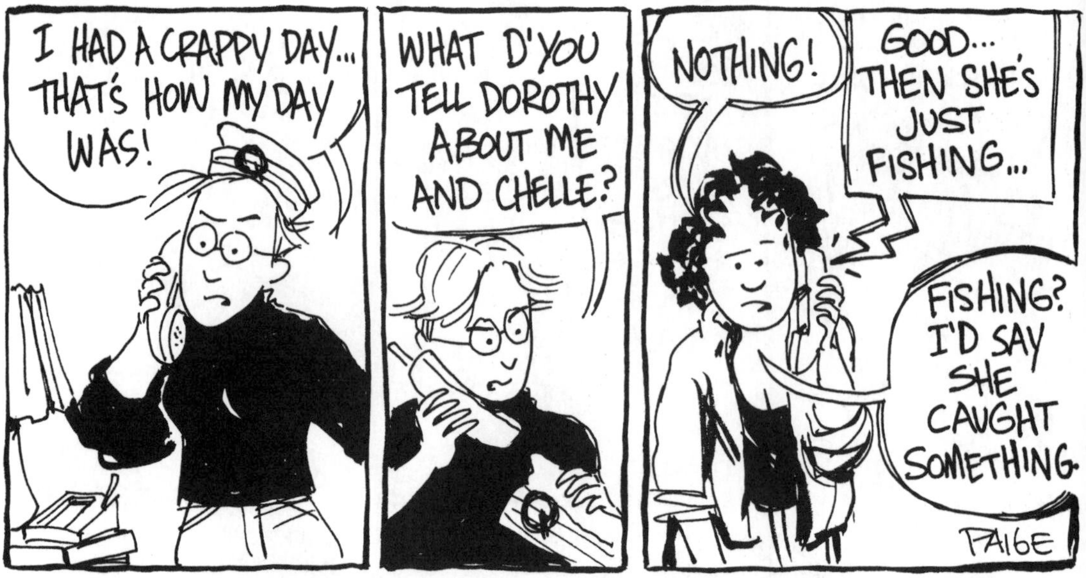
I HAD A CRAPPY DAY... THAT'S HOW MY DAY WAS!
WHAT D'YOU TELL DOROTHY ABOUT ME AND CHELLE?
NOTHING!
GOOD... THEN SHE'S JUST FISHING...
FISHING? I'D SAY SHE CAUGHT SOMETHING.
PAIGE

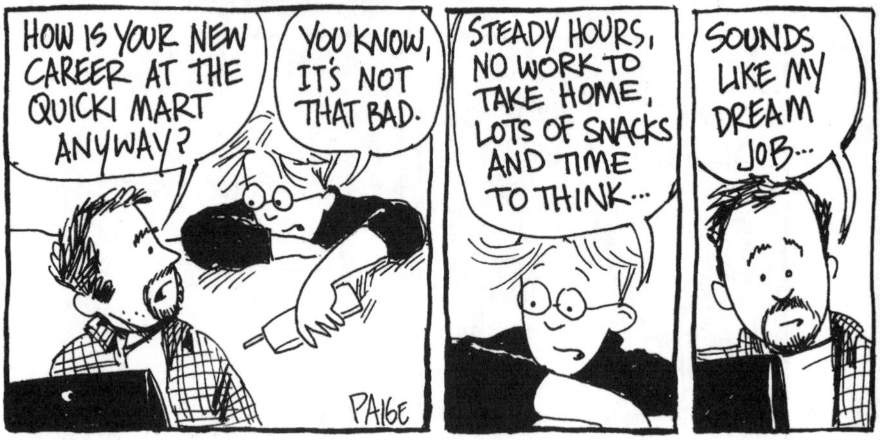
HOW IS YOUR NEW CAREER AT THE QUICKI MART ANYWAY?
YOU KNOW, IT'S NOT THAT BAD.
PAIGE
STEADY HOURS, NO WORK TO TAKE HOME, LOTS OF SNACKS AND TIME TO THINK...
SOUNDS LIKE MY DREAM JOB...

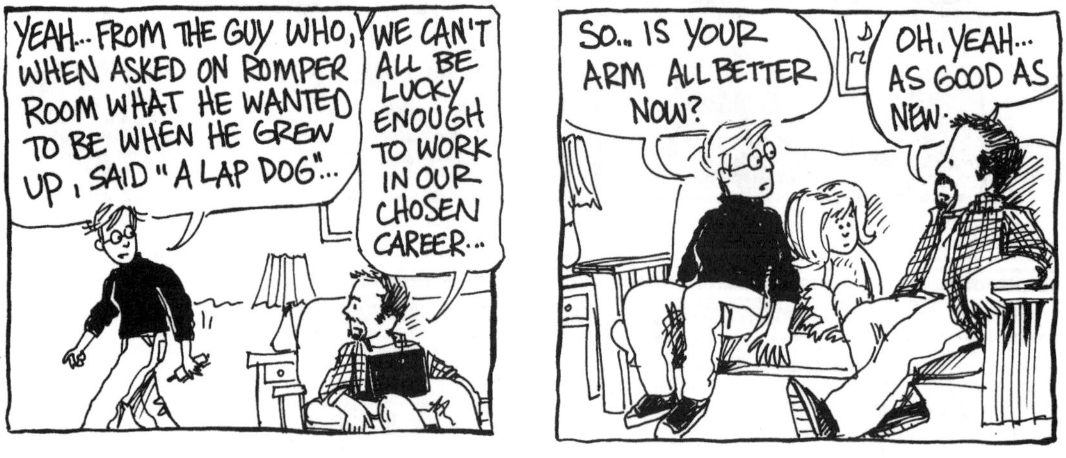
YEAH... FROM THE GUY WHO, WHEN ASKED ON ROMPER ROOM WHAT HE WANTED TO BE WHEN HE GREW UP, SAID "A LAP DOG"...
WE CAN'T ALL BE LUCKY ENOUGH TO WORK IN OUR CHOSEN CAREER...
SO... IS YOUR ARM ALL BETTER NOW?
OH, YEAH... AS GOOD AS NEW.

GOOD... THEN MAYBE YOU CAN FIND A FEW MOMENTS TO TAKE OUT THE TRASH...
OH, SURE... SORRY, I HADN'T NOTICED.
PAIGE

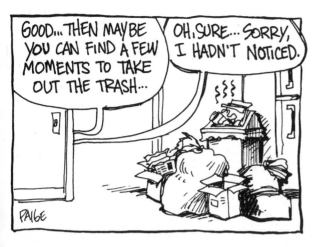

Back in the newsroom, Chelle contemplates her next steps...

I CAN GET PAST THIS... I'M BIGGER THAN THIS...
WHAT I NEED IS A DISTRACTION...
HEY, STRANGER.
I WAS WONDERING IF YOU HAD PLANS FOR LATER...
PAIGE

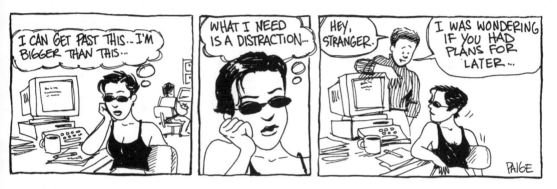

The next night, at the cafe, Jane is having her usual latte with Dorrie, when Evelyn walks in.

"Since when did this become her hang out?!" said Jane, annoyed... "Scoot down in your chair... maybe she won't see us."

"If you were really my friend, you'd get her number for me," Dorrie taunted, trying to guilt Jane into action.

"No..." Jane quipped, "If I was really your friend, I wouldn't."

"Trust me on this," added Jane, "She's one of those feminist theorist types... She'll just rail on neo-feminism and sip organic herbal tea..."

DO YOU EVEN KNOW WHAT NEO-FEMINISM IS?
OKAY... HERE IT COMES ..THE LECTURE ABOUT HOW I NEVER PAID ATTENTION IN MY WOMEN'S STUDIES CLASSES...

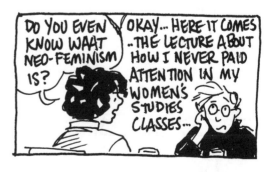

Jane loses the argument and slinks off to do Dorrie's bidding...

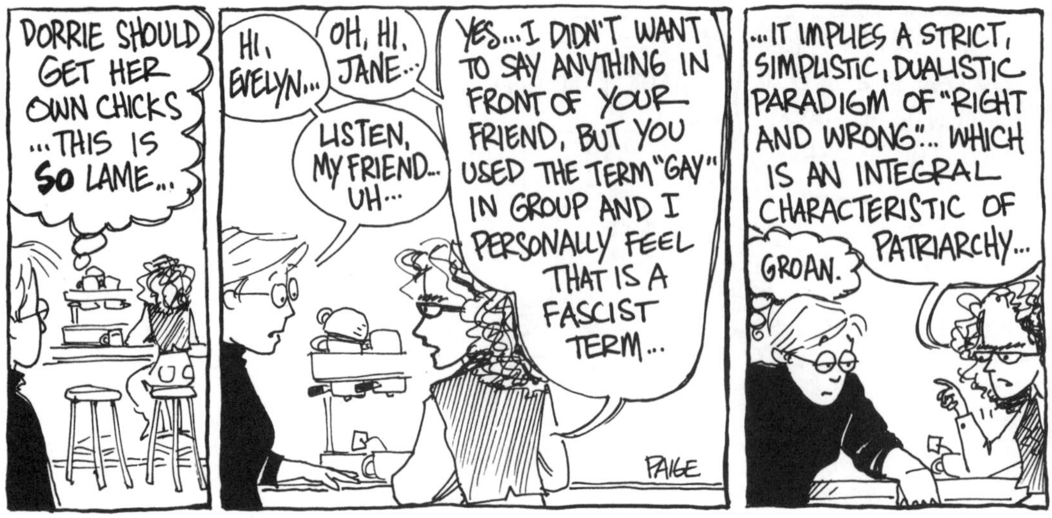
DORRIE SHOULD GET HER OWN CHICKS ...THIS IS SO LAME...
HI, EVELYN...
OH, HI, JANE...
LISTEN, MY FRIEND... UH...
YES...I DIDN'T WANT TO SAY ANYTHING IN FRONT OF YOUR FRIEND, BUT YOU USED THE TERM "GAY" IN GROUP AND I PERSONALLY FEEL THAT IS A FASCIST TERM...
PAIGE
...IT IMPLIES A STRICT, SIMPLISTIC, DUALISTIC PARADIGM OF "RIGHT AND WRONG"... WHICH IS AN INTEGRAL CHARACTERISTIC OF PATRIARCHY...
GROAN.

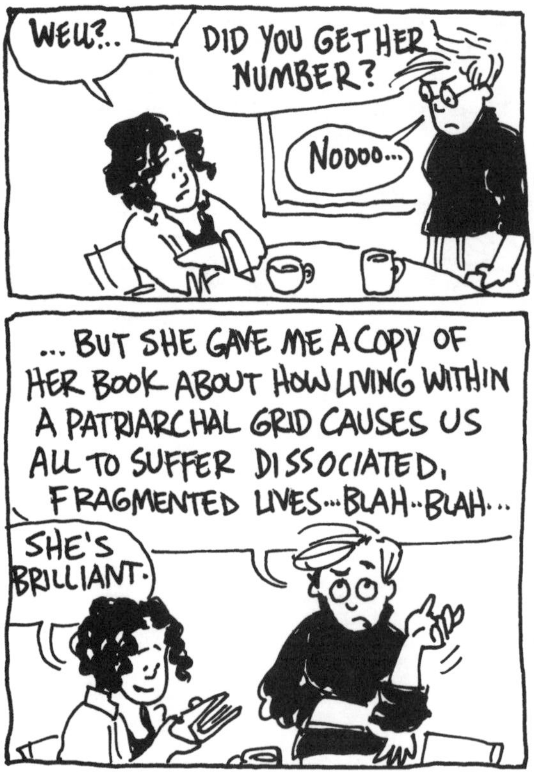
WELL?..
DID YOU GET HER NUMBER?
NOOOO...
... BUT SHE GAVE ME A COPY OF HER BOOK ABOUT HOW LIVING WITHIN A PATRIARCHAL GRID CAUSES US ALL TO SUFFER DISSOCIATED, FRAGMENTED LIVES...BLAH..BLAH...
SHE'S BRILLIANT.

Dorrie discovered later that Evelyn had written her name inside the book... with a little sleuthing, Dorrie was able to get Evelyn's number herself. A few days later, Jane bumped into Dorrie and got the update...

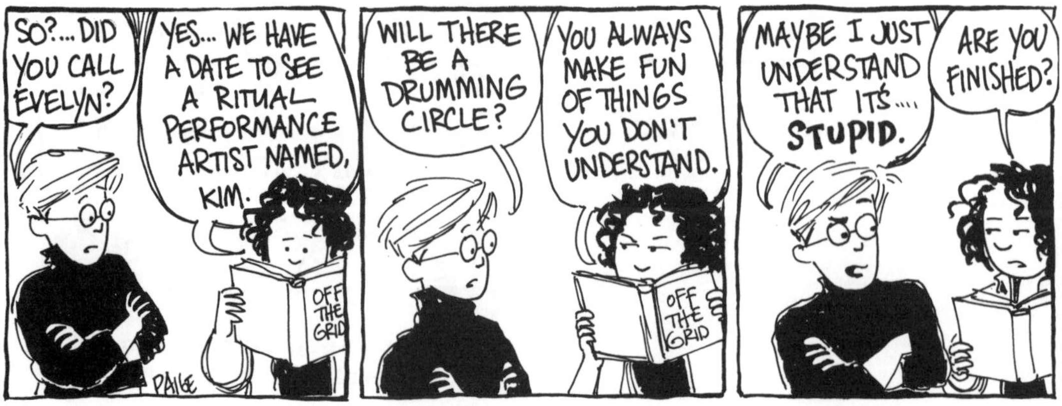
SO?... DID YOU CALL EVELYN?
YES... WE HAVE A DATE TO SEE A RITUAL PERFORMANCE ARTIST NAMED, KIM.
OFF THE GRID
PAIGE
WILL THERE BE A DRUMMING CIRCLE?
YOU ALWAYS MAKE FUN OF THINGS YOU DON'T UNDERSTAND.
OFF THE GRID
MAYBE I JUST UNDERSTAND THAT IT'S.... STUPID.
ARE YOU FINISHED?

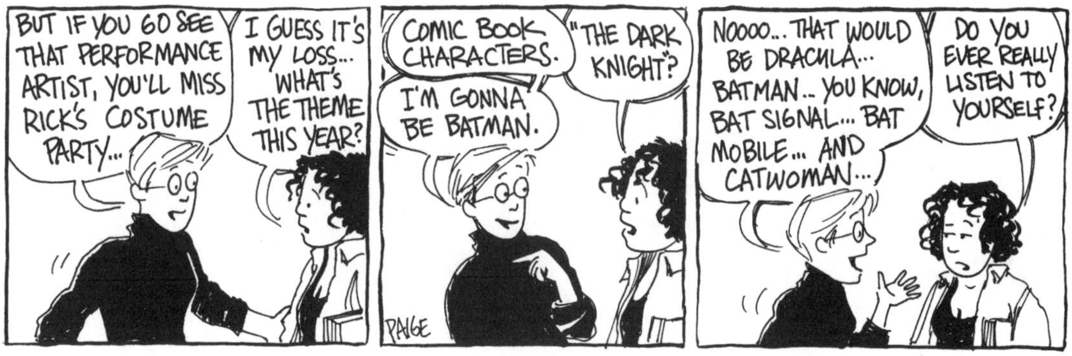
BUT IF YOU GO SEE THAT PERFORMANCE ARTIST, YOU'LL MISS RICK'S COSTUME PARTY...
I GUESS IT'S MY LOSS... WHAT'S THE THEME THIS YEAR?
COMIC BOOK CHARACTERS.
I'M GONNA BE BATMAN.
"THE DARK KNIGHT"?
PAIGE
NOOOO... THAT WOULD BE DRACULA... BATMAN.. YOU KNOW, BAT SIGNAL... BAT MOBILE... AND CATWOMAN...
DO YOU EVER REALLY LISTEN TO YOURSELF?

Needless to say, Dorrie decides to skip Rick's annual costume party extravaganza...

...and Ethan mistakenly agrees to let Jane pick their costumes for the event...

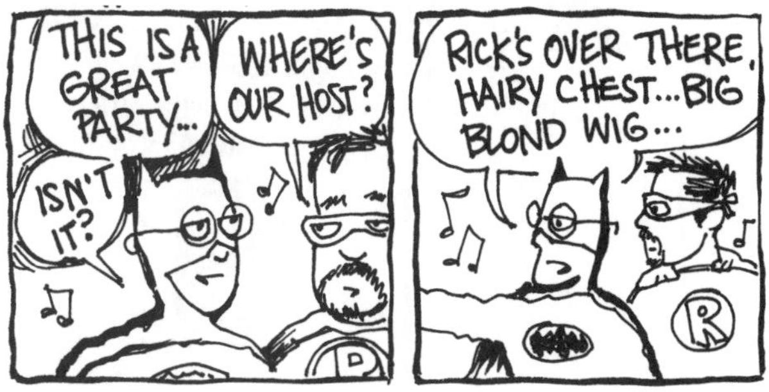
THIS IS A GREAT PARTY...
ISN'T IT?
WHERE'S OUR HOST?
RICK'S OVER THERE, HAIRY CHEST...BIG BLOND WIG...

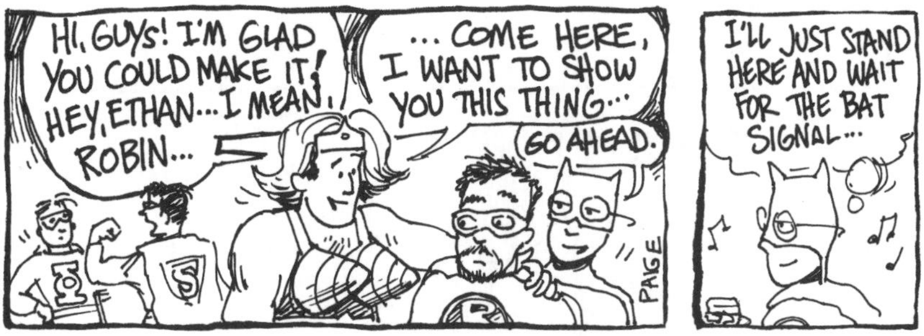
HI, GUYS! I'M GLAD YOU COULD MAKE IT! HEY, ETHAN... I MEAN, ROBIN...
... COME HERE, I WANT TO SHOW YOU THIS THING...
GO AHEAD.
PAIGE
I'LL JUST STAND HERE AND WAIT FOR THE BAT SIGNAL...

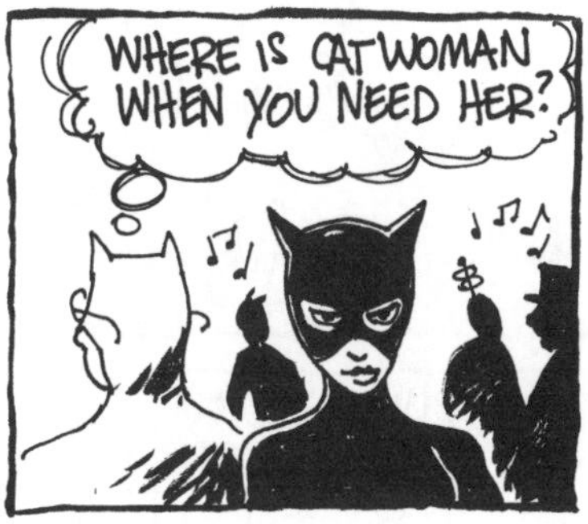
WHERE IS CATWOMAN WHEN YOU NEED HER?

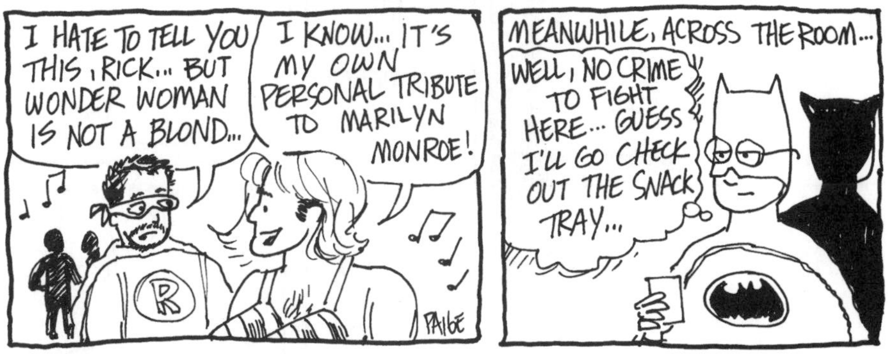
I HATE TO TELL YOU THIS, RICK... BUT WONDER WOMAN IS NOT A BLOND...
I KNOW... IT'S MY OWN PERSONAL TRIBUTE TO MARILYN MONROE!
PAIGE
MEANWHILE, ACROSS THE ROOM...
WELL, NO CRIME TO FIGHT HERE... GUESS I'LL GO CHECK OUT THE SNACK TRAY...

Panel 1: UMPH! / HEY! / BUMP

Panel 2: OH...JEEZ...I'M SO SORRY...I'LL GET YOU ANOTHER DRINK...

Panel 3: CATWOMAN IS SUPPOSED TO TAUNT BATMAN!...NOT THE OTHER WAY AROUND... / CHELLE?!

Panel 4: I KNEW I SHOULDN'T HAVE LET YOU PICK THE COSTUMES!

Panel 5: I WAS ONLY **ROBIN** BECAUSE YOU WANTED TO BE **BATMAN**...NOW ALL THE GUYS THINK I'M A GIRLIE-MAN!

Panel 6: I CAN'T GO THERE WITH YOU RIGHT NOW, ETHAN... I JUST RAN IN-TO CATWOMAN... ...LITERALLY...

Panel 7: "EVEN THE LOSERS GET LUCKY SOMETIMES"...

Panel 8: I DON'T KNOW WHY YOU ARE SO FREAKED OUT ABOUT CHELLE...

Panel 9: YOU KNOW ABOUT CHELLE AND ME?! / **EVERYBODY** KNOWS EXCEPT...

Panel 10: ...SARAH! INTERESTING COSTUME... / I DIDN'T GET THE MEMO...

Panel 11: WHERE'S SARAH? / LOOKING FOR YOU...

Panel 12: WHY ARE YOU HERE WITH SARAH AFTER WHAT HAPPENED BETWEEN **US?**...

Panel 13: ARE YOU **REALLY** INTERESTED IN HER?! / IT WAS SOMETHING TO DO... ...I.. I GUESS I WAS LONELY...

Panel 14: WHAT ARE WE DOING HERE?... / ...LEAVING...

PAIGE

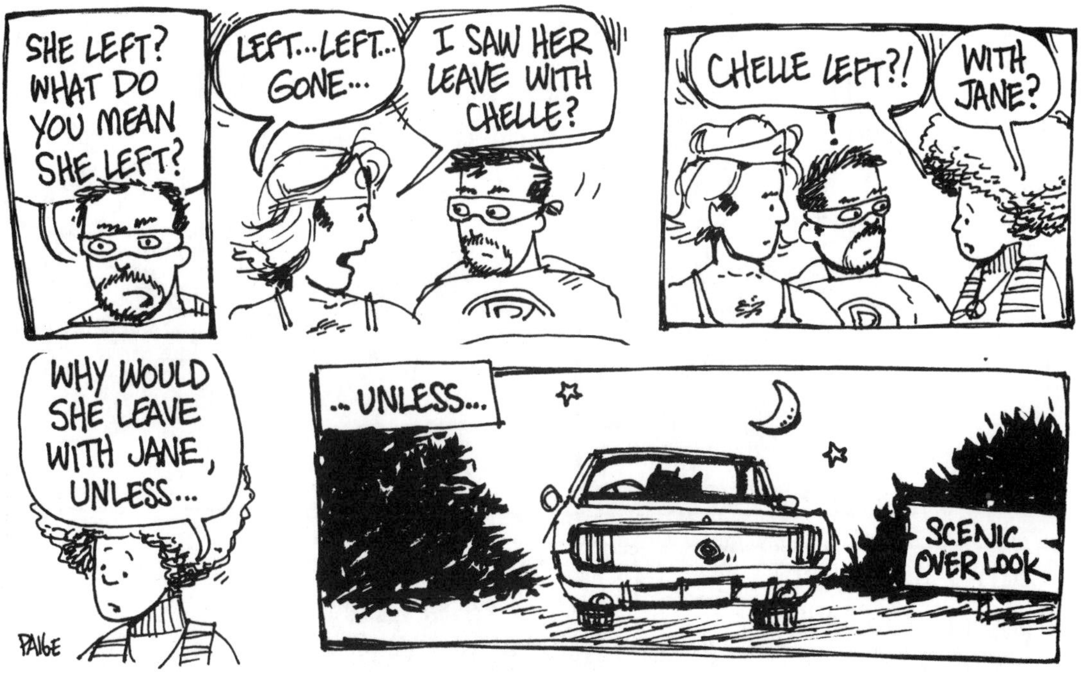
SHE LEFT? WHAT DO YOU MEAN SHE LEFT?
LEFT...LEFT... GONE...
I SAW HER LEAVE WITH CHELLE?
CHELLE LEFT?!
WITH JANE?
!
WHY WOULD SHE LEAVE WITH JANE, UNLESS...
PAIGE
...UNLESS...
SCENIC OVERLOOK

Poor Sarah... Ethan and Rick try to help her find comfort in "comfort food" at an all night diner after the party...

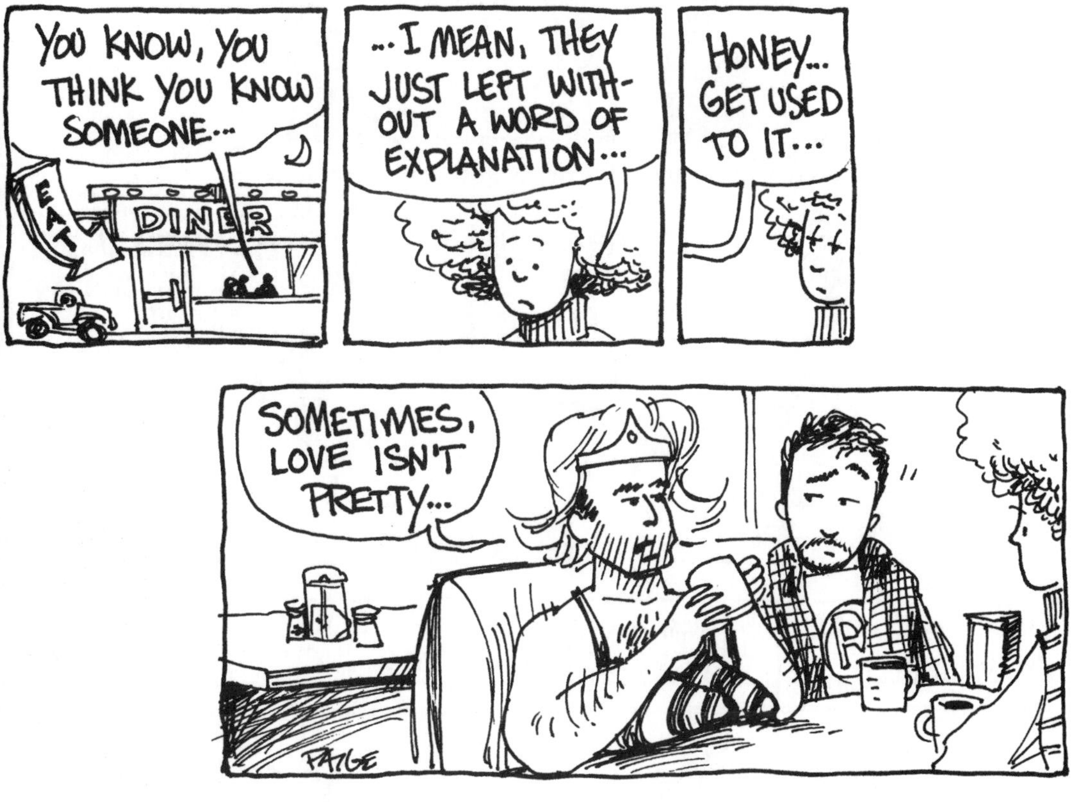
YOU KNOW, YOU THINK YOU KNOW SOMEONE...
EAT
DINER
...I MEAN, THEY JUST LEFT WITH-OUT A WORD OF EXPLANATION...
HONEY... GET USED TO IT...
SOMETIMES, LOVE ISN'T PRETTY...
PAIGE

The next day at work, the hours seem to drag, but...

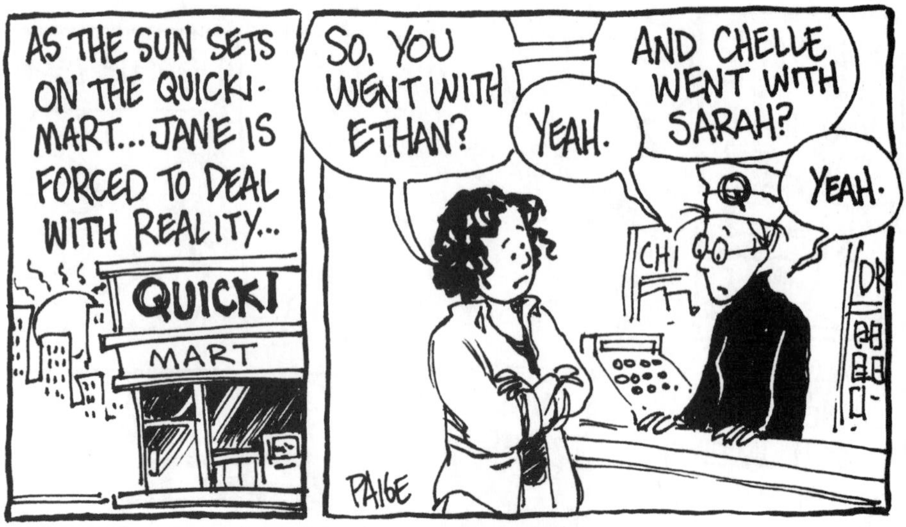
AS THE SUN SETS ON THE QUICKI-MART... JANE IS FORCED TO DEAL WITH REALITY...
QUICKI
MART
SO, YOU WENT WITH ETHAN?
YEAH.
AND CHELLE WENT WITH SARAH?
YEAH.
PAIGE

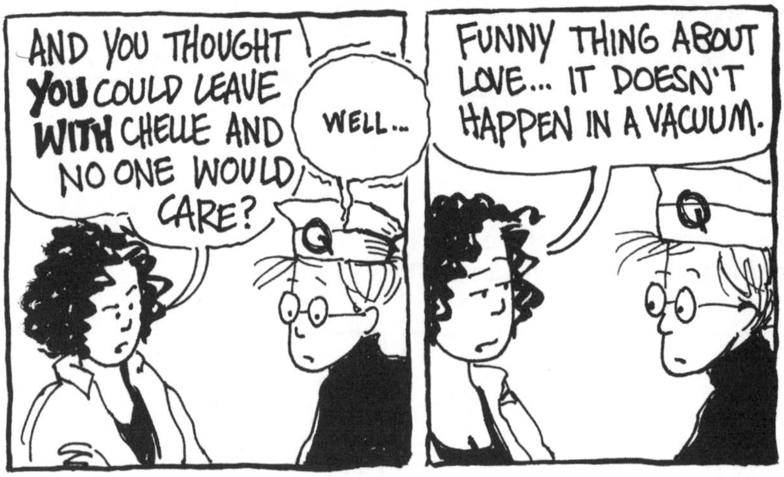
AND YOU THOUGHT YOU COULD LEAVE WITH CHELLE AND NO ONE WOULD CARE?
WELL...
FUNNY THING ABOUT LOVE... IT DOESN'T HAPPEN IN A VACUUM.

Jane leaves work and a bit of introspection finally sets in...

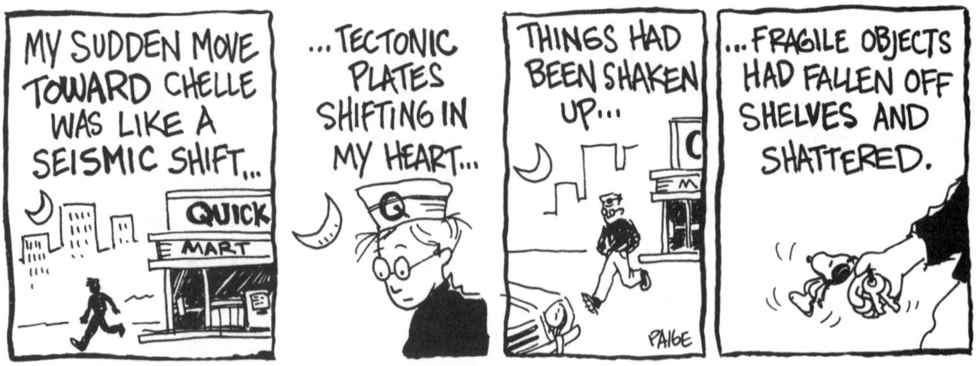
MY SUDDEN MOVE TOWARD CHELLE WAS LIKE A SEISMIC SHIFT...
QUICK
MART
...TECTONIC PLATES SHIFTING IN MY HEART...
THINGS HAD BEEN SHAKEN UP...
PAIGE
...FRAGILE OBJECTS HAD FALLEN OFF SHELVES AND SHATTERED.

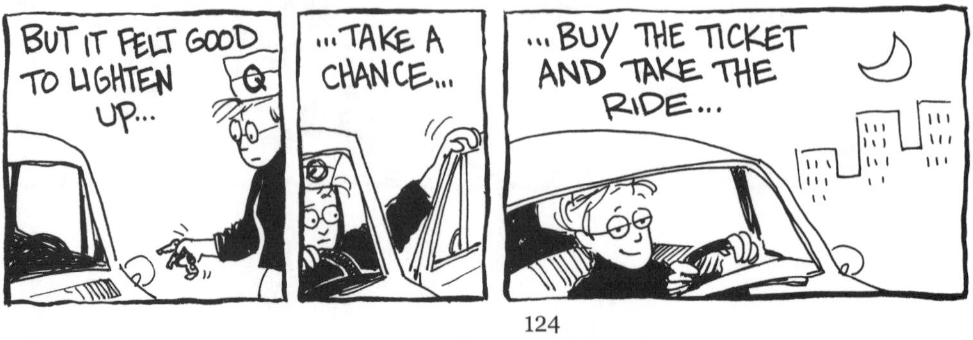
BUT IT FELT GOOD TO LIGHTEN UP...
...TAKE A CHANCE...
...BUY THE TICKET AND TAKE THE RIDE...

... but before she pulls away in her car, she notices a folded scrap of notebook paper...

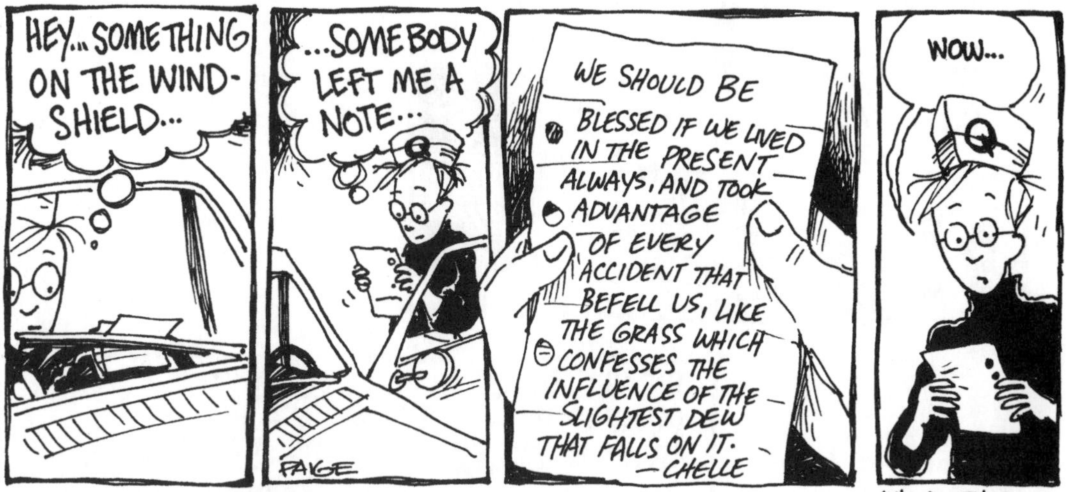
HEY... SOMETHING ON THE WIND-SHIELD...
...SOMEBODY LEFT ME A NOTE...
PAIGE
WE SHOULD BE BLESSED IF WE LIVED IN THE PRESENT ALWAYS, AND TOOK ADVANTAGE OF EVERY ACCIDENT THAT BEFELL US, LIKE THE GRASS WHICH CONFESSES THE INFLUENCE OF THE SLIGHTEST DEW THAT FALLS ON IT. —CHELLE
WOW...

*HENRY THOREAU

Jane sits at the wheel of her car... such a surprising note made her feel a bit light-headed... and all the sensations of that unexpected night together on the river came rushing back... Meanwhile, at the Cafe, Mia bumps into Sarah, finding a little solace in Marcel Proust... who else?!

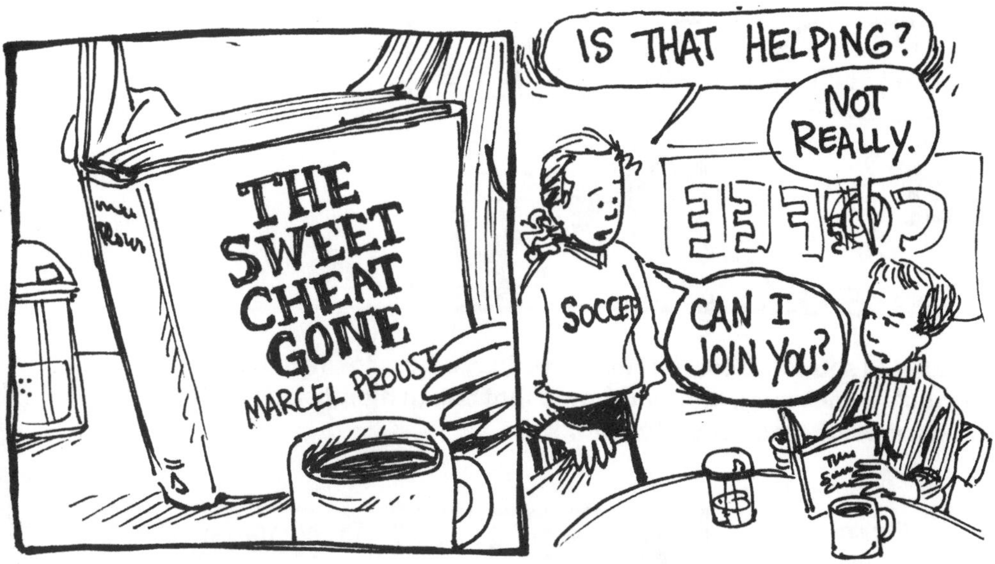
THE SWEET CHEAT GONE
MARCEL PROUST
IS THAT HELPING?
NOT REALLY.
SOCCER
CAN I JOIN YOU?

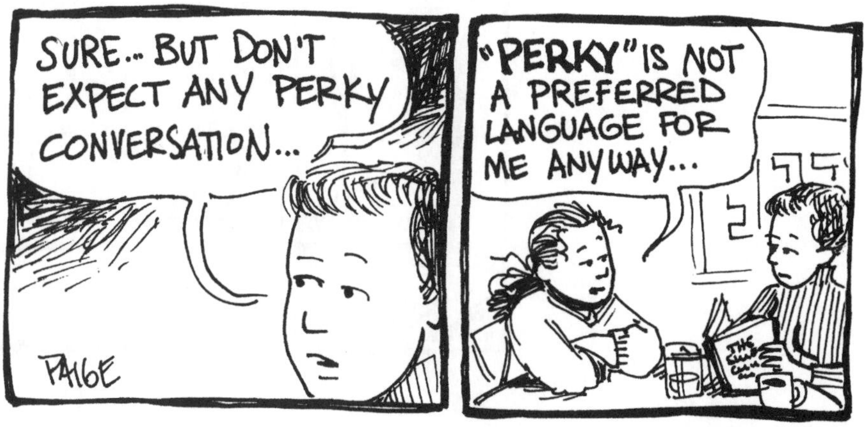
SURE... BUT DON'T EXPECT ANY PERKY CONVERSATION...
PAIGE
"PERKY" IS NOT A PREFERRED LANGUAGE FOR ME ANYWAY...

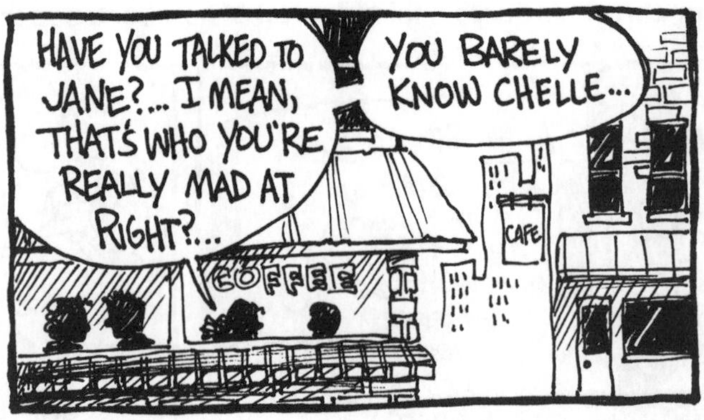
HAVE YOU TALKED TO JANE?... I MEAN, THAT'S WHO YOU'RE REALLY MAD AT RIGHT?...
YOU BARELY KNOW CHELLE...
CAFE
COFFEE

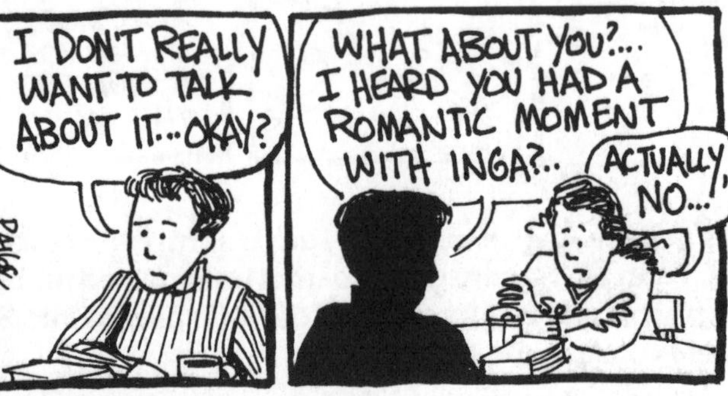
I DON'T REALLY WANT TO TALK ABOUT IT...OKAY?
PAIGE
WHAT ABOUT YOU?... I HEARD YOU HAD A ROMANTIC MOMENT WITH INGA?..
ACTUALLY, NO...

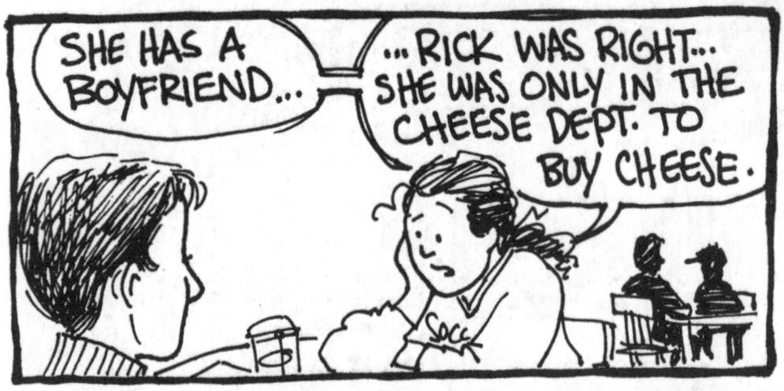
SHE HAS A BOYFRIEND...
...RICK WAS RIGHT... SHE WAS ONLY IN THE CHEESE DEPT. TO BUY CHEESE.

...as troubled souls find comfort in each other, across town, in Jane and Ethan's living room, another drama that began months ago on the flatlands of Oklahoma begins to unfold...

... the chimp who once was...

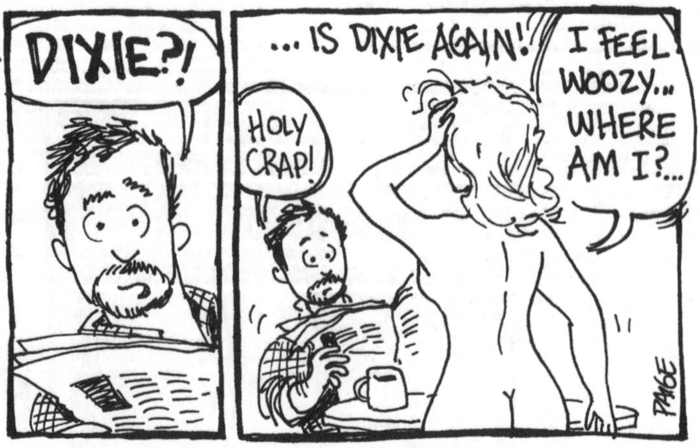
DIXIE?!
... IS DIXIE AGAIN!
I FEEL WOOZY... WHERE AM I?...
HOLY CRAP!
PAIGE

Chapter 6
Chimp striptease

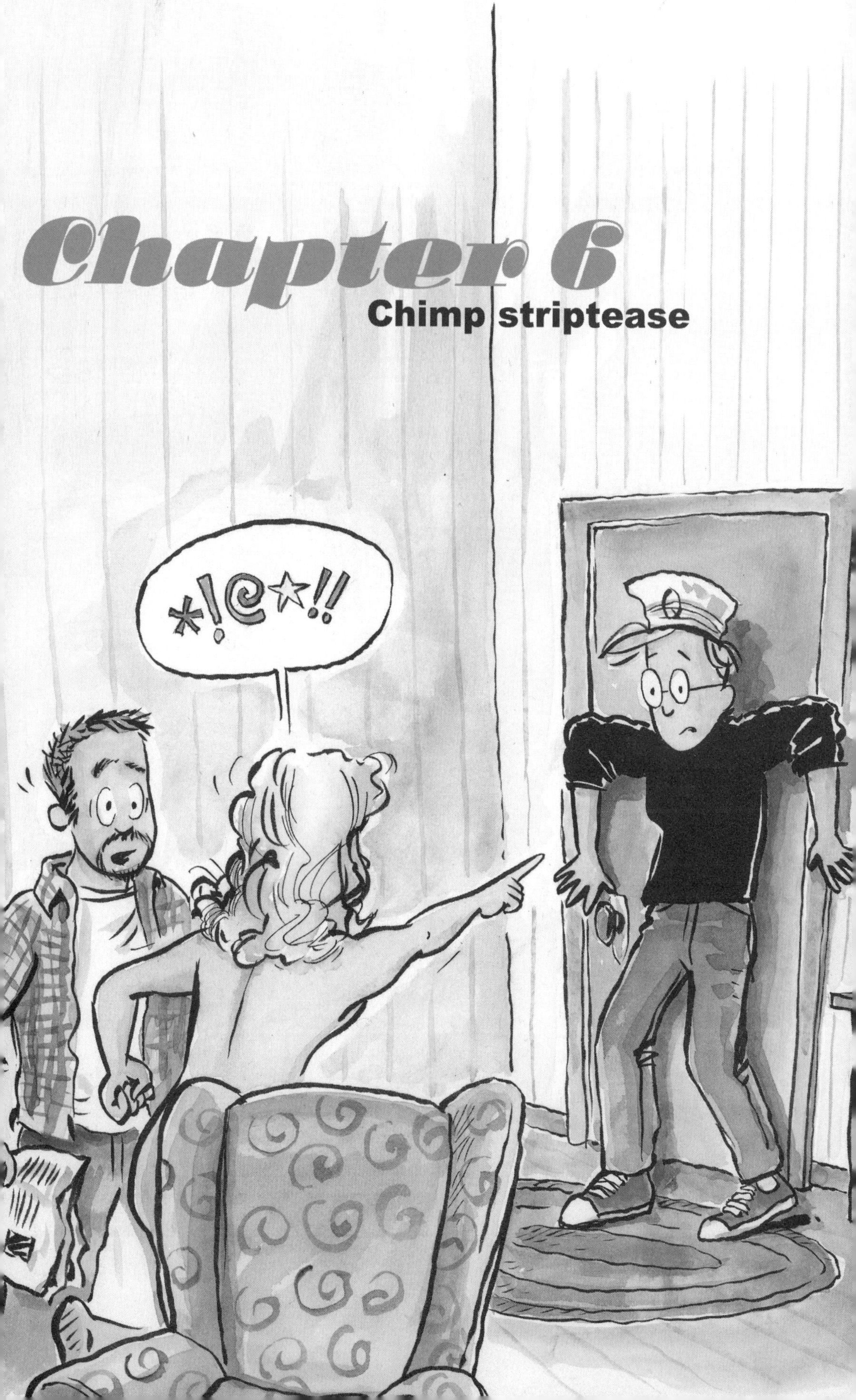
*!@★!!

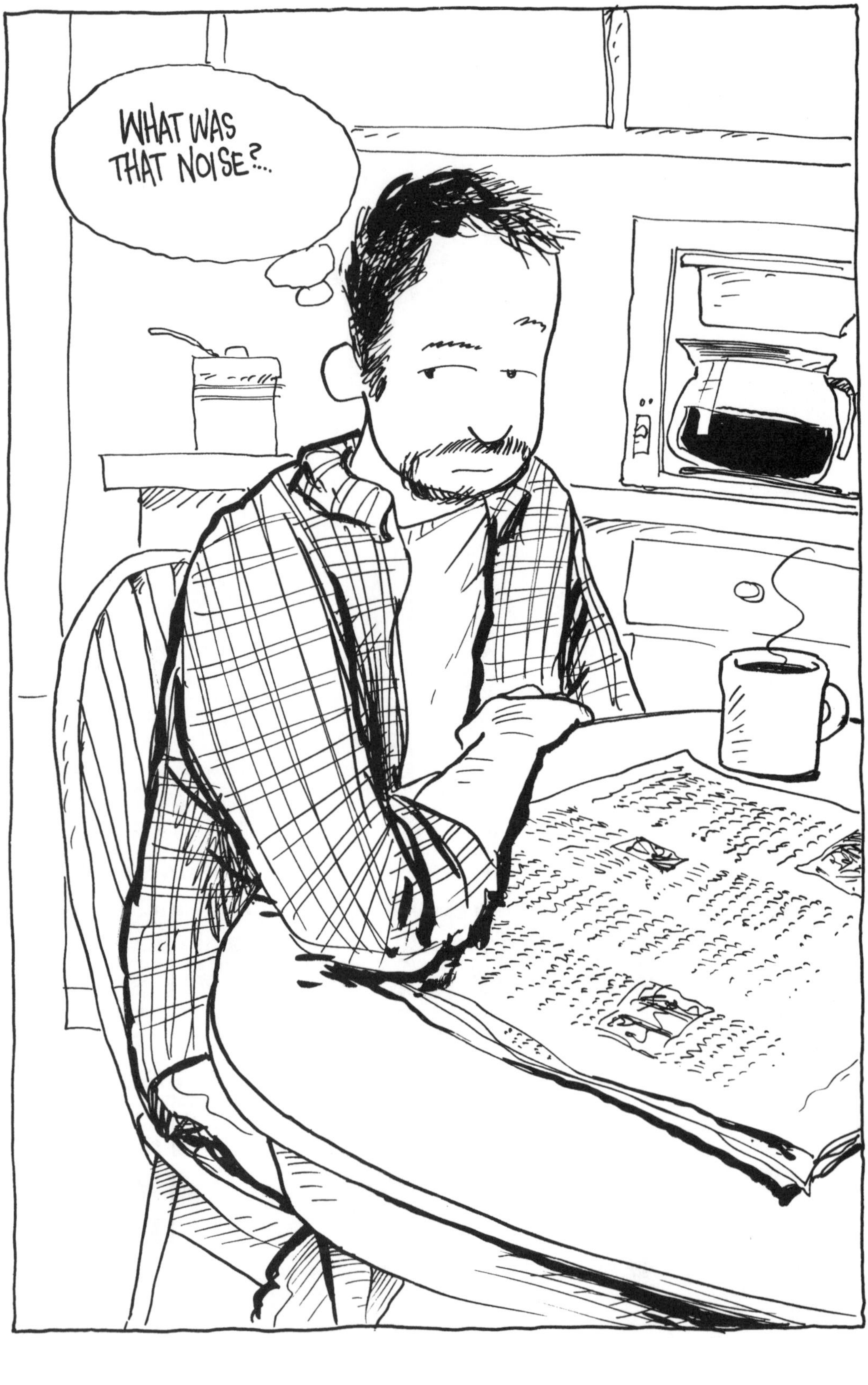
WHAT WAS THAT NOISE?...

While Ethan sips his afternoon coffee in the kitchen, a wonder of chromosomal reformation takes place in the comfort of Jane and Ethan's living room. Dixie returns, wearing nothing more than Chanel No. 5

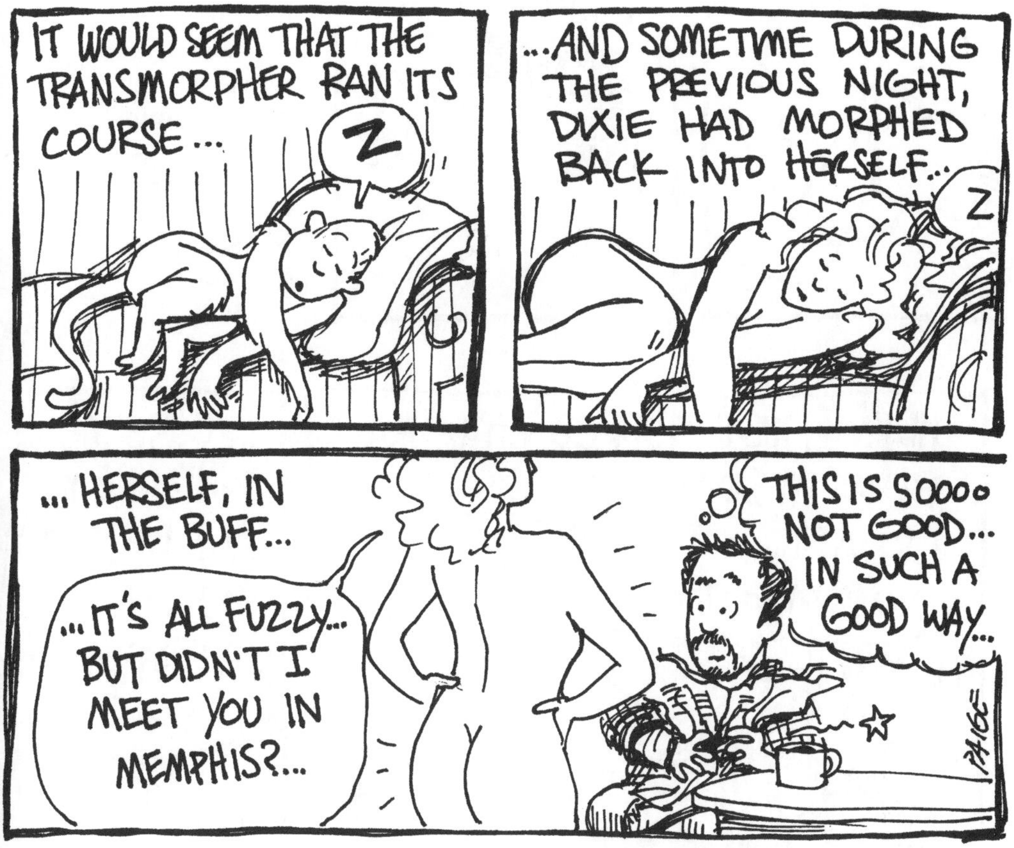

IT WOULD SEEM THAT THE TRANSMORPHER RAN ITS COURSE...
Z
...AND SOMETIME DURING THE PREVIOUS NIGHT, DIXIE HAD MORPHED BACK INTO HERSELF...
Z
... HERSELF, IN THE BUFF...
...IT'S ALL FUZZY... BUT DIDN'T I MEET YOU IN MEMPHIS?...
THIS IS SOOOO NOT GOOD... IN SUCH A GOOD WAY...
PAIGE

JANE SHOWS UP, JUST AS DIXIE'S MEMORY COME'S RUSHING BACK...

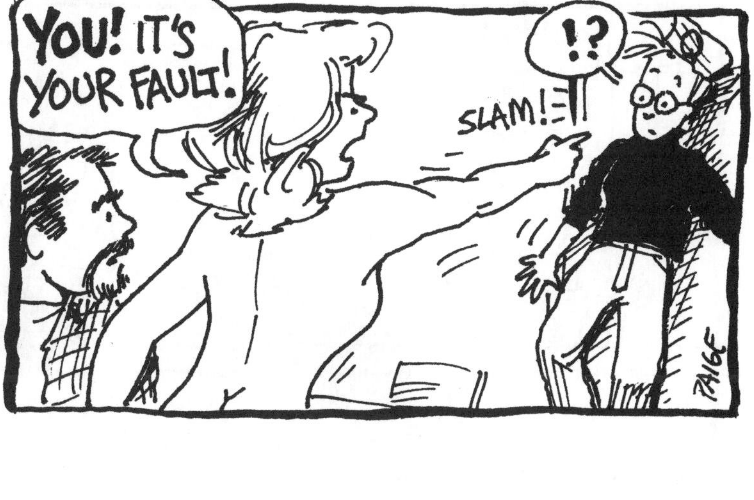

YOU! IT'S YOUR FAULT!
!?
SLAM!
PAIGE

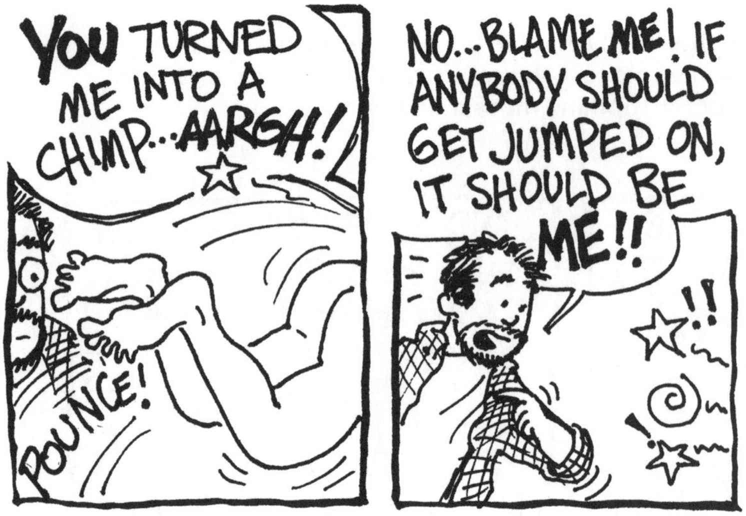
YOU TURNED ME INTO A CHIMP...AARGH!
POUNCE!
NO...BLAME ME! IF ANYBODY SHOULD GET JUMPED ON, IT SHOULD BE ME!!
!!

Dorothy, thinking that the love nest is still her domain, stops by with a frozen, dairy treat for her recently rediscovered boyfriend...

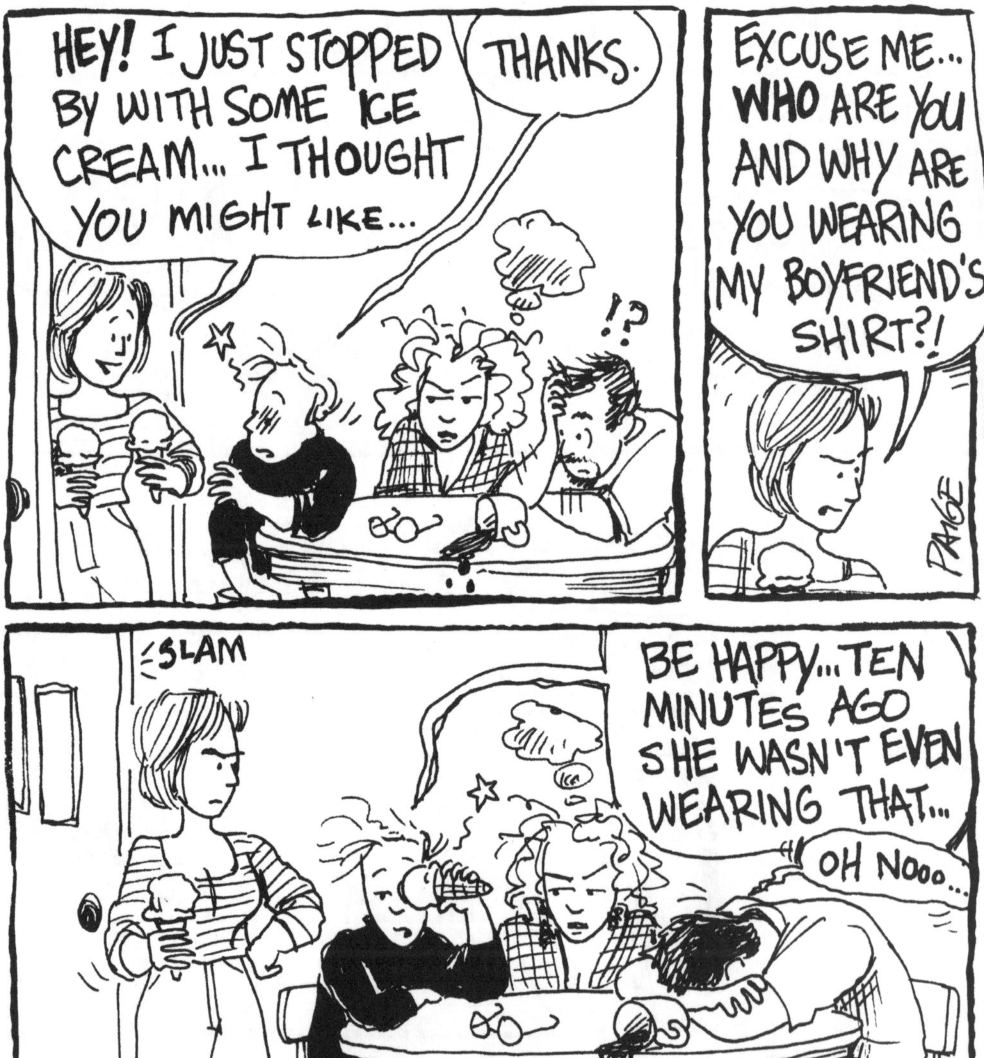
HEY! I JUST STOPPED BY WITH SOME ICE CREAM... I THOUGHT YOU MIGHT LIKE...
THANKS.
!?
EXCUSE ME... WHO ARE YOU AND WHY ARE YOU WEARING MY BOYFRIEND'S SHIRT?!
PAIGE
SLAM
BE HAPPY... TEN MINUTES AGO SHE WASN'T EVEN WEARING THAT...
OH NOoo...

Thinking this is all somehow Jane's fault, and following the tried and true technique of punch first, ask questions later, Dorothy is about to pummel Jane....

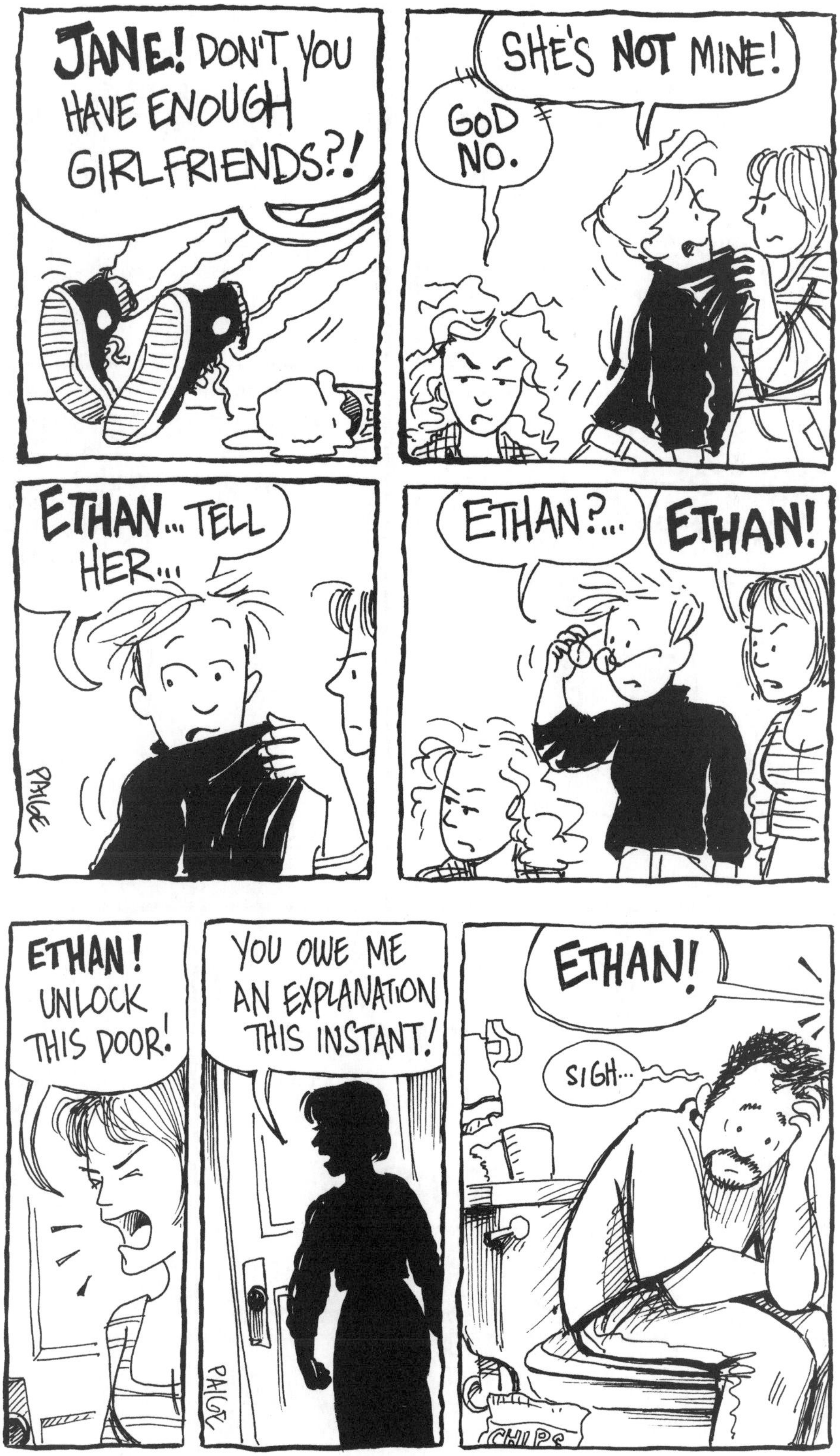
JANE! DON'T YOU HAVE ENOUGH GIRLFRIENDS?!
SHE'S NOT MINE!
GOD NO.
ETHAN... TELL HER...
PAIGE
ETHAN?...
ETHAN!
ETHAN! UNLOCK THIS DOOR!
YOU OWE ME AN EXPLANATION THIS INSTANT!
PAIGE
ETHAN!
SIGH...
CHIPS

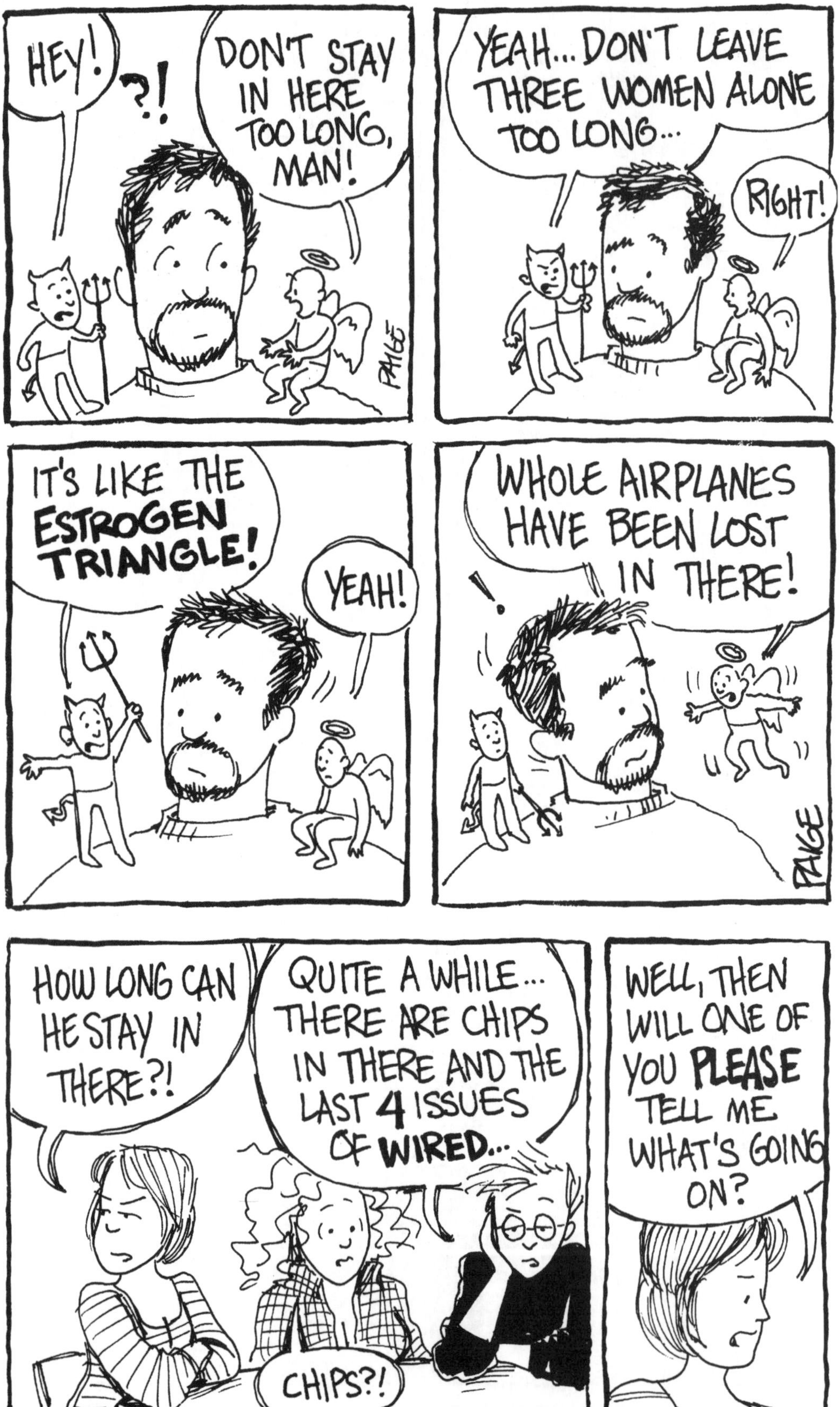
HEY!
?!
DON'T STAY IN HERE TOO LONG, MAN!
PAIGE
YEAH... DON'T LEAVE THREE WOMEN ALONE TOO LONG...
RIGHT!
IT'S LIKE THE **ESTROGEN TRIANGLE!**
YEAH!
WHOLE AIRPLANES HAVE BEEN LOST IN THERE!
!
PAIGE
HOW LONG CAN HE STAY IN THERE?!
QUITE A WHILE... THERE ARE CHIPS IN THERE AND THE LAST **4** ISSUES OF **WIRED**...
CHIPS?!
WELL, THEN WILL ONE OF YOU **PLEASE** TELL ME WHAT'S GOING ON?

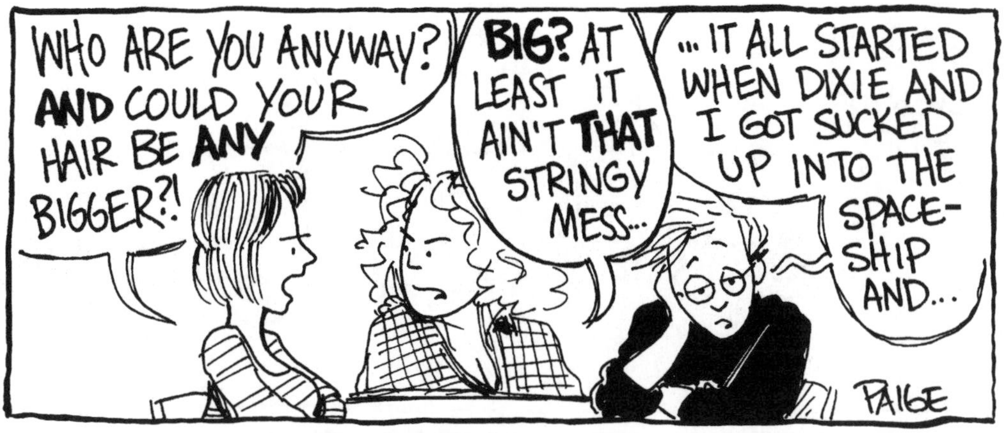
WHO ARE YOU ANYWAY? AND COULD YOUR HAIR BE ANY BIGGER?!
BIG? AT LEAST IT AIN'T THAT STRINGY MESS...
... IT ALL STARTED WHEN DIXIE AND I GOT SUCKED UP INTO THE SPACE-SHIP AND...
PAIGE

Jane explains the whole story (see chapter three) and convinces Ethan to come out and face the truth...

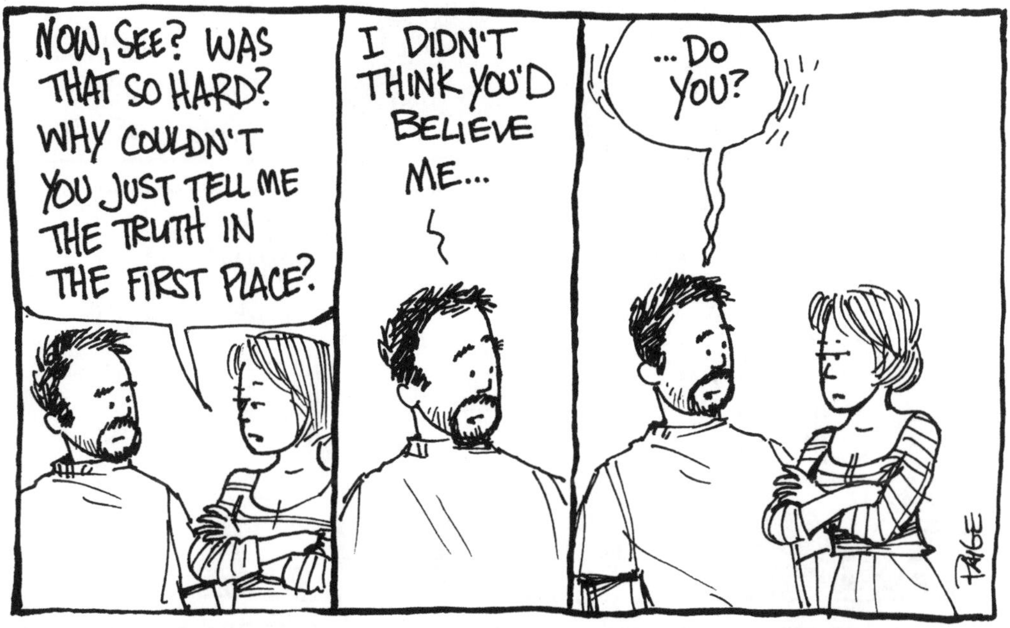
NOW, SEE? WAS THAT SO HARD? WHY COULDN'T YOU JUST TELL ME THE TRUTH IN THE FIRST PLACE?
I DIDN'T THINK YOU'D BELIEVE ME...
... DO YOU?
PAIGE

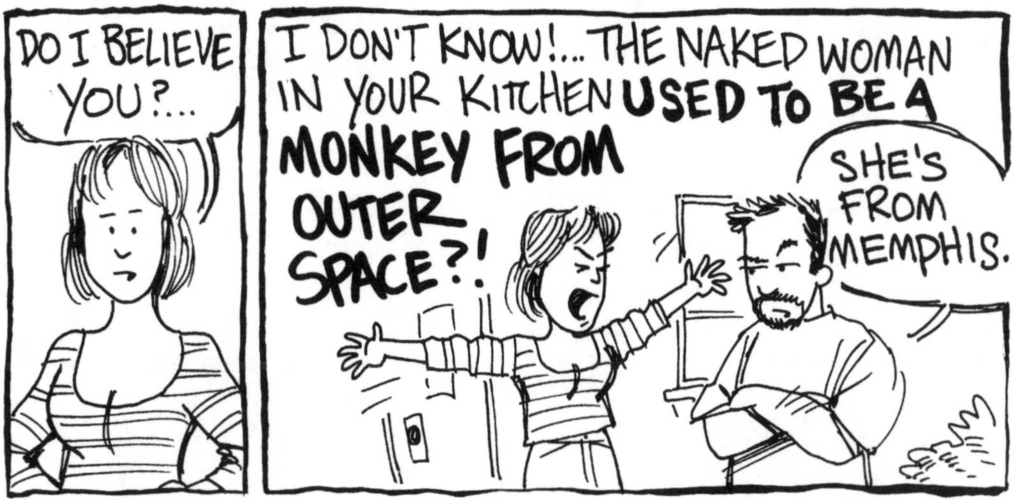
DO I BELIEVE YOU?...
I DON'T KNOW!... THE NAKED WOMAN IN YOUR KITCHEN USED TO BE A MONKEY FROM OUTER SPACE?!
SHE'S FROM MEMPHIS.

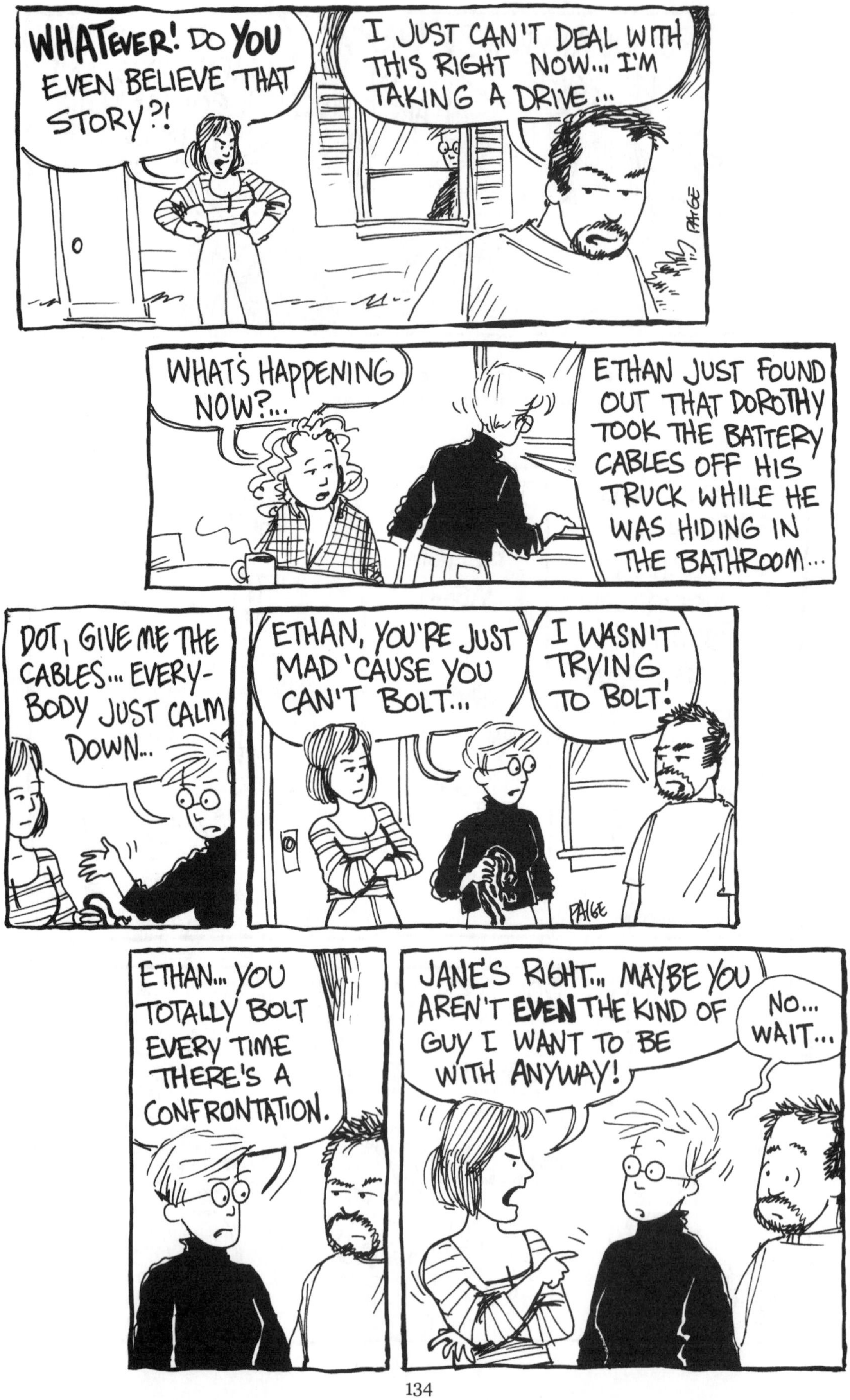
WHATever! DO YOU EVEN BELIEVE THAT STORY?!
I JUST CAN'T DEAL WITH THIS RIGHT NOW... I'M TAKING A DRIVE...
PAIGE
WHAT'S HAPPENING NOW?...
ETHAN JUST FOUND OUT THAT DOROTHY TOOK THE BATTERY CABLES OFF HIS TRUCK WHILE HE WAS HIDING IN THE BATHROOM...
DOT, GIVE ME THE CABLES... EVERY-BODY JUST CALM DOWN...
ETHAN, YOU'RE JUST MAD 'CAUSE YOU CAN'T BOLT...
I WASN'T TRYING TO BOLT!
PAIGE
ETHAN... YOU TOTALLY BOLT EVERY TIME THERE'S A CONFRONTATION.
JANE'S RIGHT... MAYBE YOU AREN'T EVEN THE KIND OF GUY I WANT TO BE WITH ANYWAY!
NO... WAIT...

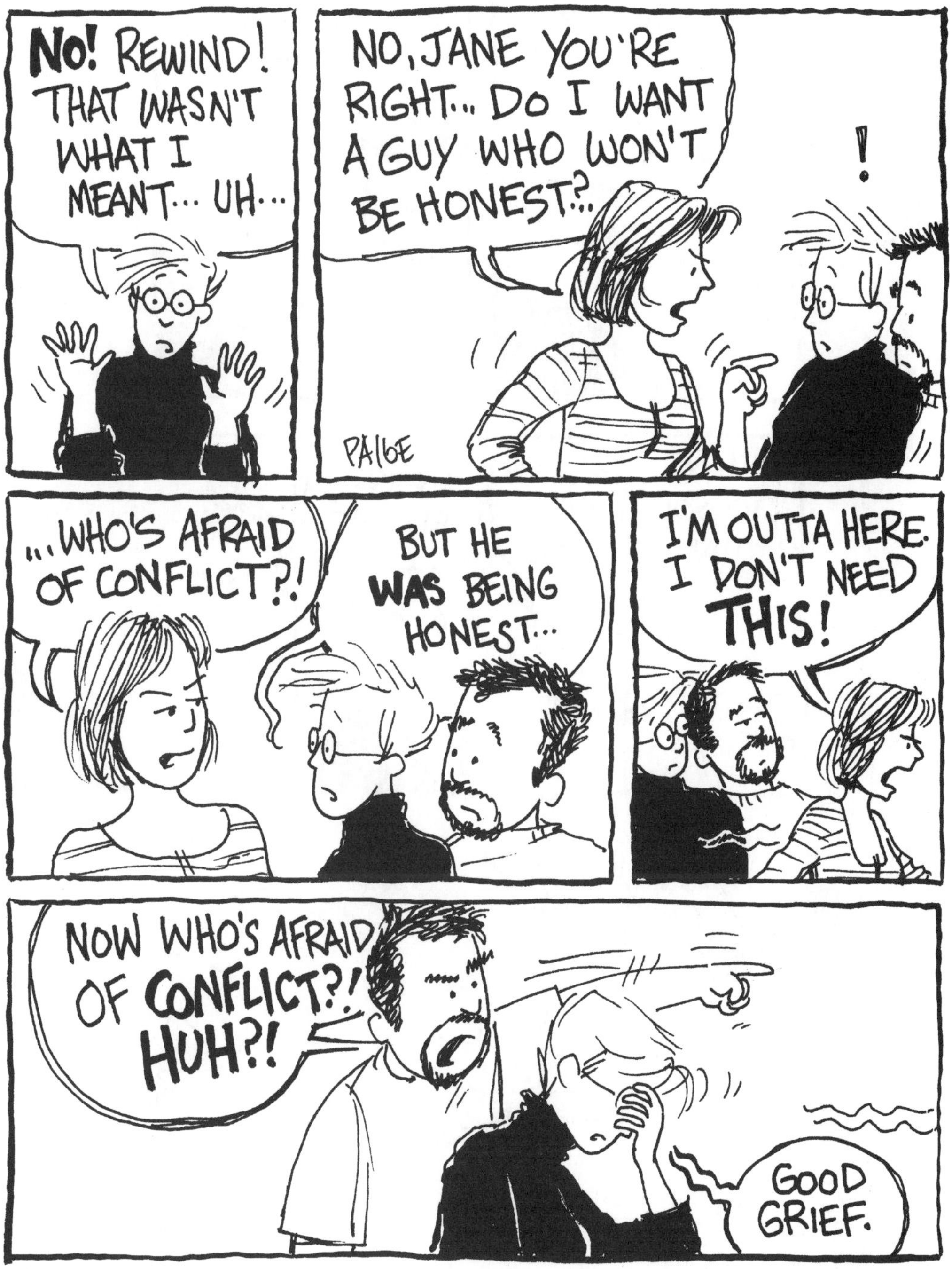
NO! REWIND! THAT WASN'T WHAT I MEANT... UH...
NO, JANE YOU'RE RIGHT... DO I WANT A GUY WHO WON'T BE HONEST?..
!
PAIGE
...WHO'S AFRAID OF CONFLICT?!
BUT HE WAS BEING HONEST...
I'M OUTTA HERE. I DON'T NEED THIS!
NOW WHO'S AFRAID OF CONFLICT?! HUH?!
GOOD GRIEF.

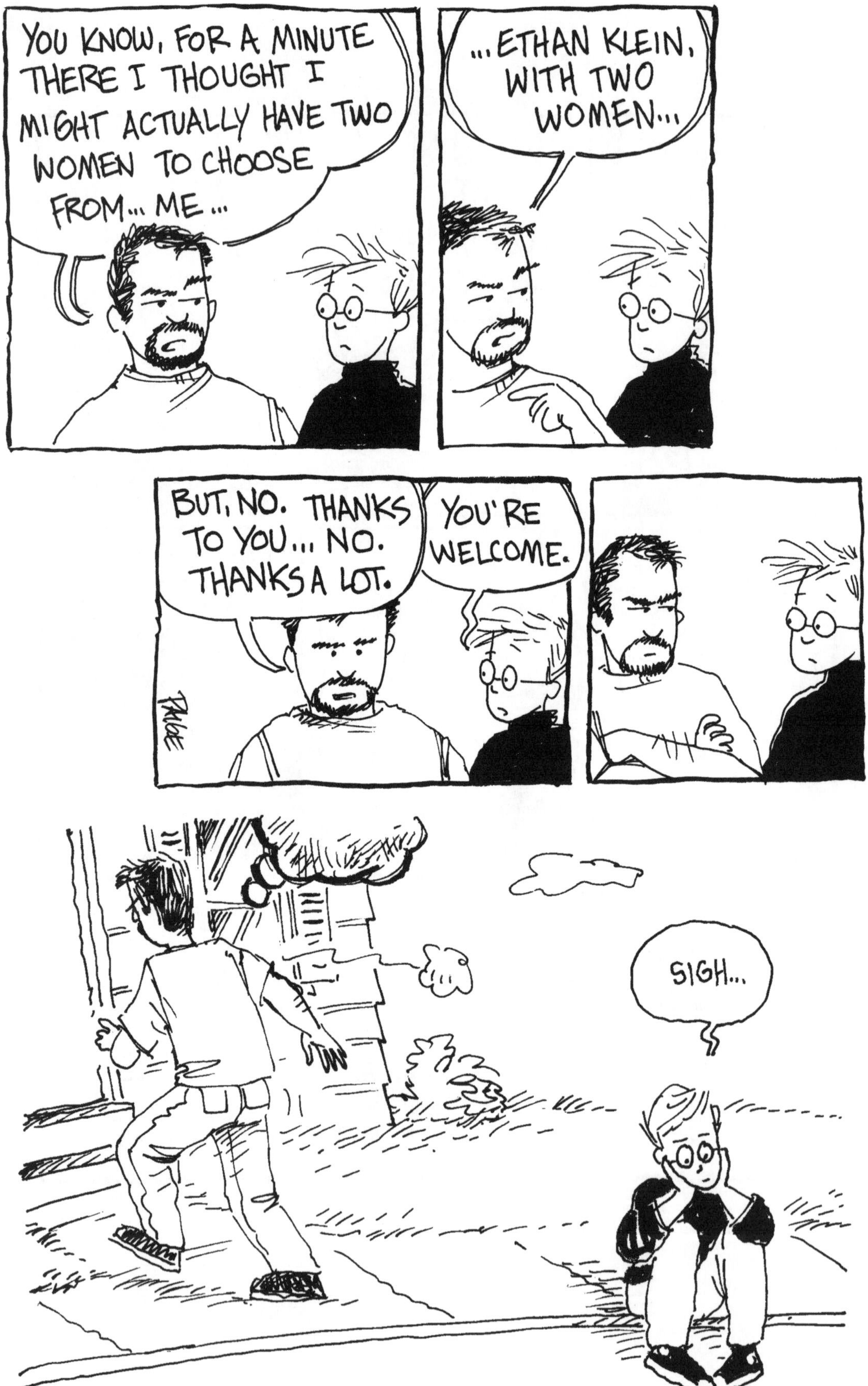
YOU KNOW, FOR A MINUTE THERE I THOUGHT I MIGHT ACTUALLY HAVE TWO WOMEN TO CHOOSE FROM... ME...
...ETHAN KLEIN, WITH TWO WOMEN...
BUT, NO. THANKS TO YOU... NO. THANKS A LOT.
YOU'RE WELCOME.
SIGH...

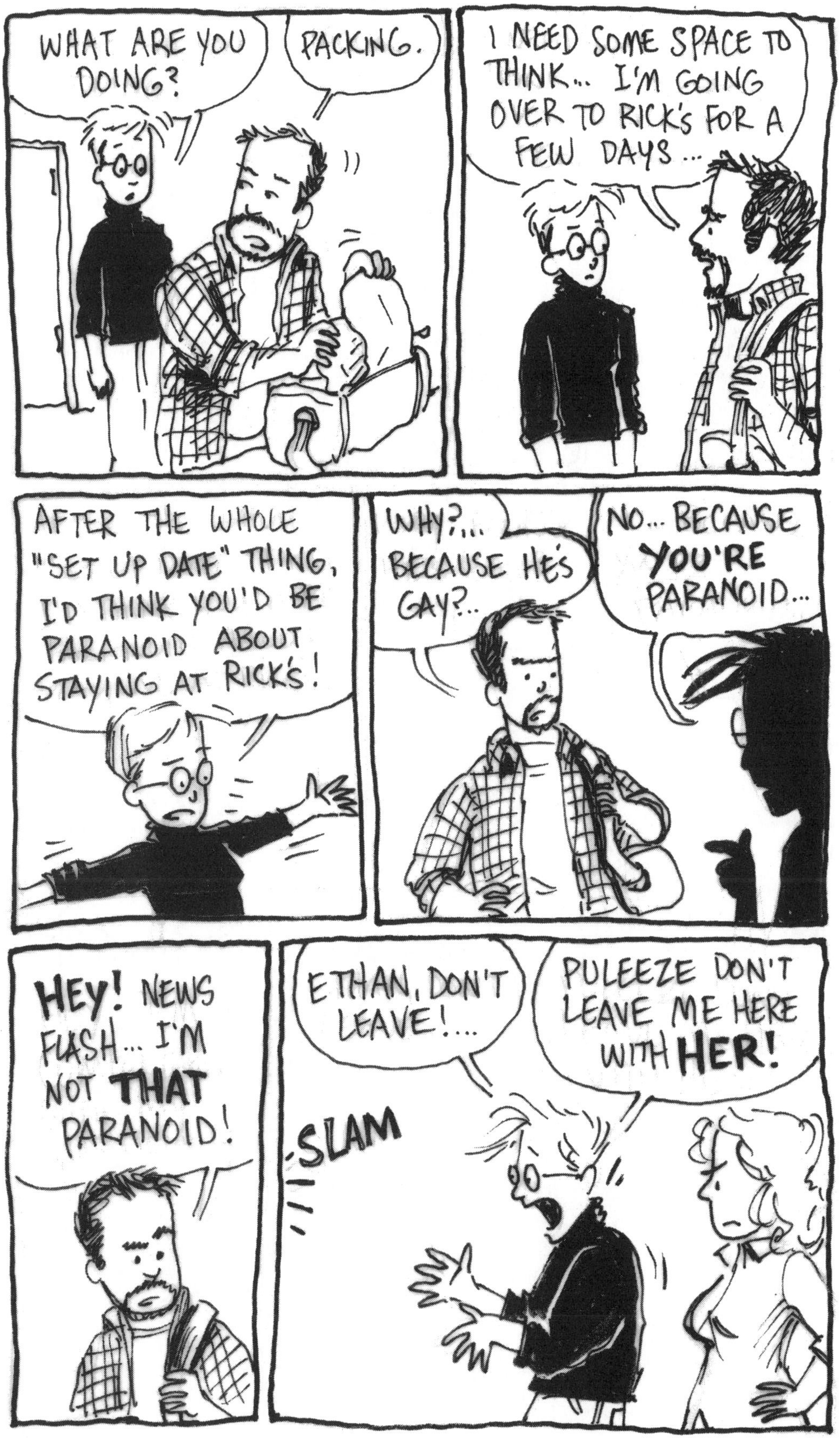
WHAT ARE YOU DOING?
PACKING.
I NEED SOME SPACE TO THINK... I'M GOING OVER TO RICK'S FOR A FEW DAYS...
AFTER THE WHOLE "SET UP DATE" THING, I'D THINK YOU'D BE PARANOID ABOUT STAYING AT RICK'S!
WHY?... BECAUSE HE'S GAY?...
NO... BECAUSE YOU'RE PARANOID...
HEY! NEWS FLASH... I'M NOT THAT PARANOID!
SLAM
ETHAN, DON'T LEAVE!...
PULEEZE DON'T LEAVE ME HERE WITH HER!

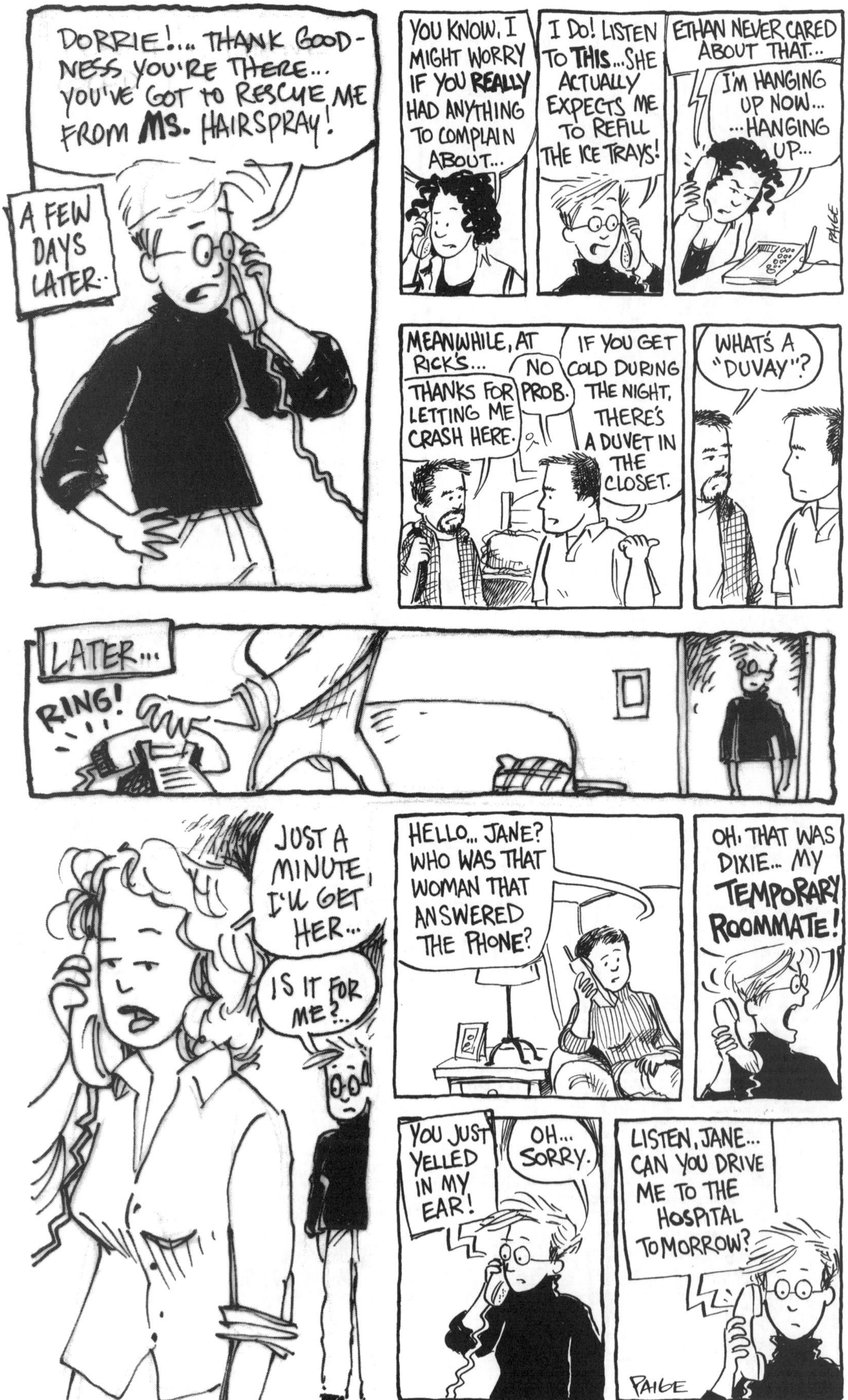
DORRIE!... THANK GOODNESS YOU'RE THERE... YOU'VE GOT TO RESCUE ME FROM MS. HAIRSPRAY!
A FEW DAYS LATER...
YOU KNOW, I MIGHT WORRY IF YOU REALLY HAD ANYTHING TO COMPLAIN ABOUT...
I DO! LISTEN TO THIS...SHE ACTUALLY EXPECTS ME TO REFILL THE ICE TRAYS!
ETHAN NEVER CARED ABOUT THAT...
I'M HANGING UP NOW... ...HANGING UP...
PAIGE
MEANWHILE, AT RICK'S...
THANKS FOR LETTING ME CRASH HERE.
NO PROB.
IF YOU GET COLD DURING THE NIGHT, THERE'S A DUVET IN THE CLOSET.
WHAT'S A "DUVAY"?
LATER...
RING!
JUST A MINUTE, I'LL GET HER...
IS IT FOR ME?...
HELLO... JANE? WHO WAS THAT WOMAN THAT ANSWERED THE PHONE?
OH, THAT WAS DIXIE... MY TEMPORARY ROOMMATE!
YOU JUST YELLED IN MY EAR!
OH... SORRY.
LISTEN, JANE... CAN YOU DRIVE ME TO THE HOSPITAL TOMORROW?
PAIGE

Jane processes the phone call with Archie...

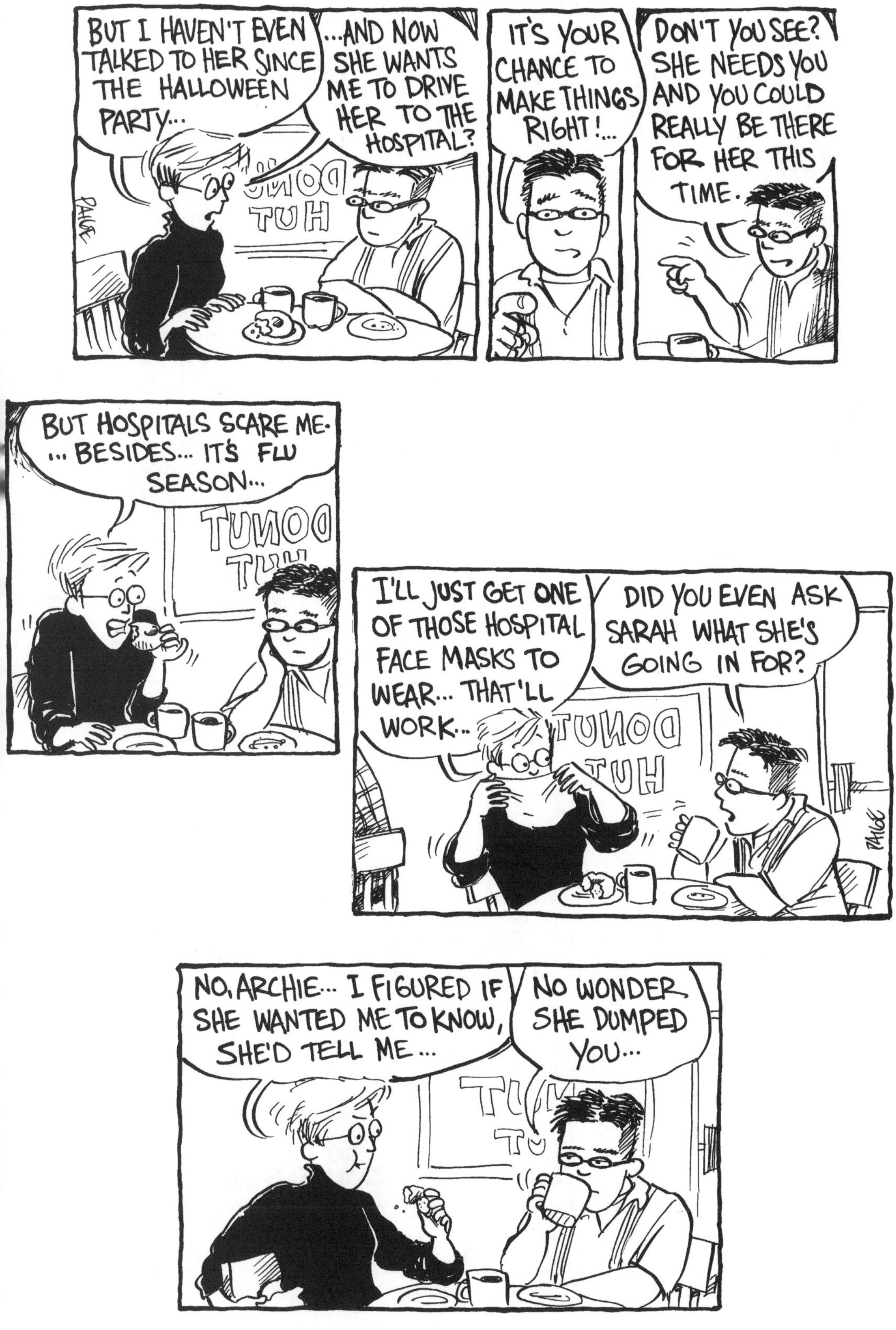

BUT I HAVEN'T EVEN TALKED TO HER SINCE THE HALLOWEEN PARTY...
...AND NOW SHE WANTS ME TO DRIVE HER TO THE HOSPITAL?
IT'S YOUR CHANCE TO MAKE THINGS RIGHT!...
DON'T YOU SEE? SHE NEEDS YOU AND YOU COULD REALLY BE THERE FOR HER THIS TIME.
BUT HOSPITALS SCARE ME. ... BESIDES... IT'S FLU SEASON...
I'LL JUST GET ONE OF THOSE HOSPITAL FACE MASKS TO WEAR... THAT'LL WORK...
DID YOU EVEN ASK SARAH WHAT SHE'S GOING IN FOR?
NO, ARCHIE... I FIGURED IF SHE WANTED ME TO KNOW, SHE'D TELL ME...
NO WONDER SHE DUMPED YOU...

ALRIGHT, MAN. I GOTTA GO... I'M SUPPOSED TO PICK SARAH UP IN A FEW.
THANKS FOR THE DOUGHNUT...
NO PROBLEM.
HUT
PAIGE

LISTEN, JUST BE UM... WELL... TRY AND BE SENSITIVE.
YOU REALLY LIKE HER DON'T YOU?
ONUT HUT
YEAH...

At the hospital...

JANE... I KNOW I CALLED OUT OF THE BLUE...
HOSPITAL ENTRANCE
PAIGE
THANK YOU FOR COMING WITH ME...
SURE
UM... ARE YOU NERVOUS?
WAITING AREA
SARAH...

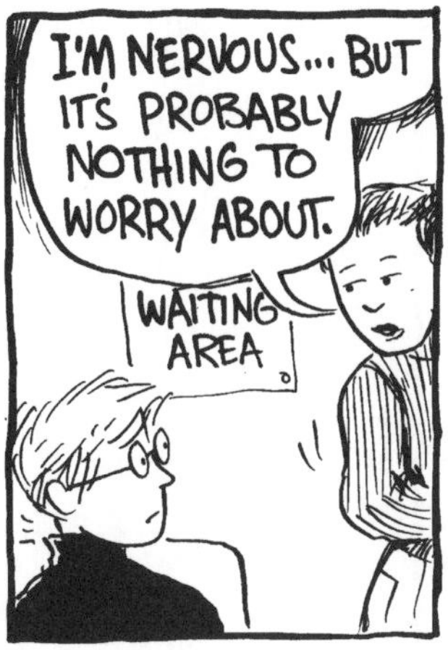
I'M NERVOUS... BUT IT'S PROBABLY NOTHING TO WORRY ABOUT.
WAITING AREA

Jane waits for word, while across town Ethan gets a taste of what it's like to live with a guy in touch with his feminine side...

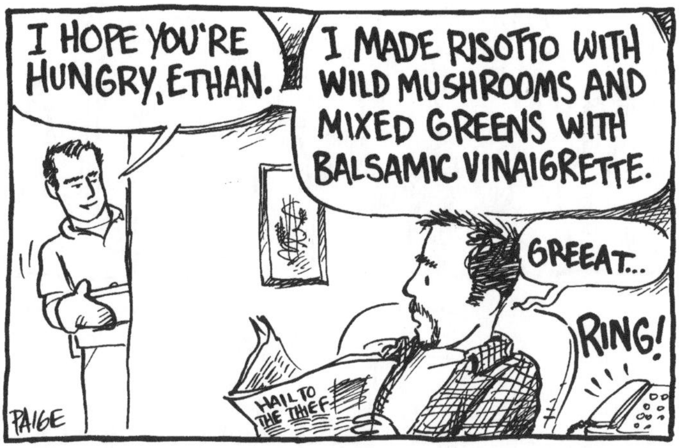
I HOPE YOU'RE HUNGRY, ETHAN.
I MADE RISOTTO WITH WILD MUSHROOMS AND MIXED GREENS WITH BALSAMIC VINAIGRETTE.
GREEAT...
RING!
HAIL TO THE THIEF
PAIGE

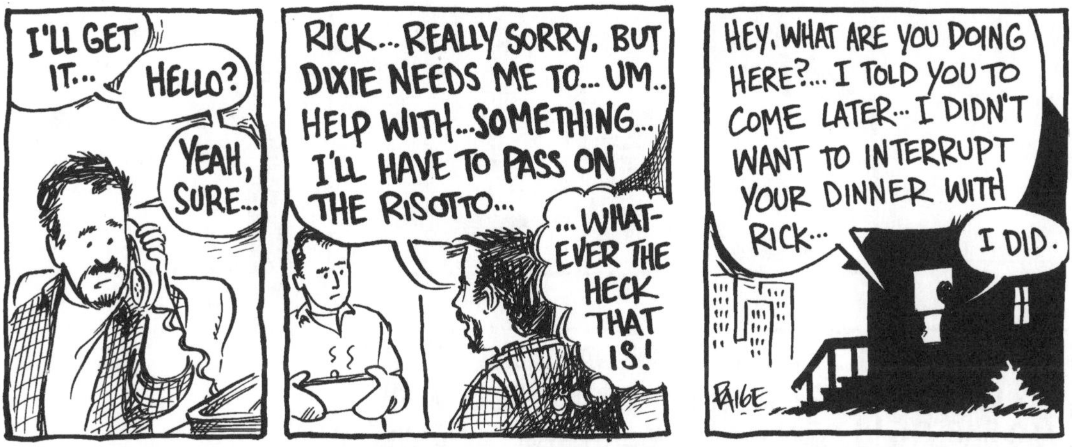
I'LL GET IT...
HELLO?
YEAH, SURE...
RICK... REALLY SORRY, BUT DIXIE NEEDS ME TO... UM.. HELP WITH...SOMETHING... I'LL HAVE TO PASS ON THE RISOTTO...
...WHAT-EVER THE HECK THAT IS!
HEY, WHAT ARE YOU DOING HERE?... I TOLD YOU TO COME LATER... I DIDN'T WANT TO INTERRUPT YOUR DINNER WITH RICK...
I DID.
PAIGE

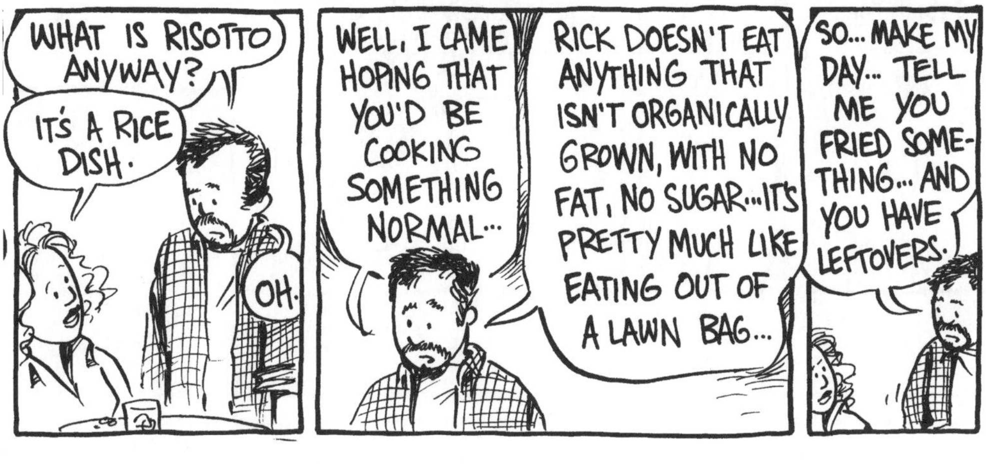
WHAT IS RISOTTO ANYWAY?
IT'S A RICE DISH.
OH.
WELL, I CAME HOPING THAT YOU'D BE COOKING SOMETHING NORMAL...
RICK DOESN'T EAT ANYTHING THAT ISN'T ORGANICALLY GROWN, WITH NO FAT, NO SUGAR...IT'S PRETTY MUCH LIKE EATING OUT OF A LAWN BAG...
SO... MAKE MY DAY... TELL ME YOU FRIED SOME-THING... AND YOU HAVE LEFTOVERS.

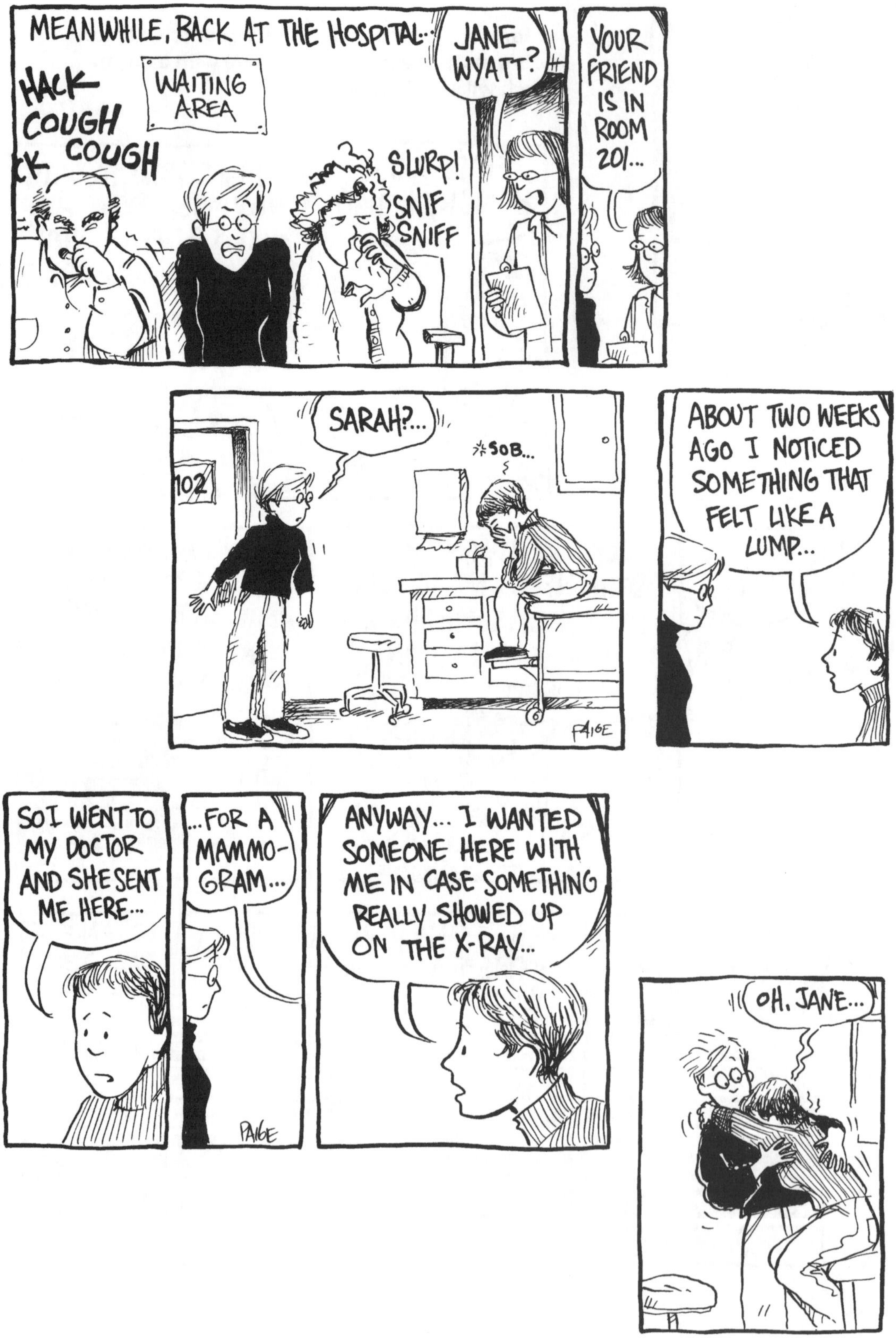
MEANWHILE, BACK AT THE HOSPITAL...
WAITING AREA
HACK
COUGH
CK COUGH
SLURP!
SNIF
SNIFF
JANE WYATT?
YOUR FRIEND IS IN ROOM 201...
SARAH?...
102
SOB...
PAIGE
ABOUT TWO WEEKS AGO I NOTICED SOMETHING THAT FELT LIKE A LUMP...
SO I WENT TO MY DOCTOR AND SHE SENT ME HERE...
...FOR A MAMMO-GRAM...
PAIGE
ANYWAY... I WANTED SOMEONE HERE WITH ME IN CASE SOMETHING REALLY SHOWED UP ON THE X-RAY...
OH, JANE...

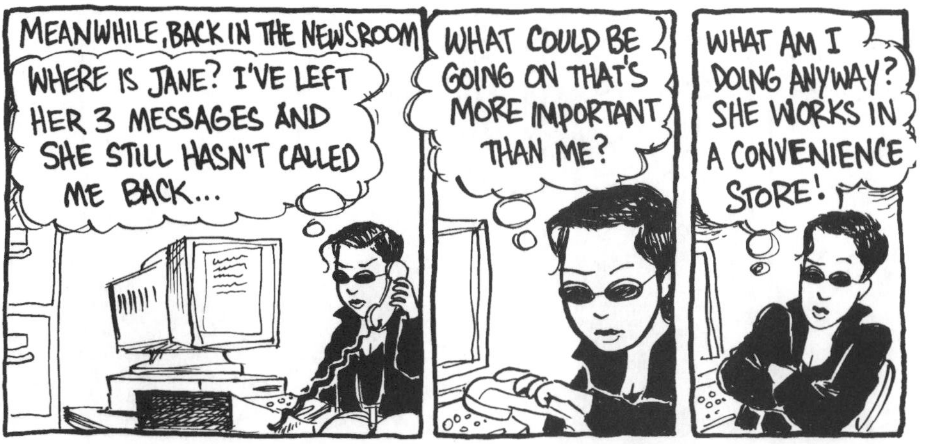
MEANWHILE, BACK IN THE NEWSROOM
WHERE IS JANE? I'VE LEFT HER 3 MESSAGES AND SHE STILL HASN'T CALLED ME BACK...
WHAT COULD BE GOING ON THAT'S MORE IMPORTANT THAN ME?
WHAT AM I DOING ANYWAY? SHE WORKS IN A CONVENIENCE STORE!

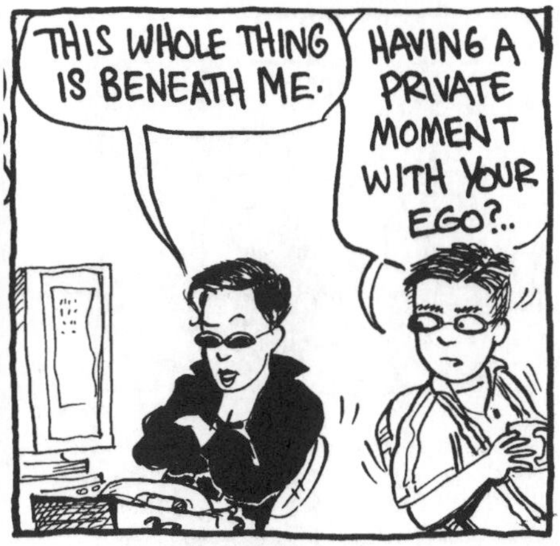
THIS WHOLE THING IS BENEATH ME.
HAVING A PRIVATE MOMENT WITH YOUR EGO?..

Being the good pal that he is, Archie stops by to ask after Sarah...

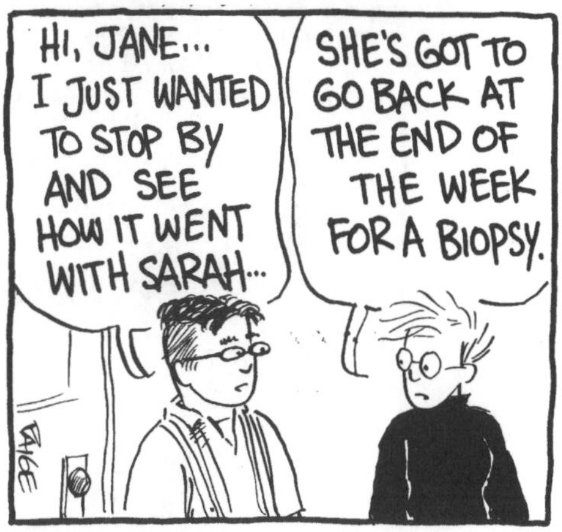
HI, JANE... I JUST WANTED TO STOP BY AND SEE HOW IT WENT WITH SARAH...
SHE'S GOT TO GO BACK AT THE END OF THE WEEK FOR A BIOPSY.
PAIGE

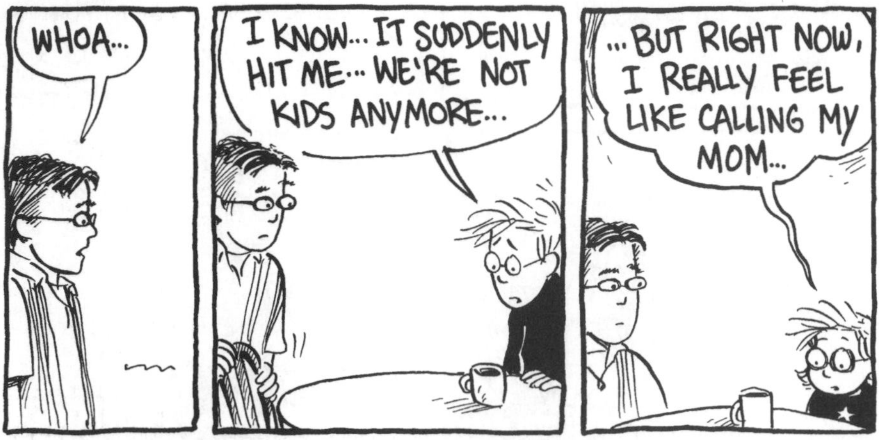
WHOA...
I KNOW... IT SUDDENLY HIT ME... WE'RE NOT KIDS ANYMORE...
...BUT RIGHT NOW, I REALLY FEEL LIKE CALLING MY MOM...

The next morning Jane stops for coffee on her way to the Quicki-Mart. It's a double latte kind of day...

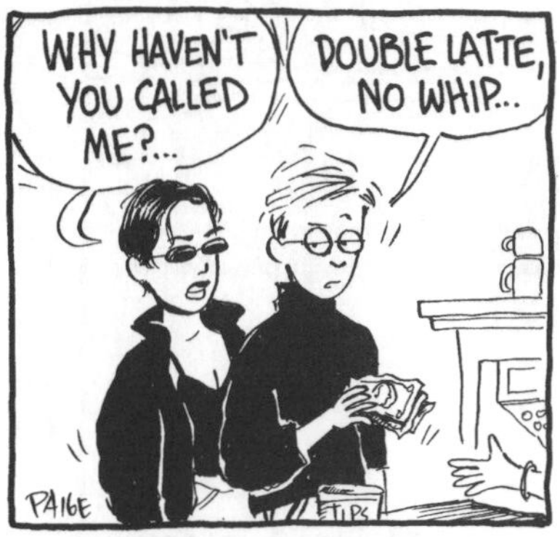
WHY HAVEN'T YOU CALLED ME?...
DOUBLE LATTE, NO WHIP...
PAIGE
TIPS

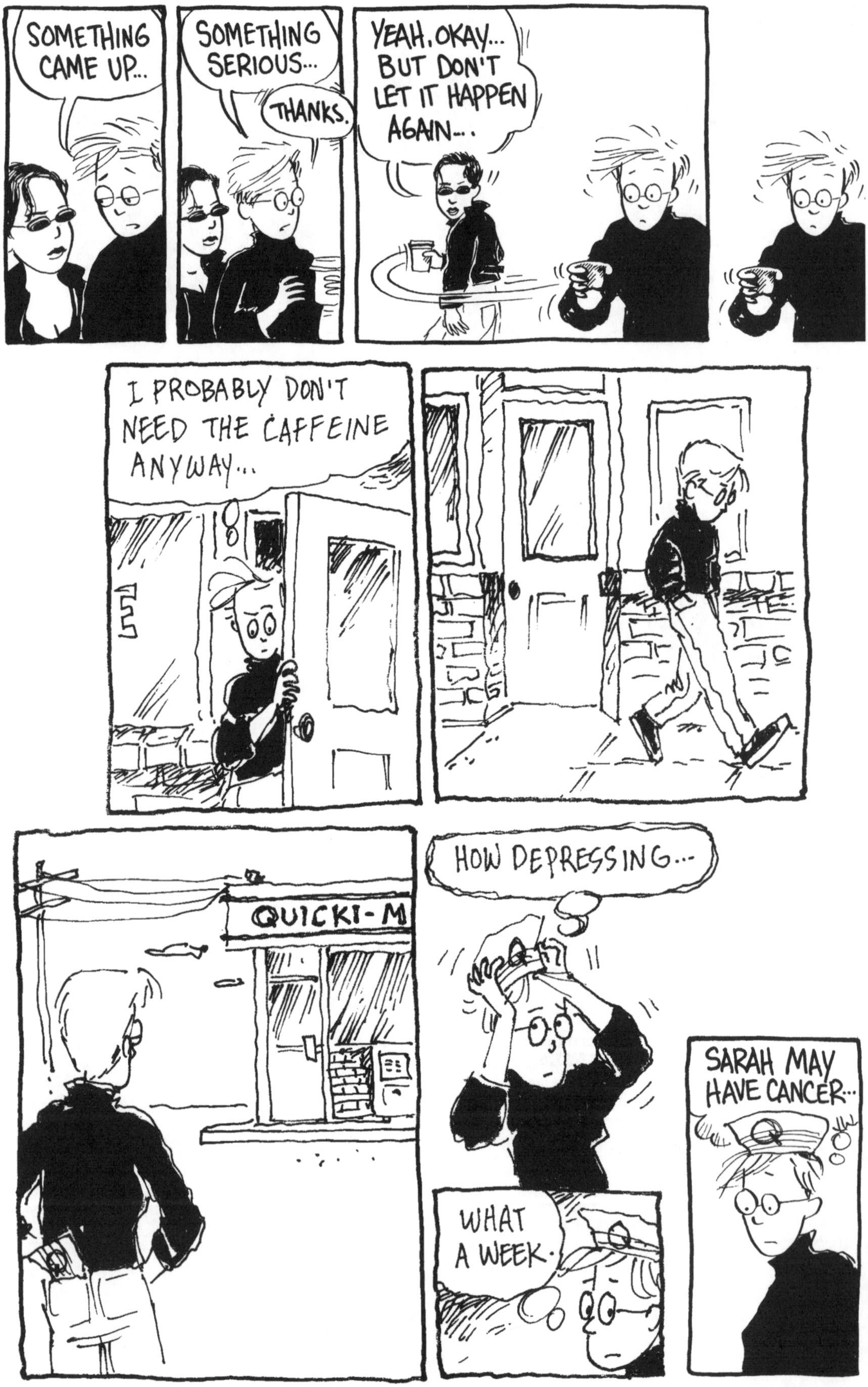
SOMETHING CAME UP...
SOMETHING SERIOUS...
THANKS.
YEAH, OKAY... BUT DON'T LET IT HAPPEN AGAIN...
I PROBABLY DON'T NEED THE CAFFEINE ANYWAY...
QUICKI-M
HOW DEPRESSING...
WHAT A WEEK.
SARAH MAY HAVE CANCER...

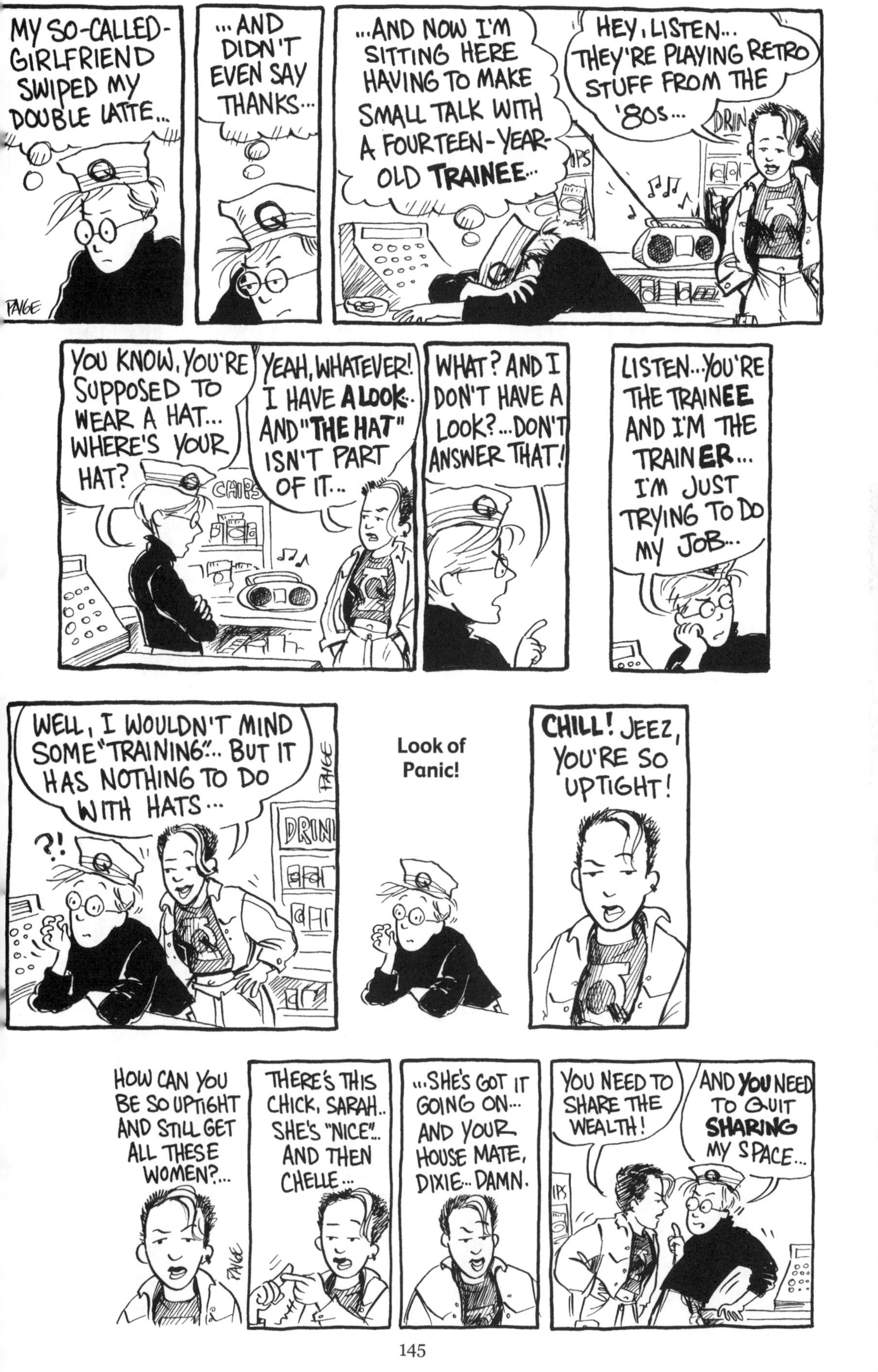
MY SO-CALLED-GIRLFRIEND SWIPED MY DOUBLE LATTE...
...AND DIDN'T EVEN SAY THANKS...
...AND NOW I'M SITTING HERE HAVING TO MAKE SMALL TALK WITH A FOURTEEN-YEAR-OLD **TRAINEE**...
HEY, LISTEN... THEY'RE PLAYING RETRO STUFF FROM THE '80S...
PAIGE
YOU KNOW, YOU'RE SUPPOSED TO WEAR A HAT... WHERE'S YOUR HAT?
YEAH, WHATEVER! I HAVE **A LOOK**... AND "**THE HAT**" ISN'T PART OF IT...
WHAT? AND I DON'T HAVE A LOOK?...DON'T ANSWER THAT!
LISTEN...YOU'RE THE TRAIN**EE** AND I'M THE TRAIN**ER**... I'M JUST TRYING TO DO MY JOB...
WELL, I WOULDN'T MIND SOME "TRAINING"... BUT IT HAS NOTHING TO DO WITH HATS...
?!
PAIGE
Look of Panic!
CHILL! JEEZ, YOU'RE SO UPTIGHT!
HOW CAN YOU BE SO UPTIGHT AND STILL GET ALL THESE WOMEN?...
PAIGE
THERE'S THIS CHICK, SARAH.. SHE'S "NICE"... AND THEN CHELLE...
...SHE'S GOT IT GOING ON... AND YOUR HOUSE MATE, DIXIE... DAMN.
YOU NEED TO SHARE THE WEALTH!
AND **YOU** NEED TO QUIT **SHARING** MY SPACE...

After what seemed like a never-ending shift at the 'Mart, Jane heads for home...

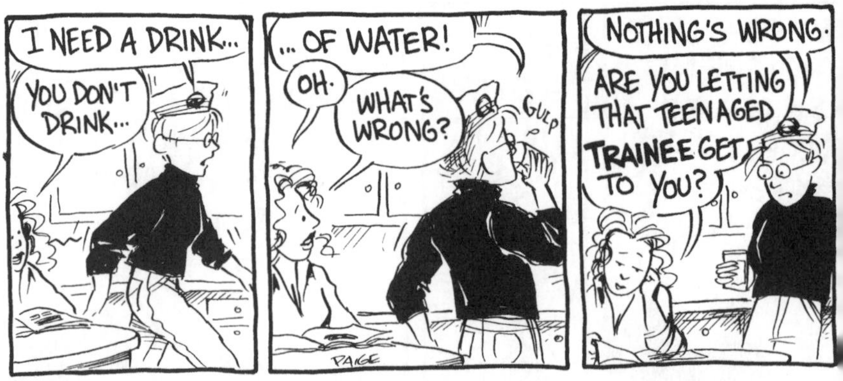
I NEED A DRINK...
YOU DON'T DRINK...
... OF WATER!
OH.
WHAT'S WRONG?
GULP
NOTHING'S WRONG.
ARE YOU LETTING THAT TEENAGED TRAINEE GET TO YOU?
PAIGE

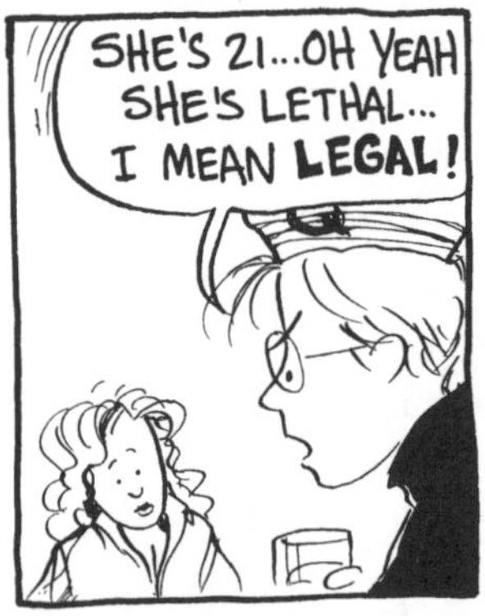
SHE'S 21...OH YEAH SHE'S LETHAL... I MEAN LEGAL!

... then, for the next trip to the hospital, Jane has to do the undesirable...

...ask Natalie for a favor...

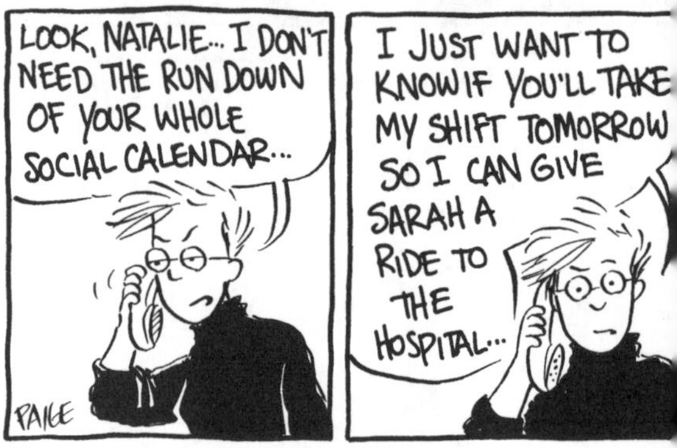
LOOK, NATALIE... I DON'T NEED THE RUN DOWN OF YOUR WHOLE SOCIAL CALENDAR...
I JUST WANT TO KNOW IF YOU'LL TAKE MY SHIFT TOMORROW SO I CAN GIVE SARAH A RIDE TO THE HOSPITAL...
PAIGE

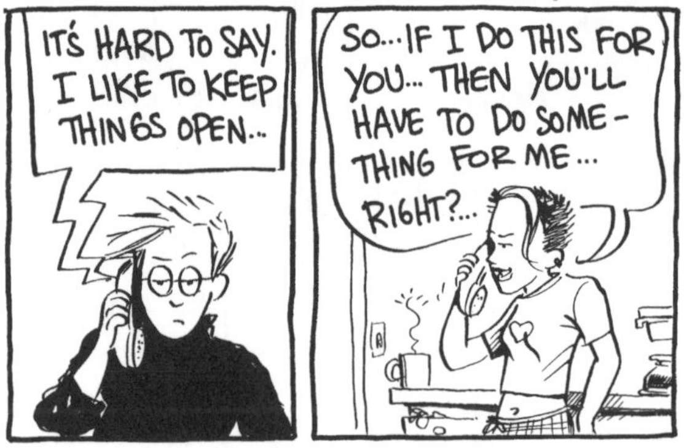
IT'S HARD TO SAY. I LIKE TO KEEP THINGS OPEN...
SO... IF I DO THIS FOR YOU... THEN YOU'LL HAVE TO DO SOME-THING FOR ME... RIGHT?...

The next day...

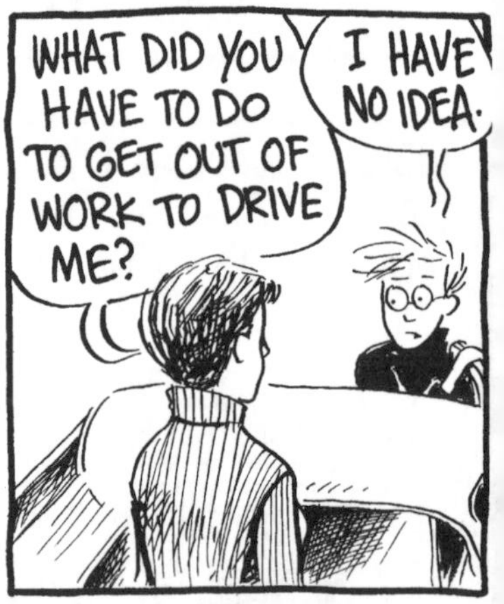
WHAT DID YOU HAVE TO DO TO GET OUT OF WORK TO DRIVE ME?
I HAVE NO IDEA.

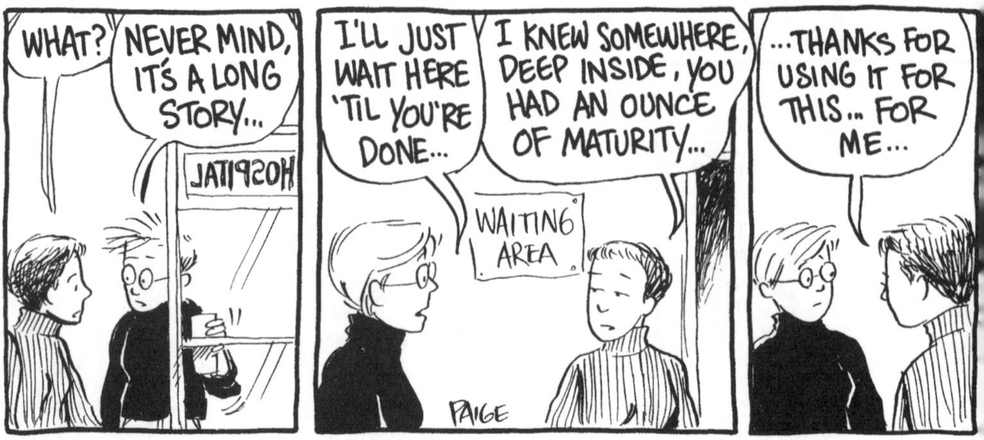
WHAT?
NEVER MIND, IT'S A LONG STORY...
HOSPITAL
I'LL JUST WAIT HERE 'TIL YOU'RE DONE...
I KNEW SOMEWHERE, DEEP INSIDE, YOU HAD AN OUNCE OF MATURITY...
WAITING AREA
...THANKS FOR USING IT FOR THIS... FOR ME...
PAIGE

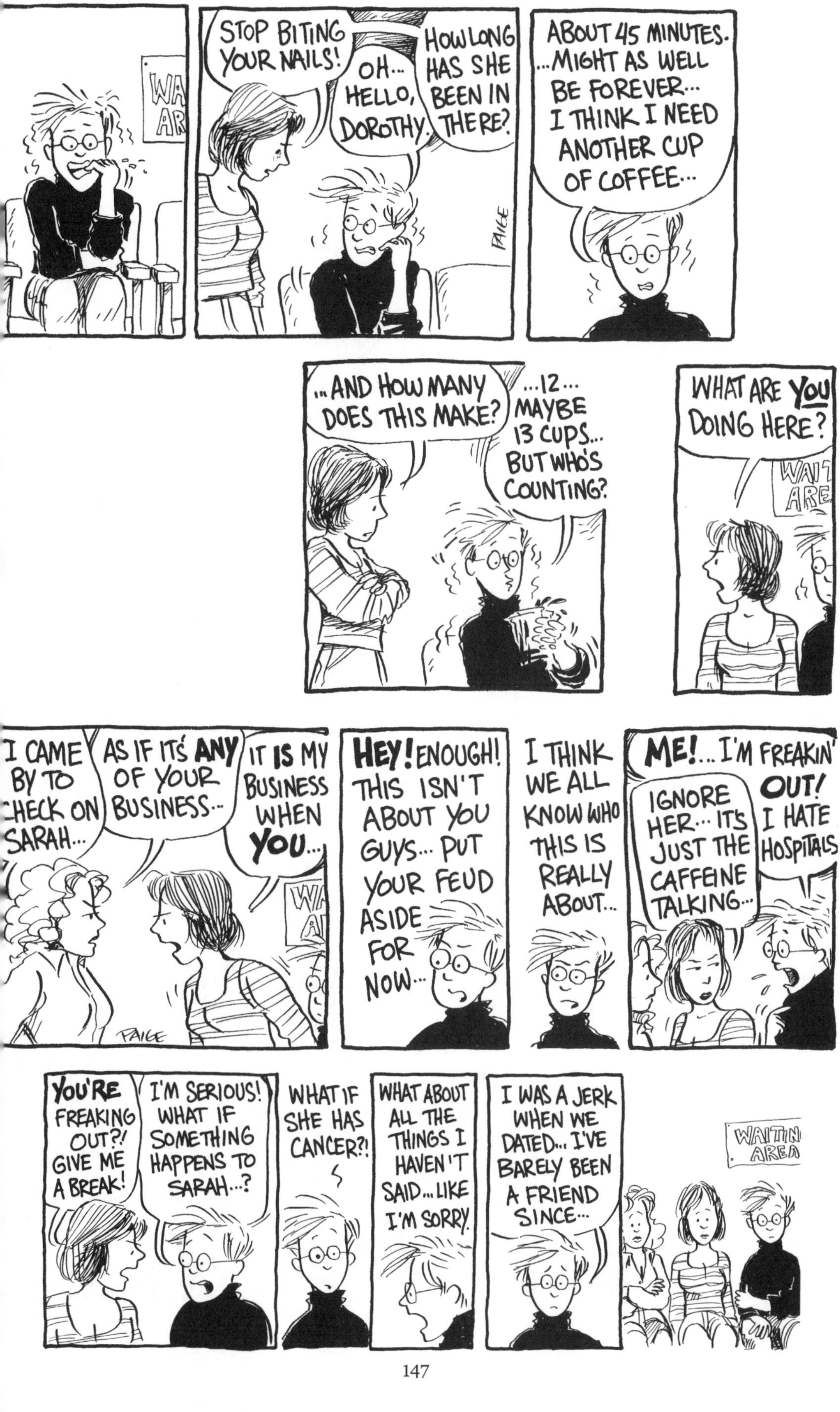

STOP BITING YOUR NAILS!
OH... HELLO, DOROTHY.
HOW LONG HAS SHE BEEN IN THERE?
PAIGE
ABOUT 45 MINUTES. ...MIGHT AS WELL BE FOREVER... I THINK I NEED ANOTHER CUP OF COFFEE...
...AND HOW MANY DOES THIS MAKE?
...12... MAYBE 13 CUPS... BUT WHO'S COUNTING?
WHAT ARE YOU DOING HERE?
I CAME BY TO CHECK ON SARAH...
AS IF IT'S ANY OF YOUR BUSINESS...
IT IS MY BUSINESS WHEN YOU...
PAIGE
HEY! ENOUGH! THIS ISN'T ABOUT YOU GUYS... PUT YOUR FEUD ASIDE FOR NOW...
I THINK WE ALL KNOW WHO THIS IS REALLY ABOUT...
ME!... I'M FREAKIN' OUT! I HATE HOSPITALS
IGNORE HER... IT'S JUST THE CAFFEINE TALKING...
YOU'RE FREAKING OUT?! GIVE ME A BREAK!
I'M SERIOUS! WHAT IF SOMETHING HAPPENS TO SARAH...?
WHAT IF SHE HAS CANCER?!
WHAT ABOUT ALL THE THINGS I HAVEN'T SAID... LIKE I'M SORRY.
I WAS A JERK WHEN WE DATED... I'VE BARELY BEEN A FRIEND SINCE...
WAITING AREA

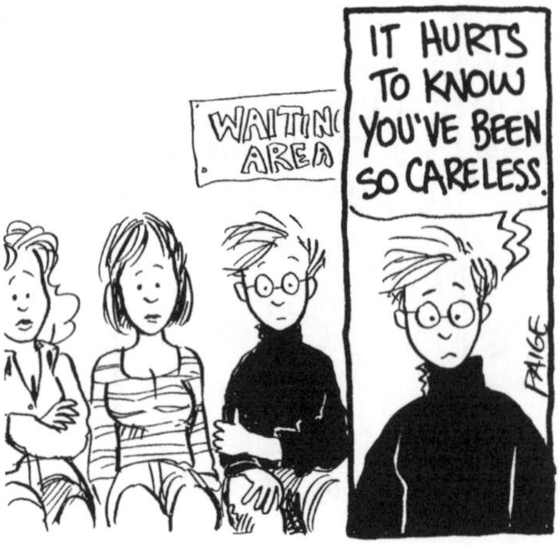
WAITING AREA
IT HURTS TO KNOW YOU'VE BEEN SO CARELESS.
PAIGE

The tension is thick between Dorothy and Dixie in the waiting area... eventually, they both leave Jane alone with her thoughts...

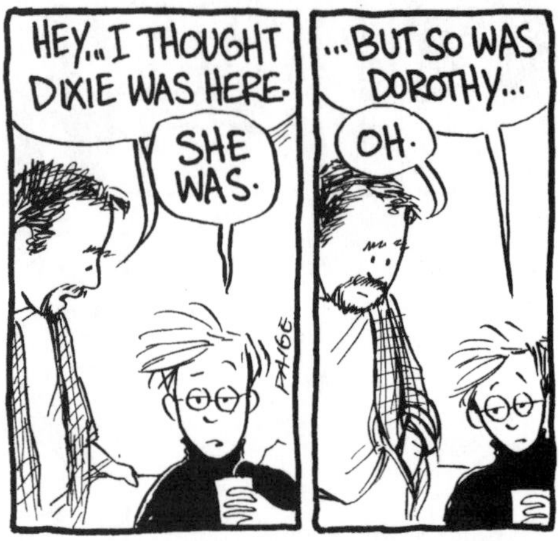
HEY... I THOUGHT DIXIE WAS HERE.
SHE WAS.
...BUT SO WAS DOROTHY...
OH.
PAIGE

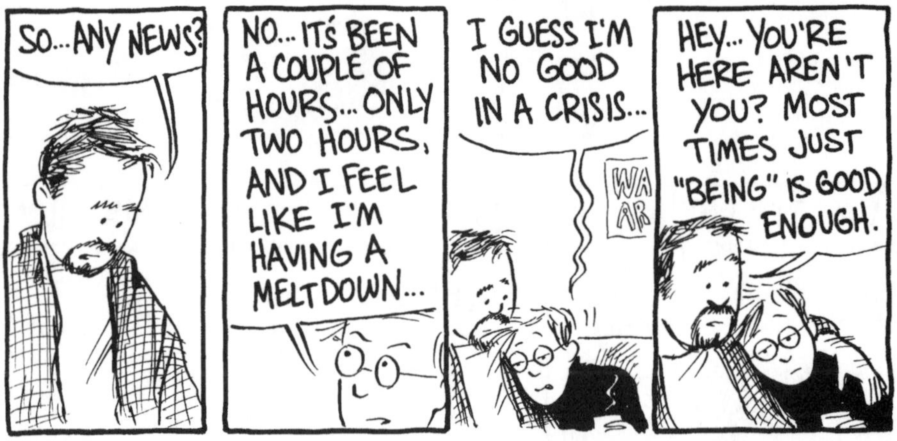
SO...ANY NEWS?
NO... IT'S BEEN A COUPLE OF HOURS... ONLY TWO HOURS, AND I FEEL LIKE I'M HAVING A MELTDOWN...
I GUESS I'M NO GOOD IN A CRISIS...
HEY... YOU'RE HERE AREN'T YOU? MOST TIMES JUST "BEING" IS GOOD ENOUGH.

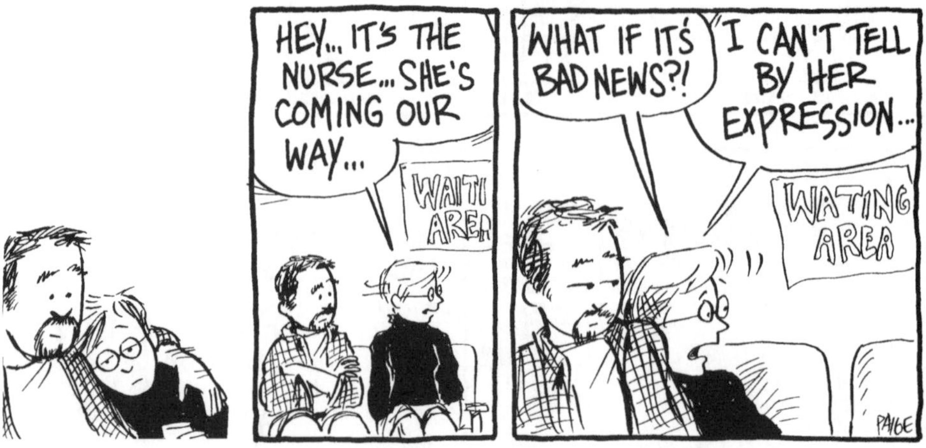
HEY... IT'S THE NURSE... SHE'S COMING OUR WAY...
WHAT IF IT'S BAD NEWS?!
I CAN'T TELL BY HER EXPRESSION...
WAITING AREA
PAIGE

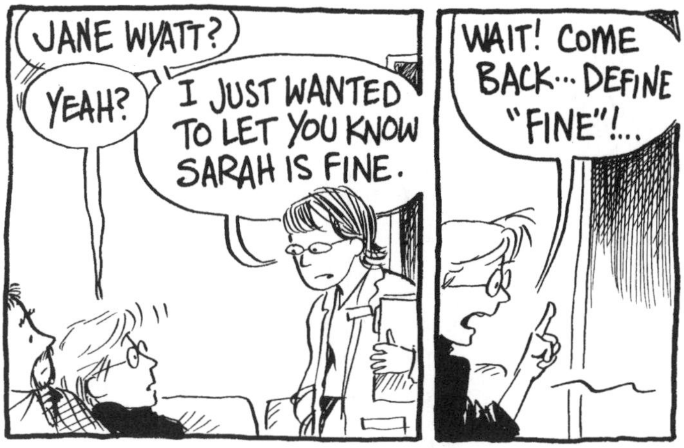
JANE WYATT?
YEAH?
I JUST WANTED TO LET YOU KNOW SARAH IS FINE.
WAIT! COME BACK... DEFINE "FINE"!...

The crisis is over... the biopsy came back with good news... and while none of the experience could be classified as "good," at least it got Jane and Sarah talking again... and you know what talking leads to... ex-girlfriend drama...

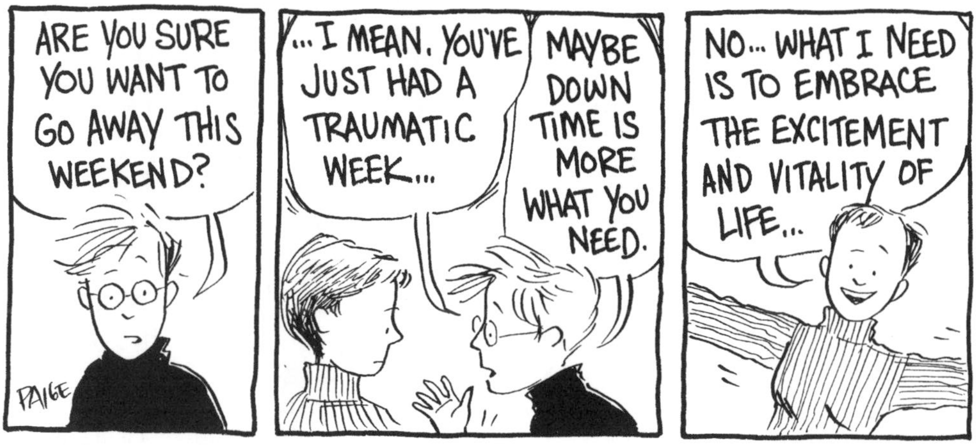
ARE YOU SURE YOU WANT TO GO AWAY THIS WEEKEND?
PAIGE
...I MEAN, YOU'VE JUST HAD A TRAUMATIC WEEK...
MAYBE DOWN TIME IS MORE WHAT YOU NEED.
NO... WHAT I NEED IS TO EMBRACE THE EXCITEMENT AND VITALITY OF LIFE...

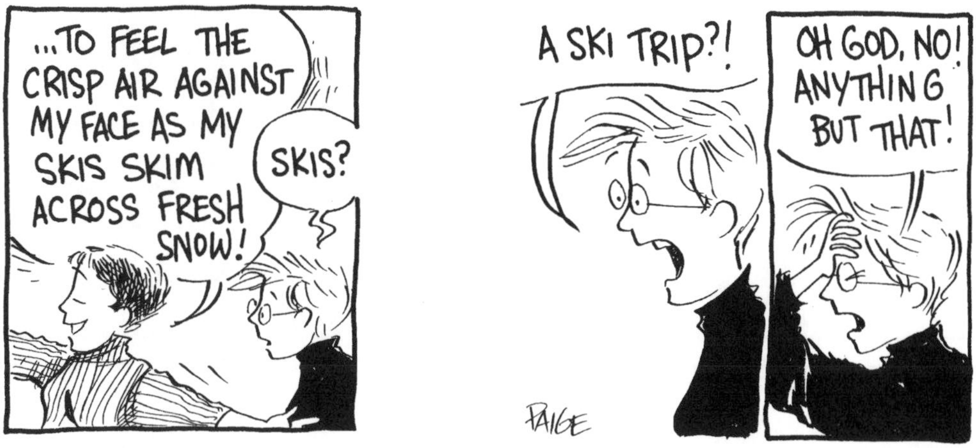
...TO FEEL THE CRISP AIR AGAINST MY FACE AS MY SKIS SKIM ACROSS FRESH SNOW!
SKIS?
A SKI TRIP?!
OH GOD, NO! ANYTHING BUT THAT!
PAIGE

REMEMBER THE CANOE TRIP? THAT WAS A TRAGIC BIT OF TOGETHERNESS!
THIS WILL BE DIFFERENT.
YEAH... FROST BITE AND BROKEN BONES!
ARE YOU CALLING CHELLE, OR AM I...?
THIS IS GOING TO BE A DISASTER! MY EX AND ME AND CHELLE IN A SECLUDED CABIN...
DUDE! SKI TRIP! ROCK ON...
SARAH WAS AT THE 'MART, FILLING THE TANK AND SHE SAID YOU NEEDED A FOURTH...
PAIGE
I'M GAME.. BESIDES, YOU OWE ME A FAVOR...
OH, JEEZ...

To be continued!

Some random sketches for future story lines...

Jane's World
Vol. 1

Paige Braddock
Story and art

Snail mail:
Jane's World
c/o Paige Braddock
P.O. Box 88
Sebastopol, CA
95472
Email: janetoon@mindspring.com

Visit our website:
www.JanesWorldComics.com

Jane's World, Vol. 1, June 2003. Paige Braddock, P.O. Box 88, Sebastopol, California, 95472. $12.95 U.S./$16.60 in Canada. **Jane's World** © Paige Braddock 2003 / Distributed by United Feature Syndicate, Inc. All rights reserved. **Jane's World** logo, symbols, prominent characters may not be used without written consent of author. With the exception of artwork for review purposes, none of the contents of this publication may be reprinted without the express permission of Paige Braddock.

Special thanks to Terry Moore, without his help and encouragement, this book would never have happend.

PRINTED IN CANADA

GIRL TWIRL
COMICS

PAIGE

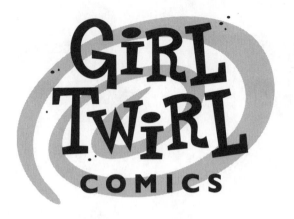

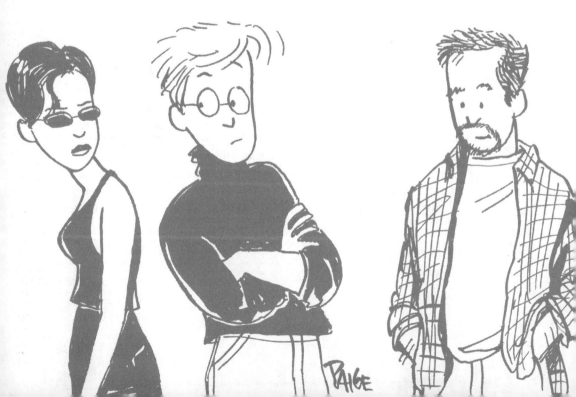